STATE
AND LOCAL
GOVERNMENT
AND POLITICS

Morris J. Levitt
Howard University

Eleanor G. Feldbaum
University of Maryland

Dryden Press
901 North Elm
Hinsdale, Illinois

Date Due

MAY 13 1977		
NOV 24 1980		
OCT 26 1983		
OCT 16 1989		
MAY 18		
OCT 12 1992		
MAR 11 1999		

DEMCO NO. 38-298

To Mary and Harold Levitt
and to Ronald, Merle, Mindy, Miriam, and Audrey Feldbaum

Library of Congress Catalog Card Number: 73-1800

ISBN: 0-03-084348-0

Printed in the United States of America

3456 090 987654321

Preface: A Program Guide to Participation

On many campuses throughout the nation, the cry has been heard for student participation. The students of many institutions of higher education are demanding a voice in the planning of programs which are affecting their lives. We concur with their belief that courses should not be planned for them but with them.

A major step in implementing a program to bring students into the planning and teaching processes is the participation of students in the writing of a textbook. This text is the result of such a joint undertaking. At the beginning of this project several points were considered. First, it was felt that a student should be involved in writing the text. Second, since the text would be designed for an undergraduate course, the student selected was an undergraduate. (Because this project was conducted over a period of years, the student has now completed her undergraduate and graduate course requirements.) Third, it was believed that meaningful participation demanded equal status; thus, she was invited to be a coauthor. Last, other undergraduate students were involved in the execution of the project. They have read each draft of the manuscript to assure that the analysis was understandable and the material was relevant for the student of state and local politics courses.

A project of this nature requires extensive planning. We have looked to those researchers who have contributed a vast array of ideas, data, and analysis to advance the state of the discipline. They have showed us the extent of the studies that have been made, the nature of political phenomena that can be studied, and the kinds of subjects that need to be explored in the future. Their names appear in the footnotes to the text. We acknowledge our debt to them. One of them, Clarence N. Stone, deserves particular mention; he has given advice and made suggestions, in addition to his own scholarly contributions.

Those who have experience in public service have also been called upon for assistance. They have shared their knowledge and have provided us with invaluable data. In acknowledging their contribution, we are pleased to dispel the notion that all bureaucrats are insulated and unresponsive. One former public servant, Daniel Gordon, deserves special thanks for his willingness to answer questions and obtain material which was inaccessible to us.

Several people were instrumental in the processing of the manuscript. Whenever possible, student help was enlisted. Those students who merit particular mention are: Jack Buchanan for his editing, and Davella Major and Greta Weiner for their typing. Shirley Norton and Judith Rife undertook the Herculean task of typing the major portion of the text.

Any attempt at being innovative involves the risk of being criticized. Thus, we would advise anyone planning such an endeavor to seek financial and personal support. Howard University has granted research funds to conduct preliminary studies to begin this book and sabbatical leave for its completion.

Unmeasureable support and encouragement has come from Ron and "our" girls. They have been patient, understanding, and loving throughout the duration of our project.

August 1972   M.J.L.
                                                               E.G.F.

Contents

Preface

Introduction 1

Part One. The Settings of the Subnational Political Systems

I. Structures and Forms of State and Local Governments

State and Local Political Systems 9
Structure of State Governments 13
Structure of Local Governments 23
Factors Relating to the Forms of Government 31

II. The Basic Rules

State Constitutions 36
Basic Rules of Local Governments 44
Intergovernmental Influences on the Basic Rules 48
Constituency Influences on Basic Rules 52

Part Two. The Functions of Expression

III. Interest Articulation | Part 1: Individual Actions

Prerequisites for Articulation 59
Demographic Characteristics and Interest Articulation 63

Direct Channels of Interest Articulation 65
Direct Articulation Initiated by Public Officials 71
Indirect Channels of Interest Articulation 73
Voting as an Indirect Channel of Articulation 80
New Channels and Revitalized Old Channels of Articulation . . . 89

IV. Interest Articulation | Part 2: Collective Actions

Types of Organized Associations 96
Pluralism and the Fluidity of Group Relations 100
Motivations for Joining Associations 101
The Factors of Group Strength 102
Channels and Techniques 109
Lobbying the Executive Branch 117
Lobbying the Judicial Branch 118
Groups and the Electoral Process 120
Recent Trends in Collective Articulation 124

V. Interest Aggregation

Political Parties and Interest Aggregation 134
Reforms and Interest Aggregation 139
Parties as Agencies of Interest Aggregation 144
Interest Groups and Interest Aggregation 151
Bureaucrats and Interest Aggregation 154
The Chief Executive and Interest Aggregation 155
The Legislators and Interest Aggregation 157

VI. Political Recruitment

Citizen Attitudes toward Public Office 163
Agents Performing the Function of Political Recruitment 165
Recruitment of Inflos 170
Recruitment of Service Personnel 175
Recruitment of Bureaus 177
Recruitment of Centros 181
Motivations for Seeking Centro Positions 195
Characteristics of Centro Nominees 197

Part Three. The Satisfaction of Needs and Demands

VII. Rule-Making | Part 1: The State Level

Formal Factors in Legislative Rule-Making 202
The Procedure of Legislative Rule-Making 216
Informal Factors in Legislative Rule-Making 222

The Executive in Rule-Making 228
The Administrators in Rule-Making 235
The Judges in Rule-Making 237
Intergovernmental Effects on Rule-Making 240
- Local Influence upon State Rule-Making 243
- Influence of the Media on Rule-Making 247
- Citizen Participation in Rule-Making 248
The Relationship of Rule-Making to the Public 253

VIII. Rule-Making | Part 2: The Local Level

Factors and Formal Limitations 257
Legislative Rule-Making Bodies 259
Apportionment and Districting 261
Financial Factors in Local Rule-Making 263
The Procedure of Legislative Rule-Making 267
Structural and Electoral Factors in Local Rule-Making 268
Legislators' Effect on Rule-Making 276
The Executive in Rule-Making 279
The Administrators in Rule-Making 281
The Judges in Rule-Making 285
Intergovernmental Influences on Rule-Making 287
- Influence of Community Power on Rule-Making 297
- Citizen Participation in Rule-Making 300
The Relationship of Rule-Making to the Public 305

IX. Rule Execution

Doctrines of Administration 312
Rule Execution and the Citizenry 334

X. Rule Adjudication

Agencies of Adjudication 354
Procedures of Adjudication 355
Factors Influencing the Performance of the Adjudication Function . 358
Public Attitudes toward the Function of Rule Adjudication . . . 390

Program Guide to Participation

Objective:

On many campuses throughout the nation, the cry has been heard for student participation. The students of many institutions of higher education are demanding a voice in the planning of programs which are affecting their lives. We concur with their belief that courses should not be planned for them but with them.

Implementation:

The major step in implementing a program to bring students into the planning and teaching processes has been completed. The product of this undertaking has been the enclosed text.

First, it was felt that a student should be involved in the writing of the text. Second, since the text would be designed for an undergraduate course, the student selected was an undergraduate. (NOTE: As this project was conducted over a period of years, the student has completed her undergraduate and graduate course requirements.) Third, it was believed that meaningful participation demanded equal status. Thus, she was invited to be a co-author.

Last, other undergraduate students were involved in the execution of the project. They have read each draft of the manuscript to assure that the analysis was understandable and the material was relevant for the student of state and local politics courses.

Planning:

A technical project of this nature requires extensive planning. We have looked to those researchers who have contributed a vast array of ideas, data, and analysis to advance the state of the discipline. They have showed us the extent of the studies which have been made, the nature of political phenomenon which can be studied, and the kinds of subjects that need to be explored in the future. Their names appear in the footnotes of the text. We acknowledge our debt to them. One of them deserves particular mention. Clarence N. Stone has given advice and suggestions, in addition to his own scholarly contributions.

Those who have experience in public service have also been called upon for assistance. They have shared their knowledge and have provided us with invaluable data. In acknowledging their contribution, we are pleased to dispel the notion that all bureaucrats are insulated and unresponsive. One former public servant, Daniel Gordon, deserves special thanks for his willingness to answer questions and obtain material which was inaccessible to us.

Other technicians were instrumental in the processing of the manuscript. Whenever possible, student help was enlisted. Those students who merit mention are: Jack Buchanan for his editing, and Davella Major and Greta Weiner for their typing. Shirley Norton and Judith Rife undertook the herculean task of typing the major portion of the text.

Support:

Any attempt at being innovative involves the risk of being criticized. Thus, we would advise anyone planning such an endeavor to seek support. Howard University has granted research funds to conduct preliminary studies to begin this task and sabbatical leave for its completion.

Unmeasurable support and encouragement has come from Ron and "our" girls. They have been patient, understanding and loving throughout the duration of our project.

Introduction

The justification for the study of state and local political systems customarily has been that the foundation of viable democratic political systems is an enlightened citizenry, for where governments regularly call upon the community to make political choices there is the assumption that citizens are aware, knowledgeable, and informed. It is our belief that, from a student's perspective, such study is a vital and an exciting venture. Through understanding political phenomena, students will recognize the necessity to become active and interested participants in their state and local political arenas. For it is in these arenas that decisions are made which intimately affect the choices available to those planning for the future of themselves and their families.

The choice to be made concerning one's college education, for example, may not appear to be affected by the decisions and policies of state and local political systems. Yet, the actions of public officials which have established the numbers, types, and locations of state or community colleges; which have set tuition rates, and the number and types of scholarships, fellowships, and loans; and which have prescribed the standards and requirements for entrance and graduation will determine for many whether they can afford or be admitted into an institution of higher education. Moreover, whether prospective students decide to attend a public college may be determined by its reputation and caliber, factors which are influenced by the amount of financial and academic support given by public agents.

Public policies may also affect one's decision about the acceptability of a job. Any consideration of an employment opportunity must take into account

1

where the individual will live as well as where he will work. Such questions as these would be considered: How long will it take to travel to work? Are the roads free from traffic tie-ups? Is there mass public transportation? What is the housing situation? Are zoning regulations such that housing prices are not prohibitive, that there is a wide choice of available types of dwellings, and that there is nearby shopping? Is the tax burden too heavy? Are residential neighborhoods free from crime and streets safe to walk during the evening and night hours? Are there facilities which enable one to spend his leisure hours pleasantly—such as parks, recreation centers, libraries, and cultural attractions? How free from pollution are the rivers, streams, and the air? Are the schools readily accessible and do they provide quality education? The answers to such questions, which influence the ultimate decision, are arrived at in the arenas of state and local political systems.

The dynamics of active and ever changing state and local political systems makes study of them an exciting venture. Governmental forms change, constitutions and charters are altered, and localities are created or annexed or merged out of existence. The opportunities for citizens to participate in governmental affairs add to the excitement of the political scene. There are frequent elections enabling people to cast ballots to affect the selection of officials who will fill the myriad governmental offices and to affect the outcome of public policy issues which appear as referenda and initiative questions. The proximity of subnational governmental arenas permits citizens to attend hearings and meet with their public agents. For those who wish to engage in group activities, there are political parties and civic associations to join. And for those who wish to express themselves in a dramatic fashion, there are the channels of peaceful or disruptive protest.

How can the study of state and local governmental systems in the United States be approached? Such study is an arduous task, replete with manifold obstacles. For there are over 80,000 state, county, city, town, township, borough, and special district governmental units to investigate.[1] And there are many significant differences between the units: organization, structure, powers, division of power, financial resources, service provided, political patterns and processes, and political traditions and culture. Thus, a framework is necessary to order the vast data, one that provides a blueprint for understanding general patterns of organization and political activity.

The framework selected for this book is the structural-functional approach. This approach is derived from the studies of Gabriel A. Almond and his associates.[2] They have been endeavoring to provide a frame of reference for the comparative description and explanation of observable political systems. By focusing on whole systems as unit of analysis, they have identified what they believe to be inherent activities, processes, and purposes. In doing so, they have shown that common features exist which can be used to compare disparate political systems.

There are three basic characteristics all political systems have in common. First, political structures are found in all systems. Comparisons of the systems may be made according to the type, form, purposes, permanence, and degree of structural specialization. Second, similar functions are performed in all systems. The systems may be compared through analysis of how frequently the functions are performed, by which structures they are performed, and how they are performed. Third, each political structure is multifunctional. Comparisons may be made according to the extent to which each structure is related to a particular function.

The universal functions which Almond and others have identified are:

1. Political socialization and recruitment
2. Interest articulation
3. Interest aggregation
4. Political communication
5. Rule-making
6. Rule application
7. Rule adjudication[3]

The common set of categories of functions identified within the structural-functional approach are useful for the study of the myriad, disparate American state and local political systems. However, this approach must be modified for our purpose. This framework has not been applied to a comprehensive study of subnational systems. Almond and his associates had proposed that it be used to study *inter*national political systems, rather than *intra*national ones. Thus, for us to apply the framework to a particular intranational context, it had to be altered.

Several observations and assumptions directed the development of our conceptual scheme. Within each state and local unit, relatively regularized patterns of governmental forms and structures can be observed. Moreover, the citizens of the states and localities accept and adhere to formal fundamental rules. The first part of our investigation focuses upon these settings of the subnational systems. Chapter I is a descriptive analysis of the forms and structures of the governments and governmental institutions. Chapter II is an examination of the basic rules of the systems, as embodied in the state constitutions and the local charters. These rules are considered basic, for they are the underlying ones which establish the institutions and forms of government and provide a framework for the powers of public agents, as well as for the relationships between and among the various sets of public officials and the citizens.

Inherent in the structural-functional approach is the implicit (if not explicit) assumption that the purpose of political systems is to satisfy those needs and demands that members of the community cannot satisfy for themselves. For such a purpose to be accomplished, interests must be expressed and channeled to the public agents operating the governmental institutions. The second part of our investigation is composed of those chapters dealing with the functions of expression—the *function of interest articulation* and the *function of interest aggregation*—and *political recruitment*. Needs and demands may be articulated individually or collectively. Motivations, strategies, techniques, channels, and targets of individual interest articulation are elaborated in Chapter III, and those for the collective articulation of interests in Chapter IV. The function of interest aggregation, that is, the mediation and combination of diverse and conflicting expressions of interests into policy recommendations which are transmitted to appropriate public agents, is the subject of Chapter V. Chapter VI, "Political Recruitment," focuses on the selection process of the various principal political actors. We discuss the methods of and factors relating to the recruitment of "inflos" (party leaders and interest group representatives), "bureaus" (the top level administrators), "centros" (the chief executives, legislators, and judges), and other public agents.

The types of satisfaction of needs and demands provided by the political system constitute the third part of this undertaking. Satisfaction may be derived from the making of rules, the implementation of rules, and the adjudication of controversies which arise under the rules. The *function of rule-making* is the focus of the discussions found in Chapters VII and VIII. The first of the two chapters is devoted to state rule-making, and the second to rule-making at the local level. The use of two chapters permitted a comprehensive overview and an in-depth treatment of a complex process. The evolution of administrative doctrine, practice and problems is emphasized in Chapter IX, "Rule Execution." "Rule Adjudication," the function performed to provide conflict resolution and conflict minimization, is the subject and title of the last chapter. In this third part of the book, the discussions include the attitudes, motivations, roles, procedures, problems, and limitations surrounding those actors participating in the performance of each function. Special emphasis is placed on the relationship of the citizens to those functions discussed in the seventh through tenth chapters.

We hope that readers of this book will see the dynamic quality of state and local politics, for this is the aim of the structural-functional framework. By focusing on functions, we have been able to cut across the traditional divisions of studying institutions and political activity. Thus, we selected this framework not merely to introduce a new terminology, but also to order the data systematically so that political phenomena could be better understood. This scheme allows the interrelatedness of the parts of the social and political systems to be appreciated. Change does not occur in one part of the systems without affecting the other parts. We have been able to see that when one structure does not perform its specialized function, another might. And if no structure performs the function to the satisfaction of citizens, we have been able to see the impact of inaction on the attitudes and activity of the community. The structural-functional approach is not the only conceptual scheme to enable comprehension, but we expect it will prove to be a valuable framework for the study of American subnational systems.

Introduction Footnotes

1. U.S. Bureau of the Census, *Census of Governments, 1967, Vol. I, Governmental Organization* (Washington, D. C.: Government Printing Office, 1968).
2. Gabriel A. Almond and James S. Coleman (eds.), *The Politics of the Developing Areas* (Princeton: Princeton University Press, 1960); Gabriel A. Almond, "A Developmental Approach to Political Systems," *World Politics*, XVII (January 1965), pp. 183–214; and Gabriel A. Almond and G. Bingham Powell, Jr., *Comparative Politics: A Developmental Approach* (Boston: Little, Brown and Company, 1966).
3. Almond and Coleman, *Politics of Developing Areas*, p. 17.

Part One

The Settings of the Subnational Political Systems

Chapter I

Structures and Forms of State and Local Governments

The functional approach utilized in this book is predicated upon three basic premises. First, similar functions are performed in all state and local political systems within the United States. Second, within each system there exist political structures. Third, there is a relationship between the functions and the political structures.

The relationship is an intricate one because each structure performs several functions. Yet, in viewing the performance, one sees that a specific structure is principally associated with a specific function. For example, the rule-making function is primarily performed by legislatures, and the rule adjudication function by courts. Thus, before discussing the functions of government, it is necessary to delineate the political structures and the systems in which they operate.

State and Local Political Systems

There are 81,299 political systems in the United States.[1] These include the national government, the fifty state governments, and the sum total of local governmental units. The average number of political systems per state is 1,626, with the range from 6,454 in Illinois to 20 in Hawaii. The governmental units within each state are classified as: counties, municipalities, townships, school districts, and special districts. Table I.1 presents the total number of governments found within each of these categories.

9

TABLE I.1

Political Systems in the United States

Type of Government		Number
National government		1
State governments.		50
Local governments		81,248
Counties	3,049	
Municipalities	18,048	
Townships	17,105	
School districts	21,782	
Other special districts	21,264	
Total		81,299

Adapted from: *Census of Governments, 1967, op. cit.,* p. 1.

The States

The states are constituent units of the American federal system. That is, they are recognized in the United States Constitution as delineated legal political entities. Thirteen states predated and ratified the formation of the federal union, and subsequently, from 1791 to 1959, thirty-seven joined to expand the system.

The legitimate recognition of what constitutes a state is vested in Congress. Article IV of the United States Constitution provides that "new states may be admitted by the Congress into this union." While there is no prescribed procedure for admission to statehood, there is a general pattern that is followed. The residents of the prospective state first petition Congress for admission. Thereafter, Congress passes an "enabling act" authorizing the writing of a state constitution. The petitioners then draft a constitution, and submit it to Congress for approval. The document is then studied, and if objectionable provisions are found, approval may be denied until changes are made. The final step is the passage of a congressional act of admission, and the signature of the President.

Upon admission, a state obtains full and equal constituent status. It's political and territorial integrity is protected under provisions of the United States Constitution. The national government may neither alter the form of government established in the state nor alter the territorial boundaries without the consent of the state legislature.

The Localities

Local governments are creatures of the states. The state constitutions and statutes provide for the establishment of such units, their territorial boundaries, and the extent and nature of their powers. The national constitution contains no reference to such entities.

The dependent relationship between the localities and the states has been enunciated by a series of national and state court decisions.[2] Generally, the decisions have reiterated the principle expounded by Iowa Justice John Dillon (which is referred to as "Dillon's Rule"): "Municipal corporations owe their origin to, and derive their powers and rights wholly from, the [state] legislature. It breathes into them the breath of life, without which they cannot exist. As it creates, so it may destroy. If it may destroy, it may abridge and control."[3]

The dependent status of counties was clearly set forth in a decision of the Ohio Supreme Court: "Counties are local subdivisions of a state, created by the sovereign power of the state, of its own sovereign will . . . County organization is created almost exclusively with a view to the policy of the state at large . . . and [is], in fact, but a branch of the general administration of that policy."[4]

Counties

Counties are the basic geographic subdivisions of the state. Counties are to be found in every state, although in Alaska they are officially designated as "boroughs," and in Louisiana as "parishes." There are 3,137 county-type areas scattered throughout the nation; of those, 3,049 have organized county governments. Two factors account for the numerical difference. Connecticut and Rhode Island have completely abolished county governmental units, although each has retained the geographical areas for state administrative purposes. In several additional states, some county-type areas are governed by such other units as cities or metropolitan governments. The number of county governments per state ranges widely, from 3 in Delaware and Hawaii to 254 in Texas.

Municipalities

Municipalities is the general term for governmental units officially designed as cities, villages, towns, and boroughs. Such designations, as prescribed by statuatory provisions, vary among the states. These may reflect local customs, size of the population, or the complexity of the structure of government. There is a wide variance in the number of municipalities per state. There are seven states with more than 850 municipalities each, and seven with fewer than 40. Illinois, with 1,256, has more such political entities than any other state; Hawaii, with 1, ranks lowest in number.

The largest municipalities in all states are referred to as cities. Any state may, however, designate any incorporated area as a city, regardless of population size. Thus, Spring City, Tennessee, with an approximate population of 2,000, and New York City with nearly 8,000,000 residents, both bear the same municipal nomenclature. The smallest municipalities are commonly called villages. Yet large urbanized communities, such as several of Chicago's most populous suburbs, retain (either because of custom, reluctance to have official change made or inaction) the legal designation of village.

Towns, as municipal political entities, are generally the basic units of rural incorporated areas. In several states, as in Iowa, smaller urbanized areas of a state may legally be called towns. Historically, New Jersey, Connecticut, and Pennsylvania have applied the term *boroughs* to some small municipalities. In addition, boroughs may be component parts of large cities. The city of New York, for example, is divided into five boroughs: Manhattan, Brooklyn, Queens, Bronx, and Richmond.

Townships

Townships, as particular forms of localities, are found in twenty-one states, predominantly in the northeastern and north central regions of the United States. Townships are usually the smallest rural governmental units; more than three fifths have populations of less than 1,000 inhabitants, and another fifth includes those having between 1,000 to 2,500 residents. In some states, principally in New England, townships (or "towns," as they are known legally) are the basic units of local government. In nearly half of the states having townships, there is some geographic overlapping between the townships and other municipalities. For example, in Kansas, Nebraska, and New York (among others), cities operate within territory that is served also by township governments.

Special Districts

Special districts are established to perform a special service; almost exclusively it is a single special service. The territory encompassed within a special district, as provided for by state legislation, may coincide with the geographic boundaries of other localities. However, most often special districts are not coterminous with any other governmental unit: they overlap counties, municipalities, or, in a few instances, states.

The largest number of single special districts have been established for the purpose of public education. Of the 23,390 public school systems in the United States, 21,782 (in forty-six states) are operated by independent school districts (the others are administered by departments of counties, municipalities, townships, or states). In twenty-five states, responsibility for all public education (from elementary school through institutions of higher learning) rests solely with the school district government; and in five states, this responsibility extends only from elementary school through high school levels. A "mixed" situation exists in sixteen states, where some public school systems are operated by such districts, and others are operated by the local

TABLE I.2

Services of Special Districts

(Exclusive of School Districts)

Service	Number	Percent
Natural resources	6,539	30.7
Soil conservation	2,571	12.1
Drainage.	2,193	10.3
Irrigation, water conservation.	904	4.2
Flood control	662	3.1
Other and composite resource purposes . .	209	1.0
Fire protection	3,665	17.2
Urban water supply	2,140	9.9
Housing and urban renewal	1,565	7.4
Cemeteries	1,397	6.6
Sewerage	1,233	5.7
School buildings	956	4.5
Highways	774	3.6
Parks and recreation	613	2.9
Hospitals	537	2.5
Libraries	410	1.9
Other single-service districts	982	4.9
Multiple-service districts	453	2.1
Total	21,264	100.0

Source: *Census of Governments, 1967, op. cit.,* p. 5.

government. Nearly 47 percent of the school districts are organized for the operation of a single school; and an additional 11 percent operate only two schools. Indeed, merely 8 percent of the school districts operate ten or more schools.

The special services performed by districts, other than those concerned with public education, cover a wide spectrum of governmental activities. Table I.2 summarizes the activities of those 21,264 special districts. As can be seen, a small percentage of special districts performs multiple services. Most often, those districts provide some combination of urban water supply with other services, such as sewerage.

Structure of State Governments

Although there is diversity in the manner by which the functions of government are performed within the states, the structure of state governments follows a basic pattern. The theory which guided the creation of American governments was that of a separation of powers. This meant that for each governmental function a separate institution was to be formed. Thus, in each state one finds a set of legislative institutions, of executive institutions, and of judicial institutions.

The Legislative Institutions

The prevailing legislative structure is a bicameral (that is, two-house) legislature. Only in Nebraska is the structure unicameral (that is, one-house). The official designations of legislative bodies vary among the different states. More than half refer to the structure as the "State Legislature." In nineteen others, it is known as the "General Assembly." The legal name is the "General Court" in Massachusetts and New Hampshire; and the "Legislative Assembly" in Oregon, Montana, and North Dakota. The upper chamber of each legislature is labeled the "Senate," a name also adopted by the Nebraska legislature to designate its unicameral body. A variety of titles is used for the lower chambers. Most often the term is the "House of Representatives." The "Assembly" is used in California, Nevada, New York, and Wisconsin; the "House of Delegates" in Maryland, Virginia, and West Virginia; and the "General Assembly" in New Jersey.

The bicameral form of structure predates the formation of the federal union. Only three of the original states entered into the union with unicameral legislative bodies. However, two of those effected the change to bicameralism shortly thereafter (Georgia in 1789, and Pennsylvania in 1790); and the third within four decades (Vermont in 1836). The pattern of two chambers continues until the present time. The one deviation is found in Nebraska. In 1937, the voters of that state ratified a state constitutional amendment which changed the bicameral legislature into a unicameral institution.

The Nebraska effort has been widely studied, but unicameralism has found few supporters outside of "good government groups" in other states. One such group is the National Municipal League, which has advocated a unicameral system since its inception, and has incorporated provisions for unicameral bodies in every edition of its *Model State Constitution* since 1921. Although no other state has followed Nebraska's example, the unicameral concept has received serious consideration as a result of the decision in *Reynolds v. Sims* (1964).[5] In that case, the United States Supreme Court ruled that the districts from which legislators in both houses of a bicameral state legislature are elected must contain populations of equal size. The ruling caused many to raise the question whether the equal population requirement for both houses made for duplicate chambers, and thus made bicameralism obsolete.[6]

Both the proponents of change and the supporters of the status quo ably argue the merits of their respective positions. Two-house bodies are said to permit a check against the passage of hurried and ill-considered legislation; to provide more time in which the public may act to combat undesired legislation; to be more secure against special interest lobbies; and to allow for more representation of diverse interests, needs, and demands. The merits of unicameralism are said to include: the concentration of responsibility; the enhancement of the public's ability to focus attention on legislative action; the simplification of cumbersome organization; the expedition of legislative matters; the elimination of "buck-passing" (that is, the placing of blame by members of one house on the members of the other house); and the reduction of operating costs.

Although the question of change has been raised in several recent constitutional conventions (as in Rhode Island and Maryland), no change has occurred. In every instance the weight of a bicameral tradition, of long experience with two houses, and of political considerations (for example, party leaders would oppose any change which would reduce the number of elected offices or affect partisan bases of strength within the chambers) was sufficient to maintain the status quo. Moreover, it was agreed that a bicameral system which incorporated differences in the lengths of terms and in the size of districts could provide different constituencies. Therefore, each house would have distinctive characteristics and one house would not be a carbon copy of the other.

The Executive Institutions

The executive institutions in each state are headed by a governor. In all state constitutions, he is charged with the duty of "faithfully executing the laws of the state" or transacting "all executive business," or both. Yet rarely do the constitutional provisions assign him exclusive control over the administrative structure. Rather, the constitutions and statutes of most states provide for the placement of many executive agencies under other independent executive officials, boards, and commissions.

In every state one or more other officials of the state administration are directly elected by the voters, and are not in any way subordinate to the chief executive. Most commonly, the offices to be filled in this manner include the following: attorney general, secretary of state, treasurer, auditor, and superintendent of public education. Each presides over an important agency, which is thus largely removed from the direct supervision of the governor. The attorney general, the state's chief legal officer, prosecutes and defends cases to which the state is a party, and serves as the legal advisor to the governor, state agencies, and the legislature. The secretary of state is responsible for the certification and keeping of public documents, the supervision of state elections, the issuance of corporation charters and various other licenses, and so on. The state's treasurer acts as custodian of the state funds and is responsible for their proper disbursement. The primary task of the auditor is to determine the fidelity and legality of expenditures that have been made. The oversight of the administration of education mainly rests with the superintendent of public education. The position of lieutenant governor is found in forty states. In all of those states, except Tennessee (where he is elected by the state senate), the office is filled by popular election. The lieutenant governor's principal task is to preside over the upper house of the state legislature. On occasion, by the appointment of the governor, he heads advisory boards and commissions. In the absence of the governor, the duty of supervising the execution of rules becomes his.

In many states, major departments or agencies are controlled by boards or commissions. The members are often independent of the governor, for they may be elected by the people or appointed by the legislature. Often when they are appointed by the governor, provisions for staggered terms and longer tenure than that of the chief executive establish their potential independence from his control.

For many decades, the performance of major states services has been the responsibility of part-time commissions or boards. The members of such boards select an individual to devote himself full-time to the administration of that group of offices. Such services include highway planning and construction, social welfare, administration of hospitals and prisons, and so forth. Boards have also been widely used for the regulation of agriculture, the conservation of resources, the administration of labor laws, the promotion of business, and so on. In the area of regulation of the rates and profits of public utilities, the states have developed the pattern of establishing independent regulatory commissions. In addition, state corporations have been created to administer public business ventures, such as liquor stores and electric power facilities.

Since 1949, much concern has been focused on the organization of the executive structures of state governments. The concern was directed toward rectifying the proliferation of administrative agencies, the fragmentation of administrative activities and programs, and the diffusion of administrative responsibility that had become the characteristics of the executive branch in every state. Each state had a plethora of departments, agencies, boards, commissions, authorities, offices, and councils, which varied widely in size, jurisdiction, organization, and relationships to the governor and to the related executive agencies. Figure I.1 illustrates the organization of the executive branch in Maryland (prior to the reorganization of 1970), and is typical of the structure that has been found in many states.

The incoherent pattern of organization, replete with duplication of services, devoid of central leadership, and lacking coordination of activities, has been the result of several historical developments and pressures. First, provisions

Organisation of the Executive Branch*

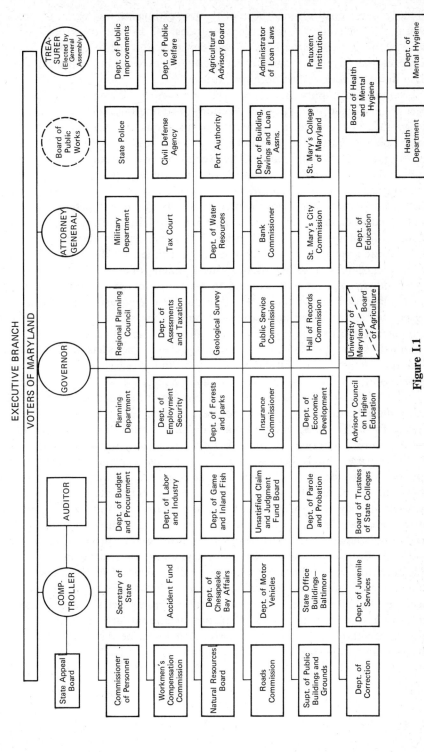

Figure I.1

* Chart copied from *Maryland Manual*, 1967–1968.

of early state constitutions (those of the late eighteenth and early nineteenth centuries) reflected the prevailing attitudes of distrust of strong central leadership, as well as the lack of confidence in and the low esteem for the office of the governor. Thus, executive activities were decentralized rather than unified under a chief administrator.

Second, the supporters of popular democracy during the Jacksonian period advocated the popular election of numerous state officials. The acceptance of the belief that public officials should be directly accountable to the people led to the adoption of the "long ballot" as the mode for the selection of state administrators. The executive power was diffused among the variety of elected top-level administrative personnel.

The third historical development was the movement to divorce administration from politics. This movement received its greatest impetus during the mid to late nineteenth century, a period marked by graft, corruption, and scandals involving many state legislators. The persistence of popular fear of concentrated executive power, coupled at that time with the popular distrust of the legislators, resulted in the establishment of autonomous agencies. Independent agencies were created in an effort to prevent interference by politically based public figures. In addition, these agencies were to be staffed by personnel appointed and promoted on the bases of merit and technical competence, rather than through political patronage procedures.

Fourth, since the end of the nineteenth century, there has been a gradual accretion of new responsibilities, activities, and services performed by the state executive structures. As these increased in response to the rising demands of industrialization, urbanization, and economic depressions, states established new boards, commissions, offices, independent regulatory agencies, and so forth. The rationale for creating a new agency instead of expanding the task of existing ones is complex. Often an agency was created as a new problem arose, simply because this was the most expedient manner of response. Moreover, it would appear that some action was being taken to solve the problem. On occasion, the public agents' intent in creating a separate agency was to emphasize the importance of and to focus public attention on a problem. A new program may not have fitted precisely within traditional departmental jurisdictions or into existing program structures, and so a new agency was deemed necessary. Or administrators in an existing structure may have been deemed insufficiently interested to execute new and innovative programs energetically. Recently the national government has become the catalyst for some proliferation of agencies. Several federal grant-in-aid programs require that organizational arrangements, if not available within existing state executive structures, be instituted to oversee the administration of specific grant programs.

Reorganization of the Executive Structure

The reorganization of the national executive branch, following the re-commendations of the Commission for the Organization of the Executive Branch of Government (the Hoover Commission) in 1949, provided the impetus for reorganization movements at the state level. One state after another has established study commissions (little Hoover Commissions) to review existing administrative organization and make suitable recom-mendations for improving structural arrangements and procedures. Study groups in at least seventeen states issued their reports during the 1968–1969 period. In addition, groups in twelve other states issued reports during 1970–1971. Illustrative of the titles of such groups were: The Commission for Reorganization of the Executive Branch of the Indiana State Government, The Arkansas Program Planning Project, The Vermont Committee on Administrative Coordination, and the Oregon Governor's Project '70's Task Force.[7]

The recommendations of such commissions have not always been adopted. The suggestions have principally called for a consolidation of various agencies performing similar services, under the direction of a strong central executive. But existing patterns of power and relationships are not easily altered. Bureaucrats, especially those within autonomous or independent agencies, oppose direct supervision from a politically based chief executive. And they look unfavorably upon the disruption of their procedures and methods of operation. Moreover, agents may feel that their status, positions, professional independence, and influence would be threatened if they were subsumed into a larger administrative structure.

Similarly, those enjoying special relationships with existing agencies may oppose reorganization proposals. Clientele groups, which have developed relationships with specialized agencies over a period of years, may view structural changes as possibly obstructing their channels of rapport, com-munication, and influence. Legislators may feel that their influence over select agencies would be diminished by a reorganization or by the introduction of strong centralized gubernatorial leadership. Thus, they also may attempt to abort plans for reform.

Despite opposition, several states have taken steps to reorganize their executive branch structure. The trends have been toward greater consolida-tion and central direction. In some states, a specific activity, the performance of which had been fragmented among different offices, has been consolidated within one agency. For example, in Rhode Island all education levels (kinder-gartens through universities) have been brought under the jurisdiction of a board of regents. And in Minnesota, the highway patrol, crime bureau, fire marshal, civil defense, and motor vehicle licensing activities have become the responsibility of a newly established public safety department.

In other states, reorganization has reflected awareness of the growing interdependency of state programs. For example, health and welfare have come to be considered two aspects of a broad social service activity, rather than separate specialities. Thus, a department of social services has been established in Utah, departments of health and social services in New Mexico and Wyoming, and a department of health and rehabilitative services in Florida. Similarly, such activities as the regulation of airports, highways, mass transportation, and motor vehicles have been combined into departments of transportation (as in, for example, Connecticut, Oregon, and Hawaii). Natural resources is another area of consolidation. For example, Colorado and Utah have united such agencies as those responsible for water and air resources, parks, forrestry, fish and game, and other conservation-oriented agencies. Consolidation or coordination has begun for such areas as community affairs, law enforcement, and manpower development.

A far-reaching reorganization has occurred in California, Maryland, and Massachusetts with the introduction of the cabinet form of executive structure. The cabinet form in Massachusetts, which went into effect in April 1971, placed all existing agencies within nine executive offices. These offices, each headed by a secretary, are: Administration and Finance, Communities and Development, Consumer Affairs, Educational Affairs, Environmental Affairs, Human Services, Manpower Affairs, Public Safety, and Transportation and Construction.

The other major trend has been toward centralized direction of the administrative establishment. The principal beneficiary of many successful reform efforts has been the governor. His immediate control and direction over top-level bureaucrats has been expanded. The appointment power of the governor has been enlarged to include appointment of a number of persons previously appointed by boards or elected at the polls. For example, statutory provisions in Utah now permit the governor to appoint the heads of departments, who were formerly selected by boards. In addition, the removal power of the governor has been increased. The constitution of Hawaii, for example, has been altered to allow the chief executive to remove department heads without the consent of the state senate.

In eight states governors have been granted authority to initiate reorganization plans and to implement them. In Minnesota, the governor may put reforms into effect without the approval of the legislature; but in the other seven states, such authority is subject to the veto of either one or both legislative houses within a short, specified period of time.

The Judicial Institutions[8]

The third major set of state institutions is the judiciary. A review of the fifty state systems would show a most complex and bewildering pattern of structural arrangement. This complexity arises from the fact that: "Each state has the right to establish its own set of courts on whatever principles it chooses, each has the authority to set up a body of law for use in these courts, drawing on whatever tradition it feels appropriate."[9] Each system is marked by internal confusion and overlap and conflict of jurisdictions and procedures. Yet despite the dissimilarities among the various state judicial systems, there exist sufficient similarities to permit discussion.

The general structure can be described as being hierarchical and pyramidal. It is hierarchical in that the judicial structure has levels of courts, which differ in the nature and the scope of their respective jurisdictions and final adjudication powers. It is pyramidal in that the numbers of courts and judges decrease at each ascending level of the hierarchical order.

At the lowest level of the judicial structure are courts of limited jurisdiction. Predominantly these courts are considered to be local courts. The most informal and limited is the office of the justice of the peace. This judicial agent settles petty civil (that is, controversies where the matter at issue is valued under $300), and minor criminal matters (that is, misdemeanors), issues warrants, and performs marriage ceremonies. Nowadays the office of justice of the peace is a rural phenomenon. The urban counterpart is the magistrate's court, sometimes termed "police court." Generally, these courts are tended to by part-time judges, with little or no law training, and are informal in the nature of their proceedings and record-keeping.

By state statuatory or local charter provisions, municipal or county courts have been established for the enforcement of local ordinances. Included within their legal jurisdictions are controversies involving zoning violations, tenant–landlord disputes, and violations of building codes. In many large cities, municipal courts have been organized for specialized purposes. Thus, one finds separate courts for handling traffic violations, domestic relations, juvenile offenses, probation of wills, and so on.

General trial courts, known by a variety of titles (for instance, superior courts, circuit courts, and district courts) constitute the next level of the judicial hierarchy. Every state is divided geographically into judicial districts, in each of which is found at least one such court. These are mainly courts of original jurisdiction (that is, cases in controversy are initially brought there for settlement), although they may, on occasion, hear appeals from the lower level of courts.[10] Their jurisdiction extends over persons accused of major crimes, over civil controversies of unlimited value, and over matters in equity. These courts are presided over by full-time judges, with legal training, and operate with formal procedures and accurate record-keeping. It is at this level that controversies may be conducted before juries (unless waived).

Appellate courts make up the top level of the judicial hierarchy. At the apex of the pyramid in every state court system is a court of last resort. This is usually called the "State Supreme Court"; but is sometimes known as the "Court of Appeals" (in Kentucky, Maryland, and New York), the "Supreme Judicial Court" (in Maine and Massachusetts), and the "Supreme Court of Appeals" (in Virginia and West Virginia). Each court is comprised of a number of judges who sit as a group to deliberate cases. The number of supreme court judges ranges from three in Delaware to nine in Alabama, Iowa, Mississippi, Oklahoma, Texas, and Washington. Nearly half of the states have seven judges, and one third have five judges presiding over the highest court. Only three states have an even number of judges (six in Connecticut and Maine, and four in Wyoming), a deviation from the generally accepted concept that an odd number prevents stalemate arising from an even division of judicial votes. One member serves as the chief justice, who presides over the court and supervises its administrative machinery.

These courts of last resort primarily act, upon request, to review the records of cases heard originally in lower courts. In order to reduce the large case load of the supreme courts, twenty-three states have established in this level intermediary courts of appeal. Thus, in those states, appeals from the general trial level would first be directed to the intermediate courts. Only if one party in a controversy were dissatisfied with the decision would further recourse be made to the supreme court.

The intermediate courts of appeals may be partitioned along geographic or jurisdictional lines. For example, they may be divided so as to serve designated judicial districts or to hear either civil or criminal appeals. The judges of these courts group into panels which sit to hear arguments or review the records of the appeals before them.

Reorganization of the Judicial Structure

Concern over the confusion, overlap, and conflict of jurisdictions and procedures has led to reform proposals to promote efficiency within the court system. One such proposal has been the unified court plan. The essential characteristic of that plan is the consolidation of the numerous and various courts of limited juridiction within the general trial level. This would provide for a statewide integrated structure, subdivided into clearly specialized areas of jurisdiction (for example, equity, criminal law, juvenile offenses, and so on). Appeals would be heard by an intermediate court of appeals, and then by a court of last resort. All courts would follow standardized procedures, and all judges would be under the central supervision of the chief justice of the highest court. In addition, the chief justice would be empowered to transfer judges from courts with light case loads to those with crowded dockets, so as to aid in reducing any backlogs which might develop.

A second proposal has been the centralization of court administration. As administrative head of the system, the chief justice would be responsible for the recruitment, training, and supervision of auxiliary personnel (clerks, secretaries, reporters, and so on); the financial affairs of the judicial branch (preparation of budgets, supervision of expenditures, and so on); the scheduling of trials, and the impaneling of jurors. To assist him with such tasks, administrative officers would be employed. Such an officer, also, would be responsible for gathering and reporting judicial statistics on case loads, case dispositions, and related matters throughout the state judicial system.

In most states the need for reform has been recognized. Between 1968 and 1970, for example, extensive reorganization of the court structure has occurred in Colorado, Idaho, Rhode Island, Pennsylvania, Ohio, and Oklahoma. Intermediate courts of appeals have been established in Maryland, Oregon, and Washington. Maine, Pennsylvania, and Rhode Island, in establishing administrative offices of the court, have joined the thirty-four states which previously had done so.[11]

Structure of Local Governments

Although the functions of rule-making and rule execution are performed in every local unit of government, there is not always a clear set of institutions responsible for the performance of each. Thus, the structures of local governments are more readily discussed in terms of forms and patterns.[12]

Town Meeting

The earliest form of local government, still found primarily in New England, is the town meeting. Adhering most closely to the principle of direct democracy, the town meeting is an assembly of all the qualified voters of the community. At such meetings, rules are made and the manner by which they are to be executed is decided. The assembly is held annually, and meetings may be called more frequently as deemed necessary.

Citizens are chosen, by those assembled, to be responsible for the administration of the rules between the meetings. Usually a group of three (although the number ranges as high as nine in various localities) are elected to be a board of selectmen for that purpose. One of them may be selected to be presiding officer of the group and to act as the ceremonial leader of the community. In addition, other officers may be chosen to perform specific activities. The town clerk acts as secretary of the board, keeps public records records deeds and licenses, and so on. The town treasurer is the collector, custodian, and disburser of the town taxes and funds. The town assessor evaluates property for purposes of taxation, and the town auditor reviews the public financial records for accuracy. The town constable or attorney is engaged in the locality's law enforcement activities. Other minor officers may include: "The Overseers of the Poor," "The Fence Viewers" (who settle controversies arising over the proper location of fences), and "Sextons" (who oversee the maintenance of the cemeteries).

In many areas of New England, as the population of the community increased, a modification of this form of government was instituted. It is referred to as the representative town meeting plan. Under this plan, the voters choose a number of citizens (usually one hundred or more) to represent them at the meetings. Any voter may still attend and participate in the discussions, but he may not cast a vote at the meetings. In such localities, selectmen and other officers are elected to supervise the administration of the local rules.

In some mid-Atlantic and western states, a form of government comparable to the New England town meeting is used. Township meetings constitute the basic institution for the performance of governmental functions. The assemblies are presided over by a township board (known by such titles as board of trustees, board of supervisors, or board of auditors). The members of such boards (usually numbering three to five) and other minor officials (such as those found in towns) attend to the administration of local affairs between the township meetings.

Executive-Council Pattern

The executive-council pattern is the oldest form of government that is most commonly found in localities today. The plan has been adopted by all sizes of municipalities and by several urbanized counties; but it is predominantly found in the most populous municipalities (over 500,000 population) and in the smaller cities (5,000–10,000 population). The executive-council form of government is similar to that found at the national and state levels of government, in that a distinction is made between institutions primarily responsible for the performance of the rule-making and those mainly responsible for rule execution. Hence separate legislative and executive institutions are established.

Since the last quarter of the nineteenth century, the legislatures have almost universally been unicameral bodies. The number of councilmen (also known as aldermen) ranges from two to fifty, generally with the larger councils being in the larger cities. The council may be composed of members elected at large or on a ward or district basis, or by a combination of the two The setting may be either a partisan or nonpartisan one.

This pattern has been categorized into the weak executive-council plan and the strong executive-council plan. The principal characteristic differentiating the two categories is the position of the chief executive within the executive institution. The weak executive form, an outgrowth of the period of distrust of strong centralized power, is marked by a decentralization of administrative responsibilities. The mayor or county executive does not directly control or supervise bureaucratic activity. His supervision is limited because the principal heads of administrative agencies are appointed by the council, or, in a few instances, appointed by the chief executive but not subject to his removal. Other officials are similarly independent of executive control, for they are elected by the people. Among those most often elected are: the city clerk, treasurer, comptroller, and assessor.

The weak executive may participate in the planning of administrative programs, for his office affords him positions on panels charged with such activities. The budget may be drafted, for example, by a board of estimate, which might be composed of the mayor, comptroller, treasurer, superintendent of public education, and the council president. The mayor may sit as a member of such groups as the board of public welfare, library board, board of public safety, planning commission, and so on. Yet he is merely a coequal member, with only one vote. In some localities, the weak executive may be no more than the ceremonial leader for the community, or the presiding officer of the council, with no power to vote or veto.

Adoptions of the strong executive-council system began in the late nineteenth century. As the number of local services and the size of communities increased, it was recognized that a system of more central leadership was needed. The model of this pattern provides for only one elected administrative officer. This executive alone directs the administrative activities, may appoint and dismiss top-level bureaucrats, and speaks as the sole voice of the executive structure.

Most localities having an executive-council plan have adopted some form between the very weak and very strong patterns. The "average" executive has broad powers of appointment and dismissal, and, thus, has the potential for control over his branch of government. However, his powers are not unlimited, for he may have to share some administrative authority with a few top-level bureaucrats who are elected (for example, the comptroller, attorney, and treasurer). He may also have to share his initiative prerogative with others; for example, the budget may be drafted by him and a small committee composed of other elected agents and some of his appointed personnel.

The Commission or the Board Pattern

The obverse of a separation of powers in a multi-institutional form is the integration of powers in a single institutional form of government. In the board commission pattern a small body of agents collectively exercise the rule-making and rule execution powers. Boards or commissions were instituted because it was believed that efficiency could be promoted by granting to the agents, who are responsible for surveying the full spectrum of public problems, the power to legislate relevant programs and to oversee their implementation. In addition it was hoped that deadlock which could occur between two bodies (executive and legislative) having approximately equal powers would be eliminated.

The commission form of government on the municipal level was adopted and gained popularity in the midwest and southwest during the early decades of the twentieth century. The governmental structure is headed by a small board of commissioners. The board is usually composed of between three to seven members, with five being the average size. The members are generally elected at large and on a nonpartisan basis.

The administrative agencies are under the collective supervision of the board. Centralization of administrative responsibility is structurally accomplished because the commissioners are generally the only officials elected in the community, and the top-level bureaucrats are appointed by them. Although the commissioners are meant to work as a committee, the usual practice is for each to work independently, as head of a specialized area of service. Thus, an allocation of activities among themselves leads to a commissioner responsible for public safety, another for parks and recreation, a third for public works, a fourth for health and welfare, and so on. The division of activities among the members, obviously, depends upon the number of commissioners.

In addition to their administrative activities, the commissioners come together periodically (weekly, monthly, or as the need arises) as a rule-making body. At such meetings, general policy or pressing public problems are deliberated. Although the board makes rules collectively for all administrative activities, deference is accorded to the proposals of the commissioner concerned with the specific area under consideration.

The chairman of the board is looked upon as the "mayor" of the community for ceremonial purposes. Though he presides over the meetings of the commission, he has no greater executive or legislative powers than his colleagues. Such an individual may be elected by the people to be the "mayor," may obtain the title by virtue of being the commissioner receiving the most votes at the election, or may be selected to so act by his fellow commissioners.

At the county level, the traditional and almost universal form of government is the commission pattern. Although some counties have commission boards which perform functions similar to those in the municipalities, variations exist throughout the country. These variations are outgrowths of the historical developments of county governments.

Originally, counties were established as administrative subdivisions of the state, and governmental units were created to oversee the local administration of state responsibilities. Such units were headed by a group, acting as commissioners, who were charged with directing the general administrative activities within their jurisdiction. The boards of commissioners were composed of: (1) individuals who were appointed by the state; (2) individuals who were chosen by the municipalities in the county, and were also officials in their respective localities; (3) state-appointed commissioners, with a county judge acting as the presiding officer; or (4) one county judge and several justices of the peace. In addition to the commissioners, separate boards were often established or officials elected to oversee specific administrative activities. Among the diverse independent boards often were those specifically responsible for libraries, hospitals, elections, and recreation. The list of elected officers has included: the sheriff, prosecuting attorney, coroner, clerk, treasurer, and assessor.

In many counties the powers of the government were expanded to include the performance of the rule-making function, and in these cases the commission pattern was perpetuated. The administrative structure, however, remained decentralized because there was no consolidation under the board of commissioners. Rather, the rule execution function continued to be performed and directed by the already existing diffusion of boards and independently elected officials.

The commission form of government on the municipal level and in some urbanized counties has lost its popularity. In the decades after the 1930's, almost no adoptions of the pattern took place. Instead, especially since the mid-1940's, many of the commission cities have changed to other forms. For example, the number of such cities has decreased from over 500 in the period of the commission form's greatest popularity (around 1915) to less than 200 by 1970. Even Galveston, Texas, the first city to adopt the commission government (in 1901), and the one that provided the working model which other cities followed, abandoned the form by popular referendum in 1960.

The principal reason for the decline in the number of localities with the commission pattern was the inability of the structure to adapt to the pressures brought about by the expanded scope of governmental activities. As the number of governmental services increased, it became necessary to allocate and distribute the additional obligations among the limited number of existing agencies. Each commissioner heading a major department had to assume the responsibility for directing unrelated or loosely related activities. In large communities, that practice proved to be administratively unwieldy. To increase the number of commissioners to oversee additional departments was considered an infeasible alternative, for a large board could not operate efficiently or effectively. Hence, in many localities the decision was made to abandon the form.

The prevailing pattern among special districts is the board form. The boards are generally small and the members are selected in one of three ways. First, they may be appointed by the governor, with or without the consent of the legislature. Second, governmental units which fall within the jurisdiction of special districts may appoint members to serve on the board, who may or may not be officers of the respective constituent units. The third method of selection is election by the voters. The type of special district which most frequently utilizes this last method of selection is the school district. The members meet to make rules collectively and to oversee implementation. Some boards assign each member to a specific area of concentration so as to facilitate task performance and expedite the work load.

The Professional Administrator Pattern

The need to introduce expertise and professionalism into the local governmental process was propounded by some reformers of the early twentieth century. They believed that even the able politician may not be trained or experienced in administration of government, or may not necessarily be interested in the mechanical and detailed aspects of public administration. Indeed, skill in political affairs and skill in administrative management are not often attributes found in the same individual. Talents useful in winning public office and knowledge of technical matters (engineering, construction, planning, sanitation, personnel) needed to conduct the public duties of the office are dissimilar. Hence, a form of government was advocated and widely adopted which provided for a professional administrator, who would hold a central position in the structure.

Such professionals are hired on the basis of their training. The first individuals to hold these positions were experienced civil engineers. Those hired in recent years have been graduates of business administration or urban administration programs. In some plans, the administrator is appointed by and responsible to the council or board; in others, he is appointed by the chief executive and is accountable to him. The former pattern (emanating from the weak executive-council form) is known as the council-manager plan; and the latter (arising from the strong executive-council form) is called the executive–chief administrative officer plan.

The council-manager plan was first established in Staunton, Virginia, in 1908.[13] By 1970, nearly half of the cities had adopted this form of government. The characteristics of this plan are a small (five to nine members), part-time council, a manager reporting to it, and the administrative agencies supervised by him. The council acts as the executive and legislative body. Where a "mayor" is present, he performs a ceremonial role and may preside over the council.

The manager is responsible and accountable only to the council (which can hire and dismiss him). His basic tasks are to supervise and coordinate administrative activities, review the plans and programs of the various agencies, prepare the budget, present reports, and offer advice to and prepare the agenda for the council. In addition, he is empowered to appoint and remove administrative heads of departments.

Modifications of this pattern are found in several municipalities and counties. The manager may have to share administrative authority with one or more elected executive officials. These may include a mayor who has some administrative power and other agents (such as the attorney, auditor, and comptroller) who head separate departments.

In some counties, there is found the quasi-manager, the administrative-officer, or the administrative-assistant plan. The full-time professional is utilized to assist the board of commissioners in such administrative activities as coordination of agencies, purchasing, and supervisory tasks. However, he does not have those full appointive, administrative, and budget-making powers as described above.

Occasionally, one finds a manager in towns and townships. He may be a member of the township board or be appointed by the board of selectmen. In addition to performing other administrative tasks, this individual may act as the town treasurer, road commissioner, water commissioner, and so on. Some New England towns too small to afford or need a full-time professional have hired managers jointly with other units of local government. Special district boards often hire an administrative officer to direct the day-to-day activities. For example, school boards employ a superintendent for public education.

The executive–chief administrative officer plan was first adopted in San Francisco in 1931. More recently it has been instituted in such cities as Boston, Los Angeles, New York, Newark, New Orleans, and Philadelphia. In those cities and the few counties which have adopted this pattern, the belief was that for the executive to exert strong central administrative and political power, he needed the services of a professional assistant. The position and tasks of the chief administrative officer are similar to that of a manager; however, he is structurally within the executive branch. He is responsible and accountable to the mayor or county executive who appoints and can fire him. The chief administrative officer supervises and coordinates the daily administrative tasks of agencies, and may act as ceremonial "vice-mayor."

Metropolitan Governments

In recent years, concern has been expressed that the existing system of local governments is neither efficient nor totally effective in providing all necessary services; for the plethora of localities, each with prescribed jurisdictions and burdened with limited resources, are increasingly unable to cope with the complex and regional nature of problems. Thus, new attempts at seeking solutions to problems have led to proposals for the creation of metropolitan governments.

By 1970, five major metropolitan reorganization proposals had been implemented. These represent rearrangements of relationships between a county and the local governments found within its territorial limits. The five are Baton Rouge with East Baton Rouge Parish (that is, county), Louisiana, in 1949; metropolitan Miami with Dade County, Florida, in 1957; Nashville with Davidson County, Tennessee, in 1963; Metropolitan Jacksonville with Duval, Florida, in 1967; and Indianapolis with Marion County, Indiana, in 1969.

These reorganizations have instituted new governmental arrangements rather than new governmental forms. Although no two of those areas adopted exactly similar systems of institutions, two basic forms of government were utilized: the executive-council form, and the council-manager form. The former was the pattern adopted in the Baton Rouge area, for example. There, the legislative institution is composed of two councils—a Baton Rouge city council and an East Baton Rouge Parish council. The membership of the two bodies overlaps, in that the parish council is composed of the members of the city council plus two members elected from the outlying rural districts. The central executive official is the mayor-president, who presides over both councils and is the chief administrative officer for the entire area. The council-manager form was utilized, for example, in the metropolitan Dade County area. While the twenty-six municipal governments within Dade County retained their respective institutional systems, the county governmental unit was restructured under the new reorganization scheme. The existing commission form at the county level was changed into an enlarged council, which hired a manager to oversee the county administrative agencies. The basic characteristic of the five reorganizations was that the county government was granted broader powers (often of the home-rule type) to handle regional problems and to provide services throughout the metropolitan area. The government of each city, which remained incorporated within its county, was responsible for matters solely of a municipal nature.

In some areas, intergovernmental coordination has been attempted through the creation of councils of governments. These are unions of neighboring localities which have combined for overall program planning and for cooperation in providing services (for example, control of air and water pollution, transportation, parks and recreation). The board form is the pattern utilized by councils of governments, with members almost always being appointed by the constituent localities. Of the nearly one hundred and fifty councils of governments, only the Twin Cities Metropolitan Council (in Minnesota) has some effective powers of review and implementation. The others lack coercive force in that they have no authority to levy taxes, pass ordinances, or regulate the activities of local governments. The increase in the number of councils of governments since 1965 demonstrates that local officials have recognized the advantage of approaching metropolitan problems through regional voluntary associations (which pose little threat to the integrity of their existing political jurisdictions).

Factors Relating to Forms of Government

It is a basic assumption that political systems are created in response to political environments. Yet two major conflicting themes have existed regarding the forms of American state and local governments. The first, maintained by the traditionalists, is that an already established form can adapt to changes which may occur within the political environment. The second theme, espoused by the reformers, is that structural alterations equatable with efficiency and economy best enable government to adapt to change.

On the state level, the reformers' drive for efficiency and economy has been manifested in proposals to reorganize the structures of the branches of government. Reformers have sought centralization through consolidation of administrative agencies under a governor; integration of the diverse components of the court system into a uniform hierarchy; and unicameralism of the legislative institution. Thus, the proposals were for making improvements in the existing forms of state government. On the local level, although similar proposals were made to restructure the institutions, the main thrust of the reform movement was directed to changing the forms of government. Hence, in the twentieth century, arguments have persuasively been propounded for the commission form, the council-manager form, and, most recently, metropolitan governments.

At the turn of the century, the mayor-council form was the universal pattern of government found in the cities. In the seven following decades, dynamic changes have taken place. This dynamic quality has been reflected in the hundreds of cities (often the same ones) which have abandoned and adopted new forms. In some cities, the mayor-council form was abandoned and then reinstituted. Commission forms were abandoned in favor of the council-manager pattern. Even the council-manager form, which has continued to enjoy great popularity (and is today the second most frequently utilized pattern in the cities), has been abandoned by some localities. The various proposals for change, the changes, and the continuance of traditional patterns have led researchers to study the various factors which relate to the forms of government.

Many studies have attempted to relate the demographic characteristics found within the environment to forms of government.[14] Mayor-council forms are most often found in northeastern and midwestern cities having populations of over 1,000,000 or below 50,000 persons. The environment is characterized by social, ethnic, racial, and economic heterogeneity. Council-manager forms tend to be in rapidly growing cities of the western, southern and border states. The residents are generally employed in white collar or professional occupations, have a relatively high level of education, are native-born, and are geographically mobile. The commission form is associated with cities having a declining or static population that is relatively homogeneous, characterized by low socioeconomic-educational levels, and little ethnic, racial, and religious diversity. The pattern is not predominant in any particular region, although the highest percentage of cities with this form is found in the south and the northeast.

People tend to hold political attitudes that influence their preferences for one kind or another of political forms. Several studies have attempted to associate types of attitudes with socioeconomic characteristics. It has been suggested that the mayor-council pattern is preferred by those in a heterogeneous society, for in a community marked by ethnic, racial, social, and economic cleavages, conflicting claims and diverse interests are transmitted into the political system. This necessitates strong political leadership that can arbitrate struggles for power and arrange compromises. In addition, the perspective of such groups as blue collar workers and immigrant and racial minorities has often appeared to be parochial in nature. These groups look to public agents for recognition and for help and favors. Thus, the need for leadership and arbitration could be satisfied by a strong mayor; and the demands for aid could readily be met by a large ward-based council, which could reelect and provide access points for the diverse groupings.

In contrast, in those communities where the "middle-class ethos" prevails, consensus is sought by minimizing cleavages through concentration on city-wide issues. The middle-class, white collar, and highly educated individuals place a premium on efficiency, professionalism, impartiality, long-term and comprehensive planning, and so on. They believe that such objectives could be best met by a council-manager form, for it represents a "businesslike" pattern (with a council as a board of directors and a manager as presiding executive) that adheres to "businesslike" principles.

In those communities with homogeneous populations, there are fewer diverse and competing interests and more acceptance of a common public interest. Therefore, the commission (as well as the council-manager) form appears well-suited to meet the emphasis on able administration and efficient provision of services. The absence of cleavages negates the need for excessive concern over political negotiation.

Research has also been undertaken to outline the factors which are conducive to changes in or maintenance of governmental forms.[15] Sudden growth in population often places stress upon a city's existing political structure. Administrative and technical problems increase as enlarged populations require additional new streets, schools, libraries, hospitals, parks, police protection, sewers and sanitation, and so on. Should the governmental pattern be unable to cope with stress, it is likely that an atmosphere conducive to change will be created. The new cities, which in recent years have been developed with an expectation of rapid growth, also have focused on selecting the governmental form apparently best able to adapt to accelerating demands. Thus, the search in both situations usually tends to lead to the adoption of the council-manager form with its emphasis on professional administration.

Similarly, change is more readily accepted in cities with highly mobile populations, because these cities have less stable political groupings and looser social and political ties. Moreover, highly mobile individuals (usually those in the higher levels of socioeconomic strata) tend to favor the "efficient, businesslike" governmental patterns, rather than a form geared to provide representation and access for traditional parochial groupings. Interest in change is often promoted by such individuals, who have been exposed to and are familiar and experienced with other political forms.

Optimal conditions for change exist in those communities where there is a preponderance of residents with civic-minded attitudes and organizational abilities. Here, there are found those with the time and inclination to join and be active in many community-wide civic and service associations, which are necessary in the mobilization for governmental reform. In addition, proximity to localities which have recently instituted changes in governmental patterns may provide the impetus for imitative change. Interaction among local public officials and newspaper support are catalysts facilitating acceptance of innovation.

Despite the many changes that have occurred, traditional forces have acted to prevent change in many localities. Where populations are stable, people may have grown accustomed to their government, may be satisfied with the level of services provided, and may feel that their interests are being accommodated by the existing political pattern. Thus, they may not desire change.

Inertia may also be caused by apathy and indifference. Unaware of and lacking political knowledge of the relative merits and consequences of adopting one governmental pattern rather than another, residents may not feel moved to organize or support proposals for new forms. Heterogeneity in the community may cause difficulty in obtaining consensus for either the need for modification or the type of alteration.

Many groups find it strategically and politically advantageous to maintain and defend the status quo, for the alteration of governmental forms involves a change in complex political arrangements of long standing. Interest groups may fear that restructuring would jeopardize their established relationships with governmental agents and agencies. Ethnic and racial groups may wish to maintain the mayor-council form, for it permits them to obtain minority representation and gives them a chance to maximize their political resources. The mayor-council form may also be preferred by political party leaders, especially in a competitive party situation; for this pattern provides more opportunities to recruit for and fill public offices and, thus, greater likelihood of obtaining ensuing rewards and privileges. Other groups, such as governmental officials and employees, align with those described above to man the bastions against change.

The retention of existing governmental forms may be due to factors other than popular considerations. Economic considerations may be a deterrent to change. For example, small cities or towns may not be able to afford a full-time manager or a full-time board of commissioners. Legal considerations may be another important factor. State constitutions and legislative enactments often inhibit change by requiring municipalities to conform to particular prescribed patterns or by preventing populations from adopting other forms.

Certainly there has never been a consensus on one perfect form of government agreeable to everyone, at every time, in every situation. Thus, changes occur or do not occur regardless of whether the legal system permits, optimal conditions exist, or some groups have more influence in innovating reforms than others. Governmental patterns reflect a combination of legal, political, social, and economic environmental factors. Only in recognizing the interrelationships of many factors will one understand the relationships between these factors and the forms of government.

Chapter I Footnotes

1. The Bureau of the Census conducts a census of governments at five-year intervals. The figures of governmental units found within this chapter were selected from the 1967 census of governments. See: U.S. Bureau of the Census, *Census of Governments, 1967,* Vol. I, *Governmental Organization* (Washington, D.C.: Government Printing Office, 1968).
2. See for example: *Ewing v. Hoblitzelle*, 85 Mo. 77 (1884); *Booten v. Pinson*, 77 W. Wa. 412 (1915); *Hunter v. Pittsburgh*, 207 U.S. 161 (1907); and *City of Trenton v. the State of New Jersey*, 262 U.S. 182 (1923).
3. *City of Clinton v. the Cedar Rapids and Missouri River Railroad Co.*, 24 Iowa 455 (1868).
4. *Commissioners of Hamilton County v. Meghels*, 7 Ohio St. 109 (1857).
5. 377 U.S. 533 (1964).
6. Talbot O'Alemberte and Charles C. Fishburne, Jr., "Why a Second House?" *National Civic Review*, LV (September 1966), pp. 431–37.
7. Current data on administrative reorganization are from *The Book of the States 1970–1971* (Lexington: The Council of State Governments, 1970), pp. 135–65.

8. Although in many states local courts have been established with limited jurisdiction (predominantly local in nature), all courts are theoretically part of state judicial systems. Hence, the discussion of the judicial structure is treated as a single unit in this section.

9. John P. Roche and Leonard W. Levy, *The Judiciary* (New York: Harcourt, Brace and Jovanovich, 1964), p. 2.

10. Quite often these cases must begin anew in the general trial courts, for the absence of record-keeping in the lower courts requires that evidence and testimony be presented again.

11. Current data on judicial reorganization are from *The Book of the States 1970–1971*, pp. 117–19.

12. Current data on forms of municipal government were from *The Municipal Year Book 1968* (Washington, D.C.: The International City Management Association, 1968).

For county data see Herbert S. Duncombe, *County Government in America* (Washington, D.C.: National Association of Counties, 1966).

13. For a brief historical account of this plan see Richard S. Childs, *The First 50 Years of the Council-Manager Plan of Municipal Government* (New York: National Municipal League, 1965).

14. See, for example, John H. Kessel, "Governmental Structure and Political Environment," *American Political Science Review*, LVI (September 1962), pp. 615–20; Charles Liebman, "Functional Differentiation and Political Characteristics of Suburbs," *American Journal of Sociology*, LXVI (March 1961), pp. 485–91; Leo F. Schnore and Robert R. Alford, "Forms of Government and Socioeconomic Characteristics of Suburbs," *Administrative Science Quarterly*, VIII (June 1963), pp. 1–17; Edgar L. Sherbenov, "Class Participation, and the Council-Manager Plan," *Public Administration Review*, XXI (Summer 1961), pp. 131–35; James Q. Wilson and Edward C. Banfield, "Public-Regardedness as a Value Premise in Voting Behavior," *American Political Science Review*, LVIII (December 1964), pp. 876–87; Raymond E. Wolfinger and John O. Field, "Political Ethos and the Structure of City Government," *American Political Science Review*, LX (June 1966), pp. 306–26; Robert L. Lineberry and Edmund P. Fowler, "Reformism and Public Policies in American Cities," *American Political Science Review*, LXI (September 1967), pp. 701–16; and Robert R. Alford and Harry M. Scoble, "Political and Socioeconomic Characteristics of American Cities," *The Municipal Year Book 1965* (Chicago: The International City Managers' Association, 1965), pp. 82–97.

15. See for example, in addition to the studies cited in note 14, Thomas M. Scott, "The Diffusion of Urban Governmental Forms as a Case of Social Learning," *Journal of Politics*, XXX (November 1968), pp. 1091–1108; Brett W. Hawkins, "Public Opinion and Metropolitan Reorganization in Nashville," *Journal of Politics*, XXVIII (May 1966), pp. 408–18; and *Factors Affecting Voter Reactions to Governmental Reorganization in Metropolitan Areas* (Washington, D.C.: Advisory Commission on Intergovernmental Relations, 1962).

Chapter II

The Basic Rules

Every political system operates according to a set of basic rules. These rules provide the legal framework for the structures of government, the distribution of public powers among governmental institutions, and the relationships of the institutions to each other. Moreover, the set of basic rules defines the formal political roles of public agents and citizens, as well as the relationships among those political actors to each other and to the institutions of government.

Such fundamental political prescriptions are, by legal and historical traditions, written. The rules that set the framework of state government are written in documents known as constitutions. And those for local government are set forth in state constitutions, state statutes, or in special documents known as local charters.

State Constitutions

The scope of state constitutions is extensive. Each document reflects its state's unique environment; yet, all constitutions contain similar essential components. These similarities are based on several theoretical principles of government. Every constitution embodies such principles as popular sovereignty, separation of powers, checks and balances, limited government, and protection of political, personal, and property rights and liberties.

The preamble of each constitution incorporates the concept of popular sovereignty. Most of the documents begin with the phrase "We the people

. . ." as an explicit statement that the ultimate source of political authority rests with the citizens of that state. Moreover, most constitutions end with the provision that change of the basic rules requires the active consent of the people.

The concepts of separation of powers, and checks and balances, are implemented in those articles that establish the institutions of government. The executive, legislative, and judicial branches are created as separate and distinct institutions. The constitutions set forth the powers of each branch, and prescribe an overlap of institutional responsibilities in the performance of the functions of government. In that manner, checks are enumerated that establish a balance of institutional strength.

The notion of limited government means that the activities of public agencies should not be all pervasive over the daily lives of the people. Constitutional provisions specifying the powers of public agents and the relationships among the institutions act to restrict government. Yet, the concept of limited government is principally related to the protection of rights and liberties of citizens. Thus, each state constitution includes a list of individual rights upon which the government cannot transgress. Such "Bills of Rights" or "Declarations of Rights" prohibits the state from infringing upon the exercise of fundamental freedoms. The range of those freedoms, however, is not uniform in every state. Generally, each state constitution mentions the freedoms that are incorporated in the United States Constitution (e.g., speech, worship, press, peaceful assembly, etc.), but some states supplement those with other freedoms considered to be fundamental there. For example, the Bill of Rights in one state includes as a fundamental freedom the right to fish; in another, to sell one's farm produce; in a third, collective bargaining by organized workers; and, in a fourth, the right of a private club to sell alcoholic beverages.

In addition to the articles that reflect the basic theoretical principles of government, there are other provisions common to all state constitutions. Those reflect the legal, political, and historical responsibilities and activities of the states as delineated by their loci within the federal system. One such responsibility is providing for local governments. For within the federal arrangement of political systems, the creation and governance of local units are under the aegis of the states. Thus, each constitution contains provisions that pertain to the identification, structure, powers, finance, public agents, and electoral processes of the political subdivisions of the state.

Within the federal system some powers are reserved to the states or shared by them with the national government. Articles in the state constitutions outline the activities the states are empowered to perform. Historically, the reserved activities have covered what is known as the "police powers," that is, health, education, welfare, and public safety. Included within this broad category has been the power of regulation over such matters as banking, insurance, railroads, water rights, liquor, mines, and agriculture. Types of responsibilities the states share with the federal government include providing for suffrage and elections, finances and taxation, highways, licenses and incorporations, and protection of natural resources.

Many present-day state constitutions are so detailed and long that they resemble statutory codes rather than sets of fundamental guidelines. The extreme detail can be traced to the mid to late nineteenth century. Prior to that period (especially in the eighteenth century), the writers of the documents focused upon the fundamental elements of political systems, and wrote brief and flexible instruments. Indeed, the national constitution, which is considered a classic in brevity, was modeled after (and written by some of the authors of) the constitutions of the original thirteen states.

In contrast, the nineteenth-century documents were characterized by a proliferation of details regarding specific authorizations, restraints, and procedures of action. The specificity of basic rules was a manifestation of the distrust held by citizens towards their state officials. Legislators were held in especially low esteem and the provisions that placed restrictions on the legislative process are illustrative of the details used to diminish the discretion of public agents. Scandals of corruption and bribery made people aware that governmental finances and affairs were being mismanaged. Unfavorable reactions to legislative activities led to provisions that prescribed those areas in which the legislators could or could not make rules. Because the legislators had endangered the credit of the states, specific debt limits and even salaries of the officials were written into the constitution. Legislative sessions were made biennial, and the maximum number of days that those sessions were to last was specified. These last provisions reflected the philosophy that the less time the legislators spent at the capitol, the less damage they could do.

The nineteenth-century model continues to shape the conduct of most state governments today. Thirty-three states retain their constitutions adopted during that period of distrust. Although the constitutions have been amended throughout the succeeding decades, essentially the revisions continued to explicitly state modes of actions that were to apply to changing circumstances. By continually focusing on specifics, the amending process resulted in adding length to already long documents.

Several implications arise from the long and detailed nature of the constitutions. The ability of public agents to act is hampered, as actions are determined and controlled by constitutional provisions written years before a specific problem or situation had to be faced. As more matters are specified in the basic rules, fewer ones are left to be decided by the regular rule-making processes. The more complex the constitutional provisions, the more active a role the courts assume in the rule-making function. Persons with the interest, time, and money can always find a constitutional provision they believe is being violated or not properly complied with, and initiate litigation in the courts. Such litigation may lead to delay in the execution of programs, if not outright prohibition of action. In addition, rule-making exceedingly becomes a process of amending the constitution, rather than exacting legislation. Thus, as new situations arise that demand attention, the utilization of the complex and time-consuming process of constitutional revision is necessary for change.

Constitutional Change

Every state constitution contains an article that prescribes the procedure for changing the basic rules. The changes take two forms. One is partial revision, or amendments, which are additions to the basic document to alter a specified part. The second is complete revision, in which a new document replaces the old one.[1]

Initiation of Amendments

There are two stages in the amending process: initiation (i.e., proposing), and ratification (i.e., approving). One way by which amendments may be proposed is through legislative initiation. The constitutions of each of the fifty states empower the legislature to propose basic rule changes. In nearly all states, either chamber of the legislature may take the first step in this process. Another common prescription is that both houses of the legislative body must vote on the proposal, and each house votes separately. The principal exceptions to this last general practice are in Nebraska, which has only one chamber, and in Massachusetts, where the members of both chambers meet in joint session to vote.

The proportion of members required for approval of proposed amendments varies throughout the states. In eighteen states a simple majority (i.e., at least one more than half of the votes cast) is necessary; in nineteen a two-thirds majority is required; and in eight the proportion is three-fifths. Several of these states have prescriptions that base the proportion on the total number of legislators who comprise that rule-making body, rather than the number of legislators who are present and voting. Approval need be gained in only one legislative session in most of the states. However, one-fifth of the state constitutions stipulate that an amendment must pass two successive sessions of the legislature, with the similar majority required each time (except in Tennessee, where at least one more than half of all the members must approve during the first session, and two-thirds must approve during the second session; and in Vermont, where two-thirds of the senate and a majority of the house are required during the first session, but only a majority of each house the second time). An interesting variation exists in three of the fifty states. In those, a simple majority in two successive sessions is required, unless an extraordinary majority (two-thirds in Hawaii, three-fourths in Connecticut, and three-fifths in New Jersey) is attained during the first session.

Additional stipulations exist in several states that serve to restrict legislative action in proposing amendments. For example, the legislature may be limited to a certain number of amendments they may initiate in a given time period. The Colorado legislature may not propose amendments to more than six articles of that state's constitution in one legislative session. In Illinois, the number of articles that may be amended in any one session is limited to three; and if amended, an article may not be subject to further alteration unless four years have passed.

Another method for proposing amendments is the popular initiative. The constitutions of fourteen states make it possible for citizens to directly offer amendments for ratification. Persons interested in initiating change can by-pass the legislature by circulating a petition to collect a specified number of signatures. The number of signatures required varies, but it is almost always a percentage of votes cast at the election (usually for governor) prior to the circulation of the petition (except in North Dakota where the number is set at a minimum of 20,000 registered voters). In several of those states, con-stitutional provisions require that all signatures not be obtained from the same area of the state. For example, in Massachusetts, the number of signa-tures must equal 3 percent of the total vote for governor at the last election, but no more than one-fourth of the signatures may come from any one county. Florida's requirements illustrate how intricate provisions for peti-tions may be; there the number of signatures needed must not be less than 8 percent of the total votes cast in one-half of congressional districts, and 8 percent of the total votes cast throughout the state in the last election for presidential electors.

A third way to initiate change is through constitutional conventions. Con-stitutions of thirty-nine states expressly authorize the establishment of con-ventions for the initiation of amendments; yet, there are no prohibitions restricting the utilization of conventions in the remaining states. Because of the complex machinery involved in calling a convention (which will be discussed later), this method is more fully utilized for complete revision than for initiating amendments.

Of the three methods, the most extensively used is the legislative initiative. For example, between January 1, 1968, and December 31, 1969, 490 amend-ments were proposed to forty-two state constitutions. Of those, 450 (91.8 percent) were initiated by the legislatures; 6 (1.2 percent) by citizens; and

34 (6.9 percent) by special conventions. That most proposals originate in the legislature reflects the fact that this is the least complex, time consuming, and expensive of the three processes. Moreover, citizens who wish to see changes made in the constitution may more easily address their interest to their legislative representatives than to a closed convention or through a demanding petition campaign.

During that two-year period, the 490 initiated amendments covered a broad range of subject categories. Nearly one-third of the proposals were aimed at changing articles that pertained to the legislative branch, and finance, debt, and taxation. Other proposals dealt with the executive and judicial branches, suffrage, civil rights, procedures for altering constitutions, and state services (including education, health, welfare, natural resources, and public works). The largest category focused on amendments that would affect the structures, finance, and services of one or more local governments.

Revising the Constitution

Complete revisions of the state constitutions usually are drafted by constitutional conventions. The procedure for calling such conventions is prescribed in state constitutions, state statutes, state court decisions, and in precedents. In all states but one the call is initiated by the legislature. Florida is the exception, as it reserves to the electorate the power to petition the call. A simple legislative majority is required in more than half the states, and an extraordinary majority (either two-thirds or three-fifths) in approximately two-fifths of the states, to approve the resolution necessary to convoke a convention.

Once the resolution has passed both houses of the state legislature, it is usually placed on the ballot for the approval of the public. Most states, by constitutional or statutory provisions, require popular approval prior to calling a convention. However, the percentage of votes needed for passage of the referendum question varies. The requisite in most states is a majority of the votes cast on the proposition; in several, it is a majority of the total votes cast at the general election; and in the others, an extraordinary majority is required. Should the legislators not consider or pass such a resolution during a specified period, the constitutions of eleven states demand that the question of calling a convention be submitted to the electorate. That question must appear on the ballot at least every ten years in Alaska, Hawaii, Iowa, and New Hampshire; every sixteen years in Michigan; and every twenty years in Oklahoma, Ohio, New York, Missouri, Maryland, and Connecticut.

Upon popular approval, the legislature proceeds to convoke the constitutional convention, guided in many cases by the prescriptions of the basic rules. Arrangements must be made for the election of the delegates, and qualifications for candidates must be set. A consensus must be reached as to the place of the convention meetings, when it shall begin, and when it shall adjourn. Temporary officers are appointed and preliminary rules are adopted. And funds must be appropriated to cover the costs of the convention.

Once the convention convenes, permanent officers are elected and permanent rules of procedure are adopted. The delegates are assigned to subject matter committees for the purpose of initially studying and drafting provisions. The full assemblage then meets to deliberate and completely draft the revision. When its allotted time has expired or when it has completed the task, the convention ends.

Constitutional commissions have been utilized in most states to study whether a need for change exists and to recommend the type of change that might be most effective. These have been created by statutes, legislative resolutions, or executive orders. Florida is the only state that provides a constitutional basis for the establishment of such a commission. Members are generally appointed by the governor and/or the presiding officers of the legislative houses. A majority of those appointed have been legislators, former legislators, and lawyers. In the two-year period 1968–1969, for example, twenty-six constitutional commissions were operative in twenty-two states. The increased utilization of such bodies has been due, in large part, to the reluctance of legislators and constituents to meet the high cost of convening and holding a constitutional convention.

Often the commissions engage in tasks other than studying the constitutions. They assist in the preparations for calling conventions, hold orientation sessions for convention delegates, gather needed resource information, draft a complete suggested constitution, etc. Occasionally, when it is thought that a full-scale revision is unnecessary, the commission members will propose amendments to one or more articles in the existing constitution for legislative initiative.

Ratification

Constitutional changes take effect by popular ratification in all states but Delaware (where adoption occurs upon approval of two-thirds of the legislators in two successive sessions). The proposed revisions may be placed on the ballot at either a special or general election. When an entirely new set of basic rules is offered for approval, the new document may be voted on in parts or in whole, depending on the decision of the legislature or the constitutional convention. In four states, the number of amendments that may appear on the ballot at any one time is limited to two or three; and in Vermont, amendments may only be submitted to the voters at ten-year intervals. The proportion of votes required for passage may be 1) a simple majority vote (although in a few states an extraordinary proportion is required) on the amendment or constitution; or 2) a majority of the total number of voters participating in the election. South Carolina requires in addition to approval of the voters, subsequent approval of the legislators.

Concern for Reform

The fundamental principle adhered to for centuries is that the constitution is the supreme law of the state. Thus, the belief held by constitution writers is that the basic rules should be more difficult to change than ordinary rules. In pursuit of implementing that belief, provisions have been set into every state constitution that place obstacles in the path of quick and simple change. Revision encompasses a two-stage process, one which demands the involvement of both public officials and constituents. Often an extraordinary proportion of approval from both legislators and the electorate is required for, respectively, the initiation and ratification of alterations. The two-stage process, in itself, lengthens the time interval between the conception and adoption of a proposal. Yet, several states further impeded speed by requiring consideration by legislators in successive sessions. In a few instances this last requirement has had the effect of hampering (if not halting) change. Intervening elections between successive sessions may have resulted in an election of legislative personnel who were unfamiliar or unsympathetic with what had begun. Additional limitations were designed in some states to restrict the character, number, and frequency of amendments.

Yet the difficulties have been overcome; amendments have been adopted. In Alabama, 314 amendments have been added to the constitution of 1901; 358 in California since 1879; 655 in Georgia since 1945; 494 in Louisiana since 1921; 284 in South Carolina since 1895; and 191 in Texas since 1876. These extensive amendments reflected piecemeal alteration, added length to the document, and in most instances, made the basic rules more detailed and complex.

Concern over constitutional reform has been noticeably ascending over the past few decades. Both public and private groups have been studying and suggesting proposals for revision of the basic rules. Among such groups have been: divisions in state legislative reference agencies, subcommittees of state legislative councils, the United States Advisory Commission on Intergovernmental Relations, the Council of State Governments, the Committee for Economic Development, the League of Women Voters, institutions of governmental research in universities, and the National Municipal League. Most of these groups have concluded that the piecemeal approach of the amending process has been inadequate to meet the needs created by population growth, the shift of population from rural to urban and suburban areas, a changing economic base (e.g., from agricultural to industrial, as well as a movement of industry and commerce from urban centers), and increased state participation in the dispensing of social welfare services. Thus, the view most frequently espoused has been for replacing detailed sets of basic rules with brief general documents that include the fundamental principles of constitutions and which would permit flexibility and adaptability to changing needs and demands.

Perhaps the oldest and most influential of the groups concerned with constitutions has been the National Municipal League. Since 1921, the League has presented its suggestions for constitutional reform in a document called *The Model State Constitution.*[2] The Model is a complete constitution the League proposes as being the most suitable basic set of rules for states to adopt. The League has distributed copies to commission members, convention delegates, and legislators. Although the document has not been embraced totally by any state, it has been an influential guide to constitution writers. Since the advent of the League's first constitutional model, numerous of its provisions have appeared in the changes which have been made to most of the state constitutions.

Basic Rules of Local Governments

The basic rules of localities are not embodied in any single document. They are, instead, derived from state constitutional articles, state legislative enactments, and state judicial decisions. As creatures of the state, the fundamental framework of local government is set by the traditions and policies of the state.

Prescriptions for the form of government, the powers of government, the manner in which the power is exercised, and the relationships between and among the political actors and the citizens are found in the charters that create the local governing unit. There are basically four categories of charters. The major difference among them is the extent to which the form of government and the scope of public functions are prescribed by the state. The first and most limiting set of basic rules is the special charter. This, the earliest method of creating local governments, results from special enactments of the state legislature. Such a charter establishes the territorial boundaries of a locality and prescribes its form of government. The responsibility for rule-making is essentially retained by the state legislature. Any alteration in either the locality's governmental structure or its authority requires state legislative action. Although each locality has the advantage of obtaining special consideration for its own situation under this method, special charters have created several problems. Local citizens found that the collective will of the state legislature becomes substituted for that of their own. This has been particularly troublesome for the urban interests that face unsympathetic rural-dominated legislatures. The state legislatures have found that a considerable amount of time must be devoted to enacting legislation for specified cities. Because of these problems, the special charter has lost its appeal outside of the New England and southern regions.

In response to the problems of the special charter, the states adopted the general charter as the method of distributing local basic rules. Initially, the legislatures drafted uniform general charters. This meant a single type of charter for all localities. The uniform charter prescribed that the structures, powers, and privileges of each locality within the state be similar. The inflexibility of such prescriptions for highly divergent local communities with differing needs led to a modification of this second category. Flexibility was introduced by classifying localities (usually on the basis of population) and issuing a general charter specifically written for each class of localities. Those who favored a system of classification charters believed that localities of approximately the same size would have similar needs to meet and each should therefore operate under a set of basic rules made for its size. Although general charters did provide broader areas of discretion to local agents, still greater flexibility appeared necessary. For size is not the only factor to be associated with the appropriateness of basic rules; other factors (including economic resources, social composition, and rate of development) deserve consideration. Thus, the problems arising from the second method led to the creation and adoption of a third category.

The optional charter category offers to localities a number of alternative sets of basic rules from which local citizens may choose. This plan offers choices as to the form of government that may be adopted. The electorate or the council may select the form believed to be appropriate for their locality. However, they must choose from among the alternatives presented without making any variations. While the state grants more local control over exclusively local matters under this form, it still retains considerable power over the extent of rule-making that shall be permitted a local government.

The broadest authority to manage local affairs is granted under home rule charters, the fourth category. The purpose of home rule is to permit maximum flexibility in determining the structure, procedure, and powers of local governments. By this arrangement, the local constituents (through their representatives) may draft and (through the referendum) adopt and amend their own charter. This set of basic rules is the one most free from state set guidelines. Home rule cities usually have broader powers than do other cities, as they may perform all functions of local self-government. However, it is not a grant of complete autonomy. The locality is still subject to some degree of control by the state branches of government.

Tradition, usage, necessity, purpose, active local groups, local councils, and citizens are factors in determining the type of basic rules for localities.

The type of charter granted to a local unit, to a large extent, may be determined by those charters that have traditionally been written throughout the state's history and that have appeared to be successful in usage. Indeed, vested interests that have developed and flourished under a given set of basic rules may be resistant to a different type that may threaten their established relationships. Charter types also may be determined by the purpose for which the local political subdivision has been created. For example, counties that were established for the purpose of administering state activities locally have usually been granted general charters. In contrast, special districts that set up to oversee one specific activity were issued special charters.

Much of charter history has been marked by the efforts of local councils, groups, and citizens to lessen the pervasiveness of the state legislature in local affairs. Initially, the response that indicated the state's willingness to permit some local self-determination was the optional charter. By offering alternative sets of basic rules, the state allowed local councils and/or the electorate to select that set which they thought best met the needs and demands of their community. Home rule charters represented the ultimate demonstration of willingness by state legislators to divest themselves of immediate control over local matters. The larger, more highly developed, heterogeneous cities have most frequently enjoyed the advantage of having such a charter. As counties became more urbanized and states ceded to them more responsibilities for performing governmental functions, they, too, became recipients of home rule charters.

Charters and Change

So that they might delineate clearly the local units, governments, and actions, charters are detailed and inclusive. One finds such prescriptions as: the specific form of government; the titles, number, duties, salaries, terms, qualifications, and methods of selection of public officials; the nomination procedures, manner of holding elections, designations of partisanship or non-partisanship, and suffrage requirements; legislative and administrative powers and procedures; and fiscal affairs.

As is the case with state constitutions, any alterations of the basic rules of local governments must come about through amendment or complete revision. The procedure for change is prescribed in state constitutions, state statutes, or in the charter itself. The basic rules for localities that are set in the state constitutions must be altered through the regular constitutional amendment process. Those that are set by statutes are usually altered by subsequent legislative enactments. Local governments having a special, general, or optional charter, may obtain a change in the basic rules applicable to them by requesting a special local act from the state legislature, instead of a charter amendment. By means of such acts, a city is able to enjoy some flexibility in meeting the specific needs of its constituency. In addition, state legislators may amend optional charter acts to expand the alternatives available for local selection.

The electorate may directly influence the initiation and ratification of changes to state prescribed charters. Where charters are written into the constitution, changes necessitate popular ratification. Several states require that changes to legislatively created charters be presented for approval in a local referendum. In others, local commissions, empowered to draft amendments, must seek popular approval prior to state legislative action. Once a locality has adopted an optional charter package, should it decide to try a different package from among the alternatives offered by the state legislature, the action can be initiated by the local council and subsequently ratified by the constituents.

Home rule charters are distinct from the other types in that the state is not an active participant in the amendment or revision process. Amendments to such charters may be introduced by the local council. Where the state permits, proposals for change may be initiated by a petition signed by a specified number of registered voters. Thereafter, in either case, the proposed amendment is submitted to the electorate for ratification at a special or general election.

A locality may choose to completely revise its home rule charter. Should the councilmen be convinced that this would be appropriate, the question of whether revision should be undertaken is placed on the ballot. If the proposal is agreed to by the constituents, a convention is usually called and delegates elected to draft the document. Often a preliminary study commission is established, with members selected by the local executive or council. In some localities, such a commission is a permanent body that has been created to study continually the feasibility of charter change. Commission members may suggest and draft amendments or prepare arguments for complete revision. The commission may prepare a comprehensive outline, prior to the convening of a convention, to serve as the basis for deliberation by the delegates.

In addition to the suggestion of study commissions, delegates to charter conventions obtain recommendations from a variety of sources. They may invite interest or civic group representatives to submit proposals. Hearings may be held at which interested members of the community may testify. Delegates often examine the charters of similar localities and inquire into the experiences those localities may have had with specific provisions. The National Municipal League is active in providing guidelines. These have been incorporated in their *Model County Charter*[3] and the *Model City Charter*.[4] After the charter is drafted, it is proffered to the voters at a special or general election.

Intergovernmental Influences on the Basic Rules

Constitutionalism is a fundamental characteristic of the American political system, for basic rules are essential in the establishment of any governmental unit. The federal union was founded with the acceptance of a drafted constitution. Once founded, the creation of a state and its admission to the Union was contingent upon its adoption of basic rules. And localities are incorporated by basic rules.

Inherent in American constitutionalism is a hierarchical arrangement of the sets of basic rules. Integral to this arrangement is the concept of supremacy. As set by its own provisions, the national constitution is paramount. Article VI (Section 2) states that:

> This Constitution, and the laws of the United States which shall be made in pursuance thereof; and all treaties made, or which shall be made, under the authority of the United States, shall be the supreme law of the land; and the judges in every State shall be bound thereby, anything in the constitution or laws of any State to the contrary notwithstanding.

With the enunciation of eminent national authority, the subordinate status of state basic rules was constitutionally set. Provisions of the states' constitutions that are in conflict with those of the national's are unenforceable. In turn, the states, when creating political subdivisions, dictate that the basic rules of localities are subordinate to those of their own.

American legal theory, tradition, and practice have preserved the hierarchical order of the basic rules. Under the mandate of Article VI of the United States Constitution, judges became the arbiter of conflicts which arose between sets of basic rules. The case that set the legal precedent for the performance of that role was *McCulloch v. Maryland.*[5] Speaking for the Court, Chief Justice Marshall reiterated the principle of supremacy:

> This great principle is, that the Constitution and the laws made in pursuance thereof are supreme; that they control the Constitution and laws of the respective States, and cannot be controlled by them.

Thus, in finding the Maryland rule incompatible with the basic rules of the federal government, the justices declared the state rule "unconstitutional and void."

McCulloch v. Maryland also expanded the necessity for judges to perform the arbiter role. For the decision was significant in that the Court enunciated the doctrine of "implied powers" as their interpretation of Article I (Section 8) which stated that:

The Congress shall have power . . . to make all laws which shall be necessary and proper for carrying into execution the foregoing powers [as enumerated], and all other powers vested by this Constitution in the government of the United States, or in any department or officer thereof.

This meant to the Court that the national government, in pursuance of its constitutional mandates, could engage in activities other than those expressly enumerated.

This interpretation of the "necessary and proper" clause increased the potential for incompatibility between the basic rules of the nation and the states. As the national government entered into a broader range of activities, the justices were called upon to determine whether conflict existed. If conflicts were deemed to exist, the basic rules of the states had to be modified so as to comply with the higher set of rules.

Changes of the national constitution can affect the basic rules of the states and localities. Indeed, several additions to that constitution have been made expressly to alter the basic rules of the states. These have included the Thirteenth, Fourteenth, Fifteenth, and Nineteenth amendments. Yet, often a state may not act as if such changes have affected their basic rules. The state may choose to ignore such alterations, or it may wait until the vague generalities or unclear wording of the new provisions are interpreted. Such inaction inevitably has led aggrieved citizens to the courts. Hence, the federal justices are called upon to adjudicate the controversies that arise from the noncompliance with the higher law.

In adjudicating the controversies, the basic rules become those the justices interpret them to be, at a specific point in time. At a subsequent time, the same rule may be given a different meaning through judicial reinterpretation. Illustrative of this point is the "equal protection" Fourteenth Amendment:

No State shall . . . deny to any person within its jurisdiction the equal protection of the laws.

The Supreme Court was first called upon to render an interpretation of that clause in the Slaughterhouse Cases, in 1873.[6] With contemporary history and conditions in mind, the Court stated:

We doubt very much whether any action of a state not directed by way of discrimination against the negroes as a class, or on account of their race, will ever be held to come within the purview of this provision.

However, in the mid-twentieth century, the equal protection clause became the basis of alterations in the basic rules of states and localities in a variety of areas. The courts have held invalid various state rules that disenfranchised classes of people because of residence, race, property ownership, etc. And most recently, malapportionment of state and local legislatures has been interpreted by the court as being in violation of the equal protection clause.

Although the national constitution and judicial interpretations have affected local basic rules, it is the state constitution and state judicial decisions that have affected them more extensively. In most instances, the localities do not determine their own basic rules; rather, they are specified by the state constitutions and statutes. The state courts, adhering to Dillon's Rule (that the locality is the creature of the state), have viewed the political subdivisions as having only those powers expressly delegated to them. State judges have traditionally been strict in construing the provisions of charters, and frequently have imposed more constraints on the delegated powers than were originally thought to exist.

State courts have been actively involved with the adjudication of controversies arising from the conflict of state and local sets of rules. The two levels of government are engaged in similar types of activities and the responsibilities of each are not always clearly delineated. The relative ease by which taxpayers' may bring suit against local actions has made the justices active participants in state-local conflicts. In adjudicating the suits, the practice of the judges has been to closely examine the specific delegated powers within the charters, rather than the appropriate provisions within state constitutions. Thus, state justices have maintained state supremacy, and have defined the extent and substance of local basic rules.

How and when justices act as arbiters depends on their own guidelines. Generally, they wait until an actual controversy arises, one which represents a real and substantial conflict affecting the legal rights and obligations of parties having adversary interests. Yet, even when a controversy is brought before the court, the attitudes of the justices affect the extent to which state and local basic rules are influenced. Whether a case is accepted to be heard; whether the constitutionality of an issue is to be focused upon; whether the basic rules will be strictly or loosely construed; or whether prior decisions are considered binding, depends on the discretion of the justices. And such decisions ultimately determine whether a basic rule is maintained, voided, or modified.

Frequently state supreme court justices can exert influence by giving advice. In many states, the governor, legislators, and/or the attorney general may request an advisory opinion as to whether a state or local act may be constitutional. Thereby, an interpretation of the basic rules may be obtained without an actual controversy having arisen.

Although the ability of the courts to interpret the basic rules is extensive, they have no power to enforce compliance of their interpretations. Compliance rests on the willingness of the state and local officials to change their basic rules as directed. If recalcitrance is encountered, then the combined efforts of the other two branches of government must be called upon. The responsibilities for enforcement rests with the executive branch. And the legislative branch may provide for the machinery, funds, and procedures that permit the executive branch to perform its responsibilities.

The laws enacted by Congress in pursuance of the Constitution (as prescribed in Article VI) are treated as the supreme laws of the land. Their position in the hierarchical order permits them to influence the basic rules of states and localities. For example, the action of Congress in 1970, extending the franchise to citizens as young as eighteen years of age, affected state constitutional prescriptions that set higher minimum ages as a prerequisite for voting in congressional and presidential elections. In addition, congressional influence can be exerted indirectly. Often national legislative action is a catalyst that stimulates states and localities to alter their basic rules. For example, the Pendleton Act (Civil Service Act) of 1883, which prescribed "merit" as the basis for the personnel selection policies of the national government, set the example for the introduction of similar provisions in the constitutions and charters of the other levels of government.

The executive branch, charged with seeing that "the laws be faithfully executed," is integral to the maintenance of the hierarchical order. Thus, it too influences the basic rules. For example, when the U.S. Attorney General sent federal examiners into southern states to take voter registration out of the hands of local registrars, the state rules (which had for so long acted to preclude blacks from registering) were shunted aside to yield to the 1965 Voting Rights Act.

Although the state legislature's ability to affect local rules has always been extensive, its interference in such matters has been diminishing in the last half of this century. With the greatest proportion of citizens living in urban areas, the major problems to be solved have become too complex for the part-time legislators to handle. In contrast there has been an increase in the governor's power to affect local basic rules. As chief initiator of legislation, and head of the executive branch, he holds the prime position to exert such influence. Indeed, he and he alone holds the extreme power of suspending local basic rules. Through his emergency powers, he may declare martial law and, by doing so, temporarily set aside the operation of local government. On such rare occasions, military officers, under the command of the governor, tend to the administration of the city.

The extent to which states intervene in local affairs is not always related to the type of charter that had been granted. This fact can best be grasped in the case of home rule charters. Despite the relatively high degree of autonomy associated with this type of basic rules, in practice the autonomy has been exercised in the choice of forms of government, rather than in the discretion permitted to handle local problems. Home rule charters have generally been granted to large, heterogeneous cities, in which the bulk of critical, contemporary problems are found. Although the charters of these localities provide the authority and machinery, the municipalities lack the crucial political and economic resources to solve the complex problems that besiege them. Thus, the recent endeavors to seek solutions, have been transferred to the state and national governments; resulting in little local discretion.

Intergovernmental influence within the hierarchical order of basic rules is not only directed downward. Often the catalysts for change in the higher level rules come from the lower levels. For example, many state constitutions have been revised in light of the consequences of urbanization and its concomitant social problems. To meet resulting complex demands, such revisions have been made as: longer legislative sessions, expanded and centralized executive powers, restructured administrative systems (e.g., cabinet systems established to include agencies for urban affairs), and fiscal reforms (e.g., expanded debt limits and reshuffling tax bases).

Constituency Influences on Basic Rules

One of the fundamental principles of constitutionalism is that the documents are written manifestations of the sovereign will of the people. The concept of popular sovereignty is enunciated in the preambles of constitutions, and the implementation of the concept is embodied in the provisions for change. Yet, "We, the People" find themselves in a rather awkward position in regard to the constitution and constitutional revision. The average citizen finds the document remote. He is not familiar with the exact contents of the basic rules or of their practical influence on his daily life. Moreover, he finds the call to participate in the process of constitutional change in conflict with his belief that these fundamental rules, sanctified through age, should not be tampered with lightly.

Although the individual citizen may be reluctant to tamper with the basic rules, groups of citizens generally are not. Indeed, such collectivities as special interest groups, civic associations, and political parties actively focus their attention on the content of constitutions and charters. Those documents, in delineating public agencies, powers of public agents, and areas of public policy, affect their interests.

Much of the nature and content of existing basic rules have been the result of the extensive activities of groups. Provisions are to be found that reflect the interests of a variety of associations over the course of time. Under the impetus of reform groups, disturbed by the public scandals of office holders, state after state in the nineteenth century adopted articles that act to restrict the actions of state and local public agents (especially legislators). Provisions designed to provide protection of and advantages for particular economic interests were adopted as results of the efforts made by such groups as farmers, labor unions, industrialists, coal mine operators, and rail-road entrepreneurs. Political parties sought and achieved the incorporation of passages they perceived to be to their political advantage; those included such matters as nominating machinery, suffrage expansion, districting, and elective offices.

Lewis A. Froman, Jr., has studied the influence of interest groups on the development of forty-eight state constitutions.[7] His basic premise was that interest groups perceived constitutions as important instruments through which special advantages are allocated, and thus they would attempt to influence the nature, content, and amending process of the basic rules. Froman demonstrated that, the stronger the interest group:

> the greater the length of the state constitutions;
> the greater the number of proposed amendments;
> the greater the number of amendments adopted;
> the less the difficulty in amending the constitution.[8]

Moreover, he noted that certain provisions were of primary concern to interest groups, especially those related to selection procedures of public officials. Hence, he tested and confirmed that, the stronger the interest groups:

> the greater the number of state elected officials;
> the greater the number of state agencies with elected officials;
> the greater the likelihood that state public utility commissions will be elected;
> the greater the probability that judges on state courts of last resort will be elected;
> the shorter will be the terms of office of judges on state courts of last resort.[9]

Special interest groups act to exert influence at every stage of the amendment and revision process. Although legislative initiative may be simulated by a variety of sources, political parties and partisan candidates are important sources for such proposals. Parties may incorporate constitutional reforms into their platforms, and candidates for office might make constitutional reform a campaign issue. With success at the polls, these proposals are introduced into the legislative chambers. If the suggested change does not directly conflict with the interests of a legislator's constituency, then the votes will be cast along party lines. During recent years, much stimulus for change has come from gubernatorial candidates, who (after being elected) use their office and position in the party to gain the support of party affiliates in the legislature. Interest groups have not been thwarted by pervasive party influence on the legislative initiative. Groups marshal their resources to draft and submit proposals to friendly legislators, offer supporting data, appear at hearings, and endeavor to obtain support from the constituents.

In those states permitting popular initiatives, interest groups are the leading actors in conducting petition campaigns. The high costs and complexity entailed in obtaining the required number of signatures generally precludes individual action. The organized groups have the necessary funds, skill, leadership, and staff to successfully operate the petition machinery.[10]

Constituent influence is thought to be exerted most extensively on constitutional conventions. The conventions are said to be the "people in sovereign assemblage," for they are called into being by the people through referendum, and are comprised of delegates elected by the people to represent them. As such they are to be above partisan and parochial considerations. But, in practice, parties and interest groups are closely involved with such conventions.

The first major hurdle in calling a constitutional convention is obtaining the electorate's approval. Quite often the process of gaining such approval is long and difficult. To overcome apathy and the innate awe felt for the constitution, vigorous campaigns must be conducted. Repeatedly, studies have demonstrated that successful campaigns have been those that have been well organized and coordinated. The task of educating the citizens to the need for constitutional revision has been undertaken by a variety of special and civic associations. For example, the approval of the convention call in Tennessee was the result of the efforts made by the Tennessee Citizens Committee for a Limited Constitutional Convention, which coordinated the activities of such state groups as: the League of Women Voters, Bar Association, Press Association, Taxpayers Association, Manufacturers Association, Federation of Labor, Education Association, Junior Chamber of Commerce, Federation of Women's Clubs, the Congress of Social Workers, and others.[11] Similar types of groups were found working to secure the approval for a call to convene a county charter convention in Prince Georges County, Maryland. Under the coordination of the Operation Charter Draft Now committee, campaign activities were undertaken by such local groups as: Chambers of Commerce, County Civic Federation, the Council of Parents and Teachers Education, American Civil Liberties Union, the NAACP, the League of Women Voters, and AFL–CIO locals.[12]

The second step in organizing a convention is to elect delegates to the conventions. Usually the method of creating convention delegate districts is expedited by utilizing the existing state legislative districts. In most instances, the selection of candidates to appear on the ballot is made, overtly or covertly, by political parties. The ensuing election campaigns are conducted by party personnel and representatives of interests groups who desire to see the election of "friendly" members to the convention. Thus, the conventions usually are no less arenas of partisan and parochial influences than are legislative assemblies.

The characteristics of delegates to conventions are not entirely reflective of the constituencies from which they are selected.[13] There are more college or post-college graduates, more people employed in professional occupations (approximately three-fifths are lawyers), more middle aged to elderly, and more males at conventions than are proportionally found in the population at-large. More significantly, the membership is comprised of people who are more politically and civically active than the constituents they represent. Most have held party office and many have held elective office. In addition, nearly all have held office in one or more civic or interest associations. Thus, it would seem that the efforts made by parties and groups preparatory to the convening of the convention were worthwhile, for their friends were being seated.

Constitutional commissions are thought to be even less influenced by party and interest groups than are conventions. It was believed that the appointment of non-political experts to blue ribbon panels would divorce the panels from the political maneuvering of the election campaign process. Yet, the appointment process is not free of political considerations. Governors and legislators may appoint individuals with whom they have become impressed or familiar in the course of their political lives. Moreover, parties and interest groups may be requested to submit nominees for appointment. In having representatives from a variety of those groups, it is hoped that a diversity of interests will be reflected on the panel. Moreover, throughout the course of the commission's deliberations, hearings are held at which spokesmen may appear to offer their suggestions and views. Thus, it seems that partisan and parochial perspectives permeate commissions also.

Basic rule-makers, whether they be in the legislature, in commissions, or in conventions, are not free from partisan and special interests. Primarily because they operate in a political milieu, constituent influence is omnipresent. For regardless of the source of change, it is ultimately the electorate that must stand in judgment to ratify the revision. Constantly, proposals are evaluated by the rule-makers in light of perceived popular reaction. And the delegates believe that the public is negative and suspicious about change. As one constitutional writer remarked in musing over public reaction to the work of his commission:

> Collectively, it would seem, we're bigoted, prejudiced, agnostic, atheistic, subversive, perverted, secretive, dictatorial, undemocratic, anti-American, disrespectful, deceptive, and treacherous. And if you think those are strong words, you should hear what the people who didn't like our proposals said.

Moreover, the delegates recognize that the public is indifferent and apathetic toward change and needs to be pushed to accept needed revision. As that delegate remarked:

> We are convinced that what we are doing needs to be done . . . it might mean that some of our friends and neighbors will have to be dragged, kicking and screaming, into the immediate future.[14]

Thus, there is a deliberate effort to incorporate the views of many partisan and special interests. The delegates know that popular ratification may depend on gaining the support of the many groups from which the public takes its voting cues.[15]

Unless the citizen is convinced that there is a direct relationship between the defects of the basic rules, his pocketbook, and his well-being, he will not be agreeable to any change. Abstract concepts of need for revision are not sufficient motivators. People must feel that the present arrangement of governmental operations, as prescribed by their existing set of basic rules, is unsatisfactory. Unpleasant personal experiences have convinced them that their public agents and agencies are unresponsive to their needs, undeserving of their trust, and are unable to perform adequately the services required by them. Occasionally the subject of the constitutional amendment will arouse emotions that stimulate constituent concern. For example, fair housing, state lotteries, or repeal of prohibition have been such "hot issues." However, for the most part the average citizen has low levels of interest and knowledge about existing rules and governmental operations, and little awareness and concern about the implications of proposed changes.

Public apathy tends to strengthen the influence of special interests that oppose the ratification of proposals for change. Such opposition comes primarily from those groups and individuals who strive to protect the position they have enjoyed under existing constitutional provisions. The fear of loss of job positions, job security, and existing pension and retirement systems arouses opposition from political parties, city and state employees, and elected or appointed incumbents. Where electoral or district changes alter the character of partisan control, strong political organizations become activated. Economic groups such as realtors, contractors, suppliers, insurance underwriters, bankers, and unionists, may fear the loss of the special status afforded them by present governmental arrangements.[16]

Rarely do such groups organize their campaigns of opposition around their real parochial motivations, because they know that those issues may not win the support of the average citizen. Instead they gauge their arguments to appeal to the emotions of the electorate. They warn that change means the loss of freedoms, higher taxes, and alteration of the economic and racial characteristics of neighborhoods. To many of the citizens who have not been convinced that the basic rule changes would enhance their well-being, these pleas are most effective. And many either vote to maintain the status quo or stay home on election day.

Despite the many obstacles to change, the interest in revision has not diminished. In the decade of the 1960s, in almost every state some form of amendment or complete revision was proposed. Constitutional commissions, legislative study groups, and constitutional conventions have been established. The various actors in the constituency have striven to impose their will within the struggle of the pluralistic systems of the states and localities. Those who have special interests want to see them elevated to the status of fundamental rules. Reformers and civic groups press for modernization of the basic rules through streamlined and flexible provisions. Perhaps the best explanation for the continued motivation of constituent efforts comes from an active constitutional drafter and proponent of change, who sums up the efforts in this way:

> There is no choice but to try, and if we fail, to try again. Constitutional revision can be achieved through a concerted citizen effort. All we need are the right orchestra leaders.[17]

Chapter II Footnotes

1. Current data on constitutional change were from *The Book of the States* 1970–1971 (Lexington: The Council of State Governments), pp. 3–28.
2. The National Municipal League, *Model State Constitution* (New York: National Municipal League, 1963, 6th ed.).
3. *Model County Charter* (New York: National Municipal League, 1956).
4. *Model City Charter* (New York: National Municipal League, 1964, 6th ed.).
5. *McCulloch v. Maryland*, 4 Wheat. 316 (1819).
6. *Slaughterhouse Cases*, 16 Wall. 36 (1873).
7. Lewis A. Froman, Jr., "Some Effects of Interest Group Strength in State Politics," *American Political Science Review*, LX (December 1966), pp. 952–62.
8. Ibid., p. 961.
9. Ibid.
10. Raymond E. Wolfinger and Fred I. Greenstein, "The Repeal of Fair Housing in California: An Analysis of Referendum Voting," *American Political Science Review*, LXII (September 1968), pp. 753–69.
11. Tip H. Allen, Jr., and Coleman B. Ransone, Jr., *Constitutional Revision in Theory and Practice* (University: Bureau of Public Administration, University of Alabama, 1962).
12. *The Evening Star* (Washing, D.C.), September 9, 1968.
13. Jay S. Goodman, Wayne R. Swanson, and Elmer E. Cornwell, Jr., "Political Recruitment in Four Selection Systems," *Western Political Quarterly*, XXIII (March 1970), pp. 92–103; Robert S. Freedman and Sybil L. Stokes, "The Role of Constitution-Maker as Representative," *Midwest Journal of Political Science*, IX (May 1965), pp. 148–66.

14.   James H. Snowden, "A Former Senator's 'Unconstitutional' Remarks on Constitutional Revision," *State Government*, XLIII (Winter 1970), p. 65.

15.   See, for example, Norman C. Thomas, "The Electorate and State Constitutional Revision," *Midwest Journal of Political Science*, XII (February 1968), pp. 115–29.

16.   See, for example, Royce Hanson, "Maryland Proved Wholesale Change Just Won't Sell," *The Washington Post*, September 8, 1968, p. 82; and Brett W. Hawkins, "Public Opinion and Metropolitan Reorganization in Nashville," *Journal of Politics*, XXVIII (May 1966), pp. 408–18.

17.   Interview, December 4, 1971.

Chapter III

Interest Articulation, Part 1: Individual Actions

All Americans agree on the principle that the governments comprising the political system of the United States are "of the people, by the people, and for the people." Inherent in this democratic axiom are the beliefs that the people can and should express their needs and demands, and that they will be heard and satisfied by public officials. The process of communicating popular needs and demands to those within the governmental arena is known as "interest articulation."

Prerequisites for Articulation

Civic Obligation

Several factors are prerequisites for the utilization of any or all of the channels of articulation. One factor is the degree of civic obligation felt by individuals. There is a belief that one should make his viewpoint known as part of his duty as a good citizen. Thus, the more one feels that he has such an obligation, the more he is likely to utilize the various channels. Gabriel A. Almond and Sidney Verba found, in a nationwide study, that a large proportion of Americans believed that an individual should make an effort to influence or hold an attitude of interest in community affairs. Fifty-one percent of the respondents on their study agreed that a citizen should be active (by attending meetings, joining civic organizations, or political parties, etc.); and 27 percent replied that at least a citizen must be interested in keeping informed, try to understand community affairs, and vote.[1]

Interest

A second factor is the extent of interest individuals have in governmental actions. Yet, high levels of general interest are not to be found within the citizenry. When persons in Minnesota were asked how much interest they had in what was happening in their state legislature, the responses were: [2]

	Percent
Great deal of interest	22
Some interest	41
Not too much interest	30
None at all	6
No opinion	1
	100

John C. Wahlke and his associates' study of state legislators, in New Jersey, Ohio, California, and Tennessee, elicited the following statements that are illustrative of the low interest levels perceived by some state legislators to be present among the citizenry:

> There isn't much interest in my county. The local newspaper gives me the only indication as to how my constituents feel.
> I think I'd say they were disinterested. If they are not affected by the legislation, they don't care. [3]

Robert A. Dahl has stated that the average American is less concerned about the affairs of his state than of his city or county. [4] M. Kent Jennings and Harmon Zeigler empirically tested Dahl's premise. They found that, within a nationwide sample, interest in the governmental affairs of the state ranked lower than that in the localities, and both were ranked lower than the level of interest in national governmental affairs. Jennings and Zeigler have noted: "The states are caught between the immediacy of the local system and the glamour and importance of the national and international systems." [5]

Interest levels are related to the saliency of a specific governmental action. Citizens will become interested as they attach values to rules that might be made. Those citizens, for whom policy consequences are only slightly beneficial or remote to their set of priorities, tend to be indifferent toward the decisions to be made and, thus, uninterested in trying to influence them. Generally, only those who expect the outcome to have important and immediate consequences to themselves, or for those to whom they feel closely related, attempt to exert some degree of influence.

In Maryland, for example, the proposed liberalization of the state's abortion law, in 1970, stimulated extensive articulated reactions from many sectors of the population. A Maryland state assemblyman has said that the only time anyone in the legislature hears from more than a few of the constituents is when the legislature is considering a matter that has a clear and primary affect on the constituents.[6] A Philadelphia councilman has noted that public hearings at the local level, concerning such issues as zoning and housing, draw a large and vocal crowd of residents.[7]

The Charlotte, North Carolina, city council made extensive efforts to elicit public response, in 1968, by holding open meetings in six sections of the city. Though the meetings were well publicized, few citizens, regardless of socio-economic status, came to see and hear the public agents discuss a variety of issues. However, in two instances, popular participation was high. When a meeting was held in a predominantly black section of the city, the residents turned out to hear and participate in the debate over a proposed anti-discrimination ordinance; and at a meeting held in a predominantly white middle-class section, discussion of street construction projects drew a large turnout. On both of these occasions, as soon as the respective discussions were over, and the council turned to other matters, the crowds quickly left the meeting halls. William J. Veeder, in relating these events, concluded that citizens will respond with high interest to specific governmental programs that are of primary concern to them, but that such interest is not likely to be manifested for other programs.[8]

Knowledge

Knowledge is the third factor related to the utilization of channels of articulation. In order to articulate an interest, one has to be informed about issues and current problems. He must also know where, when, and to whom expressions are to be directed. At least he must know the rudiments of what his state and local governments consist of and what they do. It has been demonstrated that people are generally not well informed.

A study of a local community, undertaken one week before a municipal election, found generally low levels of knowledge present about public officials, issues, and problems.[9] A third of the respondents could not identify any or more than one public official in the community. Nearly two-fifths of the respondents could not perceive any specific community problem; and 80 percent had no specific knowledge of an election issue. The results of this study on the extent of political knowledge are presented in Table III.1.

Surveys directed toward determining the levels of knowledge about state issues and public agents have also demonstrated significant rates of unawareness. In a survey undertaken in Texas, the respondents were asked to name one problem that they thought their state legislature should handle.

TABLE III.1

Quality of Public Political Knowledge

*Identification of Political Leaders**			*Knowledge of Election Issues†*		*Perception of Community Problems‡*	
Low	0–1	33%	Don't know any	56%	Don't know	20%
	2–3	39	Personalities	18	Vague, unspecific	18
	4–5	25	Vague, unspecific	6	1–2, specific	61
High	6–7	3	"Need change"	12	More, specific	1
		———	1–2, specific	7		———
		100%	More, specific	1		100%
	(N = 178)			100%		

* Respondents were asked to identify by office and party a list of seven public and party officials in the community. Only office identification is used here.
† ". . . What would you say are the main issues in this election?"
‡ "What do you think is the main problem that this community faces today?"
Source: Smith., *op. cit.*, p. 47.

To such a question, almost any type of response could have been offered; yet, 48 percent of the sample could not state a single possible problem.[10]

In New York, when voters were asked, shortly after an election, if they remembered the name of the state assembly candidate for whom they had voted, only 8 percent in New York City, 15 percent in Buffalo, and 20 percent in Onandago County could do so. A nationwide poll, also conducted immediately after an election day, showed that only 28 percent of the respondents knew who had won the state senate race in their respective districts, and 24 percent knew who was their state assemblyman-elect.[11] In Missouri, during a legislative session, only 19 percent of a statewide sample knew who their state assemblyman was, and 11 percent could correctly name their state senator.[12]

A state legislator has offered the following statement about the level of knowledge that he perceived his constituents to have about state government:

I don't think my constituents have the slightest idea of what the legislature is for. They're very poorly informed, speaking in general terms, of course . . . . Constituents have the impression that we're in session all the time and are surprised to learn that we have only one session every two years. This is because they see Congress news all year. I am thought of like a representative in Washington. People ask me to support federal bills, and ten to one, ask me "How are things in Washington?"[13]

Political Efficacy

Political efficacy is the fourth factor that stimulates individual articulation. This is the belief that individual political action does have, or can have, an impact on the political process. Furthermore, political efficacy includes the feeling that political and social change is possible, and that the individual citizen can play a part in bringing this change about. Citizens who feel that public officials are responsive and responsible to the electorate, who think that individual political activity is worthwhile and capable of influencing public policy, and who see that the private citizen's channels of access to governmental decision makers are not confined to the ballot-box, are much more likely to be politically active than those who feel largely overwhelmed by the political process.

The belief that individuals can make direct attempts to influence the government was tested by Almond and Verba. Each respondent, in a nationwide sample, was asked whether he believed that he could do something about an undesirable rule made by his local government. Seventy-seven percent of the respondents believed that they could.[14] In addition, Almond and Verba found that a larger proportion of those who felt that it was possible to do something had made an attempt to influence governmental action than had those who did not hold such a belief (33 percent of the former in comparison with 10 percent of the latter).[15]

The study further showed that the respondents did not believe that they were able to influence all governmental agents. Most (83 percent) expected to receive equal treatment in their dealings with bureaucratic agents. However, less than half (48 percent) of the respondents believed that their expressed points of view would receive serious consideration by the bureaucrats.[16]

Demographic Characteristics and Interest Application

Recent studies have focused on the relationship between demographic characteristics and political behavior.[17] It has been demonstrated that the propensity to utilize the channels of articulation is greater among those individuals with:

high levels of formal education
professional, business, or white collar occupations
high income levels
high social standing
urban residence
homes in well-to-do residential areas
long residence in the community
and who are white, middle-aged, and male.

Moreover, such studies have shown that demographic characteristics are related to civic obligation, interest in governmental action, political knowledge, and political efficacy. For example, the well-educated person has more facts about politics at his command than does the less educated, and he has a more sophisticated manner of utilizing concepts to maintain a sense of order and meaning amid the flood of available information. The more meaning he can find in the flow of political events, the more likely it is that these events will maintain his interest. With more formal schooling, an individual is more likely to feel that he can influence political events, and he is more likely to feel a sense of civic obligation to participate in political affairs.

Those individuals who do not demonstrate the propensity to utilize the channels of articulation may be considered to be alienated, that is, not socially or politically integrated into their community. Demographic characteristics have been shown to be related to alienation. Fredric Templeton in his study of Berkeley, California, correlated this attitude with education, occupation, race, and class identification; Table III.2 presents his findings.[18]

An understanding of the relationship between demographic characteristics and political behavior is not in itself meaningful in understanding the function

TABLE III.2

Status and Alienation

(in percent)

Status Indicators	Alienation	
	High	Low
Race:		
Negro	76	24
White	39	61
Occupation:		
Manual	60	40
Nonmanual	31	69
Education:		
0–12 years	57	43
13–15 years	32	68
16 or more years	25	75
Class identification:		
Working or lower	58	42
Upper or middle	32	68

Source: Templeton, *op. cit.*, p. 254.

of interest articulation. Although the empirical studies have established that certain individuals have the resources necessary to utilize the channels of articulation, those individuals are not the only ones interested in governmental action. Nor are those individuals the only ones who articulate interests to public agents. Anyone perusing daily newspapers quickly becomes aware that women, manual laborers, young adults, black citizens, and those who are poor are articulating demands. For example, local school boards are being bombarded from these types of people about such matters as expanded or relevant curricula, free lunch programs, decentralized decision making, and recreational and community services.

Moreover, public agents are the targets of various and often conflicting expressions of interest, for different individuals have differing needs and demands that they make known. Thus, local councils will hear demands from:

> manual laborers against welfare benefit expansion, and from welfare mothers for additional funds for furniture, clothing, and telephones
>
> businessmen for urban renewal, and from blacks protesting consequential relocation
>
> property owners for lower taxes, and women for increased school expenditures
>
> the aged for reduced bus fares, and from transit companies petitioning for increased rates

Examinations of the function of interest articulation must recognize that the different interests of different people are directed toward different public agents, at different levels of government, at different times, with different styles, different degrees of intensity, and through different channels.

Direct Channels of Interest Articulation

Personal Channels of Communication

Individuals wishing to articulate interests may make an effort to contact public agents directly. The channels for direct personal communication include writing letters, making telephone calls, sending telegrams, and visiting with the officials. The advantages of such personal efforts are: 1) one may select the agent he deems to be the appropriate target for articulating his interest; and 2) one may convey the degree of importance or immediacy of the need or demand articulated.

The choice of mode of communication may be affected by the nature of the interest to be articulated. One's interest may be to influence an imminent governmental action, such as a vote to be taken in a legislative meeting. Hence, time being of prime importance, the telephone call or telegram would be the instruments for speedy articulation. A complex or intricate message may best be explained by letter. An interest intensely held may prompt an individual to take the time and make the effort of personally meeting with an official so as to be able to present his case in the strongest manner.

The choice of mode of communication may be dictated by the level of government at which the target operates, and the type of office he holds. If an individual wishes to articulate an interest to a local bureaucrat, he could conveniently do so in person or by telephone. In contrast, communicating an interest to a state bureaucrat, whose office is located in the capital city, would most likely be done by letter, unless the individual lives nearby. Governors and mayors of large cities usually may be reached only by mail and telegram.

The most accessible officials are the state and local legislators. During a state legislative session, debates or hearings on proposed bills may stimulate expressions of interests. At such times, most legislators reside at the capital, and letter writing may be the most practical mode of communicating with them. Constituents may be unable to go to the capital, or they may not care to meet the expense of a telephone call. They thus would write letters. Moreover, the typically limited facilities available to the legislators, such as lack of office space and lack of private telephone lines, may make written messages the only feasible channel. Between sessions, however, those legislators may be more accessible to personal contact at their homes, their places of employment, or at delegation offices maintained in the district.

Local councilmen perform their official tasks within the city or county in which they reside. Their proximity to constituents permits easy contact. Councilmen in large cities are usually provided with office space at the city halls. In addition, ward-based legislators might have scheduled office hours at meeting places within their constituent districts. At the least, citizens may reach them at home, or at their full-time place of business. Thus, personal visits or telephone calls will generally be the most utilized direct channel of articulation.

Only a relatively small proportion of people, however, take the step of making such direct contact. For example, a group of people in Missouri were asked: "In the past year have you talked to any public official about some problem or let him know how you stood on an issue?" Their responses demonstrated a low level of personal contact, at both the state and local levels:

4 percent talked to an elected state official (governor, legislator, etc.)
1 percent talked to other state employees
4 percent talked to an elected city or county official (mayor, councilman, county clerk, etc.)
1 percent talked to some other city or county employee
2 percent named an official who could not be identified[19]

Only 2 percent of a Missouri sample claimed they had written to their state legislator to express a stand on an issue.[20] Such a figure is a gross exaggeration according to Leonard Blondes, a state assemblyman in Maryland. He claimed that less than 1 percent of his constituents had telephoned, had sent telegrams, or had written to him. Blondes believed that this figure would have been even lower had he not been chairman of his county delegation in the assembly.[21]

It does not appear that the establishment of state delegation offices within the constituency has resulted in higher frequencies of direct contact. The state senators and assemblymen elected from Prince Georges County, Maryland, for example, have a centralized permanent office in the county. Thus, county residents might be able to personally contact their state representatives by calling one telephone number, or writing to or visiting at one address. Despite this convenience and simplification, the delegation reported that only a "minimum" number of individuals contacted them at this office. Most of those communications were for general information about how a new law affected each of them, or for requests for personal assistance. The several contacts made for articulating an interest were usually directed towards the individual delegate's home or office.[22]

On the local level the frequency of communications may, however, be higher than that directed toward the state. In Montgomery County, Maryland, for example, a review of letters mailed to the county council showed that 1,223 letters were received in an eight-month period. In many instances, an issue before the council triggered these written communications. And different types of issues provoked different levels of response. In each of six of the months during that period, the rate of letters averaged ninety. Many of the letters were reactions to council deliberations on a proposed public pool to be constructed in an upper-middle-class residential neighborhood, and proposed sites for public housing scattered throughout the wealthy county. During the month in which the council entered into deliberations on the county budget, the number of letters received doubled. As the council opened discussions on the proposed school budget, the publication of record-breaking expenditure requests provoked five times the average numbers of letters. The letters described in this paragraph were only those sent to the county hall and directed to the council as a body. Additional letters or communications were directed to the residences or offices of the individual council members.[23]

The frequency of direct, personal, interest articulation in cities, especially large ones, may be related to the districting basis for the council. The propensity of individuals to communicate with their councilmen who are elected from wards is greater than with those elected at-large. Constituents may find it more difficult to identify with or gain access to at-large councilmen than with their ward-based representative. Philadelphia provides an illustration, for it has both an at-large and a ward-based districting plan. A Philadelphia councilman has noted the affect of districting on the articulation of interests:

> The distinct councilmen, like myself, receive many letters, phone calls, and visits by individuals. We hear from our constituents either at home, in our offices here at City Hall, or at meetings held in our district. Councilmen at-large must consider the entire city and work on a different sphere. Most of what they hear comes from city-wide groups, rather than individuals.[24]

Institutionalized Channels of Communication

Town Meetings

Institutionalized processes provide means by which individuals can directly articulate interests to public officials. One of these, deeply embedded in the American governmental tradition, is the town meeting. Currently, such meetings are to be found in small, homogeneous communities, predominantly in New England. Individual citizens assemble at scheduled times to discuss matters concerning the community, such as the budget, street construction and maintenance, and parks and recreation. At the meetings, individuals may introduce resolutions and express opinions for or against issues under consideration. In so doing, the needs and demands of the residents may be made known prior to final action. However, the intimacy of the residents and the informality of the setting may act to constrain an individual from articulating a personal or controversial interest. Thus, the town meeting may, in fact, foster articulation about interests that are shared by most members of the community.

Public Hearings

A second institutionalized process is the public hearing. Hearings are conducted by a variety of public officials at all levels of government. These may be required by law, or may be called at the discretion of a particular public agent. Administrative officials, such as those in regulatory agencies, schedule hearings prior to setting rates, altering requirements for professional licensing, taking punitive actions, etc. Occasionally, governors and mayors, as they ponder over the signing or vetoing of measures, provide the public with such an opportunity to express interests. Special district board members are often required to hear members of the community for special matters such as planning, zoning, and acquiring land for schools, parks, and playgrounds. And blue ribbon commission members offer forums as part of their fact-finding missions.

Public hearings are held by state and local legislators during the deliberative stages of the legislative rule making process. Often, as at the local level, such meetings must be held before a statute can be enacted. Generally, these hearings are conducted by committees charged with the subject matter under consideration. Several state legislatures maintain interim committees that seek public sentiment on bills being prepared for the next legislative session. In small legislative bodies, at the county or municipal level, the entire membership may be present at the public meetings.

The central purpose of hearings is to inform the public officials about citizen reaction to proposed measures and actions and about the subsequent affects these proposals might have for individuals. Notices of place, date, and time of scheduled meetings are printed in newspapers, posted in public buildings, and mailed to organizations, associations, and individuals requesting them. Persons may be invited to appear as expert witnesses, or may at their own initiative offer to give testimony. Individuals unable or unwilling to give oral testimony may submit written statements that become part of the official minutes of the meeting. Often, on controversial issues, the list of witnesses scheduled to testify is so lengthy that time restrictions may be imposed (for example, two to five minutes) on each speaker. Should time not permit a witness to complete his statements, he is usually allowed to submit in writing that which he could not present orally.

Individual articulation rarely is heard at hearings. The state capitol may be too great a distance to travel, the scheduled times of hearings too inconvenient (although many local councils are holding hearings during evening hours to permit more people to attend than could during the day), or a subject too technical to attract any but group representatives. For those who do testify, such a process provides a forum at which one can express an interest to many officials at the same time.

The motivation of those who testify may be other than that of presenting information to the officials conducting the hearing. They may have come to dramatize an appeal. They hope that the hearing will receive press coverage (for example, in Washington, D.C., hearings have been televised), and, thus, the interest espoused can be conveyed to the community and to other public officials not present. A review of the record of almost any hearing shows that persons do not confine their remarks to the topic at hand, as they are supposed to do. They may use this opportunity to articulate their interest on a variety of subjects, to challenge the agents to enter into other areas, or to criticize prior actions taken.

In recent years, particularly in large cities, significant numbers of black citizens have been utilizing public hearings as their prime mode of direct communication of interest. On issues salient to them, they have found that hearings provide a forum at which the intensity and immediacy of needs and demands can be made known more conveniently, quickly, and dramatically than by any other channel of articulation. Not all who come testify, nor need everyone testify for interests to be made known. The presence of persons packing the meeting hall may be sufficient to signify that interests are strongly held. As those persons boo and hiss, applaud and shout, wave placards, and distribute handbills, they are further demonstrating the depth and direction of their demands.

Such demonstrations of interest impress those public officials present at hearings. The media, drawn by a large number of persons in attendance, transmit the proceedings to those not at the hearing. In this way other elected officials, bureaucrats, and people in general may be impressed also.

The public hearings on proposed measures for improving police community relations held by the District of Columbia city council in the fall and winter of 1968, concerned an issue highly salient to the black residents of the city. Each of the hearings drew crowds of vocal individuals. Some gave testimony, while others in the audience made outcries of support or disapproval of what was said. One white councilwoman was moved to note that it was not until she saw the attendance at the meetings and the reactions of the people who were present did she realize how great the need was to improve police–community relations.[25] As a result of the hearings, stronger bills were presented to the full council than were originally proposed. The police department personnel recognized the need for prompt action to establish ways to improve relations with the public. And the Office of the Mayor, which would be charged with implementing the bills, became aware of the deeply held attitudes that would necessitate efficient implementation.

Open Meetings

Open meetings between public officials and citizens is a third, and recently established, process of institutionalized access to public agents. The intent underlying this innovation has been to bridge the gap that has developed between public agents and the people as a result of the increased size of the population and the increased glorification of professionalism in public administration. Increased size has been manifested in a representational ratio that has grown, in many large cities, to as high as one councilman per 100,000–250,000 residents. Increased professionalism has resulted in autonomous and insulated governing boards (for example, school boards and police departments), which have control over the many aspects of the daily affairs of citizens. Thus, the opening of these channels for communication has fostered the inclusion of support and involvement by citizens in public matters. Such efforts as opening meetings to the public have enabled citizens to aid in the defining of problems and to suggest solutions perceived to be meaningful.

Councils have either opened their meetings for citizens to come and comment during the discussions, or have moved the meeting places to sites throughout the city to facilitate the involvement of citizens in the deliberations of their government. In Charlotte, North Carolina, the city council scheduled regular meetings in six parts of the city. The selection of locations was made in recognition of the principle that all residents, not only members of majority groups, have a stake in the community and should be encouraged to articulate directly to their councilmen.[26]

Special district boards, such as park and planning commissioners, have called meetings when their decisions have sparked vociferous, antagonistic reactions from large numbers of individuals within their jurisdiction. School board members, as in Philadelphia, have instituted reforms that include open meetings offering members of the community the chance to voice grievances and put forward suggestions for programs. Police departments in several cities have held meetings at which residents are invited to attend in order to pinpoint problem areas and abrasive activities on the part of policemen.

On occasion, ad hoc meetings have been called to discuss the underlying causes of civil disturbances in the hope of preventing similar crises from occurring. In Alexandria, Virginia, city officials and citizens gathered at the city hall for one such meeting. The precipitating cause was a six-day period of fire bombing and vandalism that shook the city after the shooting of a nineteen-year-old black youth by a white store manager. That meeting was organized by the Citizen Complaints Officer for the city, as a "sounding board" session, and was attended by 110 persons. The individuals present articulated complaints that were focused primarily on discrimination in housing, employment, and education, and police insensitivity to the black community. Support was expressed for the scheduling of a series of subsequent sessions to assure that suggestions made by citizens would be implemented.[27]

Direct Articulation Initiated by Public Officials

Public officials often initiate actions to elicit citizen articulation. For example, Mayor Lindsay tried during his entire first term in office to stimulate communications from the residents of New York City. He maintained a schedule of "walking tours" in various sections of the city to talk with the people. And he made use of the television media by appearing on telethons called "Ask Mayor Lindsay." During these programs people were able to telephone him at the studio with their expressions of interests and complaints.[28]

Some of the actions initiated by public officials have been in response to citizen complaints. In every large city, grievances have been expressed by residents in low income areas about deteriorating housing conditions, poor trash and garbage collection, rat infestation, and hazardous conditions in the parks and playgrounds. Such complaints have been followed, as in New York City, with visits to the neighborhoods by administrative officials seeking to apprise themselves of the actual situation and to hear about the types of improvements of services that the residents think are necessary. If complaints have been vociferous, or conditions have attracted the attention of news reporters, then visits are often made by elected officials. The heavy snowfalls in New York City of the 1969–1970 winter brought Mayor Lindsay into the residential neighborhoods to personally survey the progress of street clearance, and to ask the snowbound residents to evaluate the efficiency of the city's snow removal program. The irritations of many residents were clearly expressed to him in the form of snowballs thrown in his direction.[29]

Other initiated actions have been in response to conflicting demands raised or to conflicting reports received. Plans for public housing, road construction, and urban renewal never fail to cause a barrage of conflicting outcries, as residents in and around the proposed sites articulate strong feelings for or against the projects, or insist that the projects be built elsewhere. The first reaction of elected officials responsible for final authorization is to request bureaucrats to attempt to define or resolve the controversy. This may lead to conflicting reports being returned by the administrative agents. Or, more often, the bureaucrats report that the controversy has been resolved; yet, the councilmen, from subsequent letters, phone calls, or visits by constituents, discover that the matter had not been settled. Thereupon, they may appoint a special council committee to go into the community and meet with residents personally. In Montgomery County, Maryland, plans for urban renewal in the Sandy Spring area evoked vocal and contrasting sentiments about the need for the program. When county bureaucrats had not been able to resolve the issue, after having been sent to the area by the county council, a committee of councilmen went to meet with interested individuals. In this manner, they were able to gather the information first-hand and they reported their findings to the full council.

Initiated Action Sponsored by Groups

Elected officials, aware that retention of office rests upon electoral support, and recognizing the isolation inherent in official positions, respond to opportunities that encourage individual articulation. Some of these opportunities are sponsored by organized groups within the communities that have a stake in the electoral system. Political parties offer numerous occasions to bring officials together with the people. City councilmen or state delegates appear at ward meetings, and often are regularly scheduled to do so. County committees usually sponsor public meetings for state delegates, particularly prior to the opening of the legislative session, when individuals may present ideas for bills they would like to see introduced. Arrangements are made by party organizations for picnics and rallies where citizens are invited to meet their elected representatives. Auxiliary party associations, as the Democrat or Republican women's clubs, sponsor neighborhood teas and social events. At all such occasions, individuals can question what has or what has not been done, express support or criticisms for actions taken, or enunciate their interests for future consideration.

Where non-partisan elections are held, organized interest groups, which have stakes in the outcomes of elections, may substitute for political parties in sponsoring such events. As do the parties, these groups focus their efforts on behalf of those officials who they have an interest in seeing reelected. In non-partisan Detroit, for example, labor unions (which endorse and provide support for local officials), arrange, finance, and publicize the affairs to which the public is invited.

In many locales, a critical issue may serve as an impetus for a meeting to be called. Under such a circumstance, a local civic or business association, fraternal society, or church would arrange for an open discussion to take place. Local officials, and sometimes state or national representatives, are called to meet with the citizens. The closing of a coal mine or a military installation, or the discovery of widespread use of drugs by teenagers, are types of issues that arouse public sentiment and the desire to meet with those in public office who are looked to for solutions.

In addition to sponsoring public meetings, almost any type of organization invites public officials to address meetings of its membership. Few officials would turn down the opportunity to appear before a gathering of citizens. Elected officials might perceive this as a "ready made audience" comprised of potential voters to be courted; and administrative agents would see this as a chance to make citizens aware of the intricacies and problems of their offices, and to gain public support. Once again, these meetings provide open channels for the direct articulation of interests by individuals.

Indirect Channels of Interest Articulation

The Media

Articulation of interests may be made to public officials indirectly through intermediaries. The news media are to be included in the category of intermediaries as transmitters of interests. The media can be important transmitters of citizen sentiment because public agents perceive them to be so.

Indeed, often officials equate media reaction with public reaction. Officials rely on the media to gauge the opinions, reactions, and interpretations of the people to programs that have been proposed, enacted, or executed. Legislators, executives, and administrators may also use the media to gauge the timing and support for new programs. Moreover, being readily available and easy to use, the media serves to provide ideas and suggestions on how to solve pressing problems. Newspapers are especially important, in that they are locally based and focused; and officials at both the state and local levels can, thus, obtain from them the information desired about localized public sentiment. In addition, newspapers have the time, space, and predisposition to report public affairs in depth. In contrast, radio and television, principally media of entertainment, tend to capsulize the news. This capsulization, however, by emphasizing the highlights of selected events, may have the merit of providing clues to public officials about what the public considers important.

The utilization of the media by the public may take several forms. Letters to the editor are commonly considered to be the principal channel for individuals to express concern. However, only a relatively few people make this effort; and education has been found to be an important demographic variable in determining who will express his interest through letter writing. In a nationwide survey conducted by the American Institute of Public Opinion, only 16 percent of the respondents stated that they had ever written to an editor. That survey further showed that 38 percent of the college educated had written at least one letter to an editor, as opposed to 13 percent of those with a high school education, and 6 percent of those who attended eight or fewer years of grade school.[30]

The interests of people in a community may be articulated through the media as an outcome of routine reporting. Whenever large numbers of people gather at any one place, reporters from the media appear. Whether it be a large turnout at a hearing, a demonstration, or a street confrontation between police and neighborhood residents, reporters ask what the problem was, why the people were present, and what they thought should be done. In this manner, expressions made are reproduced and transmitted to those (especially public agents) who were not present at an event.

Through leads on stories telephoned in by citizens, and through assignments to regular "beats" (as at city hall, the state capitol, and police stations), the reporters become aware of interests or grievances held, and investigate the extent to which the basic sentiments are shared. Sometimes reporters ask "the man in the street" for opinions on topical questions or for reactions to a new legislative proposal which had recently been introduced. On occasion, a reporter will initiate investigations into some pressing problem to discover how people perceive the problems and solutions to the problems.

Documentaries on television have been produced to focus upon selected major problems. Through these, needs and demands of the citizens are dramatized. As a television network presents "special" broadcasts it offers a new perspective on problems to persons in one area who see and hear the sentiments of those in other areas faced with similar types of situations or conditions. In January 1970, "The Day They Had to Close the Schools" was broadcasted over the CBS Television Network.[31] The program focused on the defeat of a referendum in Fremont, Ohio, which was to have increased property taxes to raise revenue needed for the school system. The problem of defeat at referenda of school bond issuance or of increased school tax levies had been a widespread one in the period after the mid 1960s. During that program, the citizens of Fremont were called upon to express their opinions about the tax increase question. Their attitudes, which officials of other cities and states in addition to those in Fremont learned about, may have provided clues to explain the negative reaction of citizens in many localities to the same issue.

Political Parties

People may indirectly articulate their interests to public officials through party leaders who act as intermediaries. These party leaders, who are interested in future electoral success, communicate with the governor and the local delegation of state legislators frequently, particularly if they are of the same party or factional affiliation. To the degree that they control or greatly influence the recruitment process, have performed past services, or exist in a competitive political environment, party leaders may be a source of cues to guide the actions of rule makers. Communications through party organization leaders not only serve to suggest rules that would win local support, or to reiterate proposals that are in the party platform, but they also serve as a means by which public sentiment can be gauged.

Individuals may communicate with party leaders at party meetings, or by personal visit or by telephone. In a nonpartisan situation, however, citizens may have one less avenue through which expressions of interests may be transmitted to public agents.

Phillips Cutright conducted personal interviews with precinct committeemen in "Partisan City," which had never experienced a non-partisan system, to determine the level of interaction between these grass-root politicians and voters.[32] Each committeeman was asked how many voters had come to him for aid during a thirty-day period, and also how many voters he had come into contact with daily. The responses were compared with the replies from similar questionnaires mailed to precinct committeemen in a community that had been non-partisan for fifty years. The findings are to be found in Table III.3.

Quite often communications made by individuals to party leaders are requests for aid in obtaining some form of governmental action to satisfy some need or demand. From the table it can be seen that 41 percent of the

TABLE III.3

Table Precinct Worker Interaction with Voters in Partisan and Nonpartisan Areas

(in percentages)

Indicator of Interaction	Partisan City	Nonpartisan County
Number of requests for aid during past 30 days		
0 requests	34	83
1–3 requests	25	16
4 or more	41	1
	(N = 179)	(N = 239)
Daily contact		
0–5	24	78
6–9	13	6
10 or more	63	15
	(N = 188)	(N = 205)

Adapted from: Cutright, *op. cit.*, p. 100.

partisan committeemen had received four or more requests for assistance during a thirty-day period, while only 1 percent of the non-partisan workers had been approached. Over 80 percent of the committeemen in the non-partisan situation had not received any requests for aid, compared with only 34 percent of their counterparts in the partisan locale. That requests were so directed may be indicative of the voter's perception towards precinct workers in relation to what the politician can do for the citizen, and of the effectiveness of the politician's intervention in obtaining requested governmental action.

Partisan committeemen are residents of the neighborhood in which they perform their tasks for the party. As such, they are familiar and accessible figures. The percentages in the table appear to indicate that the individual knows who his committeeman is and where he can be located. As can be seen, 63 percent of the partisan organization men claimed to have had met with ten or more persons during daily neighborhood rounds; whereas, 78 percent of the non-partisan precinct workers had seen no more than five persons, if any, in a day. Such contact may serve as a stimulus to articulation. Those individuals who are unable or unwilling to utilize direct channels (that is, writing letters, testifying at hearings, and so on) may not hesitate to express an opinion to a "neighbor" they meet on the street. Or an off-hand remark made by a committeeman encountered by chance may prompt an individual to proffer some expression of interest.

Public agents interested in obtaining public opinion may look to partisan committeemen to provide some clues. Such a party leader may be perceived to be reflective of the residents in his precinct. Thus, his opinions may be equated with those of the constituents.

The Bureaucracy

The positions held by bureaucrats in the structure of state and local governments permit them to act as intermediaries for public sentiment. Their full-time status enables them to be accessible to the public. Their training and experience places them in positions of influence within the governmental system. Legislators and executives rely on their expertise for the suggesting of proposals, the evaluation of alternatives, and the data needed for rule making. As such, bureaucrats are attractive intermediaries through which the public may articulate interests to the elected officials.

Harry W. Reynolds, Jr., has shown that citizens will go to bureaucrats to seek their aid in getting interests translated into rules. He studied the involvement of administrators in the generating and guidance of rule-making decisions in Los Angeles. During the period of his study, thirty-one bills introduced in the city council had been initiated by private citizens. Of those bills, citizens had cleared twenty-seven through agencies prior to the proposals being transmitted to the councilmen. The bureaucrats were asked to review the technical feasibility or justification of desired objectives, or to help rewrite proposals to include needed details.[33]

The Elected Officials

Just as bureaucrats may act as intermediaries to channel interests to elected officials, so may the latter act as intermediaries to channel interests to administrative agents. Many individual interests or grievances are concerned with the manner in which bureaucrats perform their rule execution function. In addition, citizens may have cause to express themselves about the way administrators adjudicate controversies arising from the interpretation, implementation, and supplementation of the rules. Often appeals to elected officials (especially legislators) to intercede are made to supplement direct communication or as a substitute for it.

Individuals may address themselves to legislators because these are felt to be more accessible than are administrators. Unlike the level of recognition enjoyed by elected officials, most bureaucrats are virtually faceless personnel. The public may not readily be able to identify an appropriate agency to which expressions are to be directed, yet alone identify the appropriate agent, because of the complexity of governmental organization. Moreover, even if a citizen should single out a bureaucrat, the agent may not be readily accessible, for fixed work schedules sometimes do not coincide with the citizen's needs. Articulating may be an acute problem for those having to transmit expressions to state agents, most of whom are located in the state capital. In contrast, state legislators are to be found within the various constituencies at interim periods during the sessions and more frequently after the legislature adjourns. And these, as well as local legislators, can be reached at home as well as at their office.

Individuals may be more at ease in communicating with elected officials than with bureaucrats. It is the general attitude that those who are elected are obligated to heed the voice of constituents. This attitude has been buttressed by the efforts elected officials have made to court public sentiment and favor, as opposed to the lack of efforts made by appointed or merit service personnel, which lead to the appearance of indifference and isolation.

Elected officials are approached to act as intermediaries to channel interests primarily because most individuals believe that an official voice is more effective than their own. The elected officials are perceived by the public to be the overseers of the governmental establishment. The activities of the administrative agents are guided by the rules made by the legislators and directed by the executive.

Being most accessible, one's legislative representative may be enlisted to channel interests to other elected officials. Such indirect articulation may be for the purpose of having expressed interests transmitted to other legislators or to an executive.

Local councilmen may be requested to intercede in matters that are within the aegis of the state government. Thus, they may perform the intermediary role as a service to constituents. Quite often, however, expressions may have been misdirected in that the subject of the interest sent to the local councilmen was one that could only be handled at the state level. In these cases, the councilmen are enlisted inadvertently as intermediaries.

Polls

The public opinion poll may be viewed as an indirect channel for interest articulation. By examining the responses of a sample in the population, public agents may be able to infer the interests, needs, and demands of most of the constituents. Unlike many other means of communicating interests, polls are not initiated by individuals who have an interest to articulate. Nor are the topics raised in a formally structured questionnaire necessarily those on which the respondents, at their own initiative, would have focused expressions of interests. Rather, questions are selected to indicate opinions of individuals on matters relevant to the concerns of those who have initiated the poll. Polls also differ from other means of indirect articulation in that this channel is not always available, nor is it open to all those who might like to express interests. The time of the poll, the number of persons to be inter-viewed, and the method of selecting the respondents are determined by the pollsters or their sponsors.

It is costly to conduct a valid poll. Survey costs vary with many factors, but usually they cost about $8 to $10 an interview. Thus, a poll of a moderately populated state or a heavily populated city would entail an expenditure of between $5,000 and $6,000.[34] Such a financial consideration precludes the wide and frequent use of a poll by public officials on a state and local level to ferret out interests of the people. Budgets for governmental personnel and agencies do not include appropriations for opinion gathering mechanisms. Therefore, polls are usually sponsored by newspapers for feature articles, by political parties and office seekers for planning campaign strategy, or by others who have funds available for these purposes.

It has been said that public opinion polls enable the will of the people to be known. However, several considerations may affect the validity and reliability of poll results. Among these is, first, that responses are indicative of interests at a given moment in time (when the people were interviewed). Opinions change with new information, temperament, or new environmental situations.

Second, when questions are asked about specific policies in a poll, they are raised in a political vacuum. It is one thing to reply to an "iffy" pollster's question and another to a real proposition. For example, there is general agreement among non-southern whites that a black person should be able to live where he desires; yet, open housing referenda have been defeated when it became apparent that Negroes may be moving into the white voters' neighborhoods.

Third, there is a question of the truthfulness of responses. Persons may not understand a question (despite efforts made to clearly word and pre-test the interview schedule), may not know an answer, or may not care to give a true response that might embarrass them. Thus, respondents may guess, give mistaken replies, or offer responses they believe would cast them in a more favorable light.

Fourth, biased answers may be an outcome of interviewer–interviewee relationships. Bias may occur from social class disparities, or differences in race, religion, or sex. For example, pollsters have found that black inter-viewers elicited different responses from low status blacks than do white interviewers in the same situations. The establishment of too friendly a rapport may similarly create biased responses. People may be prone to respond with answers they believe their "friend" would like to hear.[35]

Though polls may be an indicator of some public interest, they may also indicate a lack of public interest. Repeatedly, surveys have demonstrated that substantial percentages of the population do not possess any opinions on public matters. Pollsters have found that for almost every question asked it is necessary to include a category for the "don't knows." For example, when persons in a nationwide survey were asked about an issue that hits one out of every four homes—whether the divorce laws in their state were too strict or not strict enough—over one-third of the respondents replied that they had no opinion.[36]

A criticism levelled against polls is that not everyone is asked to participate in the utilization of this channel of articulation. It has been estimated that the likelihood of an average person being interviewed during his lifetime would be less than one chance in ten.[37] George Gallup has calculated that, "Even if 10,000 persons were questioned every week, it would take 200 years to get around to all the nation's adults."[38] Yet, it cannot be said that polls have consistently excluded certain groups of people from having their views made known. Indeed, the use of scientific methods of sampling to strive for procedures to obtain representative respondents, has provided equal opportunities for the apathetic and less-motivated persons to express their interests, needs, and demands.

Voting as an Indirect Channel of Articulation

Voting can be viewed as an indirect channel for articulation. In casting ballots, individuals may to some extent be indicating which candidate they believe would best represent their interests in the political arena. For the most part, however, voting is a confining means by which to express interests. Individuals neither initiate nor set the time for the elections. And expressions are limited to the alternative options printed on the ballot.

Eligibility to Vote

Voting is considered to be the most utilized channel for articulation. Yet, studies have shown that the number of persons who turn out in state and local elections is substantially lower than the number of persons who may be eligible to vote. The requirements for eligibility to vote are primarily set by each state, subject to provisions in the national constitution and laws. Thus, no state can declare individuals ineligible to vote because of "race, color, or previous condition of servitude" (Amendment 15), "sex" (Amendment 19), "age" (that is, eighteen years of age or older; Amendment 26), "failure to pay any poll tax or other tax" (by the U.S. Supreme Court interpretation of Amendment 24, in *Harper v. Virginia State Board of Electors*),[39] property ownership (*Kramer v. Union Free School District*,[40] and *City of Phoenix, Arizona v. Emily Kolodziejski*[41]), or lengthy residence (*Dunn v. Blumstein*).[42]

Nor may any state deviate from the 1970 Voting Rights Act, which established eighteen years as the minimum voting age.

To be eligible to vote, one must meet the several requirements that are set by the states. These include: United States citizenship (all states); a prescribed minimum time period of residency; literacy requirements (13 states, although these are subject to suspension by provisions of the 1970 Voting Rights Act should they be used in instances of discrimination); and registration (in some form in all states except North Dakota). States have further restricted suffrage by excluding persons having mental illness, or who have been imprisoned for a specified period.[43]

The requirements just mentioned that exist as barriers to voting can account for a segment of those who do not register or vote. Several of these technicalities had been purposefully instituted to disenfranchise a part of the electorate, such as the imposition of poll taxes or literacy tests in some southern areas. That these methods were successful in disenfranchising a significant portion of the population can be seen in the increase in the number of persons registered in eleven southern states after the passage of the Voting Rights Act of 1965, which suspended discriminatory literacy and other registration tests and requirements. Table III.4 presents the percentage of voting age population registered, by race, before and after passage of that Act. The substantial rise in voter registration by blacks was accompanied by a significant increase in those actually voting. In Arkansas, for example, approximately 90,000 blacks (out of 121,000 who had registered) turned out in the 1966 general elections. This figure is significant when it is recognized that only 78,000 persons were registered before the Act took affect.[44]

Other requirements set by the states had been introduced for reasons considered to be rational. The imposition of a prescribed period of residency, for example, was thought to be necessary to assure some familiarity with local problems and political figures. An additional factor that affects the rate of registration is the convenience of the registration process and machinery. Where there are frequent dates for registration, convenient locations and hours, and permanent registration, the levels of registered persons are high.

Within the eligible potential electorate, approximately three-quarters do register. The percentage of those who register is indicative of the extent to which persons are interested in utilizing this channel of articulation. For registration is a purely mechanical action, that is, to vote one must register.

Voting Turnout and Political Factors

Whatever prompts individuals to register to vote, is not necessarily sufficient to prompt them to cast their ballot on election day. A cursory observation of any election day statistics shows that the turnout rate is lower than the

TABLE III.4

Voter Registration by Race Before and After Passage of the Voting Rights Act of 1965

State	Pre-Act Percent of Voting Age Population Registered	Post-Act Percent of Voting Age Population Registered
Alabama:		
Nonwhite	19.3	51.6
White	69.2	89.6
Arkansas:		
Nonwhite	40.4	62.8
White	65.5	72.4
Florida:		
Nonwhite	51.2	63.6
White	74.8	81.4
Georgia:		
Nonwhite	27.4	52.6
White	62.6	80.3
Louisiana:		
Nonwhite	31.6	58.9
White	80.5	93.1
Mississippi:		
Nonwhite	6.7	59.8
White	69.9	91.5
North Carolina:		
Nonwhite	46.8	51.3
White	96.8	83.0
South Carolina:		
Nonwhite	37.3	51.2
White	75.7	81.7
Tennessee:		
Nonwhite	69.5	71.7
White	72.9	80.6
Texas:		
Nonwhite	53.1*	61.6
White		53.3
Virginia:		
Nonwhite	38.3	55.6
White	61.1	63.4

* Percentages and totals by race are not available.

Adapted from: *Political Participation, op. cit.,* pp. 12–13.

registration rate. A further investigation would demonstrate that participation in state and local elections is less than that for national elections.

Turnout rates may be related to the political structure and environment and to the demographic characteristics of the population found within the states and localities. One political consideration affecting voting is the level of office to be filled at an election. Generally, fewer people vote for candidates for local offices than for those running for state offices. Moreover, certain offices attract a greater amount of attention from the electorate than do other offices. With the exception of the president and vice-president, the governor attracts the largest number of votes cast within a state. On the local level, the office for which most of the votes would be cast is that of the chief executive.

When the candidates for president appear on the ballot with those for state and local offices, the greatest number of individuals go to the polls. Yet, even on the presidential election day, all those who turn out do not vote for every state and local office to be filled. In non-presidential election years, with the absence of highly visible national candidates and issues, fewer individuals are drawn to cast their ballot. The least number of persons voting is to be found at those elections when neither an office of a governor nor of a mayor is to be filled.[4,5]

In non-partisan situations, primarily found on the local level, the turnout rate at elections is lower than in partisan situations. Elections in localities with at-large systems of electing councilmen and with council manager forms of government attract fewer voters to the polls than do ward systems and mayor council forms. George E. Berkley's study of Boston showed that when the city had ward-based elections over 50 percent of the registered persons voted in the non-partisan, off-year elections. After the change to the at-large system (in 1949), less than one-third of the electorate turned out.[46]

On primary election days, one finds the polling places less crowded than on general election days. One reason may be that in most states a person must declare an affiliation with a party to vote in a primary; therefore, the independent voters are excluded. A major factor, however, is the belief held by some individuals that primary elections are less important than the general election. In one-party states, where that party's nomination is tantamount to election, the importance of the primary is such that it draws a larger turnout than does the regular election.

Voting Turnout and Demographic Characteristics

Participation in voting requires that persons be interested and informed, and that they hold a high sense of political efficaciousness. As has been seen, these factors have been related to the demographic characteristics of the population. Voting studies have repeatedly shown that those who are most prone to vote are those with high levels of education and income, and employed in white collar and professional occupations.

Interest in participating in an election can be aroused by salient and controversial issues. Campaign issues and referenda proposals that have been surrounded by heated debates have stimulated large numbers of people to turn out. Interest may also be an outgrowth of community identification. When an individual works, resides, raises his children, and owns property in a locality, community politics become meaningful. Social status is important in determining the way individuals are integrated into their communities. People with more than adequate income, education, and possibilities of interacting with prominent persons in the community, are those prone to show up on election day. Those not yet deeply involved in the community, such as young adults, or those who are located toward the periphery rather than the center of society (such as blacks and members of other racial or ethnic minorities) are less likely to vote in state and local elections.

Information influences the desire to vote. Those who are aware of the importance of an issue or a public office may want to participate in order to exert influence. An individual who knows about the issues or the candidates may feel confident in his actions. People are more likely to turn out for an election when differences between alternatives are clearly perceived than when they are not.

Education, the leisure that comes with high income, and the contacts one has, enables an individual to obtain, perceive, digest, analyze, and utilize information. Members of the less educated, low income groups are likely to refrain from voting in the belief that politics is too complicated to understand, which stems from their inability to find a sense of order and meaning from the information available. Those having less access to the mass media that serve as sources of political information, such as rural residents, are less likely to vote.

Efficacy and concern with the outcome of an election are related to voting behavior. One is likely to cast a vote when he feels it can contribute to a candidate's success. It has been seen that voter turnout rises in competitive situations where no one candidate has the certainty of success. Moreover, it is important for one to believe that the election process is significant. When individuals in Wisconsin were asked why they had not voted, though they were eligible, 69 percent said that it was not worth the bother.[47] Such an attitude is prevalent among the less educated and lower economic groups. A study of factory workers in Linden, New Jersey, found that 75 percent of the assembly line workers, 57 percent of the repairmen, and 60 percent of the maintenance men expressed the beliefs that: elections are designed to fool the public; that politicians only care to keep themselves in power; and that public officials steal, waste public funds, suppress information, and generally do not care about the common people.[48] In addition, it is important for one to believe that an outcome of an election is significant to him before he may want to participate. Where persons believe there is no real choice between candidates, such as when southern blacks were faced with two segregationist candidates, they will not exert the effort to vote.

It is difficult for people to care about the outcome of an election when they cannot identify with any candidate. For example, wards predominantly comprised of black voters have generally had lower turnout rates than those with white voters, especially when white candidates were running. However, in recent times the increase in black candidates has tended to be a factor in the increase in black voters. The candidacy of a black man for mayor in Cleveland, Ohio (Carl Stokes), and in Gary, Indiana (Richard Hatcher), altered all previous voting turnout and voting patterns. In black wards in both of those cities, nearly 80 percent of the registered voters turned out; and, of these, nearly everyone cast a vote for the candidate with whom he most readily identified.[49]

Voting as Articulation?

Although voting may be an indirect channel for articulation, most individuals do not always consider it to be a means for expressing interests, needs, and demands. When a nationwide sample of citizens were asked what they would do to try to influence local governmental officials, only 14 percent responded that they would use the ballot.[50] When persons in Wisconsin were asked why they had voted in a state primary election, their responses (as seen in Table III.5) were revealing. While some individuals may have supported a particular candidate as a means of expressing an interest, most of the respondents did not express a reason remotely related to the function

TABLE III.5

Reason for Voting in Primary

Voting is an obligation, a duty, a responsibility	32%
Voting is a privilege, a right	7
Voting is a habit, "I always vote"	19
Wanted to support a particular candidate	28
Influenced by others, got a ride, near there anyway, friends wanted me to	2
Other	5
Don't know, not ascertained	7
	100%

Adapted from: Ranney and Epstein, *op. cit.*, p. 602.

of articulation. Nearly two-thirds voted in the primary because it was a civic duty, a privilege, or a habit.[51]

Murray B. Levin, in his study of a Boston mayorality election, also showed the difficulty of interpreting voting as a means of interest articulation.[52] The reasons given by nearly two-thirds of the Bostonians voting for the winning candidate, John Collins, were not issue oriented. Their responses, basically candidate oriented in nature, are categorized in Table III.6.

TABLE III.6

Why Did You Vote for Collins?

Any anti-opponent reason	50%
His personality	26
His sincerity	21
His program	19
Tax issue	14
Lesser of two evils	13
His courage (fight against polio)	7
He was the underdog	7
He favors the little man	5
	(N = 253)

Adapted from: Levin, *op. cit.*, p. 37.

If a potential voter is to use the ballot as a means of articulating interests, he must perceive the issues and become identified with them; he has to know which candidates are defending which issues; and then he must be able to recognize those candidates as they appear on the ballot. Party identification serves to facilitate his endeavors by offering a framework for structuring the electoral decision making. The voter has his preferences ordered, his information organized, and the alternative of candidates narrowed for him. The partisan is able to simplify his task and reduce to manageable proportions the amount of time and energy he spends on political affairs. Thus, to a highly significant extent, one's habitual attachment to a party accounts for his voting decision.[53]

Individuals who upon their own volition do not identify with political parties, or who are cast adrift from partisan elections (perhaps because they live in non-partisan communities) seem to utilize voting as an indirect channel for articulation less frequently than partisan identifiers or those in partisan situations. In addition, the voting decisions of such independents do not appear to be based upon issue orientations.

James Q. Wilson has found that in partisan situations individuals tend to vote a straight party ticket. For example, in Chicago (which is nominally non-partisan, but is in reality strongly partisan), blacks tended to support the entire Democratic ticket, regardless of the individual nominees or the stands on issues. In contrast, in non-partisan Detroit, race and ethnicity were important factors in voting decisions. Black constituents voted for black candidates (even if the nominees had never taken a stand on a racial issue) to a greater degree than for a white candidate (even if he had consistently demonstrated support for issues salient to the black community).[54]

Without the framework parties provide for structuring political facts, the citizens may be guided by irrelevant or trivial factors. Votes are often cast for a person who bears a familiar or distinguishable name, whether he be an incumbent or a celebrity in a non-political field.[55] In an election for the Detroit non-partisan council, for example, one candidate's success was attributed to his being a popular shortstop on the Detroit baseball team.[56] Another trivial factor is the effect of ballot position. The first position on a vertical list on paper ballots and the top row on voting machines are favored. In the election for minor offices, where several people with unfamiliar names compete, ballot position may be the deciding factor.[57]

Thus, votes are often cast because of a sense of civic obligation, on behalf of a candidate, or as a matter of following a party label, rather than to express support for an interest oriented issue. And politicians recognize this to be true. A study undertaken to ascertain how elected officials viewed their success in attracting votes revealed that nearly 66 percent of the statewide office holders and assemblymen in Wisconsin attributed success to their own personal characteristics. Another 20 percent of the officials felt that their party label was the most important factor influencing the voters. Only 17 percent noted that the electorate was influenced by election issues. Furthermore, only 13 percent of state legislators believed that the voters were politically interested in and informed about campaign issues.[58]

Initiative and Referendum

Elections that appear to be reflections of interest articulation are the initiative and the referendum. In these elections, the people are not confronted with candidates or party labels, but with issues for which they have to express approval or disapproval. Through the initiative, individuals are voting on a proposed measure; through the referendum, they are reacting to a measure already acted on by the legislature. The issues may be placed on the ballot by public agents or by constituents. Public agents have asked the citizens to express their interest through the vote on such matters as flouridating the water supply, permitting the sale of alcoholic beverages on Sunday, redistricting the legislature, and increasing property tax levies. For certain proposals public ratification may be required. These include changes in local charters, state constitutions, and issuance of bonds to finance libraries, hospitals, schools, cultural centers, and roads. Approximately 10,000 to 15,000 referenda and initiative questions appear on the ballot across the nation annually; about 98 percent are concerned with local matters.[59]

While individuals may initiate these issue elections, it is not likely that many will find it feasible to do so. To initiate such a procedure, individuals must possess an extraordinary amount of information, interest, feeling of efficacy, and money. Placing a proposition on the ballot requires submitting petitions that bear the valid signatures of a specified percentage of the electorate. In California, where about 500,000 signatures are required for a proposal to appear on a ballot in a statewide election, a signature collecting firm is almost always hired. The cost to qualify a single measure in this state is approximately $250,000.[60] Thus, individual articulation is limited to those issues that appear on the ballot, and to that time at which elections are held.

In referendum and initiative elections, voters have not rushed to the polls in great numbers to express interests. Turnout rates are related to the scheduling of election dates. When proposals are offered at the general elections, turnout rates are the highest. However, even at those times, many proposals fail to attract the attention of the full electorate. At many elections, fewer votes were cast for the proposals than were cast for the candidates. This may be due to several factors. One factor may be that the questions were placed in a less prominent position on the ballot than were the names of the candidates for office. Another may be the tedium brought on by the added length of the ballot.

When these proposals are to be voted on at special elections, the turnout rate is the lowest. While voting rates fluctuate considerably in different localities and with different issues, the rates rarely reach above one-third of the potential electorate and occasionally fall below one-tenth. In New Orleans, for example, it was found that from 1960 through 1965, turnout was considerably lower for these elections than for general or primary elections. The turnout never exceeded one-third of the potential electorate.[61] For school fiscal referenda the average turnout throughout the nation, over an eleven-year period, had been 36 percent.[62]

To cast an intelligent referendum or initiative vote, one necessarily must know the problem under consideration, be aware of all the possible alternatives, be cognizant of the consequences of each alternative, and be able to place a value on each possibility. One must also seek all relevant information, discuss and hear all arguments, and evaluate the data obtained. Findings of studies on initiative and referendum elections have suggested that demographic characteristics are related to voting turnout and voting decisions. These studies have concluded that there is a positive correlation between interest, information, and turnout with high socio-economic status.[63]

Several factors make it difficult to accept issue election results as accurate indicators of individual interest. Individuals may be confused as they pull the lever on election day. Confusion may arise in the minds of voters because of the wording of a proposition. For example, those in favor of a proposal may be required to vote "no," yet (thinking positively), might have voted "yes," thus defeating their intent. Even a well-meaning, reasonably informed voter may be stymied when confronted by a question veiled in legislative jargon. Moreover, a proposition surrounded by popular or unpopular proposals may receive an affirmative or negative vote merely as a result of the voter's inattentive repetition.

The outcome may not reflect the intensity or the specific attitudes of the individuals voting. For the process of this form of election limits the voter's alternatives to an expression of "yes" or "no," neither of which may reflect his interest on the measure. Moreover, in the tabulation of simple "yes" or "no" responses, there is no measurement of intensity. A "yes" voter may have held an attitude of "I don't care," while the "no" voter may have cared a great deal. Where every voter's preference, no matter how casual, is equally weighed the intensity of demands can never be known.

New Channels and Revitalized Old Channels of Articulation

The function of interest articulation is intrinsic to a democratic governmental system. Only if public officials are aware of the needs, demands, and interests of the citizenry can they act to see that these are satisfied. Though a variety of direct and indirect channels for interest articulation exist, to be meaningful they must be utilized. The channels must be utilized by all segments of the population to articulate their needs and demands. And the channels for articulation must be utilized by all public agents to hear the expressions of the community with an open ear and a will to respond.

Riots

That existing channels for articulation were not being utilized by all segments of the population and by all public agents became painfully apparent in the second half of the 1960s. Beginning in August 1965, in Los Angeles, and spreading in succeeding years, city after city in every section of the country had either been the site of or felt the threat of a riot. While the causes precipitating the disorders were complex and interacting, embedded in a tangle of issues and circumstances, the prominent causal factor was the general sense of frustration about the people's inability to have conditions changed.

Investigating the basic causes and factors leading to the riots, the National Advisory Commission on Civil Disorders found that in every city for which they obtained data, the needs and demands of the poorly educated, low income, unemployed, inner-city blacks were not being met. Though the intensity of the needs varied somewhat from city to city, all demands related to: living conditions; police practices and protection; underemployment by public (as well as private) agencies; low level of services (for example, sanitation and garbage removal, paving and lighting of streets) provided by municipal governments; and inadequate education, recreation, and welfare facilities and programs.[64]

The Commission reported that "one of the most surprising findings is that in 17 of the 20 surveyed riot cities, some formal grievance machinery existed prior to the 1967 disorders. . . ."[65] Though these channels for articulation existed, they were not utilized by the members of the black communities. They were not utilized because the demands made rarely appeared to be answered. Indeed, the Commission found a pervasive feeling of distrust toward the city government and anger at unresponsive public agents.[66]

Some have viewed the riots to be actions that articulated needs. Lacking responsive channels of communication, influence, and appeal, the frustrations of powerlessness have led some to the conviction that there is no effective alternative to violence as a means of expression. As one youth, confronting two public officials in the midst of a violent outbreak, stated:

> You came down here last year. We were throwing stones at some passing cars and you said to us that this was not the way to do it. You got us to talk with the man. We talked to him. We talked with him, and we talked all year long. We ain't got nothing yet![67]

Governmental officials unwilling to accept the alternative of violence, have in recent years established new channels or revitalized old channels of articulation to facilitate and encourage the expression of interest from those citizens unwilling or unable to utilize the existing channels. Much of this effort has been on the local level, as were the riots.

Citizen Information and Complaint Centers

One such effort has been citizen information and complaint centers. These operate to provide information to people regarding municipal institutions and services. Much of the information sought concerns how to register complaints and to whom they should be directed. Personnel at these centers may handle the complaints themselves, or may direct the citizen to an appropriate agency. In several localities specific offices have been established to hear individual grievances expressed against a public department, and to transmit that complaint to the appropriate official for satisfaction.

During and after the period of the riots, some municipalities have established new centers or have revitalized already established ones. There have been campaigns of radio and television advertisements to inform the citizens of the existence of the centers, what they do, and how to contact them. To encouarge and facilitate the citizen's use of this service, many localities permit communication to be made by telephone calls, in addition to letter writing or personal visits. To assure responsiveness (so that people will feel it is worthwhile to communicate via these channels) many of the centers are charged with the responsibility of following up all complaints until satisfaction has been given.

Most information and complaint centers are located in city halls. Philadelphia's Mayor's Information Office is located on the city hall courtyard. In Boston, the Complaints Division of the Administrative Services Department is at the entrance to its city hall. The Boston office has received about 3,000 communications annually; two-thirds of these have been by telephone, and one-tenth by personal visits.[68]

To further encourage people to express their interests, needs, and demands, several municipalities have set up "little city halls," scattered throughout the city. By decentralizing the centers, it was hoped that more people would be tempted to make efforts to communicate their interests to public agents. The operation of these offices, staffed by public personnel, sometimes by volunteers, is similar to that of the Boston center described above.

In New York City, Mayor Lindsay (after a running battle with the City Council, which annually refused to appropriate public funds) had set up six little city halls by 1970, with funds donated by private foundations. Five of these were located in public buildings in different parts of the city. A sixth was a mobile unit (a 35-foot van) set up to move throughout the city, to reach people who still were unable or unwilling to go to the sites of the other five. Complaints made to the bureaucrats in these little city halls were transmitted to the Office of the Assistant to the Mayor, who was Administrator of the Neighborhood City Halls. These were then transmitted to proper city agencies and, if a satisfactory reply was not received within a week, an inquiry would be conducted by the Administrator.

The mobile unit visited 97 different locations in 1968, and received a total of 14,327 complaints, more than twice as many as were received the previous year. A breakdown of the complaints into categories indicates the nature of expressions made. The largest number of complaints (1,841) were about sanitation and sewage problems, and were directed to the Environmental Protection Administration. The next largest number (1,710) was directed to the Transportation Administration. Others were sent to the Housing and Development Administration (1,069); to the Police Department (871); to the Human Resources Administration, especially to the Department of Social Services (278); and the remainder (8,568) were considered miscellaneous.[69]

Neighborhood Service Centers

An attempt at overcoming the fear, apathy, and hostility among those of lower socio-economic status toward the complex machinery of big public agencies has been made through the initiation of "neighborhood service centers." [70] One finds these located in store fronts, converted apartments, and rooms in public housing projects and in schools, so as to give inhabitants of inner city neighborhoods a convenient place to go for help. Indeed, the largest number of persons using the centers are "walk-ins" who come from the immediate neighborhoods.

The centers have generally been funded by private foundations or federal grants (through the Community Services Act of 1966). Though they are staffed by bureaucrats, neighborhood residents are hired to help overcome the initial reticence of individuals coming in for the first time. Services dispensed by the personnel of the centers include: on-the-spot advice for problems requiring immediate attention; referral to appropriate agencies and agents; and, in some instances, acting as intermediaries in representing residents' interests in dealing with public officials.

The subject matter of concerns held by those communicating with the centers have been primarily in the areas of jobs and income, housing, health, and legal and social needs. Staffs in these centers have been quick to recognize that an individual who comes to them has additional problems beyond the one he first stated, and they try to obtain maximum assistance for the interconnecting problems that each citizen is experiencing.

Other New Channels

Stimulated by federal financial support and requirements (after the 1964 Economic Opportunity Act), other channels were established to permit the expression of interest. These were "community action programs," and they were to be developed, conducted, and administered with the "maximum feasible participation" of residents of the areas to be served.

The underlying premise in establishing such channels was that persons to be affected by governmental actions must be included in the planning stages of any programs. The inclusion of such individuals might insure that insulated administrators do not overlook aspects of programs or set priorities that would not satisfy the types of needs the people had.

Neighborhoods would be selected in which programs for housing, welfare, education, employment, etc., would be coordinated. The programs were to be directed by boards, with some members elected by the neighborhood residents. The election of members to the board would open opportunities for participation to many who would otherwise not engage in any such action. The task of the board members was basically to convey the needs and demands of the people in the neighborhood to public agents, and to set the priority of proposals for public officials to follow. In addition, the members were to be charged with continual liaison in obtaining and transmitting neighborhood interests to the public authorities.

A recent development has been the establishment of "community control programs." Unlike community action programs, in which people are elected as members to a board (staffed also with administrative agents) and involved in planning programs, the community control boards are involved with making rules within an area of governmental operations and are comprised primarily of neighborhood residents. The few attempts instituted have involved the governing of neighborhood schools. Through this channel, individuals may articulate to their neighbors and friends, rather than to "unfriendly bureaucrats," the interests, needs, and demands of the members of the community.

All the direct or indirect channels for articulation discussed in this chapter are means by which the expression of individuals could be made known. For certain types of interests, those which are personal and immediate in nature, individual effort may be effective. However, the influence of general expressions lies in the total of all individuals' efforts. A vote cast is important when added to all other votes, and it is a majority or plurality figure that is decisive. Each letter to a public official becomes important when it is one of many similar letters received. The same can be said of telephone calls or responses to a poll. Thus, for interests that are general and long range in nature, collective expressions may be the more effective means of articulation.

Chapter III Footnotes

1. Gabriel A. Almond and Sidney Verba, *The Civic Culture* (Boston: Little, Brown and Company, 1965), pp. 126–27.
2. *Polls*, II (Spring 1967), p. 89.
3. John C. Wahlke *et al.*, *The Legislative System* (New York: John Wiley and Sons, Inc., 1962), p. 296.
4. Robert A. Dahl, "The City in the Future of Democracy," *American Political Science Review*, LXI (December 1967), pp. 953–70.
5. M. Kent Jennings and Harmon Zeigler, "The Salience of American State Politics," *American Political Science Review*, LXIV (June 1970). p. 524.
6. Interview, November 7, 1969.
7. Interview, January 13, 1970.
8. William J. Veeder, "How Much Involvement is Enough?" *Public Management*, LI (July 1969), pp. 15–16.
9. Paul A. Smith, "The Games of Community Politics," *Midwest Journal of Political Science*, IX (February 1965), pp. 37–60.
10. *Polls*, I (Summer 1965), p. 87.
11. "Voters Lack Knowledge of State Legislators," *National Civic Review*, LV (March 1967), p. 152.

12. *Polls*, I (Summer 1966), p. 82.
13. Wahlke *et al.*, *Legislative System*, pp. 301–302.
14. Almond and Verba, *Civic Culture*, p. 142.
15. Ibid., p. 144.
16. Ibid., p. 72.
17. See, for example, Bernard R. Berelson, Paul F. Lazarsfeld, and William N. McPhee, *Voting* (Chicago: University of Chicago Press, 1954); Robert E. Lane, *Political Life* (New York: The Free Press, 1959); V. O. Key, Jr., *Public Opinion and American Democracy* (New York: Alfred A. Knopf, 1961); Angus Campbell *et al.*, *The American Voter* (New York: John Wiley and Sons, Inc., 1960); and Lester W. Milbrath, *Political Participation* (Chicago: Rand McNally and Company, 1965).
18. Fredric Templeton, "Alienation and Political Participation: Some Research Findings," *Public Opinion Quarterly*, XXX (Summer 1966), pp. 249–61.
19. *Polls*, II (Summer 1967), p. 82.
20. Ibid., p. 81.
21. Interview, November 7, 1969.
22. Interviews, July 13–17, 1970.
23. Letters to the Montgomery County (Maryland) Council, January–August 1969 (in the files of the Secretary to the Council).
24. Interview, January 14, 1970.
25. Interview, October 16, 1969.
26. Veeder, "How Much Involvement?" p. 16.
27. *The Washington Post*, July 26, 1970, p. C2.
28. See, for example, *The New York Times*, August 8, 1966, p. 16.
29. *The New York Times*, February 13, 1970, p. 1.
30. *Polls*, I (Summer 1966), p. 75.
31. *CBS News Transcript*, January 27, 1970.
32. Philips Cutright, "Activities of Precinct Committeemen in Partisan and Nonpartisan Communities," *Western Political Quarterly*, XVII (March 1964), pp. 93–108.
33. Harry W. Reynolds, Jr., "The Career Public Service and Statute Lawmaking in Los Angeles," *Western Political Quarterly*, XVIII (September 1965), pp. 621–39.
34. Republican National Committee, *The Art of Winning Elections* (Washington, D.C.: Republican National Committee, 1967), p. 108.
35. See, for example, Barbara Snell Dohrenwend, John Colombotos, and Bruce P. Dohrenwend, "Social Distance and Interviewer Effects," *Public Opinion Quarterly*, XXXII (Fall 1968), pp. 410–22.
36. *Polls*, II (Fall 1966), p. 77.
37. George Gallup, *A Guide to Public Opinion Polls* (Princeton: Princeton University Press, 1968, 2nd ed.), p. 25.
38. George Gallup, "How a Public Opinion Poll is Conducted," American Institute of Public Opinion, Mimeograph, n.d., n.p.
39. 383 U.S. 663 (1966).
40. 395 U.S. 621 (1969).
41. 399 U.S. 204 (1970).
42. 405 U.S. 330 (1972).
43. *The Book of The States*, 1970–1971, p. 40–41.
44. U.S. Commission on Civil Rights, *Political Participation* (Washington, D.C.: Government Printing Office, 1968), pp. 11–17.
45. Kenneth N. Vines and Henry Robert Glick, "The Impact of Universal Suffrage: A Comparison of Popular Voting," *American Political Science Review*, LXI (December 1967), pp. 1078–87.

46. George E. Berkley, "Flaws in At-Large Voting," *National Civic Review*, LV (July 1966), pp. 370–73.

47. Austin Ranney and Leon D. Epstein, "The Two Electorates: Voters and Non-Voters in a Wisconsin Primary," *Journal of Politics*, XXVIII (August 1966), p. 601.

48. Lewis Lipsitz, "Work Life and Political Attitudes: A Study of Manual Workers," *American Political Science Review*, LVIII (December 1964), pp. 951–62.

49. Jeffrey K. Hadden, Louis H. Massotti, and Victor Thiessen, "The Making of the Negro Mayors 1967," *Trans-action*, V (January–February 1968), pp. 21–30.

50. Almond and Verba, *Civic Culture*, p. 148.

51. Ranney and Epstein, "Two Electorates," pp. 598–616.

52. Murray B. Levin, *The Alienated Voter* (New York: Holt, Rinehart and Winston 1960).

53. See, for example, Leon D. Esptein, "Electoral Decision and Policy Mandate: An Empirical Example," *Public Opinion Quarterly*, XXVIII (Winter 1964), pp. 564–72.

54. James Q. Wilson, *Negro Politics* (New York: The Free Press, 1965), pp. 21–48.

55. Charles E. Gilbert and Christopher Claque, "Electoral Competition and Electoral System in Large Cities," *Journal of Politics*, XXIV (May 1962), pp. 324–31.

56. Charles R. Adrian, "Some General Characteristics of Nonpartisan Elections," in Oliver P. Williams and Charles Press, eds.,*Democracy in Urban America* (Chicago: Rand McNally and Co., 1961), p. 263n.

57. Henry M. Bain and Donald S. Hecock, *Ballot Position and Voter's Choice* (Detroit: Wayne University Press, 1957).

58. John W. Kingdon, "Politican's Beliefs About Voters," *American Political Science Review*, LXI (March 1967), pp. 137–45.

59. Hugh A. Bone, "Easier to Change," *National Civic Review*, LVII (March 1968) p. 126.

60. Joseph P. Harris, *California Politics* (San Francisco: Chandler Publishing Company, 1967, 4th ed.), p. 115.

61. Vines and Glick, "Universal Suffrage," pp. 1078–87.

62. Richard F. Carter and William G. Savard, *Influence of Voter Turnout on School Bond and Tax Elections*, U.S. Office of Education, Cooperative Research Monograph, No. 5 (Washington, D.C.: Government Printing Office, 1963).

63. See, for example, Harlan Hahn,"Northern Referenda on Fair Housing: The Response of White Voters," *Western Political Quarterly*, XXI (September 1968), pp. 483–95; Robert L. Crain and Donald B. Rosenthal, "Structure and Values in Local Political Systems: The Case of Flouridation Decisions," *Journal of Politics*, XXVII (February 1966), pp. 169–95; and Howard D. Hamilton, "Direct Legislation: Some Implications of Open Housing Referenda," *American Political Science Review*, LXIV (March 1970), pp. 124–37.

64. U.S. National Advisory Commission on Civil Disorders, *Report* (Washington, D.C.: Government Printing Office, 1968), pp. 143–45.

65. Ibid., pp. 138–39.

66. Ibid., p. 178.

67. Ibid., p. 78.

68. Walter Gellhorn, *When Americans Complain* (Cambridge: Harvard University Press, 1966), p. 160.

69. *The New York Times*, February 18, 1969, p. 43.

70. See, for example, Robert Perlman and David Jones, *Neighborhood Service Centers* (Washington, D.C.: Government Printing Office, 1967).

Chapter IV

Interest Articulation, Part 2: Collective Actions

Individuals who are informed about the scope of governmental action and interested in influencing its direction feel that they can be more efficacious in articulating interests through collective action. Gabriel A. Almond and Sidney Verba, in a nationwide survey, found that persons would rather associate with others to exert influence than act alone, at a ratio of 3 : 1. The respondents firmly held the belief that the best or only way to articulate interests in an influential manner is through group action.[1] This belief is apparent in the following statements of respondents:

> You can't do anything individually. You'd have to get a group and all get together and go to the proper authorities to complain.
> I could discuss it with others and see how many others felt the same about it as I did. We could then write a letter each to some government person in charge and let him know how we felt, or we could write one letter and get a lot of people to sign it.[2]

Types of Organized Associations

Ad Hoc Groups

People can engage in collective action through a variety of organized associations. These groups may be either ad hoc or permanent. Ad hoc associations have a single interest and a single goal. The members concentrate on obtaining their objective quickly, and they are unhampered by

96

the problems of maintaining a complex and permanent organization. The group disbands when the objective has been obtained or the issue has been resolved. Because of the nature of the purpose and the association, individuals making the collective effort are highly motivated and cohesive.

Whenever an interest is held by a number of individuals and each of them is aware that others strongly care about that interest, there is a great likelihood that an ad hoc association would be formed. This interest may be focused narrowly on a concrete objective or broadly on a general rule to be made by the governing body. The goal may be to initiate, support, or oppose a public action.

As a general rule, ad hoc groups are more readily formed to oppose a specific proposal than to initiate or support governmental actions. Yet, such groups have been organized and have been successful in initiating and supporting governmental actions that are narrow in scope and which affect a relatively small number of individuals. For example, mothers in a neighborhood concerned about traffic may get together to collectively articulate a demand for a traffic light at an intersection their children must cross on their way to and from school. When an issue is general in nature and may affect a significant proportion of the community's residents, the rule holds true that the people most likely to organize and be successful are those opposing action. The following illustration, by describing the formation and activities of one ad hoc group, demonstrates this premise.

~ During the first week in September 1968, the Montgomery County (Maryland) council held public hearings on proposed gun control legislation. Each night over 3,000 vociferous opponents of the proposal came to jam the meeting room, while hundreds more were turned away for lack of space. This unprecedented, apparently spontaneous, demonstration of public sentiment was the culmination of a six-week mobilization effort, which grew out of a friendly discussion among three men one Sunday afternoon in July. In the short interval following, these men urged their friends in different gun and hunting clubs to set up meetings to organize anti-gun control sentiment. As their support grew, they were joined by the Maryland and D.C. Rifle and Pistol Association, the Montgomery County Citizens League, gun dealers, and the local chapter of the National Rifle Association. Calling itself the Montgomery County Citizens for Just Firearms Legislation, the ad hoc group amassed a coalition of approximately 10,000 persons, and utilized several channels of interest articulation. The group collected 20,000 signatures on a petition, and motivated letter writing and phone calls to members of the council. They distributed leaflets that analyzed and denounced the proposed ordinance. And they advertised when and where the council hearings were to be held, and urged attendance. The council, swayed by such grass-root opposition, voted to kill the measure.

Although the group had gained its objective, its members did not represent the opinions and desires of a majority of the residents of Montgomery County. One public official, defending the proposed legislation, had estimated that between 80 and 85 percent of the more than 400,000 county residents favored strict gun control regulations. Metropolitan newspapers, such as *The Washington Post* and *The Montgomery County Sentinel*, gave editorial support to gun control. Important political figures testified to support the policy, including United States Senator Joseph Tydings, who had sponsored similar federal legislation, and state delegate Leonard Blondes, who had sponsored similar state legislation. Despite the prevailing positive attitude and endorsements, gun control advocates could do little to organize support for the county measure. Their slight efforts, which brought a small turnout to a council meeting, "came late and produced few results. The hearings were filled with gun enthusiasts, who jeered down those who disagreed with them and clearly swayed the county council." [3]

Public Oriented Permanent Associations

Permanent associations are organized around a special and continuing interest. This interest may be public or private oriented in nature. Public oriented groups, which focus primarily on community affairs, are civic associations. Civic associations are comprised of persons who voluntarily join together and who have neither personal stake in nor expect any material benefit from their membership.

Some civic associations are concerned with narrowly defined community interests. One such group is the historical preservation society, whose members concern themselves with saving public landmarks. For example, when the county courthouse built in the nineteenth century is scheduled to be demolished, members of such a group articulate their opposition to such a move. Other groups specialize in issues such as zoning, parks and recreation, or housing. Any governmental action that would be concerned with land use or low income, high density housing, and so on, would stimulate articulation by the members of groups that focus on these particular issues.

There are neighborhood associations comprised of residents who are concerned with governmental actions that affect their immediate area. These residents may collectively demand such neighborhood improvements as street lighting, road maintenance, and sanitation control. They may articulate opposition to the construction of an airport, television tower, public housing, or an incinerator, in a nearby area. They may request better police protection, crossing guards, or improved bus service.

A third type of civic association is that which is concerned with community-at-large matters. This group includes city and county-wide federations of neighborhood associations that bring together a variety of localized groups to discuss area-wide issues. There are also citizens' leagues that are interested in "good government" issues, such as public employment and services. Taxpayer groups have been established to study the taxation, budgeting, and borrowing practices of the government; and to articulate for lower taxes, and fewer and cheaper activities and services. The League of Women Voters is an example of those groups that focus on educating residents on major public issues and familiarizing the citizens with candidates seeking public office. They are also concerned with presenting the findings of research to educate public officials.

Some associations attempt to direct their appeal to a small, homogeneous sector of the community. With this type of membership, the associations can commit themselves to causes that are extreme or controversial. The larger and the more heterogeneous the membership, the more general are the activities and the objectives of the association. The fear of losing membership support and the hope of attracting funds lead to the avoidance of controversial issues. The policies and activities of the large established civic associations are directed by professional staffs, hired on a full-time basis. The professionals' interests are in maintaining and enhancing the organization; thus, they tend to steer the group away from conflict and controversial issues.

Private Oriented Permanent Associations

Governmental affairs occupy only the part-time attention of permanent associations that are private oriented in nature. Economic activity is the main purpose of some of these associations. There are many groups with business or agricultural orientations, including chambers of commerce, liquor interests, real estate groups, bankers' associations, insurance organizations, and farmers' cooperatives and bureaus. Others have been established around occupational interests. There are groupings for professionals (*e.g.*, medical, dental, and accounting), for manual and skilled laborers (*e.g.*, automobile and mine workers, teamsters, and electricians), and for governmental personnel (*e.g.*, teachers, policemen, and firemen). Associations and institutions have been established for non-economic purposes, and these also are partially involved in articulating sentiments to public agents regarding governmental activities. Religious institutions (*e.g.*, the corner church, or the Council of Churches), charitable organizations (*e.g.*, United Givers Fund, or the Crippled Children Society), racial associations (*e.g.*, the National Association for the Advancement of Colored People), educational groups (*e.g.*, Parent–Teacher Association), and fraternal and service oriented clubs (*e.g.*, Lions, American Legion, or Kiwanis) are included in this category.

Generally, the members of the private oriented associations spend their energies on achieving the group's principal purpose. Thus, chambers of commerce work to promote business development; labor unions to enhance salary and working conditions; PTA's to broaden the scope of school services; and charitable institutions to improve the lives of the needy and the ill. In pursuit of their goals, it may be necessary to initiate, support, or oppose some governmental action.

On occasion, these groups may focus their efforts on civic projects outside their usual scope of interest. The Junior Chamber of Commerce may, for example, hold seminars on the youth narcotic problem to bring the seriousness of the problem to the attention of public agents and members of the community. However, repercussions may result should an association enter into articulation efforts in areas outside of its major economic or noneconomic interest. For example, church group leaders who have espoused open housing or other civil liberterian programs have received responses in the form of decreased church attendance and contributions from their members, who believe that the church activities are not to be connected with political affairs.

The above categories of associations are not necessarily mutually exclusive. A member in one may belong concurrently to another organization. Moreover, persons in public oriented associations may have private oriented priorities motivating their actions. For example, the Urban League has had a membership of blacks and whites from the business and civic communities. Although the League performs service activities of a welfare nature (as job training and youth guidance and counselling) for the black community, it also serves the interests of white businessmen who have a tangible stake in that community. The white businessmen need skilled black labor, good relations between black and white workers, and protection of capital investments in black areas; and the price they pay for these benefits is support of the Urban League's education and community organization work that promotes racial ends.[4]

Pluralism and the Fluidity of Group Relations

A multiplicity of groups performs the function of articulation in the states and localities. The broad scope of state and local governmental actions, and the wide spectrum of issues that arise within the constituencies, form the basis of a fluid system of collective action.

Not every action or issue draws the attention of every group. An educational issue will spark the interest of education oriented associations, and labor issues the interest of labor unions. But groups may choose to make their interests known on any issue. Thus, labor unions may articulate on school matters, and teacher associations may become active on labor issues.

Not all groups within a category of interest orientation will articulate similar sentiments on a specific issue. There is no singular business interest, for example. Downtown merchants may hold interests that are opposed to those held by neighborhood businessmen. Similar groups may align along a continuum of interests, but they are not continually in accord on all issues. Hence, the automobile workers and the teamsters unions most likely will agree on issues related to the betterment of working conditions and labor benefits, but they might articulate dissimilar interests on issues relating to civil liberties.

Groups that may be included in opposition categories may work together on certain issues. Big business and labor, for example, may both find it to their advantage to support urban renewal. The former may view such a proposal as enhancing the drawing power of downtown business to customers; the latter might welcome the expansion of employment opportunities.

The fluidity of the pressure group system is further seen in the coalitions that are established for groups to work together toward a positive objective, or to stalemate the effectiveness of other groups. Allies within one coalition may realign, as each wishes, in different combinations for other objectives. New coalitions appear as new groups arise or as old groups change stands on issues. Indeed, the basis of group membership may change, as individuals enter and withdraw from the associations.

Motivations for Joining Associations

Just as there is a variety of groups to join, there is also a variety of motivations held by people that account for their joining. Individuals may join groups with the intent of influencing governmental action. Economic reasons may underlie the intent of some. For example, one's business may be affected by governmental actions (*e.g.*, rate making, licensing, and zoning), and, thus, he joins to participate in exerting collective influence on governmental agents engaged in those actions. A sense of civic obligation may prompt the intention of others. They feel that they should influence governmental actions to benefit the whole community, and that they could more effectively do so through collective action.

Most individuals, however, do not join associations with the intent of influencing governmental action. Doctors, lawyers, accountants, nurses, professors, and others join professional associations as part of expanding their own breadth of knowledge and experience. Some may be pressured into joining. Blue collar workers' jobs, for example, may depend on membership in a labor union. Many become members of associations and institutions for a particular reason, without being aware and concerned that these groups are engaged in any lobbying efforts. A person may join an automobile club for roadside emergency assistance, yet not be conscious of the fact that part of his dues is being used to finance lobbying efforts for highway construction, and that he is regarded as having placed his name on the list of articulating supporters. Individuals may desire to worship at a nearby church for convenience, unconcerned that the church leaders are involved in exerting influence for the correction of social ills.

Others join for social reasons (to make new friends, or to follow the example of old friends), or for status or prestige reasons. Indeed, many Americans are "joiners," and will choose to belong to almost any type of group. Having joined, membership is a passive activity for most people, not demanding time-consuming effort or attention.

The Factors of Group Strength

Resources

The degree of influence that any group is able to exert is related to its resources. No group is without any resources, although they may be unevenly distributed. Membership can be an important resource in determining a group's strength. Associations having large numbers of people articulating similar interests can be a potentially powerful force. Yet, the quantity of members need not be as critical a factor as their quality. Groups with members who are active and politically interested would be stronger than those whose members are passive and apathetic. And those that reflect more of the variety of demographic characteristics found within a community may be more accepted by public agents on broadly based matters. With respect to narrow, specialized interests, groups having members who are experts in particular matters might be most heeded. In addition, should the list of affiliates include prestigious and socially prominent people, the possibility of the group's gaining access to officials is enhanced.

Staff is a second resource adding to the strength of permanent associations. Professional staff personnel have the time to collect, interpret, and organize the technical, legal, and social data necessary for group spokesmen to make an impressive presentation before selected targets. Moreover, their experience enables them to apply the skills necessary to make collective articulation effective. Such individuals would know to whom expressions should be directed, where public agents are to be found, and the appropriate time to make expressions known. Their repeated contacts with officials permit them to build reputations of reliability and trust, which enhances their chances of gaining access to the proper offices. A staff can crystallize and clarify salient issues, and can mobilize group members' support. Such persons are assets in maintaining an organization, and in fostering its prestige within the community; they may, thus, be able to create wider support through favorable public opinion.

Funds are a third source that may increase the strength of some associations. Money can be used to hire competent staff personnel and obtain needed facilities for successful operations. Tactics of collective articulation may be carried through with ample funding. Publicity campaigns to create favorable public opinion may be conducted, and expenses in communicating with officials may be paid. Avenues for access may be opened with financial contributions to (or paid volunteer staff assisting) candidates running for office, or to political parties seeking to conduct successful political campaigns.

Economic and Political Variables

The amount of influence that interest groups exert on public policy may be related to economic and political variables found within the states and localities. L. Harmon Zeigler and Hendrick van Dalen have classified state interest groups as strong, moderate, and weak; and they have attempted to demonstrate why interest groups will vary in strength. Their conclusion was that states with strong interest groups are likely to be 1) one-party states, 2) states that have legislative parties with weak cohesion, 3) less urban, 4) less wealthy, and 5) less industrial.[5] Table IV.1 presents those findings from that study.

Factionalism is a characteristic of one-party states, states with little party cohesion, and non-partisan localities. A consequence of the presence of factions is that candidates and public officials must rely on non-party organizations for political support. Interest groups are courted for their endorsements and resources. Thus, the groups are able to establish political credit for favors and to gain access that strengthen their efforts to articulate interests, needs, and demands. In those situations where there is no party leadership to promote programs, organized special interest groups may provide the leadership, direction, and mobilization of support for their own programs.

In urban and industrial areas, interest groups are generally weak. The heterogeneous quality of the social and economic spheres found within urban, industrial communities underlies the establishment of various interest associations. Therefore, the presence of many groups with differing objectives leads to conflict, which tends to diminish the opportunity for any one group to dominate political influence. In addition, this type of political environment usually maintains either competitive parties of strong party organizations, which further undermines the strength of the influence interest groups can directly wield on public agents.

Weaker interest group systems are also to be found in wealthy communities, many of which are suburban areas. Individuals with higher

TABLE IV.1

The Strength of Pressure Groups in Varying Political and Economic Situations

	Types of Pressure System*		
Social Conditions	*Strong†*	*Moderate‡*	*Weak§*
Party Competition:	(24 States)	(14 States)	(7 States)
One-party	33.3%	0%	0%
Modified One-Party	37.5	42.8	0
Two-Party	29.1	57.1	100.0
Cohesion of Parties in Legislature:			
Weak Cohesion	75.0	14.2	0%
Moderate Cohesion	12.5	35.7	14.2
Strong Cohesion	12.5	50.0	85.7
Socio-economic Variables:			
Urban Population	58.6	65.1	73.3
Per capita Income	$1900	$2335	$2450
Industrialization Index	88.8%	92.8%	94.0%

* Alaska, Hawaii, Idaho, New Hampshire, and North Dakota are not classified or included.
† Alabama, Arizona, Arkansas, California, Florida, Georgia, Iowa, Kentucky, Louisiana, Maine, Michigan, Minnesota, Mississippi, Montana, Nebraska, New Mexico, North Carolina, Oklahoma, Oregon, South Carolina, Tennessee, Texas, Washington, Wisconsin.
‡ Delaware, Illinois, Kansas, Maryland, Massachusetts, Nevada, New York, Ohio, Pennsylvania, South Dakota, Utah, Vermont, Virginia, West Virginia.
§ Colorado, Connecticut, Indiana, Missouri, New Jersey, Rhode Island, Wyoming.

Source: Zeigler and van Dalen, *op. cit.*, p. 127.

socio-economic status have displayed a propensity to be joiners. This partially explains the plethora of groups found in such settings. A prevailing high sense of civic obligation and a distrust of party politics further enhances the establishment and utilization of groups as media for collective articulation. Under these circumstances, the presence of many groups has the affect of each tending to balance the strength of others.

Cohesion

A group's collective articulation efforts to influence governmental action may be strengthened if the group has a membership that is cohesive and has a unity of purpose. In addition, leadership must be unified and able to offer an acceptable sense of direction for the membership. Groups with a large heterogeneous membership and whose primary objectives are not public oriented may have difficulty in achieving consensus. Often staff personnel delineate the issues for which group efforts will be summoned to articulate. These issues or the subsequent stance taken by the staff need not, however, be of concern or in accordance with the desires of all those who are affiliated. Nor may the staff seek the same objectives as the elected leadership. For example, labor union leaders are interested in winning better working conditions for their members regardless of narrow political ends. The political arm of the union, however, may be interested in specific public issues and candidates, and in pursuing those find themselves in conflict with the leaders. Internal divisiveness undermines effective collective action.[6]

Access

The extent to which an interest group may be successful in articulating its interests and in having its interests satisfied depends on the degree to which it has access to decision makers. This access is partially achieved through extensive effort to establish relationships. The effort may begin with election oriented activities. Nomination procedures, political campaigns, and campaign financing afford opportunities to establish contacts with public officials.

Generally, persons view pressure groups as issue or policy oriented, and political parties as election or personality oriented. Yet, these are not mutually exclusive. Both political parties and pressure groups seek access to government; the former wish to operate the machinery to make decisions, the latter want to influence the decisions in accord with their interests. Thus, both groups may find areas in which they can cooperate to achieve their aims. The extent or type of cooperation may depend on such factors as party competitiveness or partisan or non-partisan election situations.

In partisan situations, those persons seeking nomination may find the financial and organizational assistance of non-party associations helpful. In non-partisan elections, without party organization and party labels to identify them, pressure group endorsement or support may be crucial to candidates' success. Group endorsements are made known to the membership and to the general public through the organization's bulletins or through the press. Support may be given by means of such activities as printing and distributing literature, conducting registration or get-out-the-vote drives, or inviting candidates to speak before meetings. Where candidates for public office are designated in state party conventions (rather than in primaries), or endorsed in pre-primary conventions, interest groups try to influence the selection of the delegates to the convention and to influence their choices at the convention.

During the election campaign, an interest group may decide to support an entire ticket or to concentrate on only one or two candidates. An association's campaign effort depends on the relationship it has with a party. A group may work closely within the party organization by supplying supportive personnel and material. It may decide to operate independently from the party and establish a separate and parallel campaign organization. Or, a group may keep its separate identity while still directly assist the party. In non-partisan local elections, a pressure group may be the major organization acting on a candidate's behalf.

The extensive and rising costs of election campaigns open another arena for interest group activity. Candidates generally must go beyond their personal resources to finance their efforts. Parties cannot be relied on to finance all candidates, for they may choose to funnel their limited funds toward (what the leaders consider) the most important elective positions. Associations can fill the financial gap. Indeed, in a competitive situation, they may contribute to both parties so as to gain access to influence regardless of which party wins. Non-partisan situations pose additional financial problems for the candidate. Without party organizations behind him, the individual must establish his own connections with monied sources, such as pressure groups. As one lobbyist has stated:

> When a guy has contributed generously to your campaign, and when he comes in to see you, obviously you're going to lend a sympathetic ear.[7]

Many states have laws preventing direct contributions by interest groups. To circumvent these regulations, pressure groups donate funds through "front" organizations, by forming political action committees (which raise and expend funds separately from the association's treasury), or through ad hoc "citizens" or "volunteer" groups.

Contacts established through political efforts afford the necessary access. In the long run, relationships secured with candidates, campaign workers, and party leaders are important because they open channels to friendly officials.

Channels of communication that pressure groups find open are not created entirely by their efforts in the electoral process. The needs of officials for information and assistance also develops the creation of links between governmental agents and organized constituents.

States and local legislators may be considered examples of public officials faced with such needs. Membership in state legislatures, for example, is comprised of a significant percentage of first-termers. Unfamiliar in their new role, without the benefit of formal legislative orientation, freshmen legislators may accept the counsel and orientation offered by lobbyists. In addition, legislators are part-time public officials. They are less likely to be political professionals and more likely to regard the legislative role as a secondary aspect of their lives. As legislative amateurs, they remain full-time doctors, lawyers, farmers, businessmen, and so on.

State legislatures meet only a few months annually or biennially, and many local councils meet only monthly or semi-monthly. Brief legislative sessions allow only a short time for the great amount of work to be done. Major and minor problems facing the state or locality must be dealt with, in addition to a host of trivial matters. There are limited facilities and staffs available to gather the technical, legal, and social data needed for decision making. Lobbyists may be utilized for drafting legislation, collecting data, writing speeches, and for other services necessary to officials to fulfill their roles and to maintain a favorable image among the constituents.

There are neither facilities nor staffs to ascertain the needs, opinions, and interests of the people. The importance of information cannot be over-emphasized. The quality and quantity of information on a problem bear a strong relationship to the quality and significance of a solution.

Harmon Zeigler asked a number of legislators if they depended on information provided by lobbyists. Eighty-three percent of the sample in Oregon said that they did depend upon such information much or at least some of the time; so did 80 percent in Utah, 50 percent in Massachusetts, and 41 percent in North Carolina. The pressure group representative can present an analysis of a measure and its affects on constituents. When Zeigler asked the same legislators if they had ever sought the reactions of lobbyists who had a legitimate concern about a specific issue, two-thirds of the respondents in Oregon and Utah, and more than one-third of those in Massachusetts and North Carolina replied that they had.[8]

Problems confronting citizens cannot be solved—nor an attempt at solution made—if officials have no communications of constituent needs. In the absence of government sponsored channels of information and communication the pressure group can create the image that it is the medium of articulation.

Receptivity

Several studies of state legislatures have shown that while some legislators are not receptive to interest group activity, the majority are. Thus, legislators do not attempt to restrain collective activity; they agree that pressure groups are useful and necessary. As one has said:

> Lobbyists are a vital part of the legislative process. Without them to explain, you couldn't get a clear picture of the situation. They can study and present the issues concisely—the average legislator has no time or inclination to do it, and wouldn't understand bills or issues without them. A professional lobbyist in ten minutes can explain what it would take a member two hours to wade through just reading bills. Both sides come around to you, so you can balance off all one-sided presentations (and they're all one-sided). A definite function is performed by lobbyists. . . .[9]

John C. Wahlke and his associates have studied the attitudes of legislators toward lobbying and the awareness held by legislators of the presence of interest groups.[10] The legislative members have been classified as having role perceptions as "facilitators" (those having friendly attitudes toward group activities), "resistors" (those having hostile attitudes toward pressure groups), and "neutrals" (those having neither a strong favorable nor an unfavorable attitude toward lobbying). Wahlke noted that attitude patterns differed among legislators in different states because of political traditions, constituency demographic patterns, or economic variables. But, he emphasized, the proportions of facilitators increased (and conversely, that of resistors decreased) with legislative experience. The point raised was that behavior patterns would reflect legislators' role perceptions. Wahlke felt that by identifying these roles, one could predict the effect and influence pressure groups have on the rule-making function.

A study of city councils has shown the relevance of interest groups to local rule making.[11] Table IV.2 demonstrates that councilmen's attitudes towards such groups are basically favorable.

TABLE IV.2

*City Councilmen's Attitudes Toward Interest Groups**

Attitude	Councilmen
Groups are esteemed, are perceived as useful	43%
Groups are described in neutral terms; "They have a right to be heard"	44
Groups are resisted	13
Total	100%
(N = 112)	

* Attitudes are coded from responses to two open-ended questions; "How do you feel about efforts of groups to make their views known to you and seek your support?" and "Do you feel that, in general, you should make it easy for them to contact you, or should you try to avoid them?

Adapted from: Zisk, Eulau, and Prewitt, *op. cit.*, p. 624.

A local legislator, one perhaps with a provincial bias, has viewed the role of pressure groups on a local level in this way: "Pressure groups are probably more important in local government than they are nationally or in the state, because they're right here."[12] That statement may exemplify the deference paid to interest groups on the local level. Interest groups are courted assiduously. They are called to address council meetings (especially when technical or controversial matters are under consideration) to offer suggestions, opinions, and the views of their membership. They are routinely mailed announcements of public hearings; and their representatives often are requested to testify and offer technical data, analysis, and evaluation. When councils appoint task force committees (on an ad hoc or permanent basis) to study an issue thoroughly, representatives of associations are appointed to membership on the committee.

The favorable receptivity enjoyed by lobbyists is also due to the legislator's view that lobbying is not "pressure politics." There are several reasons for this view. First, legislators may see lobbyists as friends, or at least as familiar faces encountered somewhere during the election period. Second, legislators retain their occupational affiliation and, therefore, they may sympathetically identify as professional colleagues the representatives of some organizations or interests. Third, legislators may view pressure group proponents as persons exercising their civic right of petition, as legitimate spokesmen for segments of the community.

Simply stated, legislators do not feel that they are being pressured. If the public official and the lobbyist have similar goals, backgrounds, interests, and/or contacts, then the communications and efforts by the latter are likely to be perceived by the former as the expression of a sound point of view.

Channels and Techniques

The basic aim of interest group representatives is to reinforce the interests, ideas, and policy orientations of the public officials. They also with to influence the legislators to introduce a bill; support it off and on the floor; set up favorable hearings; or, most important, vote for its passage or activate opposition towards an unfavorable bill. Conversion, that activity designed to change a legislator's hostile frame of mind into a friendly frame of interest, is not considered an effective lobby technique, and it is not generally practiced by the experienced lobbyist. Energy is expended on the friendly or at least neutral law maker. The disadvantage of creating a situation in which the person begins to feel pressured is readily apparent.

The interest group can choose numerous alternative channels of articulation and techniques to transmit the interests, needs, and demands of its membership. These may be direct or indirect means of communication. The effectiveness of different methods of communication is indicated by Table IV.3. The table presents the ratings of selected techniques by state lobbyists, local lobbyists, and local councilmen who were the targets of local interest group representatives.

TABLE IV.3

*Ratings of Selected Techniques of Communication**

Techniques	Michigan Lobbyists	D.C. Lobbyists	D.C. Councilmen
Selected Means of Direct Communication			
Personal presentation of viewpoints	9.2	8.2	6.3
Presentation of research results . . .	7.0	6.2	7.0
Testifying at hearings	6.6	6.6	6.6
Entertaining	2.3	1.6	2.0
Giving a party	1.9	0.8	1.3
Bribery	0.0	0.0	0.3
Selected Means of Indirect Communication			
Contact by constituents	3.8	3.4	6.6
Contact by a close friend	2.7	3.4	7.6
Letter and telegram campaigns . . .	1.7	4.0	3.0
Public relations campaigns	4.8	7.0	4.3
Publicizing voting records	0.8	2.4	2.6

* The respondents were asked to rate selected lobbying techniques on a scale ranging from 0, for not effective at all, to 10, for very effective. The data presented in the Table indicates the mean (or average) scored for each technique.

Source: Data for the Michigan lobbyists were from: Malcolm E. Jewell and Samuel C. Patterson, *The Legislative Process in the United States* (New York: Random House, Inc., 1966), p. 290. Data for the lobbyists and the councilmen in the District of Columbia were obtained through personal interviews, November, 1969.

Direct Communication

Testifying at Hearings

The most highly rated techniques used by the lobbyist to transmit the interests of his organization involve direct communications. Testimony at committee hearings is one device employed. Here his stature as legitimate spokesman for the viewpoints of a group of citizens, his social, legal, and technical data derived from research, and/or his friendship, enhances the effectiveness of the lobbyist's presentation.

Interest group representatives testify at public hearings for several reasons. The minutes of the public hearings held by the city council of the District of Columbia during the fall of 1968, and subsequent interviews with group spokesmen who testified, provide information concerning lobbyists' objectives. The hearings were held on proposed regulations and resolutions concerning police–community relations. During the course of the hearings, a total of 129 presentations were given, of which 121 were statements made by group spokesmen.[13]

Seven reasons why group leaders testified were identified. Selected group spokesmen were asked to rank in order of importance those reasons why they had testified at the hearings. In addition, selected councilmen and members of the council staff were asked to rank the order of reasons why they thought groups had sent representatives to testify. The reasons and the rankings are seen in Table IV.4.

TABLE IV.4

Rankings of Reasons Why Interest Group Leaders Testified at Public Hearings*

Reasons	Group Leaders	Council- men	Council Staff
1. Influence legislation	2.2	2.0	5.0
2. Aid council in finding out information .	2.8	2.3	5.5
3. Prevent council from acting against your interest.	3.6	3.3	2.0
4. Enhance image in the community . .	3.6	4.6	4.0
5. Gain publicity.	4.4	4.3	2.5
6. Necessary for group unity	5.6	6.3	4.0
7. Raise hell so council will listen more to those supporting your view	5.8	5.0	5.0

* The respondents were asked to rank the reasons why testimony was given in the order of importance. The data presented in the Table represents the mean (or average) rank assigned to each reason by each grouping. The lower the number, the higher the reason was ranked in importance (1 being most important, 7 being least important).

Source: Personal interviews, November, 1969.

Generally, it is believed that the main objective of testimony given at public hearings is to affect the substantive nature of proposed legislation. This objective would be accomplished by offering information and presenting opinions that are in favor of or in opposition either to the entire proposal or to specific provisions of the measure under consideration. Indeed, group leaders' ranking of reasons why they testified support that belief. Several statements illustrate the attitudes of the associations' spokesmen:

> I obviously testified because I felt I could influence the Council. People are influenced by what they hear, if they hear it often enough. Public hearings are the proper forum for the presentation of a group's position, and it affords council members the opportunity to ask pertinent questions.

It is important for me to participate so I can inform the Council how the people feel.

I don't want to give up the right to testify; for though I don't feel it would do any good, there is always the chance that someone would listen to our objections.

We testify to present information, such as to show the councilmen some hidden meaning in the wording of the legislation, or the need for changing some technical details in the draft.

Still, there are other reasons for giving testimony at public hearings. A review of the minutes of the public hearings indicated that many witnesses did not make use of their five-minute time limit to try to convince the council members about the merits of their groups' positions toward the bill under consideration. One lobbyist spent the time accusing other groups of impeding progress and berating the council for moving so slowly that he questioned whether the members were really concerned. Another spoke vehemently of the "white council, white police, and white society," and demanded legislation that he knew would not be considered. For him, the only laws that the council should make, that would give black people a chance, were those which would give guns to black citizens so that they could "shoot white cops in the streets." Others questioned the authority of the council to move into police matters; or refused to talk about the subject under consideration, only about their own interests. One ancillary purpose for testifying is to "let off steam."

When representatives of interest groups were asked what benefit could be derived by utilizing their time before the council in such a negative manner, their responses showed that testimony at public hearings could provide a group with opportunities other than that of influencing the council. Group maintenance is one benefit. As one lobbyist stated:

Testifying shows the membership that the leaders are concerned about their interests, and are working on their behalf by presenting their views.

"Raising hell" may attract the attention of the news media, which, by reporting the episodes, may permit the groups to enhance their image in the community and to gain wider support. As one leader noted, her prime reason for testifying was that she could (through that forum) address herself to the citizens-at-large:

I could go speak to the councilmen before the hearings, but who knows if what I would say would come out differently. Like this, I can go and talk to the citizens. I'd like them to know how I feel about the issues.

Another spokesman reported that the publicity gained was a means for transmitting sentiments to public officials not present at the hearings:

> We didn't come to these hearings to change the minds of the councilmen. We wanted to show the Mayor that there was public outrage about police activities, and he had better forcefully do something about the situation.

In addition, one candidly admitted that he "raised hell to shake some councilmen up," so that they would listen attentively to those witnesses who had constructive suggestions to make.

David B. Truman has noted that:

> The public hearing is not without significance as a means of informing legislators, but this is probably not its primary function. For the group which enjoys satisfactory access to members of a legislative body, a hearing is not the best place to attempt persuasion.[14]

Other Personal Contact

All the lobbyists in the District of Columbia claimed that they had met with individual members of the council, in informal discussions, to present their information and their groups' viewpoints during the initiation and drafting stages of the proposals. One lobbyist explained that council members can be influenced by personal presentations made before the hearings, and that their opinions are already set before they enter the scheduled meetings with the public.

The formal testimony at a hearing is supplementary to informal conversations in the legislative offices, halls, or centers for social and dining gatherings. As has been seen in Table 4, most lobbyists rate personal conversations as the most effective technique. Face to face contact may be made by going to state delegation offices in the district, or city council offices in the various wards. In addition, groups may invite legislators to speak before the members at meetings, or may sponsor rallies, picnics, or teas, where officials may hear the articulated expressions of the groups' affiliates. Other direct transmissions of collective interests are made by telephone calls, telegrams, and letters.

One lobbyist has explained the need for good personal relationships with legislators by noting that reliability and trust are essential. He has said:

> The worst thing that can happen to a lobbyist is not to tell the truth, good or bad. If somebody told you a lie, would you believe them again?[15]

These attributes have been more effective than have threats and bribes in gaining access and influence. Stories about threats ranging from defeat at the polls to having creditors call in overdue notes are heard infrequently.

Overt bribery is extremely rare. As one lobbyist working to influence the Maryland state legislature said:

The public all thinks that you walk around with a bag full of $100 bills over your shoulder buying and selling votes. Possibly that was true 50 or 60 years ago in the days of the political bosses.

Today, with "bosses on the decline and a public more sophisticated," he continued, bribery has given way to other techniques.[16] Though "deals" are made, one New York state legislator has explained, they are based upon more subtle forms of rewards. These, he said, are conducted "in a much more sophisticated way, in the form of retainers to law firms, campaign contributions and so on."[17]

Perhaps entertaining may be considered subtle bribery, but it is quite likely used more frequently to make friends than to obtain promises of votes. One legislator has said:

Legislators aren't really influenced much by lobbyists in the way people think. We go to their parties because we like free meals and parties. But no one expects that to affect your vote. I don't know that any lobbyist ever really could buy anything.[18]

As a New York state lobbyist observed:

The guy you can influence with a steak dinner and a couple of drinks doesn't have the influence to make it worth having dinner with him.[19]

In any event, there is no wholesale entertaining to be found. It should not be assumed that the legislator's life is one continuous party, or that he can live and eat throughout the sessions on pressure group gratuities.

Lobbyists would rather not spend much time with legislators they regard as unimportant. They want to communicate with influential persons, who may be (depending upon the organization of the legislative body, or the role of the political party in determining legislative policy) legislative leaders, chairmen of standing committees (where there is a tradition of committee dominance), or party or faction leaders (where there is strong party discipline and cohesion).

Indirect Communication

Intermediaries

Indirect channels of communication may be utilized by pressure group leaders to transmit their interests, needs, and demands to legislators. One indirect channel is the intermediary. Close friends of a legislator may be able to provide access that the lobbyist does not have. A close friend may be able to establish a credibility that a group has not been able to develop with the official. If an official holds a neutral attitude on a public matter, he may be inclined to accede to the request of a friend. Spokesmen for other interest associations not immediately involved with an issue may agree to act as intermediaries with legislators with whom they have free and open access in order to build credit for future assistance in return.

Other intermediaries are elected or appointed executives and administrative personnel. A governor, mayor, or county executive may be induced, for personal or political motives, to speak to legislators on behalf of a group's interest on a particular measure. Friendly administrators, with whom relations have been established over a period of time on issues of mutual concern, may offer assistance to an interest association as the legislative body deliberates on a topic.

Grass Root Pressure

State interest groups are not usually concerned with using the technique of grass root pressure. Lobbyists do not think that having constituents appeal to the rule makers is as persuasive as their own personal communication. However, polls and petition campaigns may be undertaken. Every time the Maryland state legislature considered proposals to abolish the Board of Censors, for example, the legislators received petitions to oppose that action that were sponsored by the various "decency groups." Groups having financial resources find that the accessibility to the state house and the relative informality of the legislative process facilitate the direct personal approach. In addition, they may even assiduously avoid public notices to gain the advantage of surprise within the legislature, or to limit the possibility of the public becoming aware of the group's narrowly based interest.

On the local level, however, serious attempts are frequently made to court grass root pressure. Interest group leaders strive to get their members, as well as others in the community, active and vocal. In localities with a council comprised of members elected at-large and from wards, the groups will focus efforts on the at-large councilmen, and try to stimulate the residents to contact their ward-based councilman. Public relations campaigns may encourage the distribution of petitions to be submitted to public officials. Printed postcards to be signed and sent to the legislators may be distributed at shopping centers. Community residents may be aroused to join into demonstrations—marches, sit-ins, or attendance at council meetings and hearings. These demonstrations may be staged for the purpose of gaining free, speedy, and easy access to the mass media. Group spokesmen might invite interviews to spark reporting on specific problems. Advertisements may be placed in newspapers to influence grass root opinions; and coupons may be printed so that readers may clip, and send them to the public agents. Polls are sponsored by groups to quantify some constituent interests.

Coalitions

There may be found in a community several associations organized around similar interests. Many times, each strives to maintain and enhance its own identity, with the consequence that the energy of all is directed toward improving individual images rather than to lobby for particular objectives. The ensuing organizational rivalry undermines the possibility of influence that may have been gained by cooperative ventures.

Interest groups sometimes cooperate by combining into coalitions to enhance their opportunities to communicate with public officials. The advantage of coalition is to better utilize limited resources. The combination of staff and information gathering facilities increases the effectiveness of each group. There are more personnel to advance desired legislation and to keep vigil for unwanted legislation (perhaps something as apparently innocuous as a minor amendment that might otherwise go unnoticed). Moreover, in situations where one group does not have a "contact" who can gain access to a public official, another might. In the long range perspective, a group can obtain an extra advantage by lending assistance to a second, even if its interest is not served at the moment, so that it may call for the other's assistance when it is needed.

One interest group representative, recognizing the benefits of coalitions, has said:

> Anytime you can get other organizations or other industries to assist you in your program, then it ceases to be a selfish interest thing in the eyes of the public.[20]

Groups do not have to hold similar interests to cooperate. Those groups unable or unwilling to enter into an alliance with others holding a dissimilar interest may, nevertheless, agree to cooperate in such a manner that conflict is avoided. To avoid such conflict, one group may agree to refrain from actively opposing another's interest, in return for similar treatment in the future. In addition, groups may try to cooperate so as to display a united front when offering a package set of proposals to the legislators. This may be accomplished through mediating differences among themselves prior to presentations in the legislative arena.

Group leaders, councilmen, and council staff members in the District of Columbia and Montgomery County (Maryland) rated collaboration between groups as a very effective lobbying technique. On a scale from 0 to 10 (10 being most effective), collaboration was rated 6.8 by group leaders, 7.0 by councilmen, and 7.5 by the council staff members. As one staff assistant noted:

> When two groups with differing constituencies, who usually make conflicting demands upon the Council, get together, they're a potent force to reckon with. Take that bridge matter, for example. When the black groups and the white groups protested its being constructed (albeit for different reasons) the Council stopped its action.[21]

Lobbying the Executive Branch

In their pursuit of satisfaction for their interests, lobbyists will go beyond the legislative to the executive branch. Their activities would be directed towards obtaining 1) recognition that a problem is an important issue; 2) inclusion of the issue in the executive program, or, conversely, to have an undesirable program de-emphasized or deleted from the executive's legislative agenda; 3) needed assistance in influencing the legislature; 4) executive signature or veto; 5) favorable interpretation and execution of existing legislation; 6) desired executive orders and administrative decisions; and 7) assistance in creating public support or opposition.

As the central figures of governments, the governor, county executive, and mayor are often the targets of group activity. They may be the only full-time, at-large elected officials; and generally they have influence over patronage, the dispersal of funds, and the direction of programs. Moreover, the executive has the discretion to create blue ribbon commissions to study particular problem areas. Many times, group leaders are appointed to these commissions, and they may exert influence in this capacity. But, most often, techniques utilized in communicating interests to executives are similar to those used to transmit collective articulation to the legislators.

Lawrence D. Longley, in a study of the most active interest groups in Tennessee, noted that group leaders considered the governor's stand on a bill as either "crucial" or "important" to a bill's enactment. Indeed, their appraisal was correct. For, during a six-year period, all but one of the bills on which governors took a favorable stand passed the legislature; and all those which they opposed failed to pass. Longley concluded that, "Alliance with the governor . . . appeared to be one of the most fruitful activities of the interest group working for legislative success."[22]

The alliance between interest groups and the executive is not only of benefit to the groups. Needing to demonstrate success for his program, his administration, or himself, the executive must utilize all resources available. Thus, he will seek out or be receptive to pressure associations.

Interest groups also establish a web of interaction with full-time bureaucrats. These agents have the responsibility of day-to-day interpretation and execution of rules, drafting proposals for legislative enactment, providing information for legislators and executives, and issuing administrative rules in those areas given over to the jurisdiction of the executive branch. Often bureaucrats who lack new technological or specialized knowledge, or the interest or time to act in specialized areas, may invite the assistance of lobbyists.

Lobbyists can readily identify and seek out responsible officials in the various clearly defined areas of governmental action. Group spokesmen may meet with the bureaucrats, direct collective articulation efforts to them, or have intermediaries intercede on their behalf. Representatives from associations are appointed to advisory commissions, which are charged with working closely with bureaucrats in seeking solutions to problems.

Harry W. Reynolds, Jr., has shown, in his study of rule making in Los Angeles, that interest groups worked closely with bureaucrats in the preparation of proposals that were submitted to the council. During the period of his study, groups had initiated twenty bills. Each bill had been cleared with an appropriate administrative department prior to its introduction. Indeed, nearly half of the bills had actually been written by departmental personnel, who incorporated the groups' desires and objectives into correct legal form. [23]

Friendship may enhance lobbyists' access to administrative agents. This relationship may have been developed by the long periods of contact with the same career officials. Administrators may view interest group representatives as sharing similar interests. Many bureaucrats are members of associations during their tenure in office. Doctors, for example, who are members of state or local medical associations, serve as administrators in departments or boards of health. Administrative officials may, in turn, find their "friends" useful to lobby for the maintenance and expansion of bureaucratic affairs, security, and power.

Lobbying the Judicial Branch

The judicial system is an arena of government in which authoritative decisions may be rendered on public policy, as well as one in which conflicts are resolved. Groups that fail or are disadvantaged in the executive and legislative arenas may seek favorable action by appealing to the judiciary.

The choice of pressure group strategies in this arena is governed by what are considered ethical tactics within the judicial process. An action that might overtly appear to be "pressure politics" is forbidden. Thus, interest associations direct their energy towards the selection of judges, submitting briefs, and utilizing litigation. In addition, interest groups can attempt to mold a favorable image for themselves through publication of articles in law journals that judges respect and turn to for professional guidance.

Pressure groups enter into the nomination process to ensure that candidates for the bench hold views that are neither contrary nor detrimental to the interests of the groups. Where judicial candidates are chosen at the polls, local associations may evaluate the candidates to provide cues for the electorate. Should judges be nominated by the governor or the legislature, the groups may utilize their access to support or oppose a selection. Success in the nomination and selection process is related to the amount of influence associations wield in the party, in the electorate, or in legislative and executive institutions.

Interest groups, especially the bar associations, may be invited to participate in the selection of judges. In Missouri, and in the other six states using variations of the Missouri plan, representatives of the bar associations are members of panels charged with the selection or appointment of appellate judges. The state and local bar associations are asked to evaluate and suggest suitable candidates for the bench in almost all instances. Many of these associations have continuing evaluating committees ready to undertake such a task upon request.

In the absence of desired executive or legislative action, groups have turned to the courts to make rules of to force governmental action. They initiate litigation as a channel for articulating interests in the judicial arena. Groups have raised legal questions that have been of immediate, private concern before the courts, or questions that have been of such a nature as to affect the entire community (such as civil liberties and reapportionment). The NAACP, for example, has conceived its basic strategy in terms of court action on the local as well as on the national level.

In addition, associations may be concerned about preventing the execution of a rule or a program. To accomplish this, they turn to the courts. Neighborhood groups, for example, may wish to block the construction of a highway through a heavily populated section of the city; environmental conservation groups may wish to end the dumping of sewage in a river; and taxpayers groups may wish to prevent an "emergency" tax from being collected.

Although an interest group may not be a direct party to a case in conflict, it may be permitted to file briefs or to present oral arguments before a court. Judges have recognized that many cases raise issues that affect more than the contending parties, and, therefore, will be receptive to such briefs. As a third party, groups may supply information not presented by the immediate adversaries in the court; they may focus attention on broader interests involved; and they may present an added assessment of the probable consequences of the judicial actions. Thus, the interest group has an opportunity to intervene before a decision is made, and to affect not only the immediate conflict, but also, the thinking of the court as it will affect future decisions.

The resources of the group may determine the extent to which channels to the judiciary are utilized. A group might hire attorneys and pay expert witnesses to appear. Research studies may be commissioned for the preparation of arguments containing legal precedents and facts. The persistence to which a group may pursue judicial action may also be affected by the resources available to meet the burdensome costs of appeals. If it has the resources, a group may pursue appeals until a final decision is rendered. As is the case with lobbying campaigns to influence legislators and executives, interest groups may form coalitions to exert influence on judicial decisions.[24]

Groups and the Electoral Process

Groups may utilize the ballot as a channel for articulating interests. They may do this by working for the nomination and election of officials they believe are identified with and friendly to their interests. Or, groups may make issues seem so important to relatively large segments of the population that a public official, candidate, or party leader may conclude that electoral success is enhanced by adopting or promoting those issues.

To affect the outcome of an election, groups must be able to influence the voters' attitudes and gain their support. In order to accomplish that, associations must be established as reference groups to which members and non-members look for cues. The extent to which the electorate looks to groups for voting cues depends on the salience of the association to the individual members, or the image of the group as perceived by the general public. A member's support of the group's electoral efforts may be an outcome of his activity and involvement in the group, the closeness of his interaction with other members and with the leadership, and his perceptions of the benefits derived from the group's aims and objectives.

Non-members look to those reference groups they perceive to have aims and objectives relevant to the political arena. Thus, state and local medical associations may be looked to for cues on public matters regarding health, and labor unions on measures concerning the working man. Associations that are public oriented may serve as reference groups for those individuals who perceive the group's objectives to be similar to their own. Parents interested in increased public expenditures for schools, for example, would tend to look favorably upon those candidates for the school board who are endorsed by the PTA. Those who want "good government" would seek the position reports of the League of Women Voters on those public issues that are scheduled to appear as referenda questions. Groups that are infrequently involved with endorsing candidates and issues may, on the rare occasions when they become involved in such activity, be effective in influencing voters. Hence, the statements of church leaders on a public matter may guide an individual's political action.

Referenda and Initiative

The utilization of the ballot as a channel for articulating interests may be more direct in the issue elections. When groups are rebuffed by public agents, they may seek satisfaction of their interests by obtaining public ratification of an initiative or referendum proposal. Because of the high costs and complex procedure involved in placing a proposal on a ballot, groups have been seen to utilize this channel more frequently than any other non-governmental sponsor. During a half-century span of direct legislation in Oklahoma, eighty-four initiative and referenda questions were placed on the ballot through publicly signed petitions. Of those, 62 percent were sponsored by interest groups; the others were sponsored by public officials or private citizens. The largest proportion of group sponsors were those who had pecuniary motives (*i.e.*, retail merchants, construction companies, horse breeders, and tobacco and oil companies). Other proposals, more general in nature, were sponsored by teachers' organizations, farm associations, labor unions, civic reform groups, and church leaders.[25]

Groups may expend their energies through the electoral process to oppose action. Efforts might be made to prevent a candidate from winning an election or to defeat an issue question that would alter the status quo. Groups may more readily organize to prevent change than to propose it. In mobilizing people to articulate, groups knowing the fears and prejudices of the residents of a community could exploit these attitudes to the detriment of a candidate's or an issue's success. Several examples may serve to illustrate this point. An affluent group of lawyers and large landowners distributed an eight-page tabloid newspaper to Montgomery County (Maryland) residents in the closing days of a general election campaign. In this tabloid specific council and school board candidates were accused of having the intention of raising taxes and wasting tax funds. The lawyer–landowner group was successful; all accused candidates were defeated.[26] Flouridation referenda questions have been defeated throughout the nation after groups argued that such governmental action would be an infringement of individual liberty and religious freedom.[27] In Michigan and California, real estate groups have convinced the public that the defeat of fair housing referenda would uphold individual freedom of choice and freedom of private association.[28]

Minor Party Activity

Interest groups prefer to work with the established political parties. The existing parties, however, have to accommodate many interests, and, thus, may refuse to yield to an interest group on every issue. Groups, thwarted in their demands, may then utilize one other form of action to articulate their desires. They may challenge the two major parties on the ballot by organizing a minor or a third party (the two terms are used interchangeably).

Historically, minor parties have been basically organized around a belief or an interest. Efforts have been directed toward clarifying or simplifying issues. Emphasis has been placed on aligning voters towards support of a program rather than for an office. Pendleton Herring has said that they served as "promotional agencies for minority viewpoints."[29] Third parties have been hailed as "exponents of dissent, champions of change, and critics of major parties."[30] Operating as a political party, the pressure group is afforded an effective opportunity to educate the public. Its presence on the ballot affords mass media attention that the group might otherwise be denied.

The history of third party movements shows generally that they have been vigorous where they have reflected the local background. For example, the Farmer–Labor Party in Minnesota has roots that go back to the farmer's cooperatives and the trade unions of the state. Having used its influence on behalf of labor and agriculture by working toward concrete gains for the farmers and workers of the state, its interest group basis is clear. The party won the governorship and several state legislative seats in the 1930s. Similar successes were achieved by the Progressive Party of Wisconsin, which found support among the concentrations of immigrant groups settling there. But neither of these parties was able to find support for its ideas and organizations beyond its respective state boundaries.

Minor parties have had much of their electoral success in local communities where the population had included large blocs of people possessing similar backgrounds or interests. The Socialist Party—supported by local concentrations of German immigrants—has captured the mayoralty in Milwaukee, Wisconsin, and Bridgeport, Connecticut. In New York City, the Liberal Party's candidate was elected president of the City Council in 1951, having attracted a large bloc of urban-industrial workers, and had a more spectacular success in 1969.

In the period since World War II, the list of successful third parties has been short. There are several reasons that account for their poor showing at the polls and their lack of significant support. First, the local pockets of strength that historically had supported third parties have been disappearing with the nationalization of life in the United States. The local concentrations of immigrant strength in cities such as New York, Milwaukee, and Bridgeport have been affected by new immigration restrictions and by a new urban diversity. Second, a single-member-district electoral system, which puts a premium on majorities, works to the disadvantage of third parties. Third, when one of their "radical" ideas becomes conventional, it is absorbed into the program of a major party; the major party gets the credit and the minor party disappears. Fourth, with little chance of obtaining office and issuing rewards (*e.g.*, patronage), it is difficult to attract organization workers, or even attractive candidates. Attractive candidates or active workers will expend their energies in causes having better odds for success. Fifth, restrictive laws in many states (which, for example, regulate the number of signatures needed to place a party on the ballot, or the number of votes necessary for a party to maintain its position on future ballots) make it difficult to build a permanent third party. Sixth, the weakness of the American electorate's ideological orientation, and the strength of traditional attachment individuals have to the Democratic or Republican parties, contribute to the failure of attracting voters.

People tend to consider third party groups as "spoilers" or "extremists" or "odd." Yet, even if there were some interest for a third party's candidate or statements at a given election, many people would feel that a vote cast for a minor party is a vote wasted or misspent.

However, if a small dedicated block of voters can be found, then a minor party can be kept active in the hope of influencing a major party's position. The usual strategy is to support a major party's candidate rather than to continue an independent course (by running their own candidates exclusively) and lose. The major party, anxious to woo the potential supporters, would take a stand on issues insistently raised by minor parties.

Contemporary active minor parties can be found in New York. In 1944, trade unionists, primarily members of the garment worker unions, formed the Liberal Party.[31] The objective of this party today is to convince the Democratic or Republican parties in New York that Liberals can provide a balancing or pivotal force for success. They bargain with both major parties and try to obtain commitment from candidates to both socially and politically liberal viewpoints before granting any support. "We approach politics like trade unionists," said Alex Rose, Vice-President of the Liberal party, and President of the United Hatters, Cap and Millinary Workers Union. "We try to practice political collective bargaining."[32]

The Liberal party has generally provided the decisive margins for Democrats, but on occasion they have supported the Republicans. In 1965, the party supported Republican John Lindsay for Mayor, and provided his necessary plurality. In 1969, having lost the nomination in the Republican primary, Lindsay ran on the Liberal party's ticket, and the party replaced the Republicans as the number two party in the city council.

In many states, there has been a recent resurgence of groups sponsoring their own candidates, because they felt that the major parties had been ignoring their interests. Blacks have comprised a majority of the residents in many southern communities, but their interests have been ignored by the major parties or factions in those states. After the 1965 Voting Rights Act, efforts were made to organize blacks into their own political party to insure that the ballot could be a channel for their collective articulation. Two examples of minor parties organized by blacks are the Lowndes County

(Alabama) Freedom Organization and the Mississippi Freedom Democratic party. A specific issue that was not included in the platforms of the two major parties, that is the United States military withdrawal from Vietnam, has spurred the formation of the Peace and Freedom party in California. In 1968, it ran twenty-three candidates for the state legislature, yet received a total of less than one percent of the votes cast in that election.[33]

The success of the Liberal party's strategy in New York led to the organization of the Conservative party in 1962. Deliberately patterned after the Liberal party, and to counterbalance the liberal influence, the new organization has attempted to demonstrate the existence and importance of conservative thinkers. This effort of conservatives has been manifested in organizational efforts elsewhere. George Wallace's campaign for the presidency, in 1968, stimulated the formation of the American Independent party (or its variation, the American party) in almost every state for state and local elections. For example, forty-five American party candidates campaigned for seats in the California state legislature in 1968 and received slightly over one percent of the total votes cast in the election.[34]

Recent Trends in Collective Articulation

It has been said that organized interest groups informally act as representatives of the people—linking the public with the government. As Lewis J. Froman, Jr., has stated, "They insure that a certain segment of the public is heard with respect to economic, social, and political issues."[35] There are, however, vast numbers of Americans who are not included in that "segment of the public," and who would find it difficult to name any organized pressure group acting on their behalf.

E. E. Schattschneider has noted that the myth of pressure group representativeness is flawed by the fact that "about 90 percent of the people cannot get into the pressure system."[36] To illustrate his point, he has presented the results of several nationwide surveys that found that 66 percent of farmers belong to no farm organization; 72 percent of farm laborers belong to no organization whatever; 85 percent of veterans do not belong to the American Legion; and 99.5 percent of women do not belong to the League of Women Voters.[37]

Membership in interest associations has been primarily a middle- or upper-class phenomenon. V. O. Key, Jr., found that membership in voluntary organizations was related to occupation, education, and economic and social status.[38] Almond and Verba in their nationwide study showed that 80 percent of the respondents having had at least some college were members of associations, as compared to 46 percent of those with a primary school education or less.[39]

The least organized citizens have been the blacks, the poor, and the aged. While there has been individual articulation from these sectors of the population, there has been an absence of groups that collectively articulate the needs, interests, and demands of such citizens. In the absence of collective action, it was convenient for public agents to assume that there was general satisfaction with governmental services. But, the riots and protest demonstrations of the 1960s served to dispel such confidence. It became readily apparent that there were numerous grievances that were not being articulated in the normal course of events, or, if articulated, were not being satisfied. Blacks, or poor (and often both), or elderly citizens could not influence the course of governmental action—they were powerless without organization. Attempts to rectify this situation came from the various governments, private foundations, or from within these sectors of the community.

The Blacks

In the period after World War II, there has been a dramatic influx of blacks into northern cities. Housing patterns have resulted in all-black neighborhoods or communities within cities or counties. Despite their numbers, blacks have been disproportionately under-represented in the various political arenas. In those localities where at-large elections are held and in those states where district lines are drawn so as to dilute the number of black voters, black representation has been minimal. Where there are district based elections, with district lines drawn so that blacks comprise the majority of the electorate, black councilmen have sat on city councils and black legislators have been sent to the state capital. In those areas where there are strong political parties, the black vote has been courted and organized. But as James Q. Wilson has noted:

> Politics, to the politicians, is the art of organizing a community for the purpose of electing men to office. It is not a vehicle for the public expression of grievances.[40]

Other organizations in the black communities have not served as vehicles for the expression of grievances and needs held by the majority of black citizens. Organizations such as the NAACP and the Urban League have been primarily comprised of middle- to upper-class blacks, and have articulated the demands of that sector. Members of these strata, who would normally be expected to provide leadership for collective action for the lower strata, have not done so. Middle- and upper-class blacks have displayed an aversion to politics, and lack feelings of identification with lower-class blacks, who have the need for such leadership. Wilson has found in his study of Chicago politics that:

There is a distinct and evident aversion to politics among Negroes of the
middle and upper classes. . . . Working with, or against, a political machine
means working in an area widely believed to be "dirty" or corrupt and
coming in contact with the large numbers of lower-class people who make up
the backbone of the machine in the precincts. Politics is not respectable, and
respectability is highly valued.[41]

In the absence of such leadership, there has arisen from within the black
community new, younger, militant black leaders. Their clarion call has been
"Black Power." The term is an ambiguous one, and has many connotations.
It has been used to mean economic power, in that blacks should own their
own property and control the business in their communities. It has meant
racial pride, in that blacks must make efforts to recreate black art and history,
and recover the meaning of their African heritage and style. It has been
defined as social reorganization, in that the black male should take his
rightful place of dominance in the family and society as a whole.

Black Power has been utilized as a concept advocating separatism; that is,
that blacks must build their own independent communities within or outside
of the United States. It has been a concept of force, advocated by militant
blacks who believe that the needs and interests of blacks in the white society
can be satisfied only through the use of guns. It has meant political power,
in that blacks must obtain a voice in rule making concomitant with their
numbers in the society. But no matter how Black Power is interpreted, it
rests upon one basic premise: organization and unification are essential for
any group to exert influence within the society. As Stokely Carmichael and
Charles V. Hamilton have emphasized:

Before a group can enter the open society, it must first close ranks. By this we
mean that group solidarity is necessary before a group can operate effectively
from a bargaining position of strength in a pluralistic society.[42]

The advocates of black political power have concentrated their emphasis
on the local scene. For them, large numbers of persons residing within a
contained geographical area could exert effective influence. The influence is
to be derived from the organization of blacks into political associations
separate from existing ones. Such an orientation rejects the coalition orientation of persons such as Bayard Rustin, who believe that black people cannot
win political power by themselves.[43] To gain objectives, the coalitionists
stress that blacks must form alliances with "progressive" forces (such as
labor unions, big city mayors, and churches) and work through the established political parties (especially the Democratic party). The refutation of
the "coalitions are inescapable" argument is predicated on the belief that it
is impossible to form coalitions between people who are economically and

politically secure and those who are not. The black political power advocates emphasize that all alliances are built on self interest motivations; and when the interests of the black and white members conflict, the dominant whites will not hesitate to abandon the blacks. Moreover, the existing political parties are viewed by them to be supporters of the status quo, and not as instruments for change. As Carmichael and Hamilton have said:

> We are calling at this time for new political forms which will be the link between broadened participation and legitimate government. These forms will provide a means whereby a newly politicized people can get what they need from the government.[44]

The Poor

During the early years of the 1960s, poverty as a social problem was emphasized in America. Private foundations devoted time and effort and allotted funds for programs to help the poor. The Congress passed the 1964 Economic Opportunity Act, and in doing so declared a "War on Poverty." The explanations for the basis of poverty have been many and varied, and the philosophy of self help has conflicted with that of paternal assistance. As a consequence, recommended methods of alleviating the problems of poverty have been diverse and experimental.

Many people have viewed the basis of poverty to be solely a lack of money. Thus, the programs advocated were those that would provide training and jobs, increase educational opportunities, increase minimum wage and welfare levels, and so on. As a result, those who were poor would be able to earn or receive more money. But others have viewed the basis of poverty to be sociological and psychological. Therefore, they believe, programs should be instituted to break the cycle of apathy, alienation, self debasement, and powerlessness, through organizing the poor. They would then be able to negotiate effectively for resources and opportunities.

The Economic Opportunity Act marked the first time in the history of social welfare that the poor were to participate in the planning of assistance programs. Indeed, the law required the "maximum feasible participation" by the poor in designing the anti-poverty programs sponsored by the Office of Economic Opportunity. Yet, in some programs, only token citizen participation was encouraged. For example, almost from the inception of the Head Start programs, the planning was dominated by local school boards. The boards tended to ignore all but the educational aspects of the program, and they encouraged parent participation only in terms of PTA membership. In the few instances where parent participation was activated, parents not only took a strong interest in the Head Start program, but also in the problems of their neighborhood. This led to the formation of community councils, and to efforts to collectively articulate demands for improved local living conditions.

Community Action Programs, established by the Office of Economic Opportunity, also were to include the "maximum feasible participation" of the poor in the planning of programs for their respective communities. Once provided for, a program was to be directed by a Community Action Board. As controversy over the interpretation of "maximum" participation ensued, the formula finally agreed on was that one-third of the boards were to be comprised of individuals who were poor, and the remainder of board membership would consist of one-third professionals and one-third citizens selected from the community at-large. Thus, governmental action was aimed at the organization of the poor to permit the collective articulation of needs and demands.

Several localities have made efforts to guide the poor into collective articulation activities. One such effort has been the utilization of neighborhood schools to serve as community centers. The Ludlow School Community Center, in Philadelphia, is one example. The physical facilities have been made available to neighborhood residents during non-school hours (*i.e.*, late afternoons, evenings, and week-ends). The school has become a meeting place for the nearby residents to gather and to discuss personal problems and problems of the community. Once the neighbors uncovered common problems, they sought and received advice on methods by which they could collectively articulate demands to appropriate governmental agents.

Neighborhood Service Centers, funded by federal grants or by private foundations, have been instituted in several localities. Though their principle purpose has been to assist in obtaining information and services for the poor, they have also organized and mobilized groups. The common nature of many of the problems facing the residents, combined with the shortage of resources available to meet their needs, on an individual basis, led to the idea of organizing collective action to deal with problems and bring about changes in services and social conditions. The personnel of these centers have assisted the groups in developing strategies to confront and challenge those public officials responsible for making and executing the rules affecting conditions and services in the neighborhoods.

Groups may have a limited life, such as when they have been organized in response to a crisis or to a specific issue, or they may be formed on a more permanent basis for continuing activity. The size of the groups vary, though the number of active members is usually small, ranging from three or four individuals to two or three dozen active residents. Some groups have informal gatherings; others are highly structured with officers, regular meetings and meeting places. These may be organized on a geographical basis (such as a block, or a neighborhood), by categories of people (*e.g.*, Puerto Ricans or welfare clients), or around a common interest (such as housing conditions).

The distinction may be blurred; the Committee of Welfare Families of the Lower East Side (New York) is an issue group, a category group, and a neighborhood group. On occasion, efforts have been made to affiliate these groups with existing associations, such as the PTA's, neighborhood civic associations, or church groups.

A major objective of the neighborhood center projects have been to bring about change in the policies or practices of public agencies concerned with welfare, health, education, employment, and housing. As the authors of a report on one program in New York City wrote:

> The strength of numbers is not to be underestimated in solving some of the problems of poverty. Since some solutions fall within the domain of the public welfare structure, the marshalling of group support is an effective spur to institutional response. Public officials are attuned to the interests of solidary group representing potential voters. Political sensitivity to organized constituencies makes decision makers susceptible to the demands of participants in social action.
>
> The realization of political power requires social organization and action.[45]

Several types of group actions have been stimulated by the neighborhood service centers. Block clubs in the District of Columbia took action on the condition and management of public housing projects in the Cardoza section. Efforts of the Community Progress, Inc., stimulated 160 inner city residents of New Haven to go to the state legislature to support a state aid to education bill; and 200 participated in a statewide civil rights rally. Other groups organized in the District of Columbia, New Haven, and Syracuse have been engaged in such activities as picketing, marches, demonstrations, and sit-ins.

The Elderly

The decade that saw the "War on Poverty," and "Black Power," began to see the call for "Senior Power." The elderly, feeling the pressures of inflation diminishing the value of their fixed savings and pension incomes, have become the latest pressure group. Representing nearly one-fifth of all eligible voters, and recognizing the potential political strength of numbers, they have organized to collectively articulate their needs and demands. These demands have included such things as tax relief, food programs, lower public transit costs, better police protection, and more, better, and cheaper housing.

The organizations range from local groups to statewide associations. Among these have been the Council of Elders in Boston, the Chicago Area Council (comprised of over forty neighborhood Senior Citizen Clubs), the 14,000-member Massachusetts Legislative Council for Older Americans, and the Congress of Senior Citizens in New York (with over 200,000 members in nearly 200 clubs). Their tactics have been primarily discussing their interests with public officials, demonstrating, and picketing. The sight of the elderly picketing state or local public offices, and carrying signs with such warnings as "You'll Be Old Someday," have begun to spark responses from the public agents. Several examples of "Senior Power" success have been: reduced public transit fares (in Boston), foot patrolmen in housing projects (in Yonkers), increased old age assistance (in Rhode Island), exemption of prescription drugs from the state sales tax (in Kentucky), and lower rents (in New York). As a state senator in Kentucky exclaimed, as he saw twenty busloads of the elderly arrive at the State House, "The old people have descended on us like a swarm of locust and attention must be paid."[46]

The pluralistic system of collective articulation has been expanded in recent years, as the traditionally organized and efficacious groups have been joined by the organizations of the traditionally inarticulate. Yet, not all of the groups have equal resources and access, nor are they equally influential or effective. Moreover, vast numbers of people remain inarticulate and unorganized. For interest articulation to be a meaningful function within a democratic political system, it must be representative of all the members of the community. As governmental agents undertake the task of attempting to satisfy the conflicting interests, needs, and demands of individuals and groups, they must recognize that:

> Because half a dozen grasshoppers under a fern make the field ring with their importunate chink, whilst thousands of great cattle . . . chew the cud and are silent . . . do not imagine that those who make the noise are the only inhabitants of the field.[47]

Chapter IV Footnotes

1. Gabriel A. Almond and Sidney Verba, *The Civic Culture* (Boston: Little, Brown and Company, 1965), pp. 145–59.
2. Ibid., p. 152.
3. *The Washington Post*, September 8, 1968, pp. A1, A6.
4. James Q. Wilson, *Negro Politics* (New York: The Free Press, 1965), pp. 148–49.
5. L. Harmon Zeigler and Hendrick van Dalen, "Interest Groups in the States," in Herbert Jacob and Kenneth N. Vines, eds., *Politics in the American States*, (Boston: Little, Brown and Company, 1971), pp. 122–60.
6. See for example: Norman R. Luttberg and Harmon Zeigler, "Attitude Consensus and Conflict in an Interest Group: An Assessment of Cohesion," *American Political Science Review*, LX (September 1966), pp. 655–66.
7. *The New York Times*, February 1, 1970, p. 60.
8. Harmon Zeigler, "The Effects of Lobbying," *Western Political Quarterly*, XXII (March 1969), p. 134.
9. John C. Wahlke, *et al.*, *The Legislative System* (New York: John Wiley and Sons, Inc., 1962), p. 338. See also, Harmon Zeigler and Michael A. Baer, *Lobbying: Interaction and Influence in American State Legislatures* (Belmont, Calif.: Wadsworth Publishing Company, Inc., 1969).
10. Wahlke, *et al.*, *Legislative Systems*, pp. 323–42.

11. Betty H. Zisk, Heinz Eulau, and Kenneth Prewitt, "City Councilmen and the Group Struggle: A Typology of Role Orientations," *Journal of Politics*, XXVII (August 1965), pp. 618–46.

12. Ibid., p. 633.

13. Washington, D.C., City Council, Public Safety Committee, *Public Hearings*, September 30, 1968, November 25, 1968, and December 9–10, 1968, *passim*. All quotations in this section obtained from personal interviews conducted during November, 1969.

14. David B. Truman, *The Governmental Process* (New York: Alfred A. Knopf, 1960), pp. 376–77.

15. *The Washington Post*, March 22, 1970, p. D6.

16. Ibid.

17. *The New York Times*, February 1, 1970, p. 60.

18. Wahlke, *et al.*, *Legislative System*, p. 340.

19. *The New York Times*, February 1, 1970, p. 60.

20. Lawrence D. Longley, "Interest Group Interaction in a Legislative System," *Journal of Politics*, XXIX (August 1967), p. 644.

21. Interview, November 14, 1968.

22. Longley, "Interest Group," p. 658.

23. Harry W. Reynolds, Jr., "The Career Public Service and Statute Lawmaking in Los Angeles," *Western Political Quarterly*, XVIII (September 1965), pp. 621–39.

24. See, for example, Lucius J. Barker, "Third Parties in Litigation," *Journal of Politics*, XXIX (February 1967), pp. 47–69; and Clement E. Vose, "Interest Groups, Judicial Review and Local Goverment," *Western Political Quarterly*, XIX (March 1966), pp. 85–100.

25. Bertil L. Hanson, "Oklahoma's Experience with Direct Leglislation," *Southwestern Social Science Quarterly*, XLVII (December, 1966), pp. 263–73.

26. *The Montgomery County Sentinel*, September 3, 1970, p. 1.

27. See, for example, Harvey M. Sapolsky, "The Flouridation Controversy: An Alternative Explanation," *Public Opinion Quarterly*, XXXIII (Summer 1969), pp. 240–48.

28. See, for example, Harlan Hahn, "Northern Referendum on Fair Housing: The Response of White Voters," *Western Political Quarterly*, XXI (September 1968), pp. 483–95.

29. Pendleton Herring, *The Politics of Democracy: American Parties in Action* (New York: W. W. Norton and Company, Inc., 1965), p. 187.

30. Hugh A. Bone, *American Politics and the Party System* (New York: McGraw-Hill Book Company, 1965, 3rd ed.), p. 141.

31. The base of support was derived from the United Hatters, Cap and Millinery Workers Union, and the International Ladies' Garment Workers Union. The two unions had withdrawn from the American Labor Party, which the leaders had helped found in 1936, when it appeared that Commumist supporters had filtered in and taken control of the ALP. The American Labor Party disbanded after 1954, when it had failed to poll the necessary 50,000 votes needed to maintain its legal status in New York. See Bernard Rosenberg, "New York Politics and the Liberal Party," *Commentary*, XXXVII (February 1964), pp. 69–75.

32. *The Washington Post*, November 7, 1969, p. A2.

33. Clyde E. Jacobs and Alvin D. Sokolow, *California Government* (New York: The Macmillan Company, 1970, 22nd ed.), p. 115.

34. Ibid.

35. Lewis A. Froman, Jr., *People and Politics* (Englewood Cliffs, N.J.: Prentice-Hall, Inc., 1962), p. 101.

36. E. E. Schattschneider, *The Semisovereign People* (New York: Holt, Rinehart, and Winston, 1960), p. 35.

37. Ibid., pp. 33–36.
38. V. O. Key, Jr., *Public Opinion and American Democracy* (New York: Alfred A. Knopf, 1961), pp. 501–508.
39. Almond and Verba, *Civic Culture*, p. 249.
40. Wilson, *Negro Politics*, p. 72.
41. Ibid., p. 57–58.
42. Stokely Carmichael and Charles V. Hamilton, *Black Power* (New York: Vintage Books, 1967), p. 44.
43. See, for example, Bayard Rustin, "From Protest to Politics," *Commentary*, XXXIX (February 1965), pp. 25–31.
44. Carmichael and Hamilton, *Black Power*, p. 181.
45. As quoted in Robert Perlman and David Jones, *Neighborhood Service Centers* Washington, D.C.: Government Printing Office, 1967), p. 52.
46. Theodore Irwin, "Senior Power Is on the Move," *Parade*, September 13, 1970, p. 32.
47. Edmund Burke, as quoted in Herring, *Politics of Democracy*, p. 89.

Chapter V

Interest Aggregation

Government is a complex institution created by members of a political society to satisfy those needs and demands the people could not meet themselves. For governmental agents to provide satisfaction, they must be aware of the needs and demands of the public. Through various direct and indirect channels of interest articulation, individuals and groups make a multitude of sentiments known to state and local agents. Should such expressions be singular in orientation (*e.g.*, an individual request for a personal need, or unified demands for a public action), then the function of interest articulation could provide direction for responsive public agents. However, most articulated demands for public action are not singular in nature, but are diverse and conflicting. Thus, for public agents to provide satisfaction, some order must be imposed on the diversity of expressions heard.

Interest aggregation is that function of creating order from the conflicting interests, needs, and demands articulated by groups and individuals. The function of interest aggregation requires that 1) conflicting articulated interests be heard; 2) those conflicting interests be mediated and combined into policy recommendations; and 3) the recommendations be transmitted to the appropriate public agents.

Gabriel A. Almond and James S. Coleman have stressed that in modern, democratic political systems (such as those found within the American states and localities), political parties would be the principal agents of interest aggregation.[1] For the main objective of political parties, unlike that of other permanent organizations, is to recruit personnel to staff and control the machinery of government. In two-party systems, electoral success depends on courting extensive popular support. Consequently, the parties strive to offer candidates and issues on which the greatest number of conflicting individuals and groups can agree. Moreover, between elections they try to obtain the largest consensus on issues that arise, to maintain continuing support for subsequent elections.

Yet, a variety of actors and groups besides parties can perform the function of interest aggregation. Legislators, executives, bureaucrats, and interest groups of various types may be aggregators. Each may create opportunities by which persons may present different positions on a public issue. For example, a civic club might invite speakers to its meetings, or establish a task force committee to ferret out the opinions of residents and authorities. After hearing the expressions, the membership may discuss proposals that would combine and mediate the diverse positions. Club leaders may then transmit the agreed on policy formulations to the appropriate officials, utilizing a variety of direct and indirect channels for articulation.

On the other hand, the actors and groups may refrain from or be reluctant to enter into performing the aggregation function. Each may be interested in only a few public issues, may hold a predetermined position on issues, or may wish to avoid controversial matters. Moreover, efforts to aggregate interests may prove difficult and frustrating. Some issues arouse the articulation of conflicting demands, which are not amenable to mediation efforts. Interests may be so strongly held by groups or individuals that any attempts at mediation would be resisted. In addition, efforts to aggregate interests are bound to alienate some support. A policy recommendation that has been the outcome of combining conflicting interests might satisfy one group more than others. Furthermore, an attempt by a party to focus attention on a controversial issue may activate groups that have not previously made any demands, resulting in more vocal discontent than was present originally.

Political Parties and Interest Aggregation

Political parties may be conceived to be voluntary associations of persons whose principal purpose is to win elections, in order that they may exercise governmental power and enjoy the perquisites, influences, and advantages of public authority. One characteristic of the major American parties is that they are decentralized in organization; that is, local and state parties possess considerable autonomy. A second is the cross-sectional composition of their membership; that is, each party attempts to appeal to a variety of sectors of the population. Parties, thirdly, are competitive in nature, in that each (or factions within each) struggle to maintain or obtain control of governmental machinery. A fourth characteristic is the flexible and non-doctrinaire orientation of parties; that is, they generally advocate and adopt those issue positions they perceive to be necessary to win elections for public office.

The distinguishing characteristic of the major state and local parties is that their goal is political power. The means to that goal is popular support, and their energies are expended toward accomplishing that goal. As such, the activities party personnel engage in are: maintaining an organization, selecting leaders, attracting followers, recruiting candidates, developing and presenting issues, undertaking election campaigns, and raising funds.

Many party leaders have acknowledged that their activities are primarily directed toward the organizational and procedural matters related to elections. Local party officials in Holyoke, Northampton, and Medfield, Massachusetts, and in Durham and Greensboro, North Carolina, were asked to describe their job and their most important activity.[2] The tabulation of their responses are presented in Table V.1. As can be seen from that table, campaign related tasks were mentioned most often as their prime activity. Party organizational work was the second most frequently mentioned activity, and was viewed as necessary for successful campaigning. The study pointed out that those grassroot politicians never indicated that their task was to aggregate interests or to communicate policy preferences to elected officials.

TABLE V.1

Activities Mentioned by the Party Officials

Orientation of Activity	Description of Job	Most Important*
Campaign Related	(58.3%)	(67.8%)
Contacting voters	26.5%	43.5%
Raising money.	12.5	6.9
Getting people to register	10.6	6.9
Campaigning	3.4	6.1
Public relations	3.4	1.7
Contacting new voters	1.9	1.7
Party Organizational	(27.6%)	(19.9%)
Participating in party meetings and business	11.7%	10.4%
Recruiting and organizing workers . .	9.8	5.2
County party organizational work . .	6.1	4.3
Ideological	(8.3%)	(9.6%)
Increasing political information . . .	7.2%	9.6%
Policy formulation	1.1	0.0
Nomination	(5.7%)	(3.5%)
Getting candidates for local office . .	3.4%	2.6%
General activities	2.3	0.9

* According to the ratings assigned by the individual local party officials themselves.

Source: Bowman and Boynton, *op. cit.*, p. 126.

Party leaders in other sections of the country, also, have indicated that the aggregation of interests is not one of their principal party tasks. When party leaders in Michigan were asked whether they agreed that the role of the party was to reconcile conflicting interests, 24 percent of the respondents disagreed, and another 45 percent disagreed strongly. M. Kent Jennings and Norman Thomas noted that the Michigan party personnel tended to regard the task of the party as defining and articulating issues, rather than attempting to mediate and combine conflicting interests and translate them into policy recommendations. In addition, those respondents viewed their respective parties as groups that act to express interests along with other major groups in a pluralistic system of articulation.[3]

Similarly, Thomas A. Flinn and Frederick M. Wirt have noted in their study of state and local party personnel in Ohio that party leaders neither mediated between competing groups nor made attempts to offer compromise alternatives. Instead, the respondents seemed to hold personal policy preferences that influenced their perception of electoral necessities and their tactical decisions.[4]

Organization

There seems to be a prime equation that motivates party leaders' activities: votes = success. Performing the function of interest aggregation may advance a party's electoral success. However, party leaders need not always combine and mediate among conflicting interests to win votes. As the above studies have shown, party leaders have found that they may achieve success in courting votes by concentrating on building a strong party organization, which can effectively execute campaign oriented tasks. As David Katz and Samuel J. Eldersveld have noted, in a highly competitive situation local party activity has a great impact on determining the outcome of an election. They have concluded that "when a political party neglects its organizational activities in an area in which the other party has a strong local leader it will suffer in consequence at the polls."[5]

Party Identification

In areas having a homogeneous population, nothing might be gained by those party leaders who endeavor to perform the aggregation function, and nothing might be lost by those who do not. Where members of a community sufficiently share similar demographic characteristics (such as education, occupation, income, religion, and ethnic backgrounds), they often share a commonality of outlook on public issues. Thus, their allegiance goes to the party they perceive as being most representative of that outlook. Empirical studies have presented evidence that allegiance to a party endures over time; and that party identifiers consistently vote for their party.[6] Thus, in a homogeneous setting, a political party could win elections by virtue of constituent party identification ties rather than by its capacity to aggregate interests.

Even in communities that embrace people with diverse demographic characteristics, party leaders may be able to win electoral success without having to perform the function of aggregating interests. For district plans may divide the state or locality into areas comprised of homogeneous groupings. Thus, where elections are held in wards of compact districts, party leaders may be able to rely on traditional party allegiance for electoral support.

Non-Controversial Issues

If voter support could be won or maintained by means other than aggregating interests, then party leaders would avoid performing the function. Richard Daley, mayor of Chicago and chairman of the Democratic party organization of Cook County (Illinois), had found that attending to those issues having wide constituent consensus was a means to maintain voter support. He has energetically supported highly visible and non-controversial projects that would benefit, but not place any significant financial burden on, the taxpayers. One such project was the new convention hall used by the Democratic presidential nominating convention in 1968. Furthermore, Daley has found it politically feasible to avoid attempts at aggregating conflicting interests on such controversial issues as police brutality, corruption, and inefficiency, and poor housing conditions.[7]

Services

Historically, the success of party leaders in enticing and maintaining voting support has been through providing "services." The several waves of immigration into America during the late nineteenth century created situations in the urban communities whereby people needed the services that party organizations could provide. In the days before state-supported welfare, party leaders were the "social workers." They met the newcomers at the boat and helped them settle in a neighborhood. They saw to it that people had fuel at cold times, turkeys at bare times, jobs at hopeless times. They also mediated with the authorities at critical times, and offered gifts at happy times and condolences at sorrowful times. But most importantly, they provided the cost-free service: friendship, at lonely times.

William L. Riordon, in depicting the style of political leaders during this era, recorded a day's work of one district leader. That day began at 2 a.m. when Plunkitt of Tammany Hall was awakened to bail out a saloonkeeper. After that he gave assistance to several persons driven from their home by fire; returned to the courthouse to obtain the release of six drunks and to represent a dispossessed, poor widow and her family; successfully found jobs for four constituents; went to a meeting of election district captains; rushed to treat everyone at a church fair; returned to hold court for constituents at the clubhouse; and attended a wedding reception and dance, before turning to sleep after midnight. By such activities, Riordon emphasized,

> . . . the Tammany district leader reaches out into the homes of his district, keeps watch not only on the men, but also on the women and children; knows their needs, their likes and dislikes, their troubles and their hopes, and places himself in a position to use his knowledge for the benefit of his organization and himself.[8]

Whether the immigration was from foreign soil, or from rural areas to the urban areas, the parties provided such services. The services enabled people to adjust and assimilate into their new environment. And the cost of these services was a vote.

Political party leaders in the mid-twentieth century still derive much of their support by providing services. An account of the 1970 activities of a ward organization in Chicago strikingly resembles Riordon's 1905 account of Tammany Hall in New York. The extensive list of the ward activities included the sponsorship of Thanksgiving dinners for the elderly, Christmas parties for the children, picnics, and a baseball team in each precinct. The ward leaders also handed out dirt and grass seeds to homeowners, and awarded scholarships at Negro debutante balls. As the president of the ward organization proudly stated: "Service before politics, that's our motto." [9]

Since governments have institutionalized social welfare services to provide aid, a politician today can be found calling the social security office to inquire into the cause of a delayed check; acting to get a family into a public housing project; smoothing the entrance onto the welfare rolls; or finding an open bed in the county hospital. The politician, by intervening in the dispensation of state welfare assistance, provides a humanized and personalized touch to what is perceived as an impersonal, bureaucratic, socially distant, and legally constrained governmental process. Constituents perceive their precinct committeeman as one who understands their problems and offers assistance. And on election day, they remember their friend.

Local businessmen also turn to party leaders for special services. The politician may be asked to act as an ambassador to the governmental arena the businessman may perceive to be alien and sometimes unfriendly. For example, if at a liquor board hearing on the issuance of a new liquor license, an already established saloon-keeper appears to ask that it be denied, party-appointed commissioners would view him as someone desiring less competition. But an "ambassador" from the same party, stating (on the saloon-keeper's behalf) that there are too many bars in the neighborhood already, would be viewed as a man concerned for his community. And on election day, the businessman will remember his friend.

Similarly, the party men are called on to perform services for illegitimate businesses—those engaged in vice, crime, and rackets. Leaving morals aside, these are businesses that dispense goods and services to a market where there are people who are willing to buy. These businessmen need and demand protection from undue interference from the government. And the politician who provides a climate enabling these businesses to operate will also be remembered on election day.[10]

Moreover, the party man provides a psychological boost to the "nobodies" in the society, that is, people who work only at a subsistence level, seeing no way for improvement or no hope for opportunities, and tragically maintaining such a low self-image that they would describe themselves as "nobodies." Such a person feels that the neighborhood politician is an important man. For the latter to greet him by his first name, visit his sick mother, invite his son to join the party club, confers an identity, a sense of importance and a feeling of camaraderie to an otherwise meaningless daily existence. Moreover, the successful organization man, with whom the people could identify as having roots among them, portrays an image of one who has "made it," a success in which they can share vicariously.[11] And on election day, they remember their friend.

Reforms and Interest Aggregation

As long as political party leaders were assured of obtaining sufficient electoral support by providing services, the interests of the middle- and upper-class residents of the city could be ignored. Such residents, already assimilated and basically educated, viewed political party service assistance practices as organized bribery. They perceived the political party leaders to be engaged in smoke-filled, back room, petty, political, and often corrupt tradings which were alien to the principles of good, clean, democratic government. This feeling gave birth to the reform movement.

Objectives

Since the aims of the reformers varied from time to time and place to place, it is necessary to attempt to categorize their general objectives. The first objective was to achieve responsible local government. The reformers thought it necessary to separate the business of the city from that of state and national politics, in order that there may be a concentration of local issues. This could be accomplished by home rule, and by non-partisan elections held at times different from state and national elections. The former, it was believed, would empower local public agents to satisfy the immediate needs of members of the community; and the latter would enable the electorate to focus attention on officials and issues pertinent to local affairs.

A second objective was to promote a city-wide orientation of issues for the "common good." This would necessitate the weakening of the influence wielded by groups or individuals espousing an orientation of neighborhood, parochial, private, or special interests. Such would be accomplished by centralized decision making. Reformers advocated a strong mayor, or a city manager (with a small legislative council), or a board of commissioners having extensive authority over administrative agencies. Elected public officials would run at-large and for longer terms; and bureaucrats would be competent professionals, recruited through the merit service.

The third objective of the reformers was to promote democratic account-ability within the political process. To achieve this goal it would be necessary that the electorate be informed and influential. The short ballot would permit the voter to become more cognizant of the merits and capabilities of the most important public officials. Nomination by petition, direct primaries, initiative, referendum, and recall would be means by which the citizens could influence rule makers.

Bypassing political parties was viewed by reformers as being the most important and necessary way to reassert the principles of good government. If the above reforms were instituted, they would accomplish this fourth and vital objective. Thus, the call for responsible and accountable local govern-ment was a direct assault on party politics. In non-partisan elections, parties could not lend their name to a candidate. With a short ballot, there would be fewer offices for them to fill. With longer terms, there would be fewer cam-paigns to run. With the merit service, there would be less patronage positions to enhance their power. With off-year elections, party "hacks" could not be packaged along with more attractive state and national officials. With elec-tions at-large, traditional neighborhood support would be undermined. And finally, with an electorate armed with direct primaries, initiative, recall, and referendum, the party would diminish as an important channel for interest articulation.

Many of the reformers' proposals for change have been adopted. However, it cannot be said that such changes have produced the desired objectives. Good, clean, democratic government is not inevitably the resultant of struc-tural and electoral reforms, nor of diminished political party strength. Moreover, responsible and accountable local government is not necessarily achieved by the elimination of partisan politics.

The Effects of Reforms on Political Parties

Structural and electoral reforms have not universally eliminated or ad-versely affected political parties. The most widely instituted reforms have been non-partisanship and at-large elections. These have been adopted in two-thirds of the cities having populations of 5,000 or more.[12] In many of those localities, however, parties have remained active participants in the electoral process.

In some communities non-partisanship is merely nominal. In Chicago, for example, party labels do not appear on the ballot in the election for alderman. Yet, by no stretch of the imagination can Chicago be considered a non-partisan city. The highly effective Democratic precinct organizations, nourished by material incentives, have assured for the party complete and continued dominance in the elections for the partisan mayor and the non-partisan aldermen.[13]

In large non-partisan communities, association with a party may be necessary for a candidate's success, since such affiliation offers identification and organizational support. Candidates for the non-partisan local legislative offices in the city of Milwaukee and in Milwaukee County have been predominately party affiliates. A. Clarke Hagensick has shown that, during the period he studied, 70 percent of the candidates had either been active or officers in the local or state party organizations, and nearly half of the incumbents held important leadership positions within their party.[14]

In instances where centralization of authority has been implemented, party leaders have not found their organizations to be disadvantaged. Indeed, most centralization schemes have benefitted political parties, because the leaders have not had to divide their energies or influence among numerous public officials. In Jersey City, the commission form of government was more of a help than a hindrance to Hague's boss rule. In Kansas City, Pendergast found the council manager form wholly satisfactory for his purposes.[15]

Similarly, political party leaders found the proposals for the short ballot and longer terms of office advantageous. Under these circumstances, party leaders can make smaller expenditures of time, energy, and financial resources than before to fill the fewer elected offices at the less frequent intervals. Moreover, high administrative offices did not disappear as they were dropped from the ballot. Although these jobs were now filled by appointment, they could be given to persons selected by party leaders, thus enhancing the strength of the leaders' organization.

Reformers viewed the proposal to recruit most governmental personnel through the merit service as a means to assure that public agencies would be staffed by trained, skilled, and competent individuals. They also considered the extension of the merit system as a means to diminish the strength of political parties. As more positions were to be filled by meeting merit requirements, less would be filled through patronage. Patronage, *i.e.*, awarding jobs on the basis of political support, was seen to be currency for the politician. Patronage could be used to buy votes or to pay for party organizational workers.

Daniel P. Moynihan and James Q. Wilson have suggested that the institution of merit appointments has left parties with unattractive patronage positions. In analyzing the nature of patronage available in New York state, they had discovered that most jobs were low paying, minor positions, inconveniently located and entailing hard work.[16] However, had the merit system not been adopted, it is likely that party leaders still would fill only unattractive positions strictly as rewards for political support. The reason: the complex problems facing today's governmental agents would necessitate that most administrators be hired on the basis of training, skill, and competence.

Patronage is useful in maintaining a party organization. An organization needs people to devote full-time attention to the party's affairs, and patronage positions could pay the bill of these individuals. Some people are motivated to work for a party in the hope that this may be an avenue for securing employment. Thus, a reduction of patronage positions may reduce the number of potential workers. However, political parties can and do attract workers who participate for reasons other than material gain. Individuals may volunteer to serve for the fun of playing politics, for meeting important people, for the social aspect, or for satisfying their sense of civic obligation.[17]

Reforms and Special Interests

By ridding politics of partisan activities, reformers believed they would be eliminating the influence of special, parochial interests in the governmental arena. They failed to recognize, however, that in weakening party organizations, they were strengthening the positions of special interest groups. In those localities where parties are absent from the election process, clearly defined interest groups may nominate, endorse, and support slates of candidates. In effect, these groups become non-party-label parties.

In Detroit, for example, organized labor interests stepped into the political vacuum created when non-partisanship weakened the local Democratic party organization. Union leaders nominate and support candidates, and members perform the campaign related tasks necessary to assure the success of "friends of labor." The objective of organized labor leaders in participating in such activities is rule making and execution that favors their special interests.[18]

A candidate denied party organizational and financial resources, in a truly non-partisan situation, must turn for support to other groups. Unless he is personally wealthy, a candidate needs assurance of financial backing to even consider running, especially in at-large election campaigns (usually associated with non-partisan situations). For some reason, reformers believed that non-party groups giving money directly to candidates would exert less influence than if their funds were channeled through an intermediary party treasury. But certainly, an interest group donating money to a candidate does so with the intention of gaining access to further a particular demand.

Whether the need be for financial support or for organized campaign and voter turnout assistance, the non-partisan at-large candidate increases his reliance on civic associations, labor or business groups, churches, and newspapers. The communication media, for example, are very influential in such situations. Their favorite candidates can be highly publicized, to the detriment of other candidates who they oppose or ignore. As one newspaperman stated, "You can't tell the players without a scorecard, and we sell the scorecard."[19] The payment for group support is not the old style services—which these groups do not need—but access to the decision makers who are responsible for rule making or execution.

Other reforms have also served to enhance the influence of special interest groups. The short ballot and the centralization of authority permitted interest groups to focus their energy and resources on influencing fewer elected officials and centers of responsibility. In addition, at-large elections, by lessening the dependency of officials on neighborhood support, increased the opportunities for special interests to exert influence.

Reforms and the Electorate

The objective of the reformers to promote responsible and accountable local government was to be accomplished by deemphasizing partisan politics and reemphasizing the influence of an independent and informed electorate. They envisioned an independent voter, unencumbered by pressures of party identification, concentrating on issues and evaluating candidates on the basis of their abilities and issue statements. Thereafter, that voter would actively support his carefully selected candidate. However, empirical studies have presented evidence that independents have been less concerned, less interested, and less active than party identifiers in the electoral process.

Indeed, the proposals set forth by the reformers were based on an assumption that the electorate was sufficiently concerned about the functions of the political system that, if given opportunities to vote in meaningful situations, they would act to exert influence. The direct primary was a means by which citizens could exert influence in the recruitment function. Decisions for the nomination of public officials would be taken from party leaders and transferred to the masses. In practice, however, less than one-third of the potential electorate comprise "the masses" that have availed themselves of this opportunity.[20]

Reforms and Accountable Public Agents

When instituted, non-partisan elections, the short ballot, and the extension of the merit service have not inevitably resulted in either responsible or accountable government. The successful non-partisan candidate, unhampered by any unifying party organization or symbol, and owing no allegiance to others running (including the chief executive), is self-dependent. The probability for his reelection increases as his name becomes more familiar to the electorate. The much sought after limelight often falls on those who propose new programs, or on those who are the most vociferous dissenters. In a political situation where all public officials are courting publicity, the result is a great deal of wasted motion, ending more often in stalemate than in progress. In addition, there may be no continuity of programs, for individualistic political behavior may not be obligated to honor past promises.

In partisan situations, by contrast, people identify a candidate within the context of their party's image. Having once advocated a program, in the minds of the people the party may become committed to its continuance. This commitment is transferred to the party's candidate. Therefore a partisan office seeker's electoral success is dependent not only on his organizational campaign efforts, but also on the electorate's view of his party's programs. Moreover, if he desires reelection, the office holder must cooperate with his fellow partisan officials to insure the continuance of the party's advocated program in order to maintain and enhance the favorable image the electorate has of the party.

Should the electorate become aware and concerned that no progressive decisions are being made, or that needs are not being satisfied, they might want to vote against the incumbents. But protest voting is difficult. The first difficulty is to discover where the fault lies. Does it lie with one incumbent, with a faction, or with the entire policy making body?

The second difficulty is knowing to whom allegiance and support can be transferred without cues such as party labels. In a partisan situation, for example, if the people were dissatisfied with the Democratic incumbents, a simple solution would be to vote the Democrats out and replace them with Republicans at the next election. Without such a guideline, as in a nonpartisan election, an alternate group is not readily definable. If the fault lies with special interests unduly influencing some incumbents, how might the electorate be assured that these incumbents will not be replaced by others representing the same groups? At best, the voter may be using his ballot to replace one self-dependent candidate with another. Thus, non-partisanship does not appear to promote the accountability of the public agent.

Parties as Agencies of Interest Aggregation

The various reform proposals did not directly provide for the performance of the function of interest aggregation. This was generally not an oversight, for the reformers did not believe that the function was necessary. Instead, they held that there were values and interests that were shared by the residents of a locality. Thus, public issues could be handled and solutions to problems could be found by public agents defining the common interest. However, any "common good" is not readily defined, nor can it be assumed that such exists. For in a community comprised of a population having diverse demographic characteristics, there would be found a plurality of interests and values. These interests are often conflicting, and many may be ambiguous. Thus, some mechanism by which interests can be combined, mediated, and translated into policy proposals is needed.

If the reforms were successful in deemphasizing and bypassing political parties, then any mechanism that could perform the function of interest aggregation would be weakened or eliminated. Although political party leaders may prefer to ignore or skim over issues that arise from conflicting demands or that arouse the articulation of conflicting interests, they may not be able to do so. Pressures, such as affiliation with the national party and its stands, maintenance of the party's public image, and the need to continually strive for success at the polls, may force the acknowledgment of persistent issues. The objective of obtaining electoral success necessitates that party leaders recognize the existence of diverse interests among the people. And, to appeal to the largest number of voters, the leaders may need to combine and mediate as many interests as possible.

The services dispensed by party leaders may serve as means by which private-oriented interests and public-oriented interests might be combined. For example, while recruitment for patronage positions satisfied private needs for jobs, it satisfied public demands for services. Thus, in situations where government jobs were provided party supporters, police forces to protect the community were manned, and recruits were found to clean the streets, collect the garbage, and perform other unappealing but necessary tasks.

Direct primaries were thought to be means by which the common interest could be made known. Yet it is difficult to view the outcome of a primary election as such an expression. Generally there is a small percentage of voter turnout, and this fragments among the alternative names on the primary ballot. This political process permits a man to be elevated to the highest office in the state or locality by receiving (by ability, luck, possession of a familiar name, or by some other means) the votes of as few as 5 to 10 percent of the potential electorate. An organized effort on behalf of one candidate that can attract a small block of voters will be successful in nominating a candidate who may be unattractive to the larger electorate in the general election. Thus, a candidate's success in the primary need not have been the result of any organized effort to aggregate interests.

Party leaders may become actively involved in the nominating process by endorsing a slate of candidates in a primary election, or by selecting candidates in a pre-primary convention, caucus, or nominating convention. If they are to find the most marketable candidate, they must make efforts to aggregate interests. For in attempting to appeal to the greatest number of voters, party leaders will endeavor to mediate extremist elements and create a balance between regional, community, and diverse interests.

In partisan situations, the presence of permanent organizational personnel facilitates the performance of the aggregation function by the leaders. The precinct workers (who are on the lowest level of the party hierarchy) hear what the people want or are interested in, and can relay those sentiments to the officials at the higher levels of the organization. The precinct committeemen usually live in the neighborhoods in which they perform their party oriented tasks. They are familiar with the neighborhood residents, and generally hold interests that reflect those held by their neighbors. The people are able to readily contact the party workers at their homes or at their precinct or ward party headquarters. Thus, through the network of precinct workers, party leaders can become aware of the diverse interests that have to be aggregated.

Philips Cutright has studied the amount of daily contact that partisan precinct committeemen have with voters. His study showed that nearly two-thirds of the workers had met with ten or more persons during daily neighborhood rounds.[21] David Boesel, in his study of 15 northern cities, found that black committeemen had contact with about 75 voters each week; and the politicians, hence, became aware of the demands made by the black constituents.[22]

In non-partisan situations, there are workers who mobilize the vote and conduct campaign activities; however, they are not part of a permanent organization. The voters cannot rely on those workers to serve as channels for communication, since there is very little interaction between the two. Cutright found in the non-partisan locality he studied that over three-quarters of the grassroots workers saw no more than five persons, if any, in a day.[23] In addition to having no continuing delegate to whom he can articulate, there are no permanent district headquarters at which the resident can express his interest. Thus, in localities with non-partisan elections, there is no party-like substitute structure to aggregate interests.

Whether leaders in the higher levels of a party hierarchy (*i.e.*, city, county, or state committee levels) perform the function of interest aggregation may be determined by the extent of their like-mindedness. Should such leadership groups be comprised of men representing differing viewpoints and orientations, the very need to keep their organization from splintering, or to produce a program of issues, will force them to mediate among themselves.

For example, the unity of orientation held by the members comprising the county committees of the Democratic and Republican parties in Montgomery County (Maryland) was one factor accounting for the extent to which each party performed the aggregation function. The 1966 gubernatorial election, which saw an ultra-conservative candidate nominated as the standard bearer in the primary (yet lose in the general election), left the Democratic Party organization split into three ideological groupings: liberal, moderate, and conservative. This split forced the leaders into aggregating multi- and conflicting interests in order to get the membership to agree on any policy statement. The Republican County Committee, in contrast, had not been forced to aggregate interests because of a divided membership. As the chairman of the committee stated, "There is a Republican viewpoint toward issues which is strongly held by all the members on the County Central Committee." [24]

The Amateur Politicians

In recent years there has appeared on the political scene a new figure known as the "Amateur Politician." [25] Amateur politicians have been viewed as the modern manifestation of the turn-of-the-century reformers, in that they look on parties with disdain and espouse public oriented issues. Yet, tempered by the experience of a half century of reform movements, amateurs do recognize the utility of partisan organization as a means to achieve their aims.

Amateur politicians perceived the traditional, professional politicians as being primarily interested in self-perpetuation. Professionals were seen to insure their perpetuation through emphasis on private oriented interests and favor-trading practices. The amateurs aimed to replace professionals in the various party hierarchies, so that politics would be more issue oriented and parties could be instruments for social change. Yet the amateurs are no more concerned about being actors for aggregating interests than are their traditional counterparts. The new politician believes that the public oriented issues he espouses reflect the interests of the entire community.

Because the professional politicians have not been easily replaced, the efforts of the amateurs have created situations that force the aggregation of interests. In places where the amateurs have succeeded in obtaining some seats on leadership committees, they have made demands that contrast with those of the traditional party men. This contrast arises basically out of the fact that one group is issue oriented while the other is campaign oriented. The former focus on the interests that are basically those of the middle and upper classes; the latter (believing that people in those classes did not need inducements to turn out at the polls), focus on the interests of the lower and working classes. If the two groups could mediate and combine their different orientations, then the objectives of both may be achieved.

Where the amateurs have not been able to obtain positions of leadership in the formal party structure, they have created or joined auxiliary partisan organizations. In such cases, the amateurs could negotiate from their positions of organized strength, and inject into the party policy making process the points of view that are dissimilar to those of the professionals. The outcome of successful negotiations would be aggregated alternatives.

Articulation as the Basis of Party Aggregation

Occasionally, party leaders may desire to perform the function of interest aggregation. Yet, they may be unable to do so. For the leaders to aggregate interests, the interests must be articulated to them. The level of esteem that the parties enjoy within a community may determine whether expressions of sentiments are directed toward party leaders. In many localities, though party organizations exist to perform campaign oriented tasks, the political ethos may be anti-partisan. Robert C. Wood has found this ethos to prevail in suburban settings, where the residents are predominately educated, middle- and upper-class individuals. As he has observed:

> In most suburban municipalities, and especially in residential ones, the same conditions of suburban life that encourages non-partisanship restrain the exercise of local political leadership as it is commonly understood.[26]

In such an environment, political parties would be bypassed by groups that articulate interests. The groups would focus their energies directly to the council, or indirectly through nonparty connected intermediaries.

A study of interest aggregation in a suburban county revealed that groups generally bypassed political parties in articulating interests. During a one-year period, only two permanent special interest groups had directed articulated interests to the Democratic party, and only one group had made expressions to the Republican party. Of the nearly 450 civic clubs and voluntary organizations in that county, none had chosen the parties as targets for interest articulation. When several civic association officials were asked why they had not articulated the groups' sentiments to party leaders, their responses reflected the anti-partisan ethos of the community.[27] As three officials stated:

> We are completely non-partisan. We do not go to any party, even if our stand is similar. We lean over backwards on this. We do not wish to be associated with any party.
> We stay out of party politics as much as possible. There must be a line drawn between the two. We are strictly non-partisan. We do not take any partisan stands; and we never take our stands to any party.

The extent to which parties effectively influence the rule-making function may also determine whether expressions of sentiments are directed toward party leaders. In those communities where there is party control over party affiliated public agents, groups will include parties in efforts to obtain satisfaction of their interests. In Philadelphia, for example, party discipline over legislative affiliates is evident. Each city council member is bound by decisions made in the party caucus. Thus, groups have recognized that the satisfaction of their interests may depend on obtaining the support of party leaders. In contrast, where an anti-partisan ethos prevails, party leaders exert little control or discipline over a legislator's actions. Indeed, council members in such a community might gain more constituent support by demonstrating independence from their party organization than from yielding to the pressures exerted by the party leaders. Hence, group officials may view the articulation of interests to party organizations as wasted, needless effort.

Other factors may influence the extent to which group or individual articulation is directed toward party organizations. In a competitive party situation, groups may choose to articulate interests to both parties, perceiving that each would be anxious to gain its electoral support. In states and localities where one party dominates, those articulating interests may bypass the partisan organization because they are unsure about which faction should be addressed. The party of the chief executive may be the target of expressed demands as groups see party support as necessary for inclusion of interests in the executive's program of priorities. If a party has minority status on a legislative body, then those articulating interests may not perceive any advantage to gaining that party's support. Groups may decide to go to those party leaders who have been seen to be transmitters of articulated and aggregated interests, and who have been receptive and sympathetic to the groups' interests. Or, party organizations may be bypassed by groups and individuals who have established access to and rapport with public agents, and who see direct articulation as being more advantageous.

Mechanisms to Ferret Interests

When groups or individuals do not direct articulated interests to them, party leaders who perceive themselves as agents for aggregation would have to create mechanisms to ferret out interests. Parties have established task forces to study current issues. These committees have been charged with inviting and listening to spokesmen of groups or individuals concerned with a particular issue; weighing the merits of contrasting arguments; and transmitting to the party leadership policy recommendations that reflect a combining and mediating effort. Surveys may be sponsored by party leaders to gauge the type and depth of interests held by the residents. Precinct organizations have been utilized as centers for articulation. Efforts have been made to encourage residents to attend precinct organization meetings to articulate their needs, interests, or grievances. Particular controversial issues may precipitate the calling of special meetings between party leaders and residents of the community. Or, party leaders may visit regular or special meetings of associations. At any of these meetings, party leaders may become cognizant of the nature and the extent of conflicting interests. Such an awareness would enable them to mediate and combine differences, in order that they may transmit policy statements to the rule makers.

Nonapparent Aggregation

It may appear that party leaders do not perform the function of interest aggregation because they are not making efforts to combine and mediate contrasting interests on all issues. Yet, the function may be performed on a selective basis. The leadership may have selected to aggregate interests on those issues they consider to be crucial to their party's image and/or electoral success. These party men may be especially interested in obtaining consensus on those issues that are recurring and which are of wide community concern, such as the school budget or tax matters. Or, occasionally, party affiliated public officials request the aid of parties to resolve a particular issue conflict.

Policy statements issued by party leaders may not appear to be results of a combining and mediating effort. Or the statements may be such that it appears that all viewpoints had not been heard. However, the leaders may have heard all sides, but chose to eliminate some demands they considered unfeasible or unrealistic.

Observers of the political scene may not have detected any communication statements issued by party leaders, leading to the conclusion that no aggregation efforts had been made. While no overt statements may have been issued, the party leadership may have been covertly transmitting policy recommendations. Such may have occurred, for example, if a party has minority status on a legislative body. As a county Democratic party chairman has explained:

> For our Democratic councilmembers, who are in the minority, to have one of their positions accepted, there is a need for Republican votes. So, if the Democrats testify at a public hearing, or make a public policy statement, we are making it more difficult for a Republican to come over to our side. But we certainly are in contact with our councilmen. I call them on the phone, meet them for lunch, and so on.[28]

The absence of policy alternatives issued by party committees may suggest that aggregating attempts had not been made. Yet, efforts to mediate and combine contrasting interests may have been undertaken without success. Party leaders may have been unable to reach a decision, they may have decided that no action should be taken, or they may have concluded that aggregation should be performed by others outside the party.

Interest Groups and Interest Aggregation

Private-Oriented Associations

Leaders of groups that articulate interests may occasionally perform the function of interest aggregation. Principally, the private-oriented permanent associations expend their resources in the articulation of their own points of view. Yet some policy recommendations they transmit may reflect efforts made to mediate and combine their viewpoint with the contrasting viewpoints of others. When aggregating attempts are made, they are generally for the purpose of broadening the base of the group's support. Interest group leaders may believe that favorable action is more likely to occur when the scope of conflict facing the rule-making body is narrowed. Thus, the satisfaction of their interests would be achieved if the differing interests have been combined and mediated, allaying the opposition to a transmitted policy proposal.

Ad Hoc Groups

Specific issues stimulate the formation of ad hoc groups. Most often these groups act to oppose a policy proposal being considered by a rule-making body. However, an issue may stimulate the formation of groups wishing to initiate policy recommendations. To achieve success, these groups may try to aggregate differing viewpoints. For example, in many localities, consternation over the use of drugs by teenagers has sparked the organization of ad hoc groups. These groups have sponsored meetings at which knowledgeable individuals discuss the merits of alternative means to combat the drug abuse problem. After evaluating the various ideas, the group leaders have combined, mediated, and translated those they deemed most appropriate into policy recommendations to be transmitted to public agents.

Public Oriented Associations

Public oriented permanent associations frequently have aggregating capacities similar to those of political parties. Many of these groups have a community-wide membership, and they address themselves to a variety of community-wide issues. These are often leagues of neighborhood civic associations. Each member group may serve as a "precinct organization" of the league to which interests may be directed. Civic groups may set up task forces or committees to study issues and present alternative policy proposals to the general membership. In addition, speakers are invited to meetings to offer viewpoints for consideration. Such groups regularly transmit policy recommendations to public officials (by sending spokesmen to testify at public hearings or before the legislative council, making telephone calls or personal visits, and so on). Thus, group leaders who view their organizations as agencies for interests aggregation or who see aggregation as useful for the resolution of some public issues, have the mechanisms needed to perform the function.

Before issuing policy statements, leaders of community-wide groups may have to aggregate interests. The membership of such associations may be heterogeneous, representing diverse interests, needs, and demands. Moreover, individuals have joined for a variety of reasons, and they perceive the purposes of the group differently. Such factors mitigate against a common orientation to the solution of problems being shared by the affiliates. Thus, for a consensus to be reached on a policy statement, discussions must end with efforts to combine and mediate.

Leaders of a civic association may inadvertently mediate the conflicting interests of other groups. The interests articulated by some members may reflect the positions taken by other associations to which they belong. One may find, for example, that members of taxpayers' organizations and educational associations are also members of the League of Women Voters. Should the League of Women Voters choose to issue a policy recommendation concerning education, the different viewpoints of its members would have to be taken into account. It is not too difficult to understand that the members who also belong to the educational association would be in favor of raising teachers' salaries, while the members who also belong to the taxpayers' organization would be concerned with limiting public expenditures. Thus the League, in resolving the conflicting sentiments of its members to formulate a policy position on education, would be mediating between the contrasting positions of the two other associations.

Many community-wide organizations will not make attempts to aggregate interests on all types of issues. Generally, those are the issues that arouse divisive, emotional sentiments among the members. For example, the Civic Federation and the Allied Civic Group (leagues of neighborhood civic associations in Montgomery County, Maryland) regularly transmit policy recommendations to public agents. In 1969, however, they were conspicuously quiet on two issues that stimulated a great deal of community concern: low and moderate income housing, and gun control legislation. The Civic Federation had studied the housing issue and had heard all arguments, yet was unable to arrive at a policy recommendation. As a spokesman for the Federation stated:

As a group of civic associations, we all favor low and moderate income housing in principal; but there is always objections to where these projects should be located.[29]

Aggregation did not occur because the leaders were forced to recognize each member group's dismay in having the project built in its own neighborhood.

The gun control issue was considered to controversial by both organizations that neither made any attempt at aggregating. Both refrained from involvement so as not to fragment the alliance of their multi-membered constituency. As the president of the Allied Civic Group stated:

> That gun control issue was too controversial. We steered clear of it. We did not want to stir a hornets' nest among our membership.[30]

In addition, leagues of neighborhood associations will not attempt to aggregate on issues that immediately affect a member group. On such issues they serve to give an added dimension of support to the arguments of their concerned constituents. In those instances they perform the function of interest articulation, by acting as a special interest lobby.

Limited resources and low levels of efficacy further act to constrain group leaders. One resource that may not be readily available is a number of individuals who are willing to spend the time to study issues and seek consensus outside of the areas of their immediate concern. In addition, group leaders may not feel that it is worth their while to expend effort aggregating interests. They may perceive that the rule-making body is not receptive to their transmitted policy recommendations. As one group spokesman explained:

> The legislators don't listen to us. The main reason for this is that they do not think civic associations are representative. They feel we do not represent how citizens will react on enough issues.[31]

The extent to which public-oriented civic associations aggregate interests may be determined by the extent to which interests are articulated to them. Individuals and groups direct expressions of sentiments to those organizations they perceive as being receptive and sympathetic to their interests, and as being effective in transmitting policy recommendations. Associations having a broad-based membership and commanding wide voter support are seen to be beneficial allies by those seeking satisfaction of an interest. For example, the League of Women Voters is the target for many who seek support on an issue, for the League's policy positions are respected by both voters and public agents.

In localities where the anti-partisan ethos prevails, the ability of party organizations to aggregate interests diminishes. The civic associations may more likely become the aggregating agencies, as groups or individuals approach them rather than the parties. Elected officials, aware of this ethos, would be more receptive to (and even court) overt communications from non-partisan groups than to those from partisan ones.

Moreover, in non-partisan localities, civic associations may be the only community-wide organizations having mechanisms to perform the function of interest aggregation. In the absence of partisan organizations, these associations generally serve to offer the principal means of electoral support. In doing so, channels for access are opened to the elected rule makers, through which alternative policy recommendations may be readily transmitted. Furthermore, without party organizations available to aggregate interests, public agents may refer to civic associations for the performance of the function.

Bureaucrats and Interest Aggregation

The function of interest aggregation need not only be performed by non-governmental personnel. Bureaucrats, in fulfilling their tasks, often act as agents for aggregation. As they execute, propose, make, or adjudicate rules, bureaucratic agents are the targets of diverse and often conflicting individual and group demands.

Bureaucrats, in carrying out their administrative tasks, are permitted considerable discretion. The increased burden of governmental activities necessitates that administrators set the arrangement of priorities, the emphasis for different programs, and the utilization of resources. Their decisions are, at least to some extent, based on the degree of conflict that arises as each rule is to be executed, as well as on how successfully the conflicting demands have been mediated. In addition, administrators are often faced with the problem of executing rules that have not been clearly defined by the rule-makers. For example, the only guideline that might be present is the edict that the rule should be executed "in the public interest." The responsibility for discovering the "public interest" rests with the bureaucrats. To arrive at any consensus which may be called the "public interest," it is clear that the agents must balance the demands of the conflicting groups before them.

In making and adjudicating rules, bureaucrats must consider the various interests that will be affected and the possible consequences of their actions. Groups aware that rules are being made are prompt and prone to offer advice on the "correct" action to be taken. Groups affected by the adjudication of rules are anxious to have their viewpoints considered. The administrators attempt to mediate and combine the conflicting articulated interests so that rules or decisions may be promulgated and transmitted to appropriate agency personnel to serve as guidelines for action.

As part of their responsibilities, bureaucrats transmit policy proposals to the elected officials. In the daily performance of their assigned tasks they become aware of which public rules should be modified or made. They provide the chief executive with recommendations he may be seeking, or with ideas for his administrative and legislative programs. Similarly, they provide council to legislative officials. Recognizing that the bureaucrats are knowledgeable, trained, experienced, full-time personnel, and have the necessary information-gathering facilities, legislators call on them to suggest measures that would resolve an issue or a controversy. It is expected that the bureaucrats will be concerned not only with evaluating the feasibility of proposals and the consequences of rules made, but also with weighing the merits of and mediating among conflicting articulated viewpoints. Thus, they are being asked to perform the function of interest aggregation.

In the performance of some of their tasks, administrators are required by statute to provide mechanisms to facilitate the articulation and aggregation of interests. Many states, and several localities, have administrative procedure acts that prescribe specific routines to be followed in administrative rule-making and adjudication. These prescriptions might require that advance, published, public notice of a proposed action be given, and that public hearings be held (at which any interested person may request to be heard). In addition, the acts provide for avenues of appeal from administrative decisions. The required notices and hearings permit and invite contrasting sentiments to be directed to the officials. The instituted meetings are forums at which conflicting expressions are heard and mediating efforts are made. The possibility of appeal by those not satisfied with the outcome of the administrators' actions may influence bureaucrats to make genuine attempts at aggregating interests.

Moreover, bureaucrats have had to establish the mechanisms in order to meet the requirements of several federal grants-in-aid programs. For example, to apply for many programs sponsored by the Office of Economic Opportunity and the Department of Housing and Urban Development, state and local administrators must establish structures through which those assisted by the programs can articulate their interests, needs, and demands. One type of such structure is a community or neighborhood board comprised of residents of assisted areas. Once those are established, the bureaucrats are faced with mediating and combining the sentiments of the residents with those of the rule-maker, the taxpayers, the other private and public interest group members, and their own professional perceptions. If successful, they then transmit program proposals to appropriate agents.

The Chief Executive and Interest Aggregation

The chief executive, whether he be governor, county executive, or mayor, plays several roles that are related to the performance of the aggregation function. As the central elected figure, he must create and maintain a consensus among and a synthesis of the diverse interests that exist within the constituency and the governmental establishment. To be elected from a community-wide constituency and to fulfill his manifold tasks, the chief executive must continually be aware of and make successful attempts to combine and mediate conflicting needs and demands.

As the chief administrator, concerned about the execution of rules and the supervision of the day-to-day operation of governmental agencies, he is faced with developing cooperation between the administrative personnel and his office. The manner by which such personnel are recruited may underscore the necessity for developing cooperation. Some top-level administrators are elected to their positions. Whether they are part of the chief executive's party slate or successful candidates of the opposing party, they have independent constituencies. Thus, their objectives may not be the same as those of the central executive, and their prime concern may be satisfying the interests of their own supporters.

Other bureaucrats may be recruited through the merit service system. Their appointment, retention, and promotion are based on ability rather than on political considerations. As such, these public agents may consider themselves independent of the chief executive, and develop their own attitudes and interests. They may resist the innovations of a briefly tenured elected figure; prefer the continuation of programs and methods of operation in which they have been involved; propose ideas based on their own clientele relationships; and hold that their professional training and experience in the specialized areas of their jobs permit them to better know what is needed and how to satisfy those needs, than would a newcomer who heads the administrative hierarchy.

Moreover, each top-level administrator and bureaucrat believes that his own agency and set of responsibilities are the most important aspects of the government's activities. To maintain, enhance, and enlarge his department's independence and importance, each administrator demands that his agency's proposals be given priority in the executive program and be sufficiently funded. Thus, to construct a program and budget, the chief executive must combine and mediate the myriad bureaucratic demands placed upon him.[32]

As chief legislator, the executive is concerned with proposing rules and pressing for their adoption by the legislature. He is faced with legislators who bring into the councils their own set of priorities, proposals, and interests. Moreover, whether elected by district, or (as in many localities) at-large, each legislator has his own supporters whose articulated needs and demands he must satisfy. For the success of his program, therefore, the executive must mediate the interests of the legislators.

The executive, upon election to office, assumes the position as head of his party. This role affects his efforts to mediate between the diverse interests of the legislators. As head of his party he must provide leadership and guidance to his party affiliates in the council in order that partisan promises and issue positions are fulfilled. With respect to those legislators who affiliate with the opposition party, he must deemphasize partisan positions and mediate across party lines to achieve needed support for his programs, especially if his party has minority status in the legislature.

As the central elected official, the chief executive is the spokesman of the people. His actions and statements must be geared to prevent cleavages among the groupings found within the population. To maintain the tranquility of the society, his time and energy must be directed toward creating an overall level of consensus. Thus, he must be aware of the need to make successful attempts at aggregating interests.

Yet the chief executive does not have his own grassroots network to aid him in the performance of the function of aggregation. In his official capacity he is the target of the articulated demands of organized associations, administrators, and legislators. As he listens to those expressed sentiments, the extent of the diversity and conflict of interests becomes apparent to him. However, informal communications with constituents indicate that the interests, needs, and demands of the people are neither uniform nor necessarily in agreement with those expressed by association leaders, administrators, or legislators. Thus, he may create a mechanism by which articulated interests can be evaluated, combined, and mediated prior to his taking a rule-making action, such as initiating and transmitting a policy statement, or signing or vetoing a bill. For example, task forces and blue ribbon commissions may serve as mechanisms to aggregate interests. These committees would be comprised of individuals representing different economic, civic, or political groupings and orientations. The members may act to hear interests, initially mediate and combine them, translate them into policy recommendations, and transmit them to the chief executive.

The Legislators and Interest Aggregation

In many states and localities, the legislators are the principal agents performing the function of interest aggregation. This may be due to the political setting in which the task of aggregating is thrust upon the legislators. Such settings include those that have a non-partisan electoral system, a weak party system, or a prevailing anti-partisan ethos. Those situations mitigate against party leaders serving as agents of aggregation. Civic associations may be unable to serve as agencies for aggregation, for they do not become involved with all public issues. In addition, their policy recommendations may not be reflective of all interests within the community. In localities that have council-manager or commission forms of government, where the executive and the legislative activities are structurally unified, there is no elected executive to combine and mediate conflicting and contrasting interests. Thus, in the absence of other agents, the legislators undertake the performance of the interest aggregation function.

In addition, if the legislators are the prime targets of articulation, the task may be thrust upon them. In the above settings, the residents may be conditioned to think in terms of expressing their interests directly to their local councilmen and state representatives. The size of the legislative district may also affect the direction of articulated interests. Individuals and groups are more likely to express their sentiments directly to the legislators in those districts that are relatively small and that foster constituent identification. State legislative delegations or local councils that appear to be responsive to articulated interests may stimulate expressions being addressed to them. Legislators who perceive their role as being "delegates" (*i.e.*, those who base their decision making on instructions from constituents), encourage and solicit constituent articulation.[33] As targets of articulated interests, the legislators become aware of the diversity of needs and interests that require satisfaction, and cognizant that efforts to aggregate interests must be made.

The primary task of legislators is rule-making, and rules made are products of combining and mediating conflicting interests. Latham has depicted legislative rule-making as a process that accommodates diversity of interests:

> The legislature referees the group struggle, ratifies the victories of the successful coalitions and records the terms of the surrenders, compromises, and conquests in the form of statutes.[34]

However, the legislative arena is not only the site for aggregation of the contending articulators, but it is also the site for the contending aggregators. For, as the legislators receive the transmitted policy recommendations from the various other aggregating agents, they are faced with combining and mediating as a precondition for rule-making.

Divisive factors found within the legislature may necessitate aggregation as a requisite for action. Each legislator brings into the councils the concerns of his constituency. He brings his own values, interests, perceptions, and role orientations into the chambers. Some are spokesmen for economic interests, others for organized associations. The composition of the legislature may also be divided by informal alliances formed around committee assignments, party affiliation, leadership groups, or allegiance to the chief executive and his programs. Thus, the conflicting and contrasting interests found within the legislative body must be combined and mediated.

Various mechanisms may be utilized by the legislators to aid them in the performance of the function of interest aggregation. State d·legations hold open meetings at which their constituents can express sentiments about desired legislation. Local councilmen may visit various neighborhoods to ferret the interests of the residents. Legislative committees schedule hearings for groups and individuals to present viewpoints on specific bills under consideration. By these means, legislators may become aware of the interests, needs, and demands of constituents; may gauge reactions to proposed governmental actions; mediate and combine amongst the contrasting expressions; and transmit policy proposals to their colleagues.

In addition, the legislators may request others to reconcile conflict and to transmit the results of aggregation efforts. Citizen advisory boards and task forces may be established on an ad hoc basis to deal with an immediate, pressing problem, or on a permanent basis to handle recurring controversial matters. Those appointed may be spokesmen for groups that are affected by the issues and that represent a variety of viewpoints. Their policy recommendations could reflect the combining and mediating of their own various viewpoints and of those articulated to them as well. Administrators may be requested to listen to and make attempts at resolving conflicting demands. If successful, the bureaucrats would transmit the outcomes of their mediating efforts to the legislators.

As has been seen, there are a variety of agents in the states and localities that may perform the function of interest aggregation. However, most potential agents have the inclination to avoid attempts to aggregate, for the benefits that accrue to those who try may not be commensurate with the costs of time and energy expended. Some interests are not amenable to a mediation process. Thus, aggregation attempts might lead to stalemate, or to delay in resolving an issue. Many times the only policy recommendation that would be acceptable to all is one which is worded so ambiguously as to be meaningless. Furthermore, statements resulting from efforts to combine and mediate contrasting sentiments would always satisfy some individual or groups more than others, while never completely satisfying the interests of any contending parties.

Yet when the potential agents perceive that benefits might be derived from aggregating interests, they will undertake the performance of this function. Leaders of civic organizations may find that such efforts aid in obtaining and retaining members. Party leaders might perceive that aggregation leads to greater electoral support. For bureaucrats, their professional image and agency operations may be enhanced through satisfying the conflicting demands placed upon them. Elected officials may combine and mediate among the conflicting articulated interests to meet their public tasks, or to advance their chance for reelection.

The nature of the policy recommendations that various agents transmit may reflect their personal interests and the composition of their constituency. The issues on which civic associations transmit policy proposals will generally be noncontroversial and mirror the interests of their middle- and upper-class members. Bureaucrats focus on those issues of interest to their specialized clientele groups; and their transmitted recommendations will reflect those interests, as well as their own middle-class values and professional standards. Elected officials may concern themselves with courting the interests of their supporters (or potential supporters) during the limited periods of their tenure or election campaigns.

Political parties may not be the only agencies performing the function of interest aggregation. But, where there is a competitive party system, and where the political ethos is not anti-partisan, party leaders may be the agents who combine and mediate among the broadest range of interests. Party leaders, in contrast to other agents, have a continuing stake in courting the broadest spectrum of popular support. Thus, their aggregation attempts may be directed to include the heterogeneous interests of many groupings found within a community. In the absence of party aggregation, it is unlikely that all interests would be reflected in the policy recommendations transmitted to rule-makers.

Chapter V Footnotes

1.   Gabriel A. Almond and James S. Coleman, eds., *The Politics of the Developing Areas* (Princeton: Princeton University Press, 1960), pp. 38–40.
2.   Lewis Bowman and G. R. Boynton, "Activities and Role Definitions of Grassroots Party Officials," *Journal of Politics*, XXVIII (February 1966), pp. 121–43. For corollary findings of county party chairmen see also Samuel C. Patterson, "Characteristics of Party Leaders," *Western Political Quarterly*, XVI (June 1963), pp. 332–52.
3.   M. Kent Jennings and Norman Thomas, "Men and Women in Party Elites: Social Roles and Political Resources," *Midwest Journal of Political Science*, XII (November 1968), pp. 469–92.
4.   Thomas A. Flinn and Frederick M. Wirt, "Local Party Leaders: Group of Like-Minded Men," *Midwest Journal of Political Science*, IX (February 1955), pp. 77–98.
5.   David Katz and Samuel J. Eldersveld, "The Impact of Local Party Activity Upon the Electorate," *Public Opinion Quarterly* XXIV (Spring 1961), p. 7.
6.   See, for example, Angus Campbell *et al.*, *The American Voter* (New York: John Wiley and Sons, Inc., 1960); and Angus Campbell *et al.*, *Elections and the Political Order* (New York: John Wiley and Sons, Inc., 1966).
7.   Edward C. Banfield and James Q. Wilson, *City Politics* (Cambridge, Mass.: Harvard University Press and the MIT Press, 1963), p. 124.

8.   William L. Riordon, *Plunkitt of Tammany Hall* (New York: McClure, Phillips, 1905), p. 129.

9.   *The New York Times*, November 5, 1970, p. 27.

10.   Robert K. Merton, *Social Theory and Social Structure* (New York: The Free Press, 1957), pp. 72–82.

11.   See for example: James Q. Wilson, "Two Negro Politicians: An Interpretation," *Midwest Journal of Political Science*, IV (November 1960), pp. 346–69.

12.   *The Municipal Year Book*: 1967 (Chicago: The International City Manager's Association, 1967), p. 108.

13.   Banfield and Wilson, *op. cit.*, pp. 151–53.

14.   A. Clarke Hagensick, "Influence of Partisanship and Incumbency on a Nonpartisan Election System," *Western Political Quarterly*, XVII (March, 1964), pp. 117–24.

15.   Banfield and Wilson, *City Politics*, pp. 148–49.

16.   Daniel P. Moynihan and James Q. Wilson, "Patronage in New York State 1955–1959," *American Political Science Review*, LVIII (June 1964), pp. 286–301.

17.   For a summary of motivation for political activity in general, see: Stimson Bullitt, *To Be A Politician*, (New York: Doubleday and Co., Inc., 1959).

18.   J. David Greenstone, "Party Pressure on Organized Labor in Three Cities," in M. Kent Jennings and L. Harmon Zeigler, eds., *The Electoral Process* (Englewood Cliffs, N.J.: Prentice-Hall Inc., 1966), pp. 55–79.

19.   Banfield and Wilson, *City Politics*, p. 157. See also: M. Margaret Conway, "Voter Information Sources in a Nonpartisan Local Election," *Western Political Quarterly*, XXI (March 1968), pp. 69–77.

20.   Angus Campbell, *et al.*, *Elections and the Political Order*, pp. 134–36.

21.   Philips Cutright, "Activities of Precinct Committeemen in Partisan and Nonpartisan Communities," *Western Political Quarterly*, XVII (March 1964), pp. 93–108.

22.   David Boesel, *et al.*, "White Institutions and Black Rage," *Trans-action*, VI (March 1969), p. 29.

23.   Cutright, "Activities of Precinct Committeemen," p. 100.

24.   Interviews, November, 1969.

25.   For a full discussion on non-professional politicians, see: James Q. Wilson, *The Amateur Democrat*, (Chicago: University of Chicago Press, 1962).

26.   Robert C. Wood, *Suburbia* (Boston: Houghton Mifflin Company, 1958), p. 167.

27.   Interviews, October–December, 1969.

28.   Interview, November 13, 1969.

29.   Interview, October 21, 1969.

30.   Interview, October 19, 1969.

31.   Interview, January 27, 1970.

32.   See, for example, Donald Gerwin, "Towards a Theory of Public Budgetary Decision Making," *Administrative Science Quarterly*, XIV (March 1969), pp. 33–45.

33.   John C. Wahlke, *et al.*, *The Legislative System* (New York: John Wiley and Sons, Inc., 1962), pp. 276–77.

34.   Earl Latham, *The Group Basis of Politics* (Ithica: Cornell University Press, 1952), p. 35.

Chapter VI

Political Recruitment

Adherence to the democratic creed leads to expectations of good citizenship that cannot be realized. It is expected that each citizen will be vitally interested in all public issues and candidates. He will be informed so that his choices are made rationally. He will view issues dispassionately and consider community rather than personal interests. He will be on the alert for corruption or malfeasance in public office. However, the average citizen is not so engaged. Moreover, while he is expected to be willing to answer a call for public service, whether it be serving as a juror, a dog catcher, or a governor, he is not. Thus, there is a need to search and find citizens who can and will deal with the problems confronting the political community. The search for finding these actors in the political system is the function of political recruitment.

Living in the twentieth-century United States requires one to recognize that everyone cannot do everything. To survive, each individual has to distinguish between what he must know and what he need not know, what he can do and what others can do for him. Politics is but one aspect of life. Large numbers of people cannot act organically to deal with the problems confronting the political community. Competent leadership is needed. This means obtaining individuals who can devote their time to becoming fully knowledgeable on public matters, who can refer questions to the electorate, and who can define alternative courses of action. The electorate cannot be expected to find the time nor to possess the interest that demands full-time attention to public matters. Just as a person shops for the best pair of shoes,

162

he must shop for the best leaders. If he is dissatisfied with the results, he can "buy" elsewhere.

The political roles that must be performed in the political system are fulfilled by a variety of actors. There are those who articulate, or aggregate needs and demands, and those who are involved in translating needs and demands into policies and programs through rule making, rule executive, and rule adjudication.

The major significance of the recruitment process is that the political system meets the needs and demands of the people in relation to the quality of those who are the actors. As James David Barber said of those who are elected:

> Perhaps the survival of American democracy does not depend on recruiting the very best talents to government. But excellence in American government— the rationality of its decisions, the quality of justice it dispenses, the timeliness of its actions—these things depend profoundly on the character of those we elect.[1]

Unable to understand the extent of their problems or to meet their own needs and interests, the people entrust the affairs of government to their representatives. The awesome transference of such a trust would logically imply that the people convey deep confidence and respect to their representatives.

Citizen Attitudes toward Public Office

The respect accorded public official positions has been demonstrated by two nationwide surveys, the first conducted in March 1947[2] and the second in June 1963.[3] In both of those studies people were asked to judge a number of occupations so that jobs could be ranked according to prestige. There were ninety choices offered to the sample, and the resultant distribution of prestige rating ranged from "United States Supreme Court Justice" (ranked first) to "shoe shiner" (ranked ninetieth). Regrettably, the list only included a few select public positions, yet the study is indicative of their high esteem. The ranking of the specific public official occupations, as extracted from the two lists of those ratings, is to be found in Table VI.1.

Offsetting these high levels of prestige accorded public offices is the basic attitude of distrust toward politics, which seems to prevail among much of the population. On three occasions people across the nation have been asked if they would like to see their son pursue a career in politics. Their generally negative responses are seen in Table VI.2.

TABLE VI.1

Prestige Ratings of Public Official Occupations, 1947 and 1963

Occupation	1947 Ranking†	1963 Ranking‡
U.S. Supreme Court Justice	1	1
State Governor	2*	5*
Cabinet member in Federal Government . .	4*	8*
Mayor of large city	6	17*
U.S. Representative in Congress	7*	8*
County Judge	12*	14*
Head of a department in a State Government.	12*	21*

* Tie ranking with another occupation.

Source: † National Opinion Research Center, *op. cit.*, p. 6.
‡ Hodges, *op. cit.*, p. 290.

TABLE VI.2

"If you had a son, would you like to see him go into politics as a life's work?"

	1965	1955	1945
Yes	36%	27%	21%
No	54	60	68
No opinion	10	13	11

Source: *Polls* I (Summer 1965), p. 75.

In addition, as Barber has noted:

> The very groups which tend to be most active in voting and voluntary group participation—the high-income, college-educated, professional and managerial categories—are those least likely to see politics as a desirable occupation for their sons.[4]

When elected local government officials were asked a similar question, "If you had a son just getting out of school would you like to see him go into politics as a life work?" 68 percent said "no."[5]

Of the reasons offered by those who replied "no" in the nationwide survey on attitudes towards entering politics as a career (in Table 2), 40 percent expressed the belief that there is too much corruption in politics.[6]

The general attitude that politics is a "dirty game" is also a widespread notion held by the people. Barber has written that:

> There is in the public mind a dirty side to political candidacy, getting on the public payroll, taking part in political deals. . . . Every candidate probably has to explain to those who know him why he is getting mixed up in politics.[7]

It should not be assumed too quickly that this cynical attitude is held by the public because it is not knowledgeable about the political arena and, therefore, suspect about politics. Party precinct leaders, intimately involved with political activity, seem to hold the same deprecatory viewpoints. Samuel J. Eldersveld noted that over 80 percent of precinct leaders in Detroit admitted that politics is "dirty," and that over 90 percent were aware of irregularities and questionable campaign practices.[8]

Agents Performing the Function of Political Recruitment

Despite the existence of such negative attitudes, the political system must operate and that operation requires a vast number of public agents. The recruitment of these agents is a continual process that functions to obtain the necessary public actors who make, execute, and adjudicate rules.

Party Leaders

There are several groups that participate in the recruitment of public actors. One group closely involved is the leadership of a political party. Which leaders influence recruitment would depend on the public office to be filled and the size of the election district. In St. Louis, for example, the city council is comprised of twenty-eight members who are elected from wards. These local legislators are often selected as candidates for election by the party committeemen who control the ward organization. The party's city committeemen are generally influential in recruiting candidates to run for at-large city office, such as the council's presiding official.[9]

The chairman of the county committee has singular importance in the recruitment of local and state officials. The late William J. Green, Jr., Chairman of the Democratic City–County Committee in Philadelphia, for example, had great influence in selecting candidates for both Philadelphia and the state. A similar situation existed in Illinois, where influence has been exerted by Richard Daley, Chairman of Chicago's Cook County Democratic Organization.

A study of county party leaders in Oklahoma graphically presented the role that county leaders play in state legislative nominations.[10] County leaders were asked how they perceived their role in the selection of party candidates for the Oklahoma state legislature. The responses are seen in Table VI.3.

TABLE VI.3

Participation of Oklahoma County Party Leaders in Legislative Nominations

Nature of Participation	Democratic				Republican			
	Chairmen		Co-Chairmen		Chairmen		Vice-Chairmen	
	Number	Percent	Number	Percent	Number	Percent	Number	Percent
Actively seek well-qualified candidates	17	22.1	16	16.8	29	34.5	19	28.8
Persuade well-qualified individuals to run . . .	11	14.3	16	16.8	12	14.3	9	13.6
Encourage well-qualified individuals to run . .	31	40.3	34	35.8	31	36.9	19	28.8
Try to persuade individuals not to enter the primary against a well-qualified candidate already in the race	7	9.0	15	15.8	5	6.0	4	6.1
No part at all; individual candidates just come forward on their own to run in the primary . . .	10	13.0	13	13.7	3	3.6	11	16.7
No response	1	1.3	1	1.1	4	4.8	4	6.1
Total responses* . .	77	100.0	95	100.0	84	100.1	66	100.1

* The total number of responses equals more than the sample size for each column because some individuals selected more than one type of participation, even though the questionnaire specified that the respondent select the *most important* type of participation.

Source: Patterson, *op. cit.*, p. 348.

The role of the state committee chairman as an actor at the top of a state political organization may be seen in the illustration of John Bailey of Connecticut. Joseph P. Lyford, describing him as a "boss," noted that Bailey's decisions "Can kill candidates or nominate them. Judges are appointed or disappointed as he sees fit."[11]

Party leaders may find that their recruiting activity is simplified if an incumbent wishes to run again. Here is a candidate who has already demonstrated his vote-getting power, who has experience in public office and in campaigning, and who has already developed some support within the constituency. For these same reasons, when the incumbent decides not to seek reelection, his counsel would be an important factor in the selection of his successor.

Fund raisers within a party organization may also exert influence in the selection process. Mainly concerned with party success, they are interested in obtaining candidates who are attractive to major financial contributors. The fund raiser's position is such that he will be able to ascertain who would be attractive to the large contributors.[12]

The extent to which the party organization dominates the recruitment function is related to the degree of party competitiveness and party organizational strength or weakness. A study of party influence in sponsoring the careers of legislators in four states illustrates the point.[13] As seen in Table VI.4, the state legislators in New Jersey—where a high level of party competitiveness exists—recognize the importance of party sponsorship. In Tennessee—with a low level of party competitiveness—the party's role in legislative recruitment was not considered an important factor.

TABLE VI.4

New Jersey		Ohio		California		Tennessee	
Dem.	Rep.	Dem.	Rep.	Dem.	Rep.	Dem.	Rep.
74%	66%	12%	24%	42%	22%	15%	28%
(N = 27)	44	49	108	48	55	68	18

Adapted from: Wahlke *et al.*, *op. cit.*, p. 98.

Responses from Ohio and California legislators indicate that party support is also related to how well organizationed a party may be. Though the Democratic and Republican parties actively compete in each state, they are not equally well organized. The Republicans are organizationally strong in Ohio, yet not in California. References of the Republican legislators to their party's importance reflects this situation.

Friends and Associates

Political party personnel were not perceived as the only initial sponsor for legislative careers. Some legislators named either interest groups, or friends and associates; still others claimed that they had initiated their own efforts. Table VI.5 shows the extent to which each of these was considered to be the source of sponsorship.

In non-competitive party situations, friends and associates appear to be instrumental in influencing individuals to seek office. The high proportion of legislators in Tennessee claiming associates as sponsors may be a reflection of the one party dominant situation, wherein factions compete in the political struggles. In such a situation, when each faction attempts to recruit attractive candidates, the search may begin within its group of associates.

TABLE VI.5

Proportion of Legislators Perceiving Their Careers as Interest Group, Friends/Associates and Self Sponsored

	New Jersey	Ohio	California	Tennessee
Interest groups . . .	1%	2%	9%	16%
Friends/Associates . .	8	19	24	54
Self-started	31	55	33	23

Source: Wahlke, *et al., op. cit.*, p. 100.

The same relationship may be found in small, homogeneous districts or towns. Barber recognized that in these areas "the narrowness of social contacts, their continuity in time and the extensive overlapping of social roles" have special importance to nominations.[14] Hence, the townsmen may tend to gravitate towards their most illustrative neighbor as the best person to represent them in public office. Indeed, some individuals may have become candidates due to the importuning of some few close friends. As one California legislator has remarked:

> I attribute (my decision to run) to about four close friends—a member of the legislature, a member of the county central committee, the county super-intendent of schools, and the secretary of the election board. They said to me, "Hell, why don't you throw in your hat?" So I got my petition and away I went.[15]

Interest Groups

Relatively few legislators perceived their careers to have been sponsored by interest groups. While an interest group, on occasion, may choose to independently promote a member for public office in the hope of obtaining a "built-in lobbyist," they usually tend to focus their efforts within a party framework in a competitive situation to support the party's choices. In a non-competitive party situation, the interest group may identify with a faction or become itself an independent faction.

However, interest groups may be important in recruiting candidates in non-partisan local arenas. Edward C. Banfield notes, "It is the firms that are tied to the city—department stores, banks, utilities, office buildings, and newspapers that are most concerned with local affairs, and together they exercise a great deal of influence . . . [for] every candidate needs business friends."[16] He found that business groups were especially influential in such non-partisan cities as Atlanta, Detroit, El Paso, Los Angeles, and Seattle.

Self-Recruitment

The careers of some candidates are self-sponsored. Persons enter the arena like entrepreneurs, anxious to get ahead by their own efforts. Self-recruitment can occur in each of the many different political or community situations. In non-partisan situations, the candidates may be forced to initiate their own efforts and ultimately be responsible for the formation of a group to assist them in campaigning.

Individuals may be self-recruiters in partisan systems for several reasons. The chance of success in the dominant party and in competitive party situations may be sufficient to encourage those who entertain political aspirations to come forth. Though the chance of success is poor or non-existent for the candidate running under the banner of a minority party, there still are those who will step forward to place their name on the ticket. They do so because they are staunch party affiliates and desire to see their party sustain itself by entering a slate on the ballot; or because they are staunch supporters of the two-party system and feel that a second party should not disappear through the lack or momentary absence of alternatives.

Weak party organizations may provide an open field for self contenders. This may, first, be due to the absence of centers of organizational power, and there is no organized recruitment efforts. Secondly, some may see this as an opportunity to use their candidacy as a means to take over the party apparatus.

Self-recruitment may also be a result of community related factors. Rapidly expanding populations have upset the traditional party alignments and the nominating systems in many areas. The old "friends and neighbors politics" cannot rapidly absorb the influx of newly arrived ambitious individuals who aspire for public office. Thus, potential candidates present themselves, uninvited, for consideration. In addition, candidates may appear independently in suburban areas, for example, where the growing new electorates are interested in issue oriented politics, and are dissatisfied with the traditional style of politics.

The facility with which persons may have their names placed on the ballot encourages self-recruitment. In El Paso, Texas, candidacies for municipal elections are open to anyone willing to spend the $100 filing fee. To be a candidate for mayor in Los Angeles, an aspirant must only obtain 500 signatures and deposit a $500 bond. In Philadelphia, it takes merely the action of 100 party affiliates signing a petition.

The underlying reason for the decision to self-initiate one's career, indeed, may be that which was expressed by one typical self-recruiter:

If I had waited for the joyful sight of a party deputation urging me to make my contribution to statemanship, I would still be waiting today.[17]

The discussion up to this point has focused on the agents of recruitment for elected public officials. Other public actors in the political system are obtained through the process of appointment. It would appear that recruitment for these positions would be the sole responsibility of the public officials empowered to appoint. Yet, they are influenced or aided by other participants in the system anxious to sponsor potential personnel. These others include members of a party hierarchy, interest groups and civic associations, incumbents, and the seekers of personal positions.

Recruitment of Inflos

The political actors who are recruited can be categorized into three groups —the inflos, bureaus, and centros. How the individuals will be selected to play these roles depends on the different factors and criteria important to each.

Inflos are those who are principally engaged in the articulation or the aggregation of needs and demands. They are primarily the representatives of the permanent interest groups (the lobbyists) and the members of the political party organizational hierarchy (the party leaders).

The Lobbyists

For lobbyists, the recruiter and recruited relationship resembles that of an employer–employee relationship. In effect, lobbyists are the employees of interest groups. Interest group officials, who are responsible for directing the operations of the affairs of their organization, hire those generally to be found within their own sphere of contacts.

Potential lobbyists may be found among the lawyers retained by the association. Some advantages of engaging the services of lawyers are their flexible schedules and their familiarization with legal terminology and with the rule making, rule execution, and rule adjudication processes. The legal profession provides approximately 10 to 20 percent of the lobbyists. For example, 21 percent of the lobbyists in Massachusetts are lawyers, 19 percent in Oregon, 10 percent in Utah,[18] and 10 percent in Oklahoma.[19]

Another group associations may employ as lobbyists is the public relations experts. Public relations men are knowledgeable in promoting the aims and goals of the interest groups. They are also expert in using the tools of educating the public and influencing its opinion.

Persons having previous governmental experience are often familiar to officials of interest groups and attractive candidates for lobbying positions. Former legislators are especially in demand, for in hiring them, an organization can take advantage of a certain amount of built-in access to the legislature. Such individuals are already friendly with incumbents, are looked upon as "members of the club," and have the privileges of going on the floor during a session or into committee meetings that (in executive sessions) may be closed to the public. The extent to which these men are recruited may be seen in the numbers of former-legislator-lobbyists. Harmon Zeigler found approximately 5 percent of lobbyists in Oregon, Utah, and Massachusetts had been state legislators, and about 11 percent in North Carolina.[20] Samuel C. Patterson found 12 percent of lobbyists in Oklahoma had served in the legislature.[21]

On the other hand, quite a few lobbyists have had some form of background in the executive branch. The proportion of these men were found to be about 27 percent in Massachusetts, 50 percent in North Carolina, 34 percent in Oregon, 46 percent in Utah.[22] Former executive officials have a keen awareness of the bureaucratic maze and thus can readily pinpoint those who are involved in the day-to-day operations of policy execution. Furthermore, their former experiences in office place them in a position to be identified by the bureaucrats as colleagues.

The largest proportion of lobbyists by far, however, are recruited from the professional staff of interest associations. Figures have been offered to indicate the significant bloc of such personnel so utilized. The proportion of lobbyists holding office in the organizations they represent was discovered to be 78 percent in Utah, 62 percent in North Carolina, 59 percent in Massachusetts, 57 percent in Oregon,[23] and 44 percent in Oklahoma.[24] Quite obviously, these persons have a clear interest and personal identification with the success of their association's goals. The recruitment–employment pattern of such people can be seen by the following illustrative comment of one who was explaining how he became a lobbyist:

> I was running the public relations arm of some insurance company, and as a result of this I was hired as an assistant esecutive secretary of the insurance association. Part of the job was, I subsequently learned, saving them from spending twenty-five hundred bucks for the lawyer they had on retainer. Prior to this I had done some one-shot work in another state. If somebody had offered me a job as a lobbyist, I would have told them they were out of their skull. I just kind of fell into it.[25]

This experience is undoubtedly typical of how persons get involved as lobbyists. There is no program in educational institutions to train persons for lobbying. Unlike other professions, there is no predetermination to embark upon such a career. For one thing, state and local lobbying is not a full-time occupation. As seen in Oklahoma, for example, 82 percent of the lobbyists spent only part-time lobbying the state legislature while it was in sessions; between sessions, 98 percent of the lobbyists spent half their time or less on such activities.[26] Far more important, however, is the unfavorable image of lobbying as a profession in the eyes of the public. When lobbyists were asked how they believed the general public rated their profession on a scale from 0 (totally unfavorable) to 99 (totally favorable), they estimated that the public would rank them somewhere between 30 and 36.[27]

Thus, most persons become lobbyists as an outcome of their full-time occupation (as lawyers, public relations men, or association executives); others somehow drift into it. As one lobbyist wryly admitted:

> I don't know how I got into lobbying and I don't know how I got into trade association work. If I look back and wonder how in hell I got here, it's a mystery to me.[28]

Moreover, there is no evidence to suggest that lobbyists are motivated to be recruited in order to advance into a political office or into any more lucrative or prestigeous non-political positions. In essence, the motivation of the lobbyist is to accomplish the activities of what he considers just part of a "job."

Patterson concluded from his study of Oklahoma lobbyists that the typical practitioner is:

> Usually a middle-aged, male, well-trained and well-paid, full-time interest group staff member who resides in the capital city, and who is, at least part of his time, expected by his principals to lobby the legislature.[29]

Zeigler's findings in four other states generally support this conclusion. Thus, the articulator-inflo is atypical of the general population. The data in Table VI.6 suggests how the socio-economic status of lobbyists differ from that of the community.

TABLE VI.6

Education and Median Income of Lobbyists and General Adult Population in Selected States*

	Completed High School	Completed College	Graduate or Professional School	Median Income
Massachusetts	95% (35%)	62% (7%)	32% (6%)	$12,420 ($10,835)
North Carolina	95 (22)	73 (6)	63 (3)	18,445 (7,774)
Oregon . .	93 (35)	59 (6)	36 (5)	11,772 (9,489)
Utah . . .	95 (36)	62 (8)	41 (6)	11,384 (9,320)

* Figures in parenthesis indicate the data for the general adult population.

Source: Zeigler and Baer, *op. cit.*, pp. 41–42; population figures from: U.S. Bureau of the Census, *Census of Population: 1970.*

The Party Officials

The function of aggregating the diverse interests in the political society, as has been discussed, may be performed by political parties. Members of the party organizational hierarchy are, thus, the "aggregator–inflos."

Political parties are loosely knit confederations of precinct, ward, county, and state systems. Party organizations exist in a diversity of environments: competitive, non-competitive, partisan, and non-partisan, urban, suburban, and rural.

Within the myriad positions in the organizations are found those actors who have been recruited into their roles through several methods and have become involved because of different motives. The traditional image of persons working for political parties strictly for selfish, material gain is no longer useful to explain the motivations of most present leaders. Robert S. Hirschfield has stated that, "The political activist views his party organization primarily as an instrument for effectuating policies rather than as a source of personal gain." [30] His conclusion was drawn from interviews with committee-men in Manhattan. When the county committeemen were asked what motivated them to become party activists, most answered that their desire was to contribute to the well-being of the community; others gave social reasons, such as they enjoyed dealing with people; while only a few admitted they did it for prestige or to make job and business contacts.

Most of the local precinct chairmen in North Carolina communities and ward officials in Massachusetts communities who were interviewed, also appeared to subordinate personal gains for the goals and success of their party. Some stated that they were motivated by a desire for social relation-ships; a few had sought material rewards, such as contracts or opportunities to further their political ambitions. [31]

Perhaps it would seem that few officials claim to be motivated by the pur-suit of any selfish gain because most are not willing to admit it. Yet, the studies have shown that the responses are fairly truthful. For the ranking of material gains as a motivation does vary to the extent that such incentives are available. For example, the Liberal party committeemen in New York can honestly deny any personal motives for there are few benefits that can come to them as members of a minor party. They can sincerely consider themselves as wedded to ideas and ideals of social progress and be ideo-logically and issue oriented. Yet, in Washington County (Illinois), where the party control over the political process is virtually complete, and where precinct work is a stepping stone to elective office, precinct committeemen readily admitted that their occupancy of their party position was motivated by the possibility of acquiring a public office. And here, in contrast with those in other communities, a desire to help their party or their party's candidates was mentioned by only a few officials. [32]

An examination of how leaders became initially recruited into party office further reveals the lack of selfish gains as their underlying motivation. Overwhelmingly, local party leaders are recruited through the urgings of others. Those who hold party office are the most influential in persuading individuals to become precinct committeemen. Between 50 and 70 percent of the local party officials in the North Carolina and Massachusetts communities stated that they had been recruited into their position by other party officials.[33] Generally the recruiters are the party county leaders. On occasion, positions of leadership are extended by them to individuals in reward for or recognition of service, in addition to ability. Public office holders also act as recruiters to staff party positions, out of concern for the party organization or for personal motives of maintaining their own strength and influence over the party. In Washington County (Illinois), 80 percent of the committeemen reported that party leaders or public officials had been responsible for their seeking office.[34] By far the most common method of filling the state party chairmanship is nomination by the state chief executive.

Party members may also be prevailed upon by other groups to enter positions of leadership. An average of 11 percent of those in North Carolina and Massachusetts reported interest groups, such as unions or businesses, came to them; and a similar percentage of those in the Illinois County reported that family members, personal friends, and associates stimulated their involvement as party office holders. Others credit their own efforts for their success in obtaining leadership status. In Washington County fewer than 10 percent said they were "self-starters," while the average in the eastern communities was 29 percent.[35]

Gerald Pomper's study of county committee chairmen in New Jersey indicates that the process of recruitment is best described as "a game of musical chairs, as party leaders move from one job to another as the political situation allows or requires."[36] Nearly all the county chairmen studied held simultaneously an elective or appointive public office; and most had secured their public positions prior to their chairmanship. Thus, the necessity of filling vacancies in the organizational hierarchy may lead partisan public officials into undertaking the responsibilities because of some sense of obligation to the organization.

The premise that party leaders are primarily motivated by the desire to assist their party or their community becomes more credible as it is recognized that many of these people "are of high social status, are highly educated, and come from highly politicized backgrounds."[37] Studies have shown that these characteristics are applicable for the leadership at all party levels, and in rural and urban settings. In Ohio, over one-half the county chairmen have an average income over $7,500 per year; in Manhattan, over one-half the precinct committeemen report more than $10,000 per year; and in New

Jersey, more than one-third the county chairmen have incomes over $15,000 per year. Well over one-half of these party officials, like the county chairman in North Carolina, earn their income as professionals (primarily lawyers), business executives, or owners of small businesses. Furthermore, more than one-half of the county chairmen in Ohio, more than two-thirds of the precinct committeemen in Massachusetts communities and in Manhattan, and over three-fourths of the committeemen in North Carolina communities had attended college or had gone beyond the college degree in their education.[38]

Though party officials do not enjoy as high a socio-economic status as the lobbyists discussed above, they also are drawn from higher social and more active political backgrounds than the average population found within their communities. And, as William J. Crotty concluded, they reflect the "group characteristics of the most politically articulate elements in the community."[39]

Recruitment of Service Personnel

The number of public employees found within the state and local political systems has nearly reached the nine million mark. Of these, one-fourth are employed on the state level and the remainder are employed by the local governments.[40]

The largest proportion of these public servants (over one-half) are engaged in the education systems within the state. Local school districts employ 80 percent of these people, primarily to teach in elementary and secondary schools. State employment in education is concerned chiefly with institutions of high learning.

The second largest proportion (over 860,000 persons) is found in the area of public health. This category includes doctors, nurses, medical laboratory technicians, and attendants, and others who work in hospitals, clinics, and sanitarium that are public facilities. The third highest category (over 590,000) is comprised of those working on the construction, maintenance, and planning of highways and roads, bridges, and tunnels. These include civil engineers as well as toll bridge collectors. The protective services of the state and local governments (primarily the latter) utilize over 400,000 policemen and 250,000 firemen.

Of all the remaining personnel, over one-half million are occupied in activities of financial and general administration. These would include the executive, legislative, and judicial staffs, tax enforcement officials, lawyers, property assessors, stenographers, and clerks.

Indeed, public servants range from professionals to unskilled workers. An occupational manual might add to the above listings such non-governmental appearing occupations as carpenters, janitors, painters, electricians, pipe fitters, and bus drivers, in addition to those readily recognized as public personnel, such as forest rangers, librarians, recreation workers, sanitation and sewage employees, welfare, and social workers.

Merit Service

The recruitment of these public servants is undertaken through various merit service procedures or patronage. Requirements of employment through merit service vary with states and localities. In general, they encompass such processes as the evaluation and testing of knowledge, training, and experience.

The standards are often set outside the merit systems and accepted without modification. Governments accept the qualifications set by professional licensing boards in such fields as law, medicine, architecture, and engineering. The holding of a professional license by an applicant will be sufficient evidence of his competence without further testing to determine his knowledge and skill when he seeks employment or advancement.

In addition, the greatest impact on the establishment of merit standards is that made by the universities. By their curricula, their faculties, and their teaching, the schools define the content of each different specialization. The possession of a degree from an accredited institution or program (itself an accumulation of acceptable standards set by committees within academia) is also evidence of achievements of merit having been met. The extent, therefore, that public personnel employees enter into a selection process is in their evaluation of the applicant's grade point averages and recommendations from professors—academic, rather than public, determinants.

Patronage

Categories of merit or patronage recruitment are not mutually exclusive; indeed, labels may be misleading. The opprobrium attached to patronage is not generally deserved. The growing complexities of governmental operations require an increased reliance on skills. Thus, though jobs may be dispensed through partisan activities, standards and criteria do exist for the selection of personnel. On the other hand, placement into merit positions may remain within the spectrum of partisan activities. Certain "merit" jobs may be reserved as currency for the parties, or job seekers may be guided or assisted into openings by partisan contacts.

Furthermore, political parties are hampered in their free use of patronage as rewards by several factors. For one reason, the need for greater specialization and skills within the public service limits the potential reservoir of talent from which the party can choose. This may lead them to encourage those already in the positions to remain, even if the job holders maintain a "wrong party" affiliation. For another, the political systems also require laborers and unskilled workers to keep public service programs operating. Filling these positions may not be an easy task, for they frequently are low paying, unattractive, and physically demanding. Party officials will once again seek to retain those willing to remain and to recruit those willing to work, overlooking not only party affiliations but also the fact that such persons generally are not among the politically active. Thus, within the patronage system there is a partial merit system that flourishes with the party acting as an ad hoc civil service agency. Where patronage positions exist, they are principally dispensed by the county chairmen, or at least formally cleared through the county committee chairman's office. As patronage can be useful in maintaining party organization, county chairmen would share the recruiting function with local party officials. Realistically, however, it does not matter who makes the patronage appointments or who has the power to fill vacancies, as long as a job recipient believes that the party was instrumental in securing his position.

Recruitment of Bureaus

Also to be recruited, are those public servants who are top-level executives, administrators, advisors, and technicians in those agencies which play a decisive role in the activities of the states and localities. These are the "bureaus."

State Bureaus

The bureaus are recruited through the elective, appointive, or merit processes. Major top-level executives in the state and their method of recruitment are seen in Table VI.7.

TABLE VI.7

Methods of Recruitment of Selected State Bureaus

Office	Elected	Appointed by Governor*	Other†
Secretary of State‡	78%	14%	6%
Attorney General	84	12	4
Treasurer‡	80	6	10
Auditor‡.	54	2	28
Controller‡	22	20	16

* Includes approval by one or both houses of the state legislature, or some other board.
† Includes election by the legislature, or appointment by a state court justice, commission, special boards, etc.
‡ Office does not exist in all states.

Adapted from: *The Book of The States: 1970–1971* (Chicago: The council of State Governments, 1970), pp. 148–49.

Administrators who head departments and divisions of the fifty state governments are generally appointed. A survey has found that 46 percent had been appointed by the governors, 49 percent by a board of commissioners (generally with gubernatorial approval), and the remainder by various other agencies (*e.g.*, the courts).[41] These bureaus are presented for appointment by a variety of recruiters. Lists of names may be provided by party officials, legislators, administrative staff personnel, special interest groups, citizens groups, or occupations licensing boards. There may be certain legal qualifications that limit the alternative choices available. For example, by law, two members of the Texas Commission for the Blind must themselves be blind—and until the late 1950s, had also to be graduates of the Texas School for the Blind. In addition, talent and skills are considered in the making of such appointments. Indeed, the governor's reputation and the success of his programs may rest on the actions of these personnel. Moreover, the appointees who head staffs of professionals must be sufficiently capable to command the respect and cooperation of their subordinates.

Local Bureaus

The ranks of chief administrators on the local level are growing. They include city or county managers and city or county chief administrative officers. Such officers are to be found in over 2,100 cities with a council–manager plan, in more than 400 cities using a mayor–council–chief administrator plan; and in over fifty counties with county board and manager or chief administrative officer plans.[42]

Their recruitment and employment are the responsibilities of the city or county councils. The councilmen may act to select a candidate themselves; or they may delegate the initial screening process to a committee of councilmen, to a joint council–citizen (usually businessmen) committee, or, on occasion, to a management consulting firm. Mayors, responsible for filling chief administrator positions, may call on citizen groups or their own advisors to assist them. These bureaus are, in effect, professional employees of the locality, and outside of the politics and election processes within the local systems.

Though qualifications may vary, one basic criterion generally recognized is college training, with some concentration (or a graduate degree) in public administration and management. The International City Managers' Association counsels localities to look for individuals with "management ability and leadership qualifications," and such personal traits as honesty, force, tact, industry, vision, humor, and loyalty.

Other high-ranking personnel—assistant department heads, deputy directors, functional specialists, and managers—are recruited and appointed by such agents, mayors, managers, councils, judges, individual department heads, or merit service commissions. Though the criteria vary by necessity of function, the basic requirement remains constant—expertise or training in the area of the position. Several top-level local executives are elected. Table VI.8 indicates the percentage of selected municipal officers who are elected. The percentage of several county officers who are elected is indicated in Table VI.9.

TABLE VI.8

Percentage of Municipal Elective Offices other than Mayor and Council

(in cities with population over 5,000)

Treasurer	27.4
City Clerk	20.9
Assessor	9.1
Auditor	8.8
Attorney	6.9
Controller	3.1

Adapted from: *The Municipal Year Book* 1968, p. 63.

TABLE VI.9

Percentage of Independently Elected County Offices

Office	Number of States	
Sheriff	46	92%
Treasurer	40	80
Attorney	31	62
Coroner	27	54
Clerk of Court	32	64
Assessor	26	52
Surveyor or Engineer	27	54
Auditor	16	32
County Clerk	20	40

Source: *Census of Governments, 1967*, vol. 6. *Popularly Elected Officials of State and Local Governments*, pp. 80–212.

Attitudes toward Bureau Positions

The prestige accorded to and the attractiveness of public service on the state and local levels may have bearing on the type of persons filling public positions. Studies of college students (that group from which the bulk of bureaus is recruited) have demonstrated that they hold generally unfavorable attitudes toward governmental employment.[43] The interest in public work varied with the level of government considered for employment. State governments were considered slightly more attractive as potential employers, by the students, than were local governments; but neither was considered as appealing as private employment. Those young adults who wanted to be "really successful" did not perceive public service as the vehicle to achieve their goal. In addition, government work had an image of being more "routine" and "monotonous" than business work. A review of Leonard D. White's classic study of Chicago residents of 1929 (which demonstrated the relatively low image and prestige accorded to public in comparison to private employment) points out that these students of eastern urban and southern rural areas continue the tradition of unfavorable attitudes that were held by an earlier generation of the population.[44]

Despite the poor general images, persons are recruited into government work. A variety of reasons have been given by bureaus as to why they entered the public service. Table VI.10 reveals the range of responses from a national survey of municipal bureaus.[45]

TABLE VI.10

Reasons Given by "Bureaus" For Seeking Positions in Local Government

Motivations	Given as Primary Reason	Mentioned Most Frequently (Rank)
General nature of the work.	40%	1
Opportunity to help solve public problems	15	3
Only position available in your line of work	11	8
Opportunity for advancement	10	2
Job security	8	6
Salary	7	4
Important Responsibility	4	5
Good experience for entering private business.	3	10
Prestige	1	7
Political opportunities	1	13
Retirement benefits	1	9
Low pressure	*	14
Other fringe benefits (not retirement) . .	*	12
Co-workers	*	11

* Less than one per cent.

Source: Municipal Manpower Commission, *op. cit.*, p. 158.

The table makes it apparent that the public servants were motivated by other factors than material success or prestige. Prime inducements for recruitment appear to be the nature of the work and civic mindedness. Table VI.11 indicates, however, that though a person may enjoy working for the public, he would not advise his child to follow suit. Yet, 33 percent of a nationwide sample of state bureaus had fathers who had held either state or local elective or appointive governmental posts.[46] One might conclude that a father's political background is more influential than a father's advice.

TABLE VI.11

Municipal Bureaus' Employer Preference For Their Children

Private business	72%
Local Government	17
Federal Government	8
State Government	2
Trade or non-profit association	1
	100%

Source: Municipal Manpower Commission, *op. cit.*, p. 164.

An examination of the backgrounds of bureaus showed that, however qualified these men may be, they may not always reflect the characteristics of the general population. They are older (the average age of state bureaus being 52 years, the local bureaus 50 years); and they are more highly educated (64 percent of state bureaus need college degrees, and 40 percent held an advanced degree; 59 percent of local bureaus held college degrees, and 25 percent held an advanced degree). In addition, state bureaus have a high annual income (40 percent earned over $10,000, and 40 percent earned over $15,000); are almost exclusively male (99 percent); are overwhelmingly Protestant (76 percent) and white (99.5 percent); and were raised in small towns, rural areas, or farms (70 percent).[47]

Recruitment of Centros

The public officials who are in the center of the political systems, are to be labeled "centros." They are primarily responsible and accountable for making rules (*e.g.*, the state legislators, county commissioners, and municipal councilmen), executing rules (*e.g.*, the governors, the county executives, and the mayors), and adjudicating rules (*e.g.*, the judges).

Formal procedures for the recruitment of the centros are prescribed by state constitutions, local charters, or statutory enactments. While procedures vary in the fifty states and in the thousands of localities, they all fall within the general categories of primaries (partisan or non-partisan), conventions, or a combination of both. Of course, in most states one can initiate his own nomination by filing a petition for candidacy.

Nominating Conventions

As nominating devices, conventions have declined in importance in the twentieth century. Only two states (Delaware and Indiana) make exclusive use of the convention method to nominate candidates for state-wide office. In several cities, there still remains a caucus arrangement for nominating local candidates. In some southern states, such as Alabama, South Carolina, and Georgia, state election laws permit the political parties to choose the convention method as one alternative in the selection process. In these states, the Republican parties, because of their minority status, have chosen to do so. Third party candidates are usually chosen by conventions also.

Several other states utilize a variety of methods for nomination that combine conventions and primaries. In nine states the candidates for some state-wide offices are nominated in conventions while those for others are nominated in primaries. By election laws in some states, political parties are permitted to utilize the convention system to complement or supplement the primary. In Colorado, for example, parties hold pre-primary conventions to select the candidates whose names will appear on the primary ballot. In Connecticut, a primary election would be held only if an unsuccessful candidate at the convention (who has received at least 20 percent of the convention vote) contests the party's choice. In contrast, a convention would be held in Iowa and South Dakota if any candidate failed to receive at least 35 percent of the votes cast in a primary.

Primaries

The most widely used form of nomination is the direct primary, by which segments of the voting public have the opportunity to participate in the selection of contenders for public office. Primaries take several forms. Partisan primaries are mechanisms for selecting party labeled candidates. In most states primaries are "closed," that is, only registered party affiliates may participate. A registered Democrat, for example, would be eligible to choose only from a list of candidates seeking office under the Democratic banner; he could not make a choice for Republican candidates unless he changed his party registration prior to the primary.

An "open primary" is found in five states (Michigan, Montana, North Dakota, Utah, and Wisconsin). Unlike the closed primary, an individual need only be registered to vote in order to participate in the nomination process. Here he may choose whichever party's ballot he prefers without disclosing his party affiliation. Thus, the Democratic affiliate may request either a Republican or a Democratic primary list of candidates.

In three states (Alaska, Minnesota, and Washington) the open primary has been altered to expand the range of choices open to the voter. In this system, any registered voter appearing at the polls receives the ballots of each party. He may then vote for one person for each office, crossing back and forth between the party lists as he desires. Thus, the Democratic affiliate may select an individual for the office of governor from the Democratic nominees, and the attorney general from among the Republican nominees. In effect, this system differs from the open primary in that the voter is not restricted to only one party's selectees. This system is called the "wide-open" or "blanket" primary.

A quick review of the primary systems indicates that the "independent" voter (a person who refuses to register as a party affiliate) can participate in the nomination process in the open or wide-open primaries. He would be excluded from participating in the closed primary.

Another type of primary is the "non-partisan primary" in which the candidates seeking nomination for office have no party designation identified with them. Such a procedure is employed to nominate candidates for some local, special district, and judicial posts. Minnesota and Nebraska, in addition, hold such primaries to select candidates for the state legislature.

Several states and localities require a candidate to receive a majority of votes cast in the primary in order to be placed on the general election ballot. Should no candidate receive a clear majority, then a "run-off," or a second primary, may be required in which the top two candidates compete.

Nomination Panels

Judges generally are recruited through each of the above nominating processes. However, in several states a new procedure for their recruitment has been introduced. A select nominating panel is established by constitutional prescription to present or confirm alternative candidates in an attempt to obtain qualified and objective individuals. In the "Missouri Plan," used for selecting members of the Missouri supreme court and other major courts in Jackson County and St. Louis, a special non-partisan commission composed of seven members (the chief justice of the Supreme Court, three laymen appointed by the governor, and three attorneys selected by the bar association) offer three choices to the governor.

Similar plans are utilized in Alaska (for justices of the appellate courts); in Iowa (for the justices of the appellate and district courts); in Kansas (for the supreme court only); and in Nebraska (for the justices of the appellate and district courts, and some municipal and juvenile courts). The governor then selects a judicial candidate from the choices presented to him. A variation exists in California, where the governor's appointments for the supreme and district courts of appeals, are submitted for approval to a panel that includes the chief justice, a presiding justice of the district court of appeals, and the attorney general.

Thereafter, in each of these plans, the candidates stand for an election on a non-partisan ballot without any other name in opposition for a full term. Should they not receive a majority of affirmative votes, or should they (at the completion of a term) choose not to stand for reelection, the procedure starts anew.

Formal Qualifications

Potential centros must meet formal minimal qualifications prior to any consideration for their recruitment. These are also (but not universally) prescribed in the constitutions, charters, or state statutory enactments. In general, any person who is qualified by law to vote in terms of age, residence, and citizenship is also qualified to be a candidate for state and local office.

It is not unusual to find, however, additional qualifications specified for various positions. Residency requirements, for example, may vary. Gubernatorial candidates may have to meet a state residency requirement ranging from one year (as in Minnesota) to ten years (as in Missouri); legislative candidates may face a minimum period up to seven years in an assembly district or council ward; and the residency of judicial candidates may range from one to ten years.

The minimum age may also vary among the states from twenty-one to thirty-five years for state executives and judges, or twenty-one to twenty-five for state legislators. Furthermore, many states require that judges be "learned in the law," while others insist on prior legal experience.

Beyond the qualifications already described, several states have placed further formal limitations. South Carolina declares a person ineligible for the position of governor "who denies the existence of a Supreme Being." Clergymen are constitutionally ineligible for the legislature in Tennessee and Maryland. Yet, the most important consideration is the limitation of terms for the office of governor or mayor. Delaware and Missouri, for example, forbid anyone who has held the office of governor for two terms from ever being considered again, and in Philadelphia, an individual who was mayor for two terms cannot be recruited for a third.

The Office To Be Filled

It would be superficial to concentrate only on the formal qualifications or procedures for selecting potential candidates. The recruitment of centros is best understood through a study of informal considerations that are influential. These considerations are the office to be filled, the potentialities for obtaining the centros, and the agents of recruitment.

Of all the offices to be filled, the executive centro positions in state and local systems are the most attractive. As seen above, in Table VI.1, the office of state governors has been ranked as the fifth most prestigious occupation, and the office of mayor of a large city has been ranked seventeenth. The benefits of executive positions are attractive to potential candidates. Materially, the positions carry a more than adequate salary, perhaps the use of a mansion as an official residence, a limousine with a chauffeur, funds for travel and entertainment, and staff assistance. The office has potential political attractiveness in that it is the position on which the constituents can most readily focus, are the most knowledgeable about, and can most readily identify with—or simply identify. Moreover, the executive centro has, generally, the greatest access to the communication media, to the party organization, to civic and interest groups and associations, and to the officials at the national level of government. In addition, the singularity of the office enhances its attractiveness; for there is only one governor per state, one county executive (if any) per county, and one mayor per city.

For many, a position as a judicial centro is also attractive. Justices, too, are held in high esteem by the public. Though the number of judgeships available is greater than that of governors or mayors, the positions are relatively few. The desirability of this office can be seen in the following remarks made by (first) a public official and (second) a journalist:

> For good reasons all New York lawyers want to become judges. There is no question that the zenith of a legal and political career is a judgeship. . . . The plum of New York Democratic politics is the prestige, compensation and security of a New York judgeship. . . .
> There must be at least 3 or 4,000 Brooklyn politicos, who would give their right arms to don the black robes and the tag "judge." To these panting politicos, the bench is nothing short of heaven on earth.[48]

Numerically, the legislative centros comprise the largest proportion of elected public positions. They are found in the state capitals, county seats, and city or town halls. The number, as such, does not necessarily detract from the prestige of legislative office. However, the prestige as an attractive feature has not been sufficient to compensate for the various disadvantages accompanying such office.

Legislators are confronted by a host of adverse conditions. They do not meet often enough nor long enough. They are faced with an array of existing law, and thousands of new proposals. They are expected to know about the personnel and programs of myriad governmental agencies as well as public needs and demands. They have little technical, professional, and clerical staff assistance, and they suffer from a shortage of space and facilities at their disposal. They are overworked.

Local councilmen are restricted and hampered by state legislative primacy in most areas, and the state legislators by a lack of funds or outdated constitutional provisions. Legislators are overshadowed by an executive authority. They are buffeted by criticisms and attacks, regardless of their alternative strategies; they are dubbed "rubber stamp lackies" if they follow executive proposals, yet are called "obstructionists" if they attempt independent action. Their political achievements are shared by the group while their failure to satisfy needs and demands are individually shouldered. They are faced with a public always suspicious and cynical, quick to accuse them of a lengthy list of improprieties of office. And for this, they are generally poorly paid and incur substantial personal expense.

Local legislative positions may be more attractive than state legislative positions. The state legislator must set aside his regular employment for a period of time every year or two, disrupting his normal routine. He incurs a dual living expense, one in the capital, the other in his home city. The local legislator may find that the part-time legislative work can supplement rather than impede his regular life scheme. He lives and works in his usual surroundings, and has the potential advantage of maintaining his private contacts as he performs his public function within his constituency.

Political and Social Environment

The nature of the position to be filled may affect the quantity and quality of potential candidates, but there are other influential factors important to the recruitment function. One factor is the make-up of the constituencies represented by the elected officer. Candidates run for offices that are filled by at-large or district-type elections. Executive centros, elected judicial centros, and some legislative centros face at-large constituencies. The main challenge in the recruitment for at-large elections is finding individuals who will appeal to heterogeneous groupings within the area. The gubernatorial candidate encounters a state-wide electorate composed of varying degrees of diverse demographic, ecological, and economic characteristics. Each state, to varying degrees, has urban–rural, industrial–agricultural, ethnic, racial, and religious dichotomies. Thus, the recruitment function must be geared toward obtaining a candidate whose attributes would best overcome the conflicts inherent in such diversity. Perhaps the model candidate would be an individual free of political controversy, who possesses a name well known through either having distinguished himself in some public or other pursuit, or is the scion of an established and respected family. There are, however, environmental or sporadic factors that affect deviations from the model. For example, it has been seen that flamboyant demogogic candidates, who come from the bottom of the social ladder, appear most often in poverty-stricken social environments when an emotional issue is available.

Local executives, running at-large in big cities, face as complex a situation as that of governors. On the local level, the economic and demographic dichotomies become more crystallized with the proximity of these groupings to each other. Hence, it is important to find a candidate who can tread lightly among conflicting interests. The candidate must either come from one of the dominant economic groups; or from the largest ethnic, religious, or racial grouping. At the minimum, he should be from one grouping considered neutral or least offensive to the others. Edward C. Banfield has noted that people prefer a candidate of their own group, but one who has their attributes in association with the admired Anglo-Saxon model. Thus, the model candidate "is of Irish, Polish, Italian, or Jewish extraction, but has the speech, dress, and manner and also the public virtues (honesty, impartiality, devotion to the public good) that belong in the public mind to the upper-class Anglo-Saxon." [49] Thus, with the exception of current examples of the infrequent machine-run cities (*e.g.*, Daley in Chicago), the modern typical candidate is of the "blue-ribbon" type who strives for the "good government" appeal of the middle- and upper-class professionals (*e.g.*, Lindsey of New York). In addition, the voting participation rates of each population grouping is considered the recruitment of a mayorality candidate. If "votes = success," then it is those groups that turn out for local elections that are of major concern to the recruiters. For example, despite the large proportion of blacks in major cities, with singular exceptions the predominant mayorality candidate is not black.

In the homogeneous environments of the small town, the aspirants for executive office must meet different criteria than their "big city cousins." The search here is for those persons who embody tightly knit community values and characteristics. Here, a most distinguished and respected neighbor would be the prime choice.

Judicial candidates also, generally, have to meet such personal standards as training, experience, honesty, objectivity, sound reputation, and personal integrity. And, in most areas, they must also reflect the demographic balance in the community.

In the commission form of government, the commissioner, elected at-large, is expected to play a dual role—he is to be a member of the legislative council and administrative head of one of the city or county's major departments. The antecedent of this governmental form is the efficient business corporation where a board of directors establish managerial policies. Thus, the model for selecting candidates as commissioner is the business executive: an individual of relatively high socio-economic position, with extensive educational and managerial experience. Considering that the work is full time at part-time pay, candidates who meet such criteria are not easily attracted. Moreover, even the civic-minded executive who would be willing to devote his attention to public service may find it difficult to muster enthusiasm for such a position, as there may be no certainty as to which specific division of administration will be his to head.

The concept of at-large elections for city councilmen was included within the reform movement programs of the early twentieth century in order (among other reasons) to eliminate neighborhood or ethnic advantages and outlook. At-large councilmen represent the same constituencies as the mayors. Thus, their recruitment is also affected by the heterogeneous group characteristics found within most cities. Like the modern mayors, they must play the role of the "at-large statesmen," and look the part. The more attractive potential candidates are those who are professionals, or managers; living in the better part of town; joiners of fraternal, business or veterans clubs; and known for their achievements in civic or charitable activities.

Yet, the at-large system for electing councilmen does not eliminate favoring special constituencies. For example, in Boston, where a large Irish contingent lives, the results of the councilmanic elections between 1951 and 1963 have demonstrated their predominate influence, in that all but nine of the fifty-seven men elected have been Irish.[50] Unlike the recruitment process for a single executive centro, the recruitment for a multi-membered council allows articulate blocs of voters to be accommodated.

All state legislators and over one-fourth of the city councilmen are elected on a district basis. Here, the attempt is to recruit those individuals most nearly reflective of the characteristics of the constituencies they are to represent. To an extent this depends on the size of the district. It has been found that in those cities with small, compact districts, the councilman most closely approximates those he represents. In Chicago, for example, the councilmanic districting conforms to neighborhood boundaries clearly encompassing ethnic groupings. The potential official would be of a group, live among that group, and have a well-developed network of contacts with the group members.

State legislative districts are generally established along the lines of existing political units, such as counties, cities, or towns. Thus, the nature of some state legislative districts is predominately traditional-stabilized, while that of others is predominately modern-changing.

A traditional-stabilized district is one that would be principally comprised of rural areas and small town communities. Prevailing attitudinal patterns remain unchanged over the course of time, and they are reinforced by a limited and interconnecting network of social contacts and relationships. The level of political interest is low and its extent is narrow. The constituency does not turn to the state legislature for action or services. Citizens feel that the best agencies to satisfy their needs and demands are found in their local communities. In this type of district, offices are filled by the available business executives, lawyers, or other civic leaders who find they can fulfill their public-spirited motivations without impeding their usual occupational routine. Thus there is a scarcity of those who are capable, available, and interested in the state legislative office.

In such communities, recruitment is an informal process in which political conflict and competition are not desired. Candidates who command respect for their presonal character, caution, loyalty, sound judgment, tact, reliability, and honesty are sought. They are to be found among the old families, and long-time residents, who have cultivated a wide circle of friends and contacts who share complementary group memberships.

The modern-changing districts are those urban and suburban areas characterized by rapid population growth, industrial development, or rapid rates of social mobility. Each new wave of migration into these areas brings more educated professionals and technical specialists. These people are politically interested, and have a high degree of concern about public issues confronting each level of government. Politics is not the old-style informal friends-and-neighbors affair. It is marked by individuals and associational organizations competing aggressively for political benefits. Thus a number of issue oriented individuals would present themselves for recruitment. They would be educated, high socio-economic status professionals, belonging to several associations in the community.

Incumbency

Incumbency is another factor that will influence the potentialities for obtaining the centros. If there were one generalization that could be made about recruitment it would be: if an incumbent wanted renomination, he most likely would get it.

In partisan situations, political parties recognize the advantages accruing to them in supporting an incumbent. For one, they may be reluctant to surrender the benefits that his experience, contacts, and seniority may bring to the community or the party. For another, they already have an official whose relationship to them is known. Third, he is a proven winner. Thus where the party can nominate through convention, its members usually will renominate an incumbent. Where primaries exist, the party may openly endorse a candidate (*e.g.*, in a pre-primary convention or meeting), covertly discourage competitors, or insure that loyal party affiliates turn out on primary day to support their chosen nominee. Incumbents are favored in non-partisan situations also. Their advantage may be in their having already established campaign organizations, having maintained channels to financial support, and having claims on a variety of groups which they have assisted in the past.

The typical voter may be more readily attracted to an incumbent than to the challengers. He may perhaps feel that experience is to be rewarded; that the official should have another chance; or even that it is better to keep in office someone who is known, rather than take a chance with someone whose probable performance would be unknown. At the least, the incumbent may bear a name familiar to them.

Name familiarity can be buttressed by the incumbent's use of his official position. First, he may have access to the communication media. Second, he could create situations that would be newsworthy by issuing statements or generating reports. Third, by virtue of his position, he is invited to speak, to attend ceremonial functions, and to be present at public affairs. Fourth, he may take the initiative of establishing official communication channels with constituents, such as designating times and places to meet with them for the ostensive purpose of giving the public an opportunity to articulate its needs and demands in person.

Furthermore, potential candidates may be discouraged from competing against an incumbent because of the belief that the latter would be difficult to defeat. Should the incumbent have the strong endorsement and support of the party or important groups, the challenger may additionally conclude that the expenditure of time, energy, and money would not be worthwhile. However, in states or districts dominated by a single party, where the primary is in essence the election, the proportion of challengers to incumbents increases. For if securing the nomination is equivalent to success, the stakes may be considered worth the effort.

Financial Resources

Money as a factor will also influence the potentialities for obtaining the centros. Financial resources are necessary for both seeking the nomination and campaigning for the election. Communication with the public to make familiar one's name, qualifications, and record, and to project a favorable image, is no simple or inexpensive task. Getting messages across necessitates imagination, organization, and money. Levels of costs and types of expenditures involved in securing a nomination vary with such factors as office sought, ways of nominating candidates (*i.e.*, convention, primary, or combinations of the two), size and type of the constituency, degree of competitiveness, character of the competition, and the candidate himself.

Basically, candidates cannot rely on party organizations to finance their efforts for nomination. Parties generally utilize their limited resources for the election campaign; and they open their treasuries usually only to executive and judicial centros. Thus the individual must make use of his own ingenuity, luck, or opportunities.

The implications of this practice for recruitment are many and varied. The double sets of costs may discourage individuals from being potential candidates. Some individuals may not think that the material rewards of a public position (*e.g.*, a part-time legislative post) is worth the level of expenditure necessary to obtain the office.

Seeking the nomination in direct primaries may be as expensive as mobilizing for a general election campaign. Often, in one-party states or districts (where the struggle lies in securing the nomination), the costs of running in primaries may be as high or higher than the costs of the final campaigns in competitive party situations. An aspirant for nomination by convention does not avoid having to face the money requirement. He may receive support if he can convince the party leadership that he or his backers are able and willing to contribute to the party's treasury.

Perceived Potential for Success

Polls, too, may have a bearing on the recruitment process. Polling may be undertaken by any office seeker, but, because they are costly, usually only those running for at-large executive positions attempt to use them. The potential candidate is the principal sponsor of such undertakings, and he may choose to do so for any one of several reasons. He may wish to know if he has some basis to believe that he has a chance for success, for example, ascertaining if his name evokes any familiar response from the voters. Or, he may wish to demonstrate constituent support to the party leadership instrumental in recruitment. Favorable results of the polls may, furthermore, reinforce a candidate's efforts; while unfavorable results may influence him to withdraw from the race before extra time, energy, or money is spent.

The "coat-tail phenomenon" may affect the opportunities seen by prospective centro candidates. The presence of a popular incumbent or candidate to a major office may enhance the chances for success for everyone running on the same ticket. Thus there may be a strong desire to compete for a place on the ticket. Conversely, there may be a decline in competition should the ticket be headed by an individual considered unpopular in a specific district.

Party Competitive Systems

A factor that appears further to influence the quantity and quality of potential candidates is party competitiveness. Where there is a highly competitive party system (that is, where either major party has a good chance for election success), strong party organizations dominate the selection process. The two major parties always compete for the executive centro positions (outside of the traditional South). These are the offices that the parties are most interested in obtaining in order to acquire the benefits derived from controlling the machinery and resources of government. Thus party leaders will actively seek the most experienced, qualified, and attractive candidates.

That competitiveness affects quality can be seen, for example, in the type of state legislature candidates recruited. John C. Wahlke has concluded that:

> the more competitive the structure of the political party system the more likely it is that:
> (1) State legislators have had some prior governmental experience on the local level and in a legislative or quasi-legislative capacity . . .;
> (2) State legislators will place value on possession of particular skills thought relevant to a political career;
> (3) State legislators will have legal training and skills . . .;
> (4) State legislators will not look upon their political careers as a means for achieving personal goals—whether altruistic or selfish ones . . .;
> (5) State legislators will attribute their . . . committment to their personal involvement in the legislative job.[51]

Party competitiveness, however, is not an extensive phenomenon. Malcolm C. Jewell and Samuel C. Patterson have concluded that a realistic two-party competitive system has existed in only ten states in the period since World War II. In the remaining states there are one-party or limited two-party systems. Moreover, an examination of the legislative districts within the states shows an even more pronounced lack of party-competitiveness. For example, in Michigan the number of competitive districts is so slight that there has been party turnover in only 10 percent of the legislative seats.[52]

Urban areas have a higher degree of party competitiveness than rural areas. One reason for this is that the larger number of persons with a variety of socio-economic characteristics provide pockets of support for each party. Another is that the parties have greater financial resources and working personnel available to them. In addition, there is an incentive to maintain effective party organizational strength since larger blocs of votes are at stake for state and national elections. Yet, the competitiveness principally exists for at-large elections. In ward elections for city councilmen, there is a tendency for one party to be dominant in each district.

Where the competition is high, each political party actively attempts to find the most attractive candidates. However, where one party is assured of victory at the polls, it is the attractive candidates who seek that party. Where a party has little likelihood of victory, it may (if it does not choose to decline from entering the race) be relegated to the position of seeking or accepting any individual who is available or interested. Thus various political situations influence who are the agents of recruitment and who are recruited.

In a political situation where the majority party is virtually sure of victory, the incentive to run under its banner is widespread. Thus that party's leadership encounters little difficulty in filling a ticket. For attractive public offices, such as the central executive positions, self-recruited aspirants present themselves. Though the majority party may have little trouble recruiting men for such positions, the leaders have difficulty specifying which one should get the party's nomination. The major concern is having an attractive candidate who can maintain the party's success. Where nominations are determined by a primary, the decision may be made for them.

There are public offices, such as state legislative positions, in which local party leaders have less interest. They perceive these offices as commanding little power, patronage, or prestige. Therefore, nominations may be offered as a reward for faithful party service or to placate competing groups within the party, rather than as a means to strengthen the ticket.

In contrast, where the prospects of victory are slim, the party leadership may have to draft individuals to fill positions on the ticket. The available choices for recruitment may not always be attractive, for people with serious political intentions will strive for opportunities with the majority party. Obtaining a marketable candidate for the gubernatorial race is particularly important to a minority party. For this office, almost all minority parties have a chance for success. In recent times (1947 to 1968), the minority party in only nine states has been precluded from obtaining the office.[53]

In some districts the minority party leadership does not attempt to run candidates for the state legislature or some local offices. This may be because they cannot find candidates, or they do not feel it is worth their time and energy to combat the political realities of the traditional defeat. In some states from 50 to 60 percent of the districts have only one candidate on the ballot.[54] In some districts the absence of an opposing candidate may have been due to an agreement made with the majority party in order to assure receiving some patronage or other favors.

Minority party leaders can never choose to ignore all campaigns, however. They must keep the party alive for national elections. Thus they must always find some candidates for some of the offices. They may have to twist someone's arm to obtain a name to place on the ballot, persuading an individual who has neither interest nor time to hold the office, that it is only a matter of campaigning for a couple of weeks—if at all. Loyal and long-term affiliates, desiring to keep the party operating, may be likely to agree to lend their names for this purpose. A Connecticut politician related how one such party solved its problems:

> Came time to nominate candidates for local elections, we would put all the names of the town committee in the hat and draw them out and—"all right, you're going to run for mayor, or first selectman, and this and so forth." Year after year, the same names running for different offices.[55]

In the one-party dominant southern states, there has existed a variety of patterns of factional alignments. V. O. Key has classified them as: 1) two clearly defined factions; 2) one clearly defined faction opposed by a minority faction far less cohesive; and 3) multifactionalism, where groupings form and reform from campaign to campaign.[56] These patterns have implications for the style of recruitment.

The first pattern can be said to resemble a competitive two-party system, and the second a majority–minority relationship. Thus the styles of recruitment in each resemble fairly closely the styles discussed above.

The style of recruitment for the third category is characterized by fluid and discontinuous groupings that depend on changing candidates, reemphasized issues, and an absence of a readily defined set of traditions. Candidates run by their own exertions, with their own personal following. In such situations, individuals are principally self-recruited; or they are proposed by economic or social groupings anxious and able to expend their time and financial resources for success. Such multifactionalism places a high premium on qualities of personality that attract voter attention; and, as Key concluded, this may enhance the possibility of demagogic types of individuals presenting themselves.

Non-Partisanship

In truly non-partisan systems (*i.e.*, those uninfluenced by any political party activity), there are two main agents of recruitment: the individual himself, and formal interest or civic organizations. Candidates for councilmanic positions, running on a ward basis, probably would find that friends, associates, and personal contacts might be the only resources needed for success. Candidates running at-large for mayor or council positions of a small locality might also require little else. However, when a person seeks office in cities the size of Los Angeles, Atlanta, or Detroit, organizational backing becomes a necessity. The influence and activity of the several organizational forces (*e.g.*, business, unions, newspapers, and civic associations) in supporting candidates vary in different settings according to the relationships of political power, economic power, and citizen interest.

In Boston, candidates are self-recruited and must rely on their own resources to convey their personal attributes to the public. Aspirants for mayor and council position run at-large in a situation that finds business groups, labor unions, civic associations, and the press generally uninterested in the local elections. These groups focus on the elections for the state offices, since these officials are responsible for most of the decisions affecting Boston.

Candidates running in the Detroit mayorality or at-large councilmanic elections are also self-recruited. In a city of this size, they usually strive to get the active electoral and financial support of two or three groups. The interested groups (*e.g.*, small businesses, various unions, homeowners' associations, and ethnic leagues) are willing to make concerted efforts on behalf of a candidate to assure being represented on the council. Serious seekers of the executive position attempt to gain the electoral support of such groups as local business firms, citizen leagues, the active press, and several black organizations important within the city.

Though several candidates may run in the primary mayorality election in Los Angeles, the leading contender is likely to have been recruited by a coalition of large business, manufacturing, and utility company executives, and the publishers of the daily press (especially *The Los Angeles Times*). This coalition agrees on a candidate and sees to the organization of his campaign. The potential councilmen, running in districts, must rely on personal followings created through contacts with civic, social, and economic interest groups found within their individual constituency.

Motivations for Seeking Centro Positions

The holding of a public office on a state and local level carries with it the awesome feature of caring for the public trust. The office thrusts the individual into the limelight. He is no longer a private citizen with the pleasures of privacy of time, interests, and family life. And he can look forward to being rewarded with complex work, great inconvenience, often economic sacrifice, and a barrage of public criticism and abuse. To obtain this, the public servant has spent time, energy, and money. Why then do people run?

The prime reason overwhelmingly articulated by public figures is the concept of civic duty and service. Each official may state his reason in different words, but the basic concept can be recognized: he wanted to help "his" state or city or neighbors; he had a burning sense of cause about waste and corruption in government; he saw an opportunity to influence policy towards desirable ends; he felt that the people were not being represented well or that there were too many "forgotten men." Or, as some began: "Duty called and..."

Other motivations may be categorized as personal psychological reasons. Some individuals derive personal satisfaction from the accomplishment of effort for their neighbors; and others are caught in the pomp and ceremony of political contests and public office. Some think it is just "plain fun," and others derive pleasure from the opportunities of meeting celebrities and "important people." Some strive for the deference paid to the prestige of the position, or for the satisfaction of seeing themselves on or mentioned in the mass media; others strive for the power, influence, and authority of their political post. Some feel a sense of obligation to return something to the community that has given them a home and livelihood; others feel obligated to the party that has given them a sense of political identity. And for some, it is the sense of professional pride and achievement in obtaining what is considered the apex of a chosen career—as, for example, a lawyer may look upon a judgeship.

There are motivations that can be categorized as selfish personal reasons. A retired individual may seek freedom from boredom and cherish the chance to socialize. A handicapped person may be motivated by the hope for gainful employment. The immigrant, the minority member, or the low socio-economic status individual may see public office as the avenue of upward mobility. The struggling young professional may utilize a public office to advertise and gain publicity or contacts that will aid his private career. And there are those who would simply promote the welfare of an economic interest group.

In addition, as can be inferred from a close examination of political backgrounds, another motivation for seeking local and state positions is ambition. Many individuals realize that their interests, ability, and personality best suit them for one office at one level of government. Thus they would expend their energies to become influential in policy making or execution at that level. Yet others have a desire to use one office as a steppingstone for advancement to another that they consider more prestigious in the political systems.

However, the levels of government (local, state, and federal) are distinct systems. There is no arranged three-layer hierarchical order of escalating advancement or automatic promotion. The local governments are not, in fact, placement services for the recruitment of state officials; nor are the state governments places for recruitment to federal office.

Local executives rarely gain entrance into higher office. The exceptions to the rule can be seen in the two examples of recent vice-presidents: Hubert Humphrey, who was mayor of Minneapolis, Minnesota; and Spiro Agnew, who was County Executive of Baltimore County, Maryland. Each, of course, attained the vice-presidency after having filled other posts. Traditionally, the local council is not a stepping-stone to state or federal elective or appointive positions, though councilmen may find opportunities to transfer within the local political sphere.

One reason for this lack of upward mobility is that anyone closely identified with a city, especially a large one, is under a handicap in a statewide election, for there still exists, as part of the general political ethos, the traditional distrust of big city politics and politicians. Secondly, non-partisanship (a basically local phenomena) limits available options. Non-partisan officials, having tossed aside party identifying labels, cannot expect to be readily received back into a partisan context for state or national office.

State politicians have been more successful in moving out of their level of government, or into what they consider more important posts within that level. Governors (particularly those from politically important states) have filled the seats in the White House, in the Congress, in the federal courts (as well as state courts of appeal), in the cabinet, or in other significant national administrative agencies. State legislators have been able to advance into the position of central executive authority in the state (and subsequently use these to advance to federal office), have entered into the Congress, or served in second-level federal posts.

Characteristics of Centro Nominees

Considering the diverse factors influencing the recruitment process, it is remarkable that those recruited possess strikingly similar personal characteristics. However, they are seldom representative samples of their constituencies.

Centros are most reflective of their constituencies when they are elected from small districts. The ward apportionment of local councils allows for group, ethnic, cultural, and religious representation. With at-large elections, many of those complimentary characteristics are lost.

The characteristics of the at-large councilmen resemble closely that of a mayor. The typical local councilman and mayor have been found to be male, middle- to upper-class, white, Protestant, educated, forty-five to fifty years old, with a business or professional background.

The mayor in larger republican or non-partisan cities has been likened to the chief executive of a corporation. They are similar in social status, background, and responsibilities, but not in salary.

The pattern of similar characteristics exist also for judicial centros. They too are middle-aged, middle-class, college- and post-graduate-educated professionals. If there are deviations, it is to be found in the backgrounds and credentials of those at the lowest levels in the judicial system, where the characteristics may be less impressive than for those who sit in the general trial or appellate courts. The various systems of selection or political arenas do not tend to recruit judges with different social backgrounds.[57]

An examination of the selected social characteristics of state legislators presented in Table VI.12 shows the parallelism continued.

Perhaps a detailed comparison of the governors would be illustrative of the types of persons generally recruited. The fifty chief executives in 1968 had an average age of fifty-one years; and almost all were married men with families of from two to three children. Almost all had attended college, and over two-thirds held one or more degrees in law, liberal arts or science. More than one-half were attorneys, several others were business executives, while the remainder came from farming or ranching, education, engineering, or entertainment fields. Many had previous governmental experience, most

TABLE VI.12

Social Characteristics of State Legislators from Selected States

	Percentage College Graduates	Percentage Professionals (*e.g.*, lawyers, business executives)	Median Age
California	54	83	48.2
Massachusetts*	61	68	44.2
New Jersey	63	83	45.9
Ohio	58	83	46.9
Tennessee	46	79	44.4

* House members only.

Source: Figures for the Massachusetts House are taken from Sheldon Goldman, *Roll Call Behavior in the Mass. House of Rep.: A Test of Selected Hypothesis* (Amherst: University of Massachusetts; Bureau of Governmental Research, 1968) p. 18; and the others from Wahlke, *et al.*, *op. cit.*, pp. 489–91.

having been state legislators or state bureaus, a few having seen public service in the federal or local levels. A perusal of the backgrounds of the governors shows a startling regularity of characteristics and credentials regardless of section, party competitiveness, or the size of the state.[58]

TABLE VI.13

Social Characteristics of Governors from Selected States

State	Date of Birth	Education	Occupation	Government Experience
North Dakota .	1919	B.S., M.S.	Farmer	State Rep.
Oregon . . .	1913	B.A.	Journalist	Sec. State
Pennsylvania .	1917	B.A., Ll.B.	Attorney	Lieutenant-Gov., D.A., State Senator
Rhode Island .	1922	B.A., Ll.B.	Attorney	State Rep.
South Carolina .	1913	A.B., Ll.B.	Attorney	State Rep., Lieutenant-Gov.

Source: *The American Governors, op. cit.*

It would appear that "certain types" of persons are more prone to be recruited than others. High levels of education and socio-economic status generally relate with greater knowledge and awareness of politics, and a higher sense of citizen obligation, political efficacy, and interest.

Moreover, certain vocations are "political" in nature, that is, the practitioners of "brokerage occupations" (*e.g.*, lawyers and businessmen, as opposed to industrial wage earners, service workers, or farm laborers), interact with the political system or political decision-makers at a high frequency. Not only do prestige occupations demonstrate achievement and success, they demand skills that enhance the ability of individuals in political roles. These are verbal skills, as well as bargaining and compromising abilities. In addition, these professionals have a flexible work schedule that allows time for involvement; have economic interests that would not suffer unduly or might even profit from political activity; and have positions that encourage concern with a wide range of public problems.

Thus most of the potential candidates would logically come from these socio-economic, educational, and professional sectors of the population. And it appears that these are the sectors to which the electorate looks for its public officials. As Frank J. Sorauf noted: "Paradoxically, voters seem to want both the typical and atypical in their elected representatives.... They favor candidates with education, occupation, and general social status far above the average. They seek the successful, the respected man—the common man write large, so to speak."[59]

Chapter VI Footnotes

1. James David Barber, *The Lawmakers* (New Haven, Conn.: Yale University Press, 1965), p. 1.
2. National Opinion Research Center, "Jobs and Occupations: A Popular Evaluation," *Opinion News*, IX (September 1, 1947), pp. 3–13.
3. Robert W. Hodge, Paul M. Siegel, and Peter H. Rossi, "Occupational Prestige in the United States, 1925–1963," *The American Journal of Sociology*, LXX (November 1964), pp. 286–302.
4. Barber, *Lawmakers*, p. 5.
5. Ibid., p. 288.
6. *Polls*, I, (Summer 1965), p. 75. Other reasons offered included such beliefs as politics disrupts family life, there is too much responsibility, and it is a "thankless job."
7. Barber, *Lawmakers*, p. 222.
8. Samuel J. Eldersveld, *Political Parties: A Behavioral Analysis* (Chicago: Rand McNally and Company, 1964), p. 312.
9. Edward C. Banfield, *Big City Politics* (New York: Random House, Inc., 1965), pp. 121–32.
10. Samuel C. Patterson, "Characteristics of Party Leaders," *Western Political Quarterly*, XVI (June 1963), pp. 332–52.

11.   Joseph P. Lyford, *Candidate* (New York: McGraw-Hill Book Company; Eagleton Institute Cases in Practical Politics, Case 9, 1960), p. 4.

12.   For an extensive discussion of fund raisers see Alexander Heard, *The Costs of Democracy* (Chapel Hill: University of North Carolina Press, 1960).

13.   John C. Wahlke, *et al.*, *The Legislative System* (New York: John Wiley and Sons, Inc., 1962), pp. 98–99.

14.   Barber, *Lawmakers*, p. 123.

15.   Wahlke, *et al.*, *Legislative System*, p. 101.

16.   Banfield, *Big City Politics*, p. 59.

17.   James MacGregor Burns, *The Deadlock of Democracy* (Englewood Cliffs, N.J.: Prentice-Hall Inc., 1963), pp. 229–30.

18.   Harmon Zeigler and Michael A. Baer, *Lobbying: Interaction and Influence in American State Legislatures* (Belmont, Calif.: Wadsworth Publishing Company, Inc., 1969), p. 44.

19.   Samuel C. Patterson, "The Role of the Lobbyist: The Case of Oklahoma," *Journal of Politics*, XXV (February 1963), p. 75.

20.   Zeigler and Baer, *Lobbying*, p. 53.

21.   Patterson, "Rule of the Lobbyist," p. 78.

22.   Zeigler and Baer, *Lobbying*, pp. 51–53.

23.   Ibid., p. 64.

24.   Patterson, "Role of the Lobbyist," p. 75.

25.   Zeigler and Baer, *Lobbying*, p. 48.

26.   Patterson, "Role of the Lobbyist," p. 78.

27.   Zeigler and Baer, *Lobbying*, p. 95.

28.   William J. Keefe and Morris S. Ogul, *The American Legislative Process: Congress and the States* (Englewood Cliffs, N.J.: Prentice-Hall, Inc., 1968, 2d ed.), p. 48.

29.   Patterson, "Role of the Lobbyist," p. 76.

30.   Robert S. Hirschfield, Bert E. Swanson, and Blanche D. Blank, "A Profile of Political Activists in Manhattan," *Western Political Quarterly*, XVI (September 1962), p. 491.

31.   Lewis Bowman, Dennis Ippolito, and William Donaldson, "Incentive for the Maintenance of Grass Roots Political Activism," *Midwest Journal of Political Science*, XVII (February 1969), pp. 126–39.

32.   Phillip Althoft and Samuel C. Patterson, "Political Activism in a Rural County," *Midwest Journal of Political Science*, X (February 1966), pp. 39–51.

33.   Lewis Bowman and G. R. Boynton, "Recruitment Patterns Among Local Party Officials: A Model and Some Preliminary Findings in Selected Locales," *American Political Science Review*, LX (September 1966), p. 674.

34.   Althoft and Patterson, "Political Activism," p. 44.

35.   Bowman and Boynton, "Recruitment Patterns," p. 674; ibid.

36.   Gerald Pomper, "New Jersey County Chairman," *Western Political Quarterly*, XVIII (March 1965), p. 195.

37.   Bowman and Boynton, "Recruitment Patterns," p. 672.

38.   Thomas A. Flinn and Frederick M. Wirt, "Local Party Leaders: Groups of Like Minded Men," *Midwest Journal of Political Science*, IX February 1956), p. 86; Hirschfield, Swanson, and Blanc, "A Profile," p. 493; Pomper, "County Chairman," p. 187; William J. Crotty, "The Social Attributes of Party Organizational Activists in a Transitional Political System," *Western Political Quarterly*, XX (September 1967), p. 677; and Bowman and Boynton, "Recruitment Patterns," pp. 671–72.

39.   Crotty, "Social Attributes," p. 680.

40.   The figures in this section are taken from United States Department of Labor, Bureau of Labor Statistics, *Occupational Outlook Handbook 1968–1969* (Washington, D.C.: Government Printing Office, 1969).

41. Neil S. Wright and Richard L. McAnaw, "American State Executives: Their Background and Careers," *State Government*, XXXVIII (Summer 1965), p. 153.

42. *The Municipal Yearbook 1968* (Washington, D.C.: The International City Managers' Association, 1968), pp. 52–54; Herbert S. Duncombe, *County Government in America* (Washington, D.C.: National Association of Counties Research Foundation, 1966), p. 55.

43. H. George Frederickson, "Understanding Attitudes Toward Public Employment," *Public Administration Review*, XXVII (December 1967), pp. 411–20; Frank K. Gibson and George A. James, "Student Attitudes Towards Government Employees and Employment," *Public Administration Review*, XXVII (December 1967), pp. 429–35.

44. Leonard D. White, *The Prestige Value of Public Employment* (Chicago: University of Chicago Press, 1929). A replication of White's study undertaken in Detroit in 1954 found similar unfavorable attitudes towards public employment: Morris Janovitz and Deil Wright, "The Prestige of Public Employment: 1929 and 1954," *Public Administration Review*, XVI (Winter 1956), pp. 15–21. See also Morris Janowitz, Deil Wright, and William Delaney, *Public Administration and The Public: Perspectives Towards Government in a Metropolitan Community* (Ann Arbor: University of Michigan, Institute of Public Administration, 1958).

45. Municipal Manpower Commission, *Government Manpower for Tomorrow's Cities* (New York: McGraw-Hill Book Company, Inc., 1962).

46. Wright and McAnaw, "American State Executives," p. 151.

47. Ibid., pp. 146–53.

48. Alan Fiellin, "Recruitment and Legislative Role Conceptions: A Conceptual Scheme and a Case Study," *Western Political Quarterly*, XX (June 1967), p. 277.

49. Edward C. Banfield, "The Political Implications of Metropolitan Growth," *Daedalus* XC (Winter 1961), p. 72.

50. Banfield, *Big City Politics*, p. 144.

51. Wahlke, *et al.*, *Legislative System*, pp. 120, 134.

52. Malcom E. Jewell and Samuel C. Patterson, *The Legislative Process in the United States* (New York: Random House, Inc., 1966), pp. 143–44, 80.

53. Malcolm E. Jewell, *The State Legislature* (New York: Random House, 1969, 2d ed.), p. 12.

54. Duane Lockard, "The State Legislator," in Alexander Heard, ed., *State Legislatures in American Politics* (Englewood Cliffs, N.J.: Prentice-Hall, Inc., 1966), p. 109.

55. Barber, *Lawmakers*, p. 28.

56. V. O. Key, *Southern Politics in State and Nation* (New York: Alfred A. Knopf, Inc., 1949).

57. Herbert Jacob, "The Effect of Institutional Differences in the Recruitment Process: The Case of State Judges," *Journal of Public Law*, XIII (1964), pp. 104–19.

58. *The American Governors* (Chicago: The Council of State Governors, 1968).

59. Frank J. Sorauf, *Party and Representation* (New York: Atherton Press, 1963), p. 8.

Chapter **VII**

Rule-Making, Part 1: The State Level

> The powers not delegated to the United States by the Constitution, nor prohibited by it to the States, are reserved to the States respectively, or to the people.

This provision of the United States Constitution defines the broad scope of state activities. State governments are charged with providing for the safety, health, morals, education, and general welfare of the people. The activities with which state governments are concerned range from the vital to the trivial. Quite realistically, the state has a direct impact on the lives of its residents—between its issuance of the birth certificate in the beginning and the death certificate at the end. The state will prescribe one's educational curriculum, the color of his license plates, the number of days he may go hunting, the number of fishing lines he can use, the qualifications for his occupation, and the qualifications for those who teach him, cure him, or provide other services for him. The state's involvement in these activities are outcomes of the rule-making function. Although the function is performed by all state structures, state constitutions assign legislatures the primary responsibility for this function.

Formal Factors in Legislative Rule-Making

Despite the seemingly extensive areas of public activity, the state legislative rule-making function has many limitations imposed upon it. The limitations are imposed by the national constitution, national laws and treaties, federal court decisions, state constitutions, and decisions of state courts.

National Constitutional Limitations

The listing of limitations of legislative rule-making powers may start with provisions found in the body of the national constitution (Article I, Section 10). Among the sixteen prohibitions are:

No State shall enter into any Treaty, Alliance, or Confederation; grant Letters of Marque and Reprisal; coin Money; emit Bills of Credit; make any Thing but gold and silver Coin a Tender in Payment of Debts; pass any Bill of Attainder, ex post facto Law, or Law impairing the Obligation of Contracts, or grant any Title of Nobility.

Through the course of amending the national constitution, the states have been further restrained from acting in areas affecting individual rights. No state shall permit slavery (Amendment XIII), nor shall any state:

make or enforce any law which shall abridge the privileges or immunities of citizens of the United States; nor shall any State deprive any person of life, liberty, or property, without due process of law; nor deny to any person within its jurisdiction the equal protection of the laws (Amendment XIV).

In addition, states shall not pass laws abridging the right to vote because of race, color, or previous condition of servitude (Amendment XV); sex (Amendment XIX); payment of a poll tax (Amendment XXIV); or age (*i.e.*, eighteen years of age or older, Amendment XXVI).

The Congress in passing laws to implement provisions of the constitution, has pre-empted the field for state action on many occasions. From the time of *McCulloch v. Maryland*,[1] the United States Supreme Court has declared null and void state laws in conflict with the Constitution. In recent years, the Supreme Court has interpreted the Fourteenth Amendment as covering the provisions of the Bill of Rights and the Twenty-fourth Amendment to further restrict state legislative actions.[2]

State Constitutional Limitations

State constitutions also impose limitations of various kinds. All constitutions contain bills of rights, which basically deny the legislature the power to enact laws affecting individual rights. While the various lists include such "standard" protections as freedom of speech, press, religion and assembly, the lists may not be limited to only "inalienable" rights. For example, a bill of rights may guarantee the right to fish (as in California); the "right to work" (as in Florida); or the right to organize labor unions and engage in collective bargaining (as in Hawaii).

The state constitutions may contain prohibitions that have the effect of excluding legislative actions in certain matters. For example, lotteries are barred by the Georgia constitution, as is duelling by the Iowa constitution. Other provisions may detail specifications of actions that constrict legislative discretion. The type of hard surfacing on state roads in the city of Greenville, for example, is provided for in the South Carolina constitution.

The details and specifications are especially highlighted in regard to fiscal matters. Although the constitutions assign the legislature control of the purse, the legislature is rarely allowed free use of its fiscal powers. First, revenue sources may be delimited. Tax revenue plans may be influenced by requirements for uniformity (which prohibits graduated income tax), or by maximum tax rates set forth in a constitution. Several potential taxable sources may enjoy constitutional exemption. Generally, properties devoted to religious, educational, agricultural, or charitable purposes enjoy exemption status. In addition, some specific sources may have been included for special consideration. The California constitution excludes the taxation of grape vines under the age of three years from time of planting; Georgia's excludes art works; and Louisana's excludes athletic fields.

Debt limitations represent another restriction on state legislative fiscal powers, and limitations are found in nearly all state constitutions. Some provisions prevent a state from contracting any debt, requiring that it operate within a balanced budget or surplus every year, *i.e.*, on a "pay-as-you-go" basis. Others set specific dollar limits on the amount of debt that can be incurred. In Wisconsin, for example, the maximum allowable state debt is $100,000—a figure set in the Wisconsin constitution a century ago. In addition, a constitution may restrict borrowing through the issuance of bonds by requiring approval by voters at a special referendum.

Another common limitation is the constitutional earmarking of certain state revenues for specific programs. For example, gasoline and motor vehicle taxes can be spent only for highway purposes; or revenue from hunting and fishing licenses devoted to game and fish management. Approximately one-half of all state revenues are so earmarked to impede legislative discretion of the allocation of funds.

Constitutional provisions also structure procedures of state legislatures that affect the rule-making function. For example, provisions may specify the number of days during which bills may be introduced (as in Maryland); that each bill be given a full reading (as in Pennsylvania); that each bill be given complete readings on three separate days (as in Kentucky); or that each bill be placed before the members three calendar days prior to final passage (as in New York). Failure to follow procedures in full may lead to court tests of the validity of a statute.

The legislature is not only limited in what it can do, and how it can proceed, but also in how long a period it can operate.[3] The characteristic pattern for a significant number of states is a legislature convening in January of the odd-numbered years, for biennial sessions, and limited in length to from two to three months. In twenty-six states, annual sessions are held, although in ten of these states, the even-numbered year session is a shorter one, and it usually is restricted to considerations of the budget. Annual and unlimited sessions are found in only eleven states.

Special sessions may be called to handle some legislation not completed during the regularly scheduled period. In thirty-three states, the initiative to call a special session lies with the governor; in the others, to call one requires an extraordinary legislative majority. Moreover, in nearly one-half the states, the subject matter legislators are to consider is defined by the special call, and in some cases, so is the number of days the legislature may meet.

Certain other devices are occasionally used to circumvent the time restrictions. In some states, commissions or committees may be charged with meeting between sessions, holding hearings, and preparing bills and reports. In other states, pre-session filing processes have been instituted, or legislatures have divided their allotted number of days between the two years in split sessions. These devices, however, may not solve all of the problems imposed by restrictive time provisions. For example, attendance at interim committee meetings may be poor, or membership may not reflect the actual power structure of the regular sessions. In addition, research facilities available for the pre-session activities may be inadequate.

The length of legislative terms is another constitutional limitation on legislative rule-making. In forty-six states, the members of the lower house serve terms of only two years, and in twelve states, the members of the upper chamber serve terms of two years. The significance of short terms is reflected in the length and biennial nature of legislative sessions. In most states the members of one house, and in several the members of both houses, meet for only one short session before they must stand for re-election. The significance is amplified by the high turnover rate found for state legislators. Over half the state legislators, after each election, are freshmen. Thus the number of experienced legislators in state councils is dramatically low.

Provisions prescribing the size of legislative bodies may affect the manner and speed with which the legislators perform the rule-making function. Given an extensive amount of work in a short period of time, a large body may prove cumbersome in operation, while a small body may place heavy demands on each member. The size of councils vary without any correlation with the population in the states. A majority of states have senates of less than forty members. Delaware, with nineteen senators, has the smallest upper house, followed by Alaska and Nevada, each having twenty-member senates. Iowa, with sixty-one seats, and Minnesota, with sixty-seven seats, have the largest senates. The size of lower houses range from thirty-nine (in Delaware) to four hundred (in New Hampshire), with the majority of states having one hundred or fewer members.

Legislative Handicaps

The effects of the limitations already discussed are intensified by the handicaps under which legislators operate. For their efforts, legislative centros are paid annual salaries ranging from $100 per year in New Hampshire to $19,500 per year in California. In nearly one-half the states, salaries are less than $5,000 per year. The salaries are prescribed by constitutional provisions in nearly one-half the states. Further compensation, however, is often given in the form of travel and expense allowances.

While the salaries may be considered low, inconveniences are high. Traditionally, legislators have been provided with a desk and chair on the floor of the chamber, and little else. Less than one half-dozen states provide office space in the capitol. Thus, the chambers or the halls are the sites for the vast majority of the legislators' work. Legislators must improvise work space in their hotel rooms or, if they live nearby, in their homes or private offices. Even the typical committee may be required to improvise a place to assemble from meeting to meeting. Hearings may be held in a corner of a chamber, in a hotel room, or a vacant room in a state office building.

In most states, no staff assistance is provided to the legislators for research or for aiding in casework requests from constituents. In all states, however, there are agencies to which a legislator may go for some services. Legal assistance can be given by a legislative counsel or through the attorney general's office so that bills can be written in proper technical form and language. In almost all states, legislative library reference services exist to perform some research endeavors, yet, this is generally considered by legislators to be minimal and limited. Thus the state legislative centro must rely on his own resources, on lobbyists, on constituents, or on such help as his colleagues or committee staff may be willing and able to offer.

Secretarial services are poor. In only a few states are legislators provided with a personal secretary. The usual arrangement for clerical service is to provide a secretarial pool from which legislators draw. Correspondence becomes a major task, and even the ordinary effort of communicating by telephone becomes a time-consuming chore. Materials necessary to inform legislators about proceedings are not always readily accessible. Copies of bills or pending amendments may not be issued. Floor debates, committee reports, or committee hearings may not be printed. Calendars, agendas, or lists of the status of bills may not be provided for distribution. The storage and retrieval of information about previous actions are generally inadequate.

Apportionment and Districting

Legislative rule-making may be affected by the apportionment and districting of state legislatures. Though the terms are generally used interchangeably, there is a distinction between the two. Districting refers to the design of precise geographic boundaries for legislative constituencies. Apportionment refers to the distribution of the legislative seats among the districts. For many years, political battles have been fought over apportionment or, more precisely, malapportionment. Malapportionment means the assignment of legislators to legislative districts of unequal population in order to favor one group, political party, or interest.

The malapportionment of most state legislative bodies was apparent during the first six decades of this century, as the American population changed from a predominant rural to a predominant urban one. Though the population shifted, the legislative districts did not reflect the new pattern. In state after state, small minorities of voters (usually in rural areas) could elect the majority of legislators.

Constitutional provisions reinforced malapportionment. In several state constitutions, representation was based on factors other than population. In 1961, thirty-two of the lower houses and thirty of the upper chambers were based on geographic considerations. New England states had traditionally apportioned their lower houses by towns. The population of some of these towns has grown smaller, while in others it has grown to proportions of large cities, yet each town was entitled to the same representation. In Connecticut, for example, under the aegis of the 1836 constitution, the town of Union with 383 inhabitants and the city of Hartford with a population of 162,178 persons (in 1960) were each allotted two representatives. Many state constitutions had guaranteed each county at least one legislator in the upper chamber. Thus in California, in 1960, the population of the smallest senate district was 14,294, while the largest (Los Angeles County) had 6,038,771 residents.

Malapportionment was also able to continue because of state legislative inaction. Many state legislators had refused to apportion even if their constitution required periodic changes to reflect population shifts. They were reluctant to alter the status quo that had accommodated their positions and security, their power to influence policy decisions, their interests, their constituencies, or their parties. On occasion, when legislators did re-apportion, their plans either did little to correct imbalances in representation or were quickly outmoded by the ever-increasing population growth.

There were a few remedies by which the malapportionment problem could have been alleviated. First, the citizens could have gone to their legislators.

Yet, as was stated above, legislators, and other state officials, were reluctant to respond to such appeals. As William D. J. Boyd has said, it was "virtually impossible to find an example, from 1901 to 1962, of an apportionment fairly and equitably performed by a state legislature."[4]

Second, in twenty states, the initiative existed as a means for the public to affect the status quo. However, the difficulties attached to this petition process, and the generally low levels of success of such proposals on a ballot, proved this remedy ineffective. It was tried in only seven of the states that permitted this process; and of twenty attempts, only nine were successful.

The third remedy was court adjudication. Generally, the state courts refused to hear such cases. They held that they did not have jurisdiction over what they considered to be a state legislative matter. As it became apparent that the state courts could or would not remedy the situation, attention turned to federal courts. These courts, also, generally refused to enter into the controversy. The early period of refusal by federal courts was buttressed by the 1946 Supreme Court decision in the case of *Colegrove v. Green*.[5] The Colegrove case dealt with redistricting for the national Congress, yet it was considered a judgment that could be applied to state legislatures. The Supreme Court held that re-apportionment matters were "political thickets." Thus the outlook for correction of malapportionment appeared bleak until 1962, when the Supreme Court agreed to hear a case dealing with the apportionment of the Tennessee state legislature.

The situation in Tennessee could be said to be an illustrative—if not extreme—example of malapportionment. Though the state constitution charged legislators to reapportion both houses on the basis of population every ten years, they had not done so since 1901. By 1960, the legislature was greatly imbalanced in favor of rural areas. The House districts ranged from a population of 3,454 to a population of 79,301 persons, and Senate districts ranged from 39,727 persons to 237,905 persons.

A group of urban residents of Nashville, including a County Judge Charles W. Baker, filed a suit against Joe C. Carr, Tennessee Secretary of State, in the federal court in Nashville. They had already been rebuffed by the state legislature, and by the state courts (which claimed lack of jurisdiction). In 1960, the district court dismissed the case, citing precedents establishing its lack of jurisdiction. The plaintiffs appealed to the Supreme Court, and the Court agreed to hear the case. By this action, court adjudication became a viable remedy for malapportionment.

The decision of the Supreme Court in *Baker v. Carr*[6] made malapportionment a "justiciable" issue. The Court concluded that federal tribunals could hear such cases, for the issue was not a "political question" merely because it concerned protection of a political right. By failing to apportion itself, as prescribed by the Tennessee constitution, the legislature had created an imbalanced relationship of representatives to voters, and thus had deprived the citizens of their constitutional right to have the effectiveness of their votes maintained. In so doing, the legislature had violated the "equal protection of the law" provision of the fourteenth amendment. *Baker v. Carr* did not set any guidelines for apportionment beyond the requirement that it be "fair." The case was remanded to the district court for further proceedings consistent with the decision.

The following year, in supporting a challenge to Georgia's county unit system of voting in gubernatorial and congressional primary elections (*Gray v. Sanders*),[7] the Supreme Court addressed itself to clarifying the matter of "fair" apportionment. It declared that "within a given constituency there can be room for but a single constitutional rule: one voter, one vote."

In 1964, the Supreme Court extended the principle of "one man—one vote." In *Reynolds v. Sims*,[8] the Court held that the equal protection clause required that both houses of a state legislature be apportioned on a population basis. The decision pointed out that "legislators represent voters, not farms or cities, or economic interests." Thus, a state could not establish as a basis for districting any other criteria than "substantially" equal population.

The members of the Supreme Court had not set precise guidelines or standards for apportionment. They had hoped that state legislatures would best serve the constituencies by apportioning districts themselves. Yet, federal courts were to be wary of continued imbalances and to be ready to act to uphold the decisions of fair apportionment. A federal court could forbid elections to take place under malapportionment plans, could require all legislators to run at-large if new plans were not drawn, or—as a last resort —could set the district lines itself.

The reaction to the *Reynolds v. Sims* decision was mixed and vociferous. Fights were waged in many state legislatures and before federal courts. In Congress, several attempts were made to overturn the Supreme Court's dictates. At the state level, a drive was begun to petition Congress to call a constitutional convention for the purpose of adopting an amendment to the federal constitution that would permit a state to apportion one house on a local subdivision basis. By the end of the decade, the drive to get the necessary two-thirds proportion of states in agreement was only one state short of success.

That reapportionment had come about is irrefutable; that the consequences of the changes had met the expectations of the proponents is not so clear. Proponents had felt that malapportionment, primarily, had been the cause for the failure of state legislatures to meet the needs and interests of urban populations and to solve the problems of urban centers. They thought that, once changed to reflect the population, the legislatures would be seats of liberal and progressive policies.

Yet, several political scientists have written that malapportionment was not an effective factor influencing policy, nor was it detrimental to the solution of urban problems. Thomas R. Dye has stated that policy outputs in malapportioned state legislatures were not noticeably different from those in well-apportioned legislatures. He wrote that differences in policy that did occur between the two types of bodies were results of socio-economic differences among states rather than the consequence of apportionment practices. He concluded that significant policy output changes are not likely to be brought about by reapportionment, and certainly not in areas of education, welfare, or taxation.[9] Herbert Jacob, in his study, found little correlation between apportionment and highway fund distribution or certain welfare expenditures in the fifty states.[10]

Others, however, have been optimistic about the positive effects of reapportionment. Frank M. Bryan noted that reapportionment played a "catalytic role" in Vermont's legislature, where it "produced a mass of progressive legislation." He cited such new programs as child day-care facilities, fair housing, penal reform, regulation of outdoor advertising, reform in the state judicial system, a tax on water pollution, and the establishment of a Human Rights Commission. Indeed, the most important effect of the new system was that it brought "a mood of change and progress that has had a real influence on the actions of legislative personnel."[11] The speaker of the Colorado House of Representatives also saw changes after reapportionment, as new programs dealing with urban and suburban problems were introduced and acted on. He said that reapportionment had contributed to the new legislation significantly by having created "an atmosphere for action, not inaction; and by breaking up some long-standing internal legislative alliances which tended toward inaction."[12] A Colorado state senator's view of the change in urban versus non-urban legislators was: "We seem to be a lot less at each others' throats than we were even five years ago." The speaker of the Ohio House of Representatives noted the shifts in the type of legislators elected. He believed that they "were of a higher caliber and have a more progressive outlook."[13]

Perhaps the major benefit of new apportionment schemes has been the change of attitudes within legislative bodies. At least reapportionment has given the interests that are strong in metropolitan areas a stronger voice in the state legislatures. It may be likely that state legislators will devote more time and attention to urban problems, and that a larger share of the budget will be oriented toward the cities. But it is unlikely that there will be an "urban majority" in any state, for it cannot be assumed that urban representatives comprise a cohesive political bloc and that they would consistently vote a uniform pro-urban pattern. People in the cities are divided on a variety of political and economic policies and policy priorities, and an increased number of urban legislators would, thus, produce further diversity in terms of representation.

Moreover, in light of the greater rate of population growth within the suburbs, it is these areas that will gain more legislative seats than will their neighboring cities. "Reapportionment has suburbanized the Legislatures," said the mayor of Seattle in 1970, "and the suburbanites are as hostile to the city as the farmers ever were." It is likely that suburban representatives will align themselves with rural representatives because of a mutual dislike of the cities. Latent racial fears, and hostility created by the drug, crime, and housing problems in cities have created a major gulf between suburban representatives and their urban colleagues. "The suburbs are where you are finding so much of the opposition to urban legislation," the president of the Utah Senate has explained. The rising suburban proportion in many state legislatures has meant a rising opposition to rules benefiting cities. The measures most commonly defeated have been those for new tax revenues, educational support, and assistance for city-operated services. In 1969, a bill to permit an optional sales tax increase, needed by Salt Lake City for increased fire and police protection, was killed in a Utah Senate committee because of opposition from rural and suburban representatives. A similar bill was unsuccessful in the Minnesota legislature as rural and suburban legislators combined in opposition.[14] There were glimmers of cooperation, however, as it became clearer that urban problems do not end at the city limits. Perhaps the suburban hostility was only a transitional stage of the reapportionment revolution. If not, then one might ask: If the cities were the step-children of state legislatures—as was thought—before the court decisions of the 1960s, had they gained anything after the dust had settled?

Districting

While reapportionment has corrected certain situations, it has not been the sole answer to legislative unresponsiveness. For a state legislature to make rules that are in response to the needs and demands of the citizenry, legislative districts must be drawn in such a manner that each of the pluralist interests found within the population will be represented. The members of the Supreme Court of the United States have already begun to think in terms of "communities." Districts, the justices felt, should be so drawn as to consider the wants and desires of identifiable groups of people. In such districts, representatives would be selected who were able to present and discuss rules applicable for all socio-economic interests.

Malcolm E. Jewell has emphasized another important aspect of districting, one focused on the merits of single-member districts as compared to multi-member districts. He has noted that since single-member districts are usually smaller than multi-member districts, legislators elected from the former would be more sensitive to localized pressures than those elected from the latter.[15]

In the aftermath of the apportionment cases, several states have established single-member districts for some or all metropolitan areas. Jewell studied the legislatures in four states after the change to single-member districts and reported its effects. He pointed to the broader representation of partisan, racial, and socio-economic interests. More blacks, for example, were elected under the new districting plans. In 1966, black senators were elected for the first time from Cuyahoga and Hamilton counties, Ohio, and a total of eight black representatives went to the State House from the two counties. In Tennessee, where a single black legislator was elected at-large in Shelby County in 1964, five were elected from districts in Shelby and Davidson (Nashville) counties in 1966. The nine blacks elected to the Georgia legislature from Fulton County all represented single-member districts.[16]

The Supreme Court of the United States has sanctioned a variety of district plans in their apportionment decisions. State legislatures may establish multi-member or single-member districts, as well as flotorial districts (where two or more single-member districts are combined for the purpose of electing one or more additional legislators). The Court has also allowed for districts in which members are elected at-large, or in subdistricts (where each candidate runs for a specific numbered seat).

The Effect of Fiscal Considerations

Rule-making is affected by financial considerations. The state legislature controls the public purse, possessing the authority and responsibility to levy taxes and appropriate funds. This power is an important one, for no state monies can be spent without a legislative appropriation, and there are few governmental actions that do not involve a financial expenditure.

The rate of state expenditures has risen rapidly each year of the last half-century. Several factors may account for this. First, everything costs more each year. The ever-increasing costs for material and labor have made the administration and operation of and capital outlay for programs more expensive. Second, there are more people to be served, owing to the growth in the population. Third, the concentration of people in urban areas has spurred governmental activity. The presence of large aggregates of people in relatively small geographical areas necessitates greater concern for such problems as health, transportation, and the protection of persons and property.

The fourth factor is the life style created by industrialization. Life styles are no longer those of the agrarian, modified kinship basis that stressed the values of individual self-sufficiency and the obligations of members of small communities to each other. Instead, the style of life has changed to one of great economic interdependence. The complexities of industrial urban life, the massiveness of mutual economic needs, and the difficulties of communicating these needs among people have created a situation of individual dependence on centralized public agencies. The change of social life and attitudes have stimulated greater public expenditures. Fifth, technological advances require public spending to supplement use of the new products. Increasing automobile production, for example, requires more streets, bridges, and policemen. Sixth, there has been a change in people's attitudes toward the role of the state in individual affairs. Since the depression of the 1930s, and the ensuing social legislation of that period, people expect public agencies to enter into a number of spheres previously held as personal or family responsibilities. More and better quality services are demanded. People accept the idea that the state should deal with matters of housing, social insurance programs, public health, school lunches, and numerous others.

In several of the larger states, total annual expenditures exceed $2 billion; and at least half of the states spend $1 billion each.[17] These public funds are spent on a variety of activity classifications. The largest allocation is channeled to education, which includes aid to local governments for local schools and support of state colleges and universities. The second largest amount is spent on the construction and maintenance of roads. Public welfare programs and spending for health and hospitals are the third and the fourth largest categories.

Other programs fall within the general category of natural resources (*e.g.*, conservation and development projects for soil, water, forests, fish and game), police protection and correction (*e.g.*, law enforcement and prisons), and general control (the category encompassing the financing of the operation of government). The remaining funds are spend on such items as housing and urban renewal, airports and docks, interest on state debts, and employee retirement and employment compensation trust funds.

To meet the need for money, the states have explored a variety of revenue sources. More than half the total amount is raised by taxation. Of that, the general sales tax, used in forty-four states, provides over one-quarter of the total state tax yields. Revenues are also derived from such sources as the motor fuel sales tax, the tobacco sales tax, and the alcoholic beverages tax. License taxes are imposed on motor vehicles and motor vehicle operators, hunting and fishing, and such occupations as nursing, medicine, law, teaching, and beauty culture. Taxes are also imposed on personal income (in 38 states), and on corporation net income. Other revenues are derived from property, death, and gift taxes.

States obtain further revenue from various charges and miscellaneous sources. Among the charges are college tuition fees, highway tolls, and hospital service fees. Miscellaneous sources might take the form of sale of public property, or donations from private individuals.

Legalized gambling provides a colorful source of revenue for many states (for example, from portions of bets placed at race tracks and set aside for public treasuries). In recent years, there has been a resurgence of public lotteries as revenue-producing means. In 1964, by referendum, the voters in New Hampshire approved a state lottery. Lottery tickets that were sold were based on selected horse racing events. In the first year, the net income to the state amounted to $2.7 million. The amount did not meet the expectations of proponents, and questions were raised about the wisdom of continuing the lotteries. In 1966, the voters, however, reaffirmed their interest in this form of revenue raising in a second referendum. While the New Hampshirites were voting to continue the lottery in their state, the New Yorkers were voting to start one in theirs. Also based on horse racing events, the New York state lottery yielded a net income of $30 million in the first year. Proponents of state lotteries argued vociferously in many other states for its adoption. In 1969, the voters in New Jersey supported a referendum proposal for their own state lottery.

Some states earn money through business ventures. Seventeen states operate liquor stores. Others lease or sell the resources or mineral rights of public property to private entrepreneurs for development. Alaska's recent bonanza is illustrative of this. The discovery of extensive oil deposits in America's largest state is expected to provide for it many billions of dollars annually in payments from the sale of rights to drill, land lease arrangements, and royalty payments on barrels of oil pumped. The income, for example, from the sale of oil leases in September 1969, was $900 million.[18]

Additional revenue is received from the federal government. This comes in the form of grants for such programs as highways, education, public welfare, aid to agriculture, and conservation.

Lastly, states obtain funds through borrowing. The need to borrow may arise from emergencies and exceptional circumstances, such as those created by fire, floods, or earthquakes. States may go into debt for the construction of public improvements, for example, school and office buildings, bridges and highways, hospitals, and airports. Though the states may borrow from banks, the usual avenue is the issuance of bonds. In issuing bonds, states generally promise to repay out of general revenues. On occasion, bonds are sold for which repayments are made from the revenue received from the use of a special project, for example, sewer systems or stadiums. A popular referendum may be necessary for approval of the bond sales. A state may create special districts and authorities to borrow the funds for specific projects, such as transportation or parks.

Rule-making is closely related to the course of expenditures and appropriations. In short, there are budgetary considerations. Budgeting is the process by which program priorities are established through the arrangement of receipt and allocation of funds. However, the process of constructing a budget is not approached anew each time. Legislative rule-makers have only a small margin of discretion in which to make decisions for the budget. Perhaps less than ten percent of the budget can be considered malleable. Several factors may account for this constriction of decision making for fiscal rules.

The first factor is that in some states the legislature must accept certain provisions of the executive budget without alterations, or may decrease but not increase the proposals. Second, approximately one-half of all state revenues are earmarked for specific programs. Motor fuel tax revenue, for example, is often restricted for highway purposes. Those monies collected and set aside in trust funds for unemployment insurance, workmen's compensation, and public employee retirement are also restricted. Third, continuance of long-range programs require amounts to be allotted in each budget. Fourth, grants from the federal government are given on a matching basis, and thus the legislators are faced with allocating funds for projects that are co-sponsored. Fifth, legislators may be committed to maintaining an established ratio formula. State aid to local school districts, for example, is given in relation to the number of students enrolled. Sixth, the proportions for the refunding of indebtedness may be fixed, and thus they must be maintained from year to year.

Political considerations are equally restrictive on legislative discretion in fiscal rule-making. Previous expenditures may act as a constraint in that they provide the basis for decisions about pending operations. States maintain stability in expenditure levels, so that the tendency over a period of time is to continue the levels of previous spending. Donald Gerwin tested and confirmed the proposition that personnel and material requests for the budget will not be less than the appropriation for the previous year.[19] He found that state agency administrators would not be likely to request less money than already allotted to them, since no official is anxious to suggest that his agency is neither significant nor competent to continue or progress to expanded dimensions of effort. Moreover, legislative decision makers like to keep conflict at a minimum. Should the legislature decide to cut back existing programs, it would face obstacles from the agencies' personnel, client interest groups, and affected citizens who would resist the cuts. Thus, existing appropriations are not easily reduced.

Revenue levels tend to remain stable also. Legislators are reluctant to borrow or to raise taxes because of the weight of traditional practices. Moreover, it is not politically feasible to increase taxes. State decision makers may fear that to do so would cost them their re-election. Officials are not anxious to place a heavy burden on the major income-producing sectors of the state economy, such as natural gas, iron, or timber resources. Even if they are not pressured by economic groups to give special privileges, the legislators would not wish to "kill the goose that lays the golden eggs." Thus, Wisconsin officials give favorable tax policies to their beer industries, and those of the tobacco-producing southeastern states to their cigarette manufacturers. In addition, a low tax rate might attract new business into the area.

States generally maintain financial patterns that are similar to those of other states in a given region. Legislators may plan their activity after those of their neighbors, as they perceive patterns to be regional norms based on common historical experiences, economic conditions, or political characteristics. This tendency may be reinforced as officials get together in meetings of regional associations, or through social or political interactions. Interstate competition has long been a consideration in fiscal rule-making. The legislators may test their policies against those of their sister states to see whether a plan of action might place their state at a competitive economic disadvantage by, for example, driving industry or professionals across the borders.[20]

The socio-economic environment of the state has some implications for taxation and expenditure patterns.[21] For example, in the two important activities of welfare and education, the wealth of the state (viewed as per capita income) is directly related to the extensiveness of the programs. The wealthier the state, the greater is the ability to afford the social welfare policies and the greater the likelihood that they would be implemented.[22]

In addition, different types of societies will require different types of programs. The more industrialized and urbanized the state, the more social welfare legislation might be needed, desired, and expected by the people. Studies have shown that wealthy states are more innovative in their programs than are low-income, rural states.[23]

The Procedure of Legislative Rule-Making

The procedure by which bills become laws differs in each state. The formal rules of procedure, technically, are adopted at the beginning of each new legislative session, but the legislators generally continue to use the rules adopted in previous sessions. Though identical procedures do not exist, there are numerous similarities among all states. Thus the basic paths of bills may be seen to nearly parallel the following order.

1. Bills are drafted

Anyone can draft (*i.e.*, write) a bill. Though legislators may, few do. By far the largest group of bills comes from outside sources. The governor's staff, and other state and local officials and bureaucrats, present bills. Private organizations or citizens may be the source of bills. The state attorney general's office, or a legislative bill drafting service, may write the bills in correct form for the legislators.

2. Introduction and first reading

Only legislators may introduce a bill for the consideration of the members. This is a simple procedure, merely requiring that a copy be deposited with the clerk of the chamber. Three-fourths of the state legislatures have limited the period of the session during which bills may be introduced. After the prescribed period, a bill might be introduced only by an extraordinary majority consenting, by request of the governor, or if it is a money bill. Some states have adopted procedures whereby bills may be introduced before the session convenes. In Massachusetts, for example, bills must be introduced a full month before the session begins.

At the time of introduction, the first reading takes place. Generally, a full reading is dispensed with, and only the title, the author, and the number assigned to the bill as it is introduced is recited.

3. Referral to committee

Generally the speaker of the lower house, or president of the senate has the power to refer a bill to a committee within the respective chamber. Yet, other referral practices exist. In the lower house of Kentucky, for example, the committee on committees may refer the bills; as may the introducing member in Nevada; and a joint committee of members of both houses in Maine. In the senate of California it is the bill committee; and in that of Nebraska, it is the reference committee. However, bills are usually referred, pro forma, by the clerk; and generally, each proposed measure goes to a standing, subject-matter committee.

4. Committee action

A committee's assessment of a bill may determine the fate of the measure referred to it. Committees may agree to a bill as submitted, or they may alter it or reject it by positive or passive action. Hearings may be held. Twenty states require that hearings be public; in the others it is discretionary. Not all states have a procedure that would compel a committee to report on a bill. In about one-third of the states, committees are required to report all bills back to the floor, with favorable or unfavorable recommendations. The committee recommends action (for or against passage), and sometimes gives reasons for its recommendations. In California, Colorado, and New Hampshire all bills not acted on by the committees are referred to the floor on the last day of the legislative session.

4A. Appropriations committees

Legislation requiring the appropriations of funds may be studied by an appropriations committee concurrently with or subsequent to actions of the subject-matter committee.

5. Calendar

The calendar is a list of bills arranged in the order they were reported out of committee. In some chambers there is only one calendar; in others, there are several for different types of bills. Technically, bills must be debated on the floor in their order on the calendar, but a bill may be taken out of this order by a decision of the leadership, by a special rule, or by a motion on the floor.

6. Caucus hearing

In some states a party caucus, a factional caucus, or a policy screening committee may discuss the action or strategy to be taken on the floor for selected bills. Decisions made at this stage are important to the fate of each measure as it reaches floor action.

7. Second reading and floor action

Debates and amendments may occur on the floor, after the second reading (usually in full) of the bill.

In some states the full reading of the bill and subsequent debate occurs in the committee of the whole. This committee consists of the full membership of the house, but can operate with a smaller quorum and more informal rules of procedure than the regular legislative session. The report of the committee of the whole would be submitted to the entire membership for final action.

In the debate, the report of the standing committees may be considered routinely or as an important source of reference by the legislators. The floor manager of the bill may be the chairman of the committee reporting it or the bill's author.

8. Third reading and voting

After the third reading of the bill (usually only the title and author), the members vote to approve or reject the measure. Several methods of voting are used: a) roll call—where each member's vote is announced and recorded in the journal; b) voice vote; c) a show of hands; or d) a teller vote—where each legislator walks by a clerk who counts the vote announced by the member. In some legislative chambers electronic voting machines have been installed, which speeds up the voting and which allows for a member's vote to be made known. A simple majority of members present and voting—providing a quorum is present—is the usual practice for determining the outcome of a vote.

9. Action by the second house

After passage, the engrossed bill (*i.e.*, the one printed as agreed to by the members of the chamber) is sent to the second house for its action, where it is read (usually by title), referred to a committee, and continues through the stages 4–8 outlined above.

In Connecticut, Massachusetts, and Maine, the bills would have been referred to a joint committee in step 3; thus actions by both houses in steps 4–8 would have occurred concurrently. In Nebraska, this step and step 10 would be eliminated.

10. Conference committee

Should both houses pass a bill, yet fail to agree on details, the differences may be resolved by a conference committee. This committee is composed of members from each chamber, appointed by the presiding officer of each house. The report of the conference committee is sent back to both houses for approval. A rejection by one house would stop the bill from becoming a law. A second try, with a new conference committee, may be made.

11. Enrollment

The bill is printed in the final form as passed in both chambers, and signed by the presiding officers of both houses.

12. Governor's action

All bills go to the governor for his approval or disapproval. If he approves and signs a bill, it becomes a law. If he disapproves and vetoes a bill, it would go back to each house where an extraordinary majority (usually a two-thirds majority) may override the veto. If he neither signs nor rejects a bill, then it will become law if the legislature is still in session within a period of ten to fifteen days after it was sent to him. If he refuses to sign a bill, and the legislature is not in session, then a) in 30 states, it becomes a law after a prescribed period, or b) in 20 states, it fails to become a law (*i.e.*, by "pocket veto").

13. Effective date

A law becomes effective at a date prescribed in every state. In Maryland, for example, all laws become effective on June 1; in Texas, ninety days after adjournment; in Arkansas, as it is publicized.

The normal process of a bill becoming a law may take days or weeks. Yet, parts of the route may be bypassed. Legislative business can be expedited by unanimous consent, asked for by the leadership. At the end of a session, for example, in a rush to adjourn, bills can be pressed through a house in only a few hours.

Leadership in the Legislature

The holders of formal leadership positions in state legislatures generally have ample opportunity to influence the rule-making function. The structure of formal leadership in each state is basically similar. Yet, the leaders may differ in their power and operating techniques.

The speaker is the presiding officer of the lower house of every bicameral state legislature. He is elected by the membership, and he is someone who has experience and tenure in that chamber. In two-party states, the majority and minority party each nominates a candidate (usually in party caucus), and the vote is cast on formal party lines. In one-party states, and in non-partisan Minnesota, the nominations and votes are outcomes of dominant factional divisions.

The influence of the speaker on lawmaking is derived from his powers and his use of them. The speaker makes appointments to standing, special, joint, and conference committees. He can refer bills to committees (although custom or house rules may require other referral practices in some states). He has the power of recognition. He may apply the rules of procedure. The utilization of these powers may enhance or detract from the chance of a bill's success. For example, he may determine whether a bill goes to a favorable or unfavorable committee. He may recognize a member whom he knows will introduce a favorable or unfavorable amendment on the floor. Or, he may interpret a rule strictly or loosely.

The presiding officer of the upper body is the president of the senate (in Tennessee and North Carolina, the title "Speaker" is used). In those states that have a lieutenant governor, this officer is constitutionally charged with the duty of presiding over the senate. In states without a lieutenant governor, the body elects its own presiding officer. In addition, the senators elect a president pro tempore, who assumes the power of the president in the latter's absence.

The presiding officer of the senate may, also, have powers of appointment, referral, and recognition. However, if he is lieutenant governor, his power to affect legislation is limited. Being a member of the executive branch, he cannot wield as much influence as his counterpart in the house.

Floor leaders for the various parties or factions are elected by members of their groups. These leaders assist in planning committee assignments and in developing legislative strategy. They also act as spokesmen for their party or factions. The powers and influence of these men vary with the degree of party or factional domination or competition, and which party or faction has control of the governor's office.

Committees

Committees do most of the legislative work under the principle of the division of labor. Whether a bill will be considered by the legislature, or what form of the measure may be presented for floor debate, may rest with the committees. Or, a committee may pigeon-hole a bill. Even if rules of procedure require that they report each bill, the committeemen may adopt tactics that would defeat the purpose of the rule. They could report the bills on the last day of the session (when it would be lost in the last-minute rush), report it unfavorably, or ignore the requirement. Discharge, a procedure to force a bill out of committee, exists in some legislatures, but it is rarely used because legislators respect the authority and discretion of committees. In Florida, for example, a bill reported unfavorably requires a two-thirds vote to pass.

Yet, committees are not all independent and powerful "little legislatures." Several factors account for the inequality of committee stature or power. The work load is not generally evenly distributed. Some committees composed of members loyal to the leadership may be assigned the greatest number of bills, while others may remain inoperative or have little to do. Bills need not be referred *pro forma* to a committee, for the lines of committee jurisdiction are not always clearly defined. They may have broadly descriptive titles, for example, ways and means, or executive and legislative affairs, which allow for the leadership's discretion in assignment. Some committees' activities may also be hampered by little or no budget or staff.

Committee action may be influenced by the leadership, for its composition may be determined by them. Leaders may place themselves or loyal colleagues on important committees. They may assign inexperienced members who would rely for guidance on the more senior and knowledgeable party leadership. Moreover, leaders may exert some power of discipline over a member by threatening to remove him from a choice committee.

The size and numbers of standing subject-matter committees found in state legislative chambers vary. The average number of standing committees per chamber, however, is twenty; on occasion ad hoc committees are established and joint committees exist. There is no relationship between the size of the body and the number of committees found therein. New Hampshire's legislature is about fifteen times the size of Delaware's, yet the latter has more standing committees. The lower houses of Florida and Rhode Island are similar in size, yet Florida has three times the number of committees. The size of each committee is usually five to twenty members in the house (it may go up to over sixty), and five to fifteen in the senate (it may go up to over thirty).

Members are assigned, generally, by the presiding officers. Yet, other agents may have the formal responsibility of assignment; these include committees on committees, rules committees, minority party leadership (for members of the minority party), and the whole membership. Where the legislative body is dominated by strong party or factional leadership, membership of committees is greatly influenced by the leaders.

Membership on a committee does not always rest on the principle of seniority. There is no accepted rule in state legislatures that a member has a "right" to remain on a committee from year to year. Committees, also, do not have to be partially comprised of minority representatives in proportion to minority membership; thus important committees may be filled with majority party or factional members. Geographical and political considerations may be taken into account in assignment decisions. An important consideration is the area of interest of each new member. A frequent practice is to assign lawyers to the judiciary committee, farmers to the agricultural committee, insurance agents to the insurance committee, etc. A legislator may hold membership on several committees concurrently, and generally does.

Chairmen of committees are selected by the presiding officers, or in some states by a designated committee or by the entire membership. The bases for selection are party or factional affiliation, seniority in some cases, and personal choice of the leaders. There are generally no rules prohibiting the leaders from occupying the positions themselves.

Several states have created joint committees (comprised of members from both houses) to cut the time and effort expended by each house having to consider legislative measures individually. In Connecticut, about thirty joint committees act in place of standing committees in each house. In Maine, each house has some standing committees but the bulk of the work is done in joint committees. The usual standing committee organization exists in the Vermont legislature, but each pair of committees (*e.g.*, the agricultural committee of each house) meet jointly to consider bills.

Informal Factors in Legislative Rule-Making

There is no simple formula that can explain how state legislators make decisions. The legislator is beset by a dynamic and complex series of pressures and counterpressures that work towards conflicting objectives. These pressures are derived from many sources, both within the chambers and external to the legislative bodies. He makes his decision according to whichever of the forces, or combination of pressures, have made the strongest impression on him. Often, legislators may not consciously realize the extent of these pressures or the process through which their actions were derived. When questioned about the sources of influence, an Idaho state senator exclaimed midway through his response, "You know, I never realized how many people actually have an impact on my vote." [24]

Roles

How a legislator acts may depend on how others expect him to behave, or how he believes he ought to behave. The expectations of behavior patterns are known as "roles." These expectations are related to particular situations. Thus the legislator may find that he has several roles to play, with different sets of expected behavior patterns. He may be a member of a political party, interest group, professional organization, church, and of a formal or informal legislative group, such as a committee or a voting bloc. Day-to-day activities thrust upon the individual conflicts in roles as he finds himself in situations in which incompatible demands are placed upon him. He has to meet the demands of his constituents, his party leaders, his legislative leaders, his fellow legislators, and his own moral convictions. How he recognizes his roles and these situations, and how he resolves the role conflicts will have bearing upon how he will relate to the rule-making process.

John C. Walke defined one set of roles that relate to the way legislators are oriented toward the purposes and processes of their positions.[25] Some are concerned with the mechanics of legislative work, *i.e.*, the organization and rules of procedure. These are the "ritualists" who concern themselves more with the techniques of lawmaking than with the content of the laws. Others approach their rule-making tasks as advocates of popular needs and demands, who as "tribunes" spend their time calling attention—lest others forget—to at least the existence of the constituents. The "brokers" conceive their job as maintaining the peace, and by mediating, compromising, and negotiating conflicting interests obtain some accomplishments. The "opportunists" use the office essentially for immediate or long-term political or material gains. And some see as their major tasks the duty of creating, formulating, and initiating policy programs. They are referred to as "innovators."

James David Barber's classification of legislative roles was based on reasons given by legislators as to why each had entered into and how each behaved in office.[26] Some ran because they were attracted to the excitement and glamour of the position. Once in, they attended the sessions regularly, but participated little or not at all. These were the "spectators" who asked little of and contributed little to the legislative process. They were readily influenced by others, especially party leaders.

Others appeared on the scene as "reluctants," somehow drafted into running, but not actively ambitious. Once in office, they settled into maintaining and promoting the formal and informal rules of procedure. Policy could be made by others, but they were to see that laws were properly advanced through the routine of passage.

Men who saw legislative office as a chance to make themselves professionally or politically known were labelled "advertisers." Their activity was geared toward drawing public attention to themselves. Thus, they did not spend their time and energies working behind the scenes where the important stages of the rule-making process occur. Independent, and personally aggressive, these men are the "limelighters," not the team men.

The fourth category referred to by Barber was that of the "lawmakers." Such men sought the position because they felt that they could contribute something to public life. They worked diligently, and became experts and leaders who would influence others.

It has been noted that experiences—social and political—prior to legislative service affect the representative's concept of his role. A study of the attitudes towards roles held by California assemblymen before their election and one year after their taking office showed that pre-legislative experiences were significant for initial role orientations. Yet, at some point, further legislative experience modified or drastically altered the patterns of expectations learned in the individual's pre-legislative socialization. The changes may be due to contacts, pressures, routine, and political considerations of working in the legislature. Thus legislative experience has altered role perceptions, for it has resulted in a change of awareness of what and how much an individual can accomplish as one member in a large body, and how he relates to his constituency, his party, his fellow legislators, interest groups, and executive and judicial agents.[27]

Parties and Factions

Intralegislative stimuli from an individual's relationships with the leadership, committees, and formal and informal groups may influence his decisions. A pattern of partisan influence has been seen by some observers of the rule-making process.[28] Just as party identification serves as a reference group for the voter, so it does for the legislator bombarded by the many demands made on him. Knowledge of what the policy of the party or of the party leadership is cuts the costs of the legislator's effort by providing a set of cues for his actions. The cues provide aid in structuring information and in choosing between alternative policy proposals. This may be especially valuable for freshmen legislators who comprise nearly half the membership at each session. Newcomers may have to rely greatly on the party leaders who have acquired expertise through legislative tenure. For, as 70 percent of the Colorado legislators replied, tenure brings about experience to understand the legislative process, and to get a bill passed.[29]

In two-party systems, legislators may vote along party lines. Such party directed votes are primarily related to organizational and procedural matters within the legislative body, state election laws, apportionment, appointments and patronage, and legislation that is designed to support or embarrass the governor. Deviations from party directives may come about because of socio-economic variations of constituencies that send similar party affiliates to the legislature. Thus, a party split may occur on such issues as labor, taxation, and social welfare.

In one-party or non-partisan state legislatures, factional patterns may influence voting decisions. These patterns may develop around a program of a governor, or along regional, urban–rural, or conservative–liberal lines. Such proposals related to liquor, civil rights, agricultural, and business issues have been decided by factional voting alliances.

The influence of parties or factions is not uniform throughout the states. If party members are elected from similar social and economic constituencies, party cohesion may be strong, if they are elected from dissimilar districts, then party cohesion may be weak. Hugh L. Le Blanc, in his study of twenty-six state senates, concluded that a legislator would be more prone to support party directives when they are not in conflict with the demands of his constituency, for he would be voting with his party and his constituency at the same time.[30]

Robert J. Huckshorn's findings appear to modify this premise.[31] He asked the members of Idaho's state legislature whether they agreed with the following statement: "A member should vote with his party even though it costs him support in his home county." The responses were:

> Agreed—20 percent
> Tended to agree—28 percent
> Neutral—5 percent
> Tended to disagree—23 percent
> Disagreed—29 percent.

When they were asked if the party had any impact on legislative decision making, 40 percent of the Idaho legislators responded that the parties did, and 51 percent perceived little or no party influence. Most of those who perceived party influence believed it was present mainly in organizing the legislature and in the organization of support for policy decisions. Party cues have also been seen to be inversely related to the size of the plurality received by the legislator in his last election, the total number of years he has been active in politics, and the number of years he had been in the legislature.

The extent of party leader directives may be related to the margin between the number of seats held by each party in the chamber. Where the margin is close, the leaders may ask for cohesiveness among the party membership, the minority party hoping that the majority will split and the majority leader looking to maintain program success. Where there is a wider margin, the leadership may hope to negotiate, the minority leader looking for some success, and the majority leader looking for greater support should his party members split. Where the margin is wide, both sets of leaders may be more tolerant of deviation, and be less likely to demand unity.

Caucus

A caucus is a meeting of the members of the legislative body who (usually) belong to the same party to determine the group's action in regard to such matters as organization, procedure, or policy. Caucuses may be used as forums by which the leadership could inform or educate the members to the party views on particular bills or issues, orient new members on party policies and "rules of the game," and instruct the members on strategies and procedures. They may also be used by the members to convey their own views on policies, bills, or issues to the leadership or to other members.

In some states caucus deliberations may be integral to the decision making process. In Connecticut, New Jersey, and Pennsylvania, critical decisions on legislative programs are made in the caucuses and then ratified by the majority members on the floor. The Idaho legislators were asked about the influence of the caucus on their decision making. Eighty percent of them responded that the caucus was "usually effective," and 14 percent believed that it was "sometimes effective." They saw the importance of the caucus as providing channels for communicating information between the leadership and the membership.[32]

In non-partisan state legislatures, caucuses also are held. In Minnesota, for example, a liberal caucus and a conservative caucus meet in each house frequently, and assume the characteristics of party caucuses in other states.

In one-party dominant states, there appears to be little reason to call caucus meetings. Caucuses may be deemed unnecessary by the leadership. One reason may be that if the party or faction is a loose coalition lacking common purposes, then regular meetings would be useless. Another reason may be that if the legislative group is small, then needed communication can be accomplished by less formal means.

There are several means by which the leadership could enforce discipline for its directives. It could remove a legislator from or refuse him assignment to a committee that he finds desirable. The legislator may find that his local bills are procedurally thwarted, his few fringe benefits dwindle, or his financial or political support for reelection disappear if he deviates from the desires of the leadership. But sanctions are very rarely applied, because the legislators generally believe that it is advantageous to follow the leaders.

There are some legislators who do not consider legislative party identification as either relevant to their decisions or necessary for their interests. These are the "mavericks" who regularly take positions independently from fellow members. Indeed, their colleagues and their constituents have learned to expect this deviant and independent role. The numbers of mavericks in state legislatures is small. The appearance of such an individual occurs if the constituents in his district are atypical of the usual party affiliates, or if the constituents do not have a high emotional involvement in and attachment to a partisan label (as in some suburban areas) and prefer the style of political independence.

Informal Groups

Informal intralegislative groupings influence legislators in their rule-making function.[33] These groups serve as channels for communication and as a means of gaining support for a policy position. The groupings may be social or work oriented. The social groups are held together by ties of friendship, and the members can influence each other because of this tie. When "one friend" says that he is interested in a bill (as he tosses a card from his deck at the weekly poker game), another "friend" may say, "Okay, if it doesn't hurt me, why shouldn't I support him."

One type of work oriented association is a clustering because of similarities of constituencies. For example, urban legislators may tend to seek each other out, and to study and act on matters of concern to their similar respective districts. Another type is the clustering of members from the same multi-member district (*e.g.*, a multi-member county-wide district). They are drawn together to evaluate and vote on issues that affect their collective district. Moreover, they generally will initiate "local legislation" for their mutual area, and gain from presenting a united front to the whole body.

Groups also tend to form around "experts," or "built-in lobbyists," when an issue falling within their realm of subject specialization is under consideration. The expert is a legislator who might be a committee chairman or a man of long tenure in the capitol. Expertise is related to an issue, and an expert in one area may not be considered one in another. The respect accorded to him generally is built upon his knowledge of and his legislative effort in a specialized area of concern. The built-in lobbyist is an individual who is concerned with the advancement of some private cause. The legislative system allows for him primarily because members are part-time legislators and full-time bankers, insurance agents, doctors, farmers, and so on, who bring into the short session knowledge gained from their year-round pursuits. In addition, the occupational assignment to committees enables these men to be placed into positions of influence. Hence, the legislator may be in a key position to affect the course of a specialized bill, and decide on its being cleared or being stopped for action. He could be looked upon as one who could contribute perception, information, and experience.

Informal Rules

Group life in the state legislature is generally informal, characterized as it is by transient and inexperienced membership. Thus a flexible system of operation exists, governed by the informal rules of the game, to affect the behavior and action of legislators. These rules, which coexist with formal procedural requirements, are adopted to maintain a working relationship that is necessary to law making. They limit conflict and promote cooperation among the legislators.

Wahlke has listed forty-two such rules common to all legislative bodies. There are rules that channel and put limits upon conflict (*e.g.*, be willing to compromise, do not try to accomplish too much too quickly); or expedite legislative business (*e.g.*, do not talk too much on the floor, do not argue unnecessarily, be punctual and regularly attend, do not call attention to the absence of a quorum). Procedural rules exist (*e.g.*, go along with unanimous consent to suspend the formal rules, vote for local laws without debate or opposition when the local delegation unanimously supports them); as do rules of proper individual conduct and of personal qualities (*e.g.*, courtesy, sociability, integrity, honesty, gracefulness in defeat, caution in commitments, self restraint in goals). Other categories of rules includes those for promoting group cohesion and solidarity (*e.g.*, respect your colleagues, do not act in any manner to bring discredit upon the body); and for promoting predictability of legislative behavior (*e.g.*, keep your word, do not engage in trickery or devious maneuvering).[34]

Most legislators recognize the utility of informal rules for the legislative process, once they learn what these are. The rules contribute greatly to providing new members with cues for action and, thus, make it possible for members to fit in with the others. Informal groups, both social and work oriented, are major forces in helping to socialize members to the informal norms.

Sanctions exist to limit the extent of deviant behavior. Legislators may vote against the recalcitrant one, delay his bills, amend his proposals, demonstrate distrust by extensive questioning on the floor or in committee, or subject him to social ostracism or overt ridicule. The deviant legislator may lose some of his political perquisites and rewards of office; for example, patronage or good committee assignments may be taken away from him. Though these sanctions exist, they are seldom used. The legislators follow the rules because they believe in the purposes underlying the norms, rather than because they are afraid of the punishments.

The Executive in Rule-Making

That few legislators claim to approach their task in an innovative manner may be evidence that they themselves realize that policy initiation has shifted from the legislatures to outside agencies—especially to the offices of the executive branch. As has been noted: "The function of our legislators is not to invent new laws, but to formulate and pass judgment on the legal inventions of others. . . ."[35] Indeed, state legislatures may be "boards of review" that pass or block the concepts of other agents.

The state chief executive has in recent decades become the state's "chief legislator,"[36] as G. Mennon Williams noted while in office as Governor of Michigan. Under the pressure of increased demands, legislators have come to rely on the executive to set order and establish priorities for programs. The influence of governors on rule-making is related to constitutional provisions, political traditions, and the personalities and abilities of the men holding the office.

The gubernatorial initiation of rules occurs with the messages that are sent to the legislature. Each chief executive presents his program in the annual or biennial state of the state message at the beginning of the legislative session (either because of constitutional requirements or tradition). The message sets the tone of the expected programs for the session, and indicates the emphasis to be placed on various proposals. Thereafter, more detailed messages are sent on specific subjects. Bills may be drafted to supplement those proposals, or to initiate still others, and they are introduced through the party leadership or friendly legislators as the political situation demands.

The Budget

A principal instrument buttressing the executive initiation of rules is the budget. It is through the manipulation of funds that governors can greatly affect programs. Through provisions of new funds, new programs can be introduced. By increasing or decreasing funds set by prior allocations, programs can be emphasized by expansion or de-emphasized by contraction of monies requested. The elimination of funds from budgetary requests may have the effect of ending an activity.

In more than 80 percent of the states, the governor (with the assistance of a staff subject to his control) is responsible for presentation of the budget to the legislature. In the remaining states, the budget is prepared by a group that may or may not be subject to control by the governor. Such groups may be composed primarily of other elected state executive officials (as in Florida), or of state legislators (as in Indiana). In a few states, the original requests of the agencies must be presented to the legislature along with the governor's budget. Thus the legislature may hear both arguments, and armed with that information choose between the sets of recommendations. In some states, the administrative head of a state agency appears personally before the legislature, and may press for higher appropriations than those which the governor may have requested.

Legislators do not feel that the executive has overstepped his office in becoming the prime force in fiscal rule-making. They do not have adequate staffs or the time to hold hearings and examine budgetary requests with care. Moreover, political considerations may make fiscal decision making unattractive to them. If they decide to spend more than the governor asks, they face the prospects of provoking constituent ire for creating deficits or for increasing taxes to raise the necessary additional funds. If they try to spend less, they may hear the complaint that the figures are being "cut below what the governor says we need."

Generally, bargaining on the budget starts from the governor's figures and proposals rather than from those of the agencies, interest groups, or legislators. Major changes are seldom made. A recent study of budget requests of 592 agencies in nineteen states showed that the average legislative appropriations in each of these states were only 8 to 19 percent above or below the governor's recommendation; but, in thirteen of these states, the deviation was only 2 to 9 percent from his recommended figures.[37]

Additional ability to influence fiscal rule-making is held by the governor in forty-one states, where he has the power of item veto on appropriation bills. Thus, he may exert a final control, by striking out sections (*i.e.*, items) of funding allocations. The exercise of an item veto may come about as a control over agencies that have used direct lines of access to the legislature, or to influence a rebellious legislature. The item veto is used sparingly. The governor may be cautious in altering a fiscal decision already made, for he may fear a loss of influence should his veto be overridden (by a required extraordinary majority), or he may be unable to extract an undesirable budget request from a complex provision of funds for an entire agency.

The Veto

An executive veto enables the governor to mold legislation. The veto can be a positive instrument to influence the formulation of rules, or a negative device to stop a rule that the legislature has already passed. In forty-nine states (all but North Carolina) the chief executive has the power to stop a bill from becoming a law. The veto, whether positive or negative, is a potent force, for it is rare that a legislature can muster the extraordinary vote (usually a two-thirds majority) needed to override the executive action. The governor's political power is usually sufficient that he can maintain the support of the one-third (or two-fifths, etc.) minority needed to uphold his veto. For example, a recent study that historically traced the Arizona executive veto found that approximately 90 percent of the vetoes had been maintained.[38]

The veto power is used sparingly. Coleman B. Ransone's study showed that, over a one-year period, all governors have vetoed less than 7 percent of the bills sent to them for their approval.[39] The threat of the veto can usually get a recalcitrant legislator to modify his position, thereby making an actual veto unnecessary. Almost every legislator has at least a few bills that he would like to see become law. These pertain to benefits for his locality, to damage claims by his constituents, to the interest of some group supporting him or, simply, to matters of personal interest. No one likes a veto on his bill, nor wishes to court retalliation should he confront the governor. No one looks forward to facing the wrath of his constituents to whom the executive may appeal. The legislator can only guess at the degree of determination of the governor to carry out a threat of a veto, and may back away from calling his bluff.

The governor's control over legislation is enhanced by the fact that many bills are passed in the last days of the legislative session (especially if the length of the session is restricted by constitutional provision), and the legislators may be too rushed to consider overriding any veto. Should the executive veto a bill after the closing of the session, the matter would end there. For, in almost all states, the vetoed legislation cannot be brought onto the floor at the next regular legislative session for purposes of its being overridden.

In addition, the governor has the power of executive amendment in Alabama, Virginia, Massachusetts, and New Jersey. This means that he may return a bill with the change that he would like to see made. The change is in the form of an amendment. Should the legislature accept, it will avoid an outright veto, and the bill will be so altered. The practice, though not formally instituted in other states, is commonly used by the executive informally, and has the same effect.

Special Sessions

The executive "arsenal" of rule making influence includes the ability to call a special session of the legislature. In 70 percent of the states, the power to call a special session in his exclusively; and in the others, he or the legislature may issue the call.

In the cases where the governor issues the call, he has control over the agenda; and in forty-six states, the legislature is restricted to the topics of the call. He is able to focus the public's attention on the small number of topics discussed and thus hope to marshal additional support. If legislators want to end the session quickly, they may give in to the governor, for he might call a special session a second or third time.

Special sessions may be useful, *e.g.*, if legislators did not act on some proposals during the regular session, but the governor runs several risks by calling them. He places his prestige on the line (the legislature might rebuff his demands), he risks being blamed for the extra expense of the special session, and he faces the possibility of arousing hostility of the legislators in calling them from their normal routines. Roy D. Morey's study of the effectiveness of calling special sessions showed that governors generally have an average of 82 percent success for their proposals.[40]

Executive Relationships to the Parties in the Legislature

The mobilization of forces for a legislative program may depend on the governor's relations with political parties in the legislature. Several types of relationships may exist; for each, a different tactic is necessary.

First, a governor's party may have overwhelming majorities in both houses. In this situation, the parties may have little or no opposition to maintain cohesiveness, and factions may form. The governor must work with a faction, create his own, or try to encourage the emergence of several factions in order that no majority could be reached without his intercession. He must try to influence the officers or the key legislative leaders to build support for his program.

Second, the governor's party may have only a slight advantage of numbers in each house. The majority may be cohesive, if for no other reason than they may look foolish should they not support their governor. The governor may court the support of some minority party members, and find them receptive, for they have bills they wish to have enacted.

Third, the governor's party may have a majority of members in only one house. He must try to exert influence on the leadership of that one house, and hope that these leaders can, in turn, exert influence over those in the second house. Negotiations between top leaders in each chamber necessarily occurs, for each house needs the other to pass its bills.

Fourth, the governor's party may be a minority in each house. In this situation of divided government, he may not be able to exert sufficient policy leadership. He may have to organize the minority partisans in each house as effective spokesmen for his point of view. To achieve success, he will need to consult leaders from the opposition as well. Program proposals may have to be couched in a "bipartisan" tone, and he must constantly base his tactics on the necessity of compromise with the majority party.

Members of the legislature who are fellow partisans may follow the governor out of loyalty. If not, the executive (as head of his party) has resort to partisan sanctions. He might exert influence to deny them leadership posts or committee assignments. He might appeal to local party organizational leaders to withdraw support in future campaigns. Legislators may follow, not out of fear of these sactions, but because they recognize that their chance of re-election may be tied in the voters' minds with the success of a governor's achievements and programs.

The Governors and the Legislators

The governor's position of influence is also due to his unique place within the state political system. In a system where the legislature is part-time and ill-equipped, there is a need for central direction—and the governor may fill this need. His constituency is the whole state, and he has a claim to speak for the whole interest of the state. The dignity of the office in the minds of the people and its range of concerns allow him to tower above any other state public official. The public most readily focuses on and is most knowledgeable about the office of the governor. The governor has the singular ability of being able to obtain the attention and use of the facilities of mass communication. He is, indeed, in the center of the state political process.

The legislative session absorbs much attention and energy of the governor.

He meets with the leaders periodically, talks personally with legislators, and appears personally before a party caucus or a committee hearing. He makes generous use of his liaison staff assistance. Alliances will be formed with pressure groups during the course of a session. Groups may work for parts of his program of no immediate concern to them in return for his support on their measures.

He and his staff will work hard to cultivate goodwill with the legislators. It is rare that a governor would leave the state capitol in the midst of a legislative session. Time is spent with individual members in the privacy of his office. Indeed, there is a standing rule with every secretary that a legislator is to be admitted to see the governor at any time without any prior appointments. Being invited to the executive mansion for a meal or a social gathering is a memorable experience that leaves a lasting favorable impression upon the legislator. The governor's posing for a picture with a legislator for publication in a local paper might be a helpful asset to a grateful assemblyman.

A recent technique to win popular and legislative support is the establishment of "blue ribbon" commissions to study problems. The members of a commission lend prestige to recommendations made, attract state-wide publicity in their efforts, and even "lobby" for the program.

Legislators, on their part, will cultivate relationships with the governor. They need the services that the executive can offer. The governor (and his staff), as noted above, can supply needed information and expertise. The clemency power may be used to grant a pardon or reprieve to a legislator's client or constituent. The governor's appointments and help in deciding where facilities will be placed will enable a legislator to show some visible result of public service. The announcement of the building of a state facility in a legislative district or the appointment of a local individual enhances the local delegate's political standing in his community.

Tenure may affect the governor's policy proposals and his ability to gather support among the legislators. An executive able to remain in office for successive two or four year terms may be interested in long range development programs in the states for he might expect to be in office long enough to continually press for support of these projects or ideas. He might initiate projects whose benefits will not be clear to the public for several years (*e.g.*, highway or school construction programs) and initiate policy ideas that might not command popular and legislative support for several years. A governor limited by constitutional provision to one or two terms may not be as anxious to exhaust his effort on such types of programs, because he would not be in office long enough to assure the continuance of those programs (although, of course, such an official might propose long range and costly development projects unencumbered by fears of negative political reactions from the electorate).

A "lame duck" governor may see his influence wane in the last year of two of his term. The prohibition of a second four-year term may reduce the incumbent's period of practical power to only two or three years. Because he will already have dispensed the bulk of the rewards at his disposal (*e.g.*, patronage appointments or local projects), the executive may have lost bargaining power with the legislators who support his needs and who relate to him on the basis of perspective rewards or sanctions. In addition, before his term ends some key legislative figures (even in his own party) will begin to leave the governor's side, as each of them tries to emerge as the successor to the to the office. Such a prospective successor may find that he can gain more publicity and support by opposing the governor than by backing him behind the scenes.

Today's governor usually has a position of considerable influence over the legislator, and his maintenance of that position is important to a successful administration. As has been noted, governors take great interest in the proceedings and deliberations of the legislature. It is rare that an executive would choose to play a spectator role in the legislative process, yet a few individuals do.

Some governors may not be able to influence or want to exert influence. They do not enjoy manipulating people and situations, they cannot bargain, or they cannot take temporary defeat in stride. Some may not understand the political system, and fail to realize that a political vacuum could be created by their passive actions. Some may be incompetent to exert influence. Some may be easily diverted by the glamour of the ceremonies of office. Some may be ambitious for national positions, and be more interested in building an organization for future elections than in making a record based upon the capacity to lead from the state executive mansion.

That the modern governor is active does not mean that he has unbridled rule over the legislative process. But when he wants to, the probability is great that he will be extremely influential in rule-making affairs. Alan J. Wyner's study of fourteen state governors showed the average success of a governor's program was 71 percent.[41]

That the governor is seen by the legislators to be influential has been demonstrated by Huckshorn in his study of the Idaho legislature. The legislators were asked if they recognized that gubernatorial influence existed. All the respondents agreed that it did, but there were different conceptions of the sources of this influence. The veto power and the potential of a veto over personal bills were seen by 41 percent of the legislators to be the source. The governor's personal influence was cited as the source by 32 percent; his ability to arouse public opinion was cited by 14 percent; and his control over patronage was cited by 9 percent of the legislators.[42]

The Governor's Direct Rule-Making

There are instances in which the governors singularly perform the rule making function. In times of riots, economic crises, strikes, or labor disturbances they have exercised their established statuatory powers to provide for the peace within the community. For example, during the riots of the mid-1960s, governors issued emergency orders that had the effect of preventing the congregation of people on highways, on campuses, or in other public places; prohibiting the carrying of guns; and closing public streets after certain hours.

The Administrators in Rule-Making

State administrators are influential in every stage of the rule-making function. As full time employees with technical training, background, and experience, they are aware of the extent of operational and future needs and trends in state programs. They are often the targets of continual group and individual actions, and are thus aware of many articulated demands. Having a virtual monopoly on detailed or technical information, they are looked to by the legislators and the chief executives for the initiation of specialized measures, or the actual drafting of the bills.

Administrators are active in influencing bills throughout the legislative passage stages. They are called on to testify or report on the feasibility of suggested programs, and to study or propose alternative methods of attacking the solution of a problem. Bills may be sent to them for redrafting during the course of legislative deliberations. They are often instrumental in mustering needed public support for new actions, as the citizenry also acknowledges their expertise. Yet, it should be noted that the administrators' values and preferences color the information given for and the direction of emphasis placed on many of the measures.

Moreover, a department head may strike out on his own to influence the legislature, if not merely the chief executive. Believing that what his agency is doing for the public is vitally important, feeling that some programs are worth fighting for, or wanting to expand the prestige, scope, and power of his agency, each administrator strives to insure that he is a successful combatant in the conflict between departments. Thus, an administrator has to resort to different strategies to present his case. Often an administrator chooses (or is traditionally or administratively barred from open efforts) to operate subtly and out of the spotlight. He works through clientele allies who have no such inhibitions to openly exert influence. Road constructors, for example, able and willing to spend money to lobby, will act to get bigger highway appropriations for the state road commission. Allies of the welfare department, such as professional organizations of social workers, labor unions, and other welfare service oriented groups, will press for the department's interests. On occasion, personnel of different departments act to help each other apply pressure to the legislators.

Such administrative influence is favorably received by the legislators. They recognize that the information they are receiving has been prepared by well-equipped staffs, and respect the professional expertise of the bureaucrats. Moreover, the legislators receiving requests for assistance from constituents, are mindful of the services that the administrators can render.

Direct Administrative Rule-Making

Administrators act beyond the influence part of the rule-making function by making regulations themselves. Of the total body of legal prescriptions to which citizens of the state must give heed, a great part is to be found in the regulations promolgated by agencies acting under the authority of legislative enactments or constitutional provisions. The current evolution in administrative rule-making has been largely the result of the advance of technology and of the complexity of the work of state governments.

Administrators, first, make rules to complete legislative actions. The members of the legislature cannot foresee in advance how a law could apply to every situation, so they delegate the power to make a law or rule to the administrative agents to fit into situations as they occur. Second, because of the ever increasing areas of social and economic life that are supervised by the state government, administrators have become rule-makers. The legislators do not have the time or ability to devise rules for the many areas the laws cover; nor do they have the time or technical knowledge to debate the merits of particular devices to insure the operations of rendering public services.

In some states, the courts have held that the legislatures were free to delegate to administrative agencies almost unlimited power to make whatever rules are needed for the purpose of regulating business, occupations, or activities that are related to enhancing the public welfare or wants. Constitutions of many states provide for elected state administrators with their own mandates of power. Regulatory agencies may be established and their powers of rule making set forth in the state constitutions (as in Virginia, Nebraska, California, Louisiana, Arizona, and Oklahoma); or the constitution may permit the legislature (as in Oregon) to set up such agencies, and in this way sanctions their ensuing rule-making activities.

The range of regulation is broad. Among these are business controls (*e.g.*, banking, public utilities, and insurance), labor management, and development and conservation (*e.g.*, fish and game protection, highway construction, parks and water resources). The state board of education, for example, by administrative ruling establishes uniform curricula throughout the state, or the requirements of college training for school teachers. Insurance boards not only license companies and agents to sell policies, but participate in determining fees. Public utility boards regulate the building, rates, and operation of power and transportation companies.

Rules for welfare are set by departments of public assistance. Rules for sanitation, for the sale of mattresses and bedding, and for the production and distribution of narcotic drugs are set by boards of health. Criteria for selling goods or services are set by departments of licenses. Specialized boards govern the practices of barbers, accountants, engineers, nurses, pharmacists, optometrists, embalmers, boxers, and wrestlers. Agencies give permits to operate through franchises allowing for almost monopolistic practice in, for example, transportation; or give permits for mergers, such as to banks. Highway commissions prescribe regulations for erecting and maintaining private advertising signs or directional signs in a scenic area or near highways. Horse racing commissions make rules to govern horse races. Aeronautic commissions make regulations for flying within the state. Boards of trustees for state colleges set regulations for operations affecting administrators and students. And pollution commissions control dumping of refuse into waters.

Often members of the departments, boards and commissions are representatives of interest groups. To fill such public positions, the governor may be required by statute to appoint representatives of interest groups. For example, boards regulating professional occupations may be composed of members of professional organizations. Thus those regulating the practice of nursing, law, or public accounting are comprised of registered nurses, members of the bar, or certified public accountants.

Ronald Akers has studied the close inter-relationships between public agents and private associations, and has concluded that "it appears that their activities, personnel, facilities, and even finances overlap to such an extent that...the cooperation between the two sometimes reaches the point of near identity."[43] He noted, for example, that the Medical Practices Act in Kentucky was the product of the state medical association. The organization, through its secretary—who was the state commissioner of health—guided the writing of the law. Thus interest group representatives—as administrators—can exercise more than influence on the process as outsiders; they can, in effect, write the rules themselves.

The Judges in Rule-Making

The courts' performance in the rule-making function is partly accomplished through their review of the rules made by administrative agencies and legislative bodies. Judicial review of administrative regulations has several objectives. The courts can review the regulations promulgated by the agencies to decide if the regulation falls under the authority conferred on the agency by legislative statutes or by the state constitution. The courts could review the orders of an agency fixing rates to determine whether proper legal criteria were employed in arriving at the rates, and whether there was substantial evidence to sustain the determination made. In other areas, such as granting permits, licenses, or franchises, the court might review the discretionary rules made by administrative officials, if there were reason to believe that the officials had acted in such an arbitrary fashion as to constitute an abuse of such discretion.

Cases for review may be brought before the courts by aggrieved parties or by administrative officials. Sometimes the administrative officials go to a court to force parties to obey their rules or to have the court set the penalties for disobedience. Individuals may appeal an agency's imposed penalty or prohibitory order by asking the court for an injunction to restrain the enforcement of the regulation, or to declare the regulation invalid. The resort to the courts may be authorized by a state statute; or state judges may accept cases by asserting power to review such rules.

Should a rule be challenged on the ground that it or the statute under which it was issued by the agency is in violation of the federal constitution or a federal statute, it may be brought before a federal court. In this case, the federal court might accept it directly or, as is usually the case, indirectly after all remedies in state courts have been exhausted.

Any case taken to the courts allows for judicial scrutiny of administrative rules. Knowledge that their actions may be reviewed by the courts may affect the performance of administrators in the rule-making function. In any event, final judicial decisions made by courts of appeal significantly affect the substantive nature of these rules.

By reviewing state legislative enactments, the courts further act as participants in the rule-making function. Judicial actions may take the form of nullification, reinterpretation, or elaboration of rules. Generally the courts act when a case has been brought before them by a party that has been directly affected by a rule. Recently, however, they have accepted cases by individuals acting in "representative class actions," in which the plaintiff represents, in addition to his own interest, the interests of others similarly affected. By allowing class actions in reapportionment and civil liberties cases, for example, the courts have demonstrated that they recognize the impracticality of everyone expending the time, effort, and expense of bringing individual suits to elicit the same judicial response.

Suits brought before courts have encompassed many subjects. There have been challenges to the methods of bond financing or of raising state taxes. Challenges have been made to the use of the eminent domain power in connection with slum clearance, housing, highways, airports, and other public works projects. Questions have been raised about the granting of franchises or licenses to privately owned but publicly used facilities.

Courts have become active arenas for influencing rule-making to some extent because of the nature of state constitutions. The lengthy documents, inclusive of detail, invite litigation in the courts. For any rule made by legislators which is not in complete accordance with constitutional prescriptions is subject to judicial nullification. Legislators are aware that the courts are active in this respect and may try to adjust their actions to fit into the constitutional mold. Indeed, the legislators sometimes request the opinion of the judges of the state's highest court on the constitutionality of proposed legislative bills; and, in some instances, such may be expressly provided for by the constitution itself (as in Massachusetts).

The federal courts exert influence on the rule-making function also. They do so by upholding the "supremacy" of the national constitution and federal statutes. State rules in conflict with the "higher laws" are subject to the federal courts' review and possible nullification. The foremost publication of the analysis and interpretation of the American constitutional system lists 656 state statutes that were held unconstitutional during the period between 1809 and 1964.[44] In recent years, this activity has increased, due to the Supreme Court's expanding interpretation of the "due process" and "equal protection" clauses of the Fourteenth Amendment into areas of the states' reserved powers.

The involvement of courts in the rule-making function may place them in the position of "super legislatures." Their adherence to precedents and traditional doctrines in making decisions may result in the development and modification of laws. The judicial interpretation of statutes for specific cases may differ from the legislative intent. Yet, it is this interpretation that will set the tone of how rules will be executed. For example, a law in Maryland prohibited the sale of articles on school property by unauthorized persons. The legislature had intended it to apply to ice cream venders, but a state court in 1969 interpreted it against the sellers of an "underground" newspaper.

Paul C. Bartholomew has referred to courts' positive and active role by calling them "legislative courts."[45] When the courts have entered new policy areas, such as school integration and reapportionment, their decrees have often been the stimulus for legislative enactments. When legislatures, however, had failed or refused to act, the courts have made the prescriptions for conduct in such areas themselves.

Direct Judicial Rule-Making

That courts directly make rules is uncontestable. Despite the existence of an extensive set of legal rules, cases steadily come before the tribunals for which no applicable rule can be found. Moreover, as new interpersonal practices and technological developments have appeared, there has been a need for new rules to be made. It is rare that a statute or regulation has been drafted with such attention to detail that it would be applicable to every situation that may arise. Thus the making of new rules is an important part of the activities of judges. Yet, the frequency of their action depends on the extent to which the other public agents have left questions unanswered in advance of the situations. The frequency also depends on the extent to which individuals can financially and otherwise afford to bring the case to them on appeals.

Intergovernmental Effects on Rule-Making

Modern technological developments, speedy and visually graphic communications, and increased population mobility have caused an interchange of ideas, stimulated demands, and created problems that do not respect state jurisdictional boundaries. While, traditionally, each state has grappled with its problems alone, many current problems have proven to be too extensive to be handled in that manner. Thus, state governments have begun to cooperate with other governments for solutions.

Compacts and Commissions

One way in which states have sought the solution to their problems has been through interstate cooperative ventures. Interstate compacts and commissions are among these. Interstate compacts are arrangements between states, and occasionally with the national government, for the purpose of exercising control over specific regional problems. To attack such problems as the utilization and conservation of waterways, compacts have been entered into by states bordering the Delaware, Potomac, Ohio, and Colorado rivers. To protect forests, compacts have been made in the northeastern, southcentral, and southeastern forested areas; and for the protection of fisheries, compacts have been made among the Atlantic, Pacific, and Gulf of Mexico states. For the problems of transportation, the Port of New York Authority and the Delaware River Port Authority have been created to construct port terminals, bridges, and facilities for commerce. Representatives from each member state meet together as commissions and make regulations to implement the purposes of their compact. The existence of these compacts affects the rule making activities of the governmental officials of the member states. For example, compacts may require additional rules from each state for its successful execution, or they may preclude the states from unilateral action in that area.

Conferences

Other means of interstate cooperation are conferences and associations of state officials. These have been organized for the purposes of discussing

ins. Indeed, a significant percentage of the state
cused on the allocation of funds to support local
estimated that at least one-half of the time in the
matters concerning the political subdivisions within

ng effort for matters affecting the localities, the state
by the needs and demands that are articulated from the
ally the responsibility of the local legislative delegation
es for their own constituencies. These groups of legislators,
me district (*e.g.*, a county or a major city) often meet with
officials, or hold public hearings with citizens to ascertain
demanded. The interests articulated at those meetings are
into proposed legislation. Once introduced, such measures
ted by other legislators, provided that the constituent desires
tions are not upset or infringed upon. In addition, local
upon themselves to present their views through lobbying
ot uncommon to find state agents personally pressured by
agers, or councilmen. Representatives of associations of
also come to lobby, such as those from local leagues of munic-
ious councils of governments, the National Municipal League,
ted States Conference of Mayors. Specialized organizations, such
association of Justices of the Peace, send representatives to apply
so. Indeed, mayors of large cities, assisted by well-equipped staffs
ies, and aided by their own party organizations may place well
ed demands on the state officials.
y established blue ribbon commissions have also been utilized to
fluence upon state agents. One such committee was created by the
of Seattle and the chairman of the King County commissioners in
gton, in 1966. Under the name of "Forward Thrust," a private-public
on of 200 citizens and officials organized to look into such problems a
portation, community and recreation centers, water control, sewerag
ies, low income housing, and fire protection. Their studies, reports
suggestions secured the passage of eighteen measures in the state legis
re within one year. In addition, substantial financial support for man
their projects was elicited from the state government.[48]
State agents may be receptive to the pressures emanating from the localitie
a governor's electoral success was due to the support from a major cit
e may look with favor on the source and concentrate some of his efforts
programs for the locality's enhancement. Legislators, more intimate
related to the local situation for their elections, may view approaches fro
their constituencies with favor. The influence of local officials may be a res
of contacts established over a period of time. Individuals holding state off

common problems, gathering statistics, and suggesting model laws for passage in the individual states. In addition, as state officials meet together from time to time, they come to know how their neighbors have handled problems. The exchange of proposals, data and ideas may influence state officials as they consider ways to attack their own state problems. Legislative officials, members and staffs of legislative service agencies meet in the National Legislative Conference, the National Conference of State Legislative Leaders, or the National Conference of Commissioners on Uniform State Laws. Executive officials have their own organizations, such as the National Governors Conference, the National Association of State Budget Officers, and the National Associations of Attorneys General. Judges have their associations such as, for example, the Conference of Chief Justices. One established agency that coordinates the suggestions of the above organizations, and is engaged in research, inquiry, and information services, and in making suggestions for rules is the Council of State Governments.

National Action

One outcome of these conferences has been the recognition that the solution to many problems entails an active federal role. The concern, involvement, and influence of the national government in state rule-making has a long tradition. The federal efforts have taken many forms. In several areas the national agents were first to see the need for rules enhancing the public welfare. In the public health field, for example, Congress passed a meat inspection act; and to improve employment practices, minimum wage and work safety standards were established. Such foresighted actions of the national government were duplicated by the states, which passed similar rules. In areas where states refused to act, such as in civil rights, the federal government made rules. Provisions in the national constitution were expanded by congressional action to sustain the momentum for social change. The interstate commerce provision was referred to as buses, restaurants, and other public accommodations were officially desegregated.

Grants-in-aid

In many areas where the Congress has not intervened by legislative preemption, it has relied upon grant-in-aid programs as instruments for change in the states. The purpose of payments from the federal government has been to accomplish some nationwide objective in which it has an interest by contributing to the undertaking of state programs.

Grants-in-aid in some form were offered by the national government as far back as 1785. The early grants were in the form of land, but annual money grants for specified purposes have been in use since 1808. A major increase in the number and size of grant programs came after World War I. The greatest increase of federal action began in the 1930s and has continually risen since that period. Of all programs in which the national government has participated, two-thirds have been initiated since the depression era of the 1930s.

The areas covered by the programs are quite extensive. The 1969 *Catalog of Federal Domestic Assistance*[46] listed 581 domestic assistance programs. These were administered by 47 national departments and agencies. The categories of programs included agriculture, airports, civil defense, cultural pursuits, education, fish, game and wildlife, health and hospitals, housing, highways, labor, natural resources and pollution control, public works, recreation, transportation, veterans, and welfare. The assistance takes such forms as outright grants, conditional grants or shared revenues. Other forms of federal assistance include the offered use of federal facilities, direct construction, goods and services, and donations of surplus property. The value of the latter goods and services add greatly to the outright cash figures received by the states as cited above.

Grants of money are based upon formulas derived for specific services. They may be based on the numbers of persons who will receive benefits from the programs, the extent of need, or on the income levels to be found within each state. Quite often there are requirements that the state must match the federal funds with some of its own. For example, the state must provide 10 percent in some cases, 50 percent in others, or some specific determined amount in still others.

The impact of grants-in-aid on state rule-making has been great. First, the result has been new programs and enlarged existing state programs that might not otherwise have been undertaken because a state was not concerned or could not afford such programs. Encouraged by the funds, states have gone into new areas. For example, under the 1956 Federal Highway Act, a state legislature could obtain a modern network of roads by appropriating only 10 percent of the cost of the highways, receiving the remaining 90 percent of the money from the federal government. Second, federal grants have stimulated states to make rules regarding program execution. For example, some programs must be executed by persons recruited through the merit service, and the states have expanded this method of hiring personnel to other areas. Third, the grants have stimulated uniformity of standards in accord with national guidelines, such as, for example, in the quality of construction of public facilities and roads. Fourth, the impact of federal assistance has also been seen in ancilliary rules that states must make. In order to avoid a cutback of funds for highways, under the 1966 Highway Act, the states were required to enact legislation for such things as compulsory inspection of motor vehicles and requirements that drivers forfeit their licenses if they refuse to take a sobriety test when accused of driving when drunk.

Grants-in-aid have been used, also, as leverage by the federal government

in promoting civil r... structing scho...
In addition, gr... Appalachian Re... action. This mea... comprised of repre... bined attack on a b... hard-core poverty.

States have had to... affect their budget pla... offered by the national g... monies may entice legisla... financed programs regardle... constituencies. Of course, no... Yet, each governor wants to o... dollar allotted to his state; and... limitations on tax resources, war... the standards and regulations set... be met.

Not all state public agents react... Governor John Chafee, of Rhode Islan... federal impact on state rule-making and... following statement:

> Let me give you an example. The federal gov... help elementary and secondary education. . . . ... ment has tried to keep very close strings on thi... Rhode Island, you take the money and use it in ... think you need it most!" No, no. It says the mon... programs. And so if the state is relatively advance... reading programs and compulsory kindergarten an... money for that—it's got to go on to something else... stems from a belief, inherited from the New Deal... federal government that the states are ignorant, ineff... quently corrupt and therefore can't be trusted.[47]

Local Influence upon State Rule-Making

Much of the time and effort of the state's rule-making fun... to local legislation. In all states, the legislature has some... over matters within the counties and municipalities. Most... activities undertaken by local governments require state actio... where some semblance of home rule powers exist, the state's...

over the localities rem... fiscal rule-making is f... programs. It has been... legislature is spent or... the state.

In their rule-maki... agents are affected... localities. It is gene... to introduce measur... elected from the sa... local councils and... what is needed o... often translated... are usually acce... of other deleg... officials take i... efforts. It is... mayors, ma... governments... ipalities, var... and the Un... as the state... pressure a... and facili... coordina...

Locall... exert in... mayor... Washi... coaliti... trans... facili... and... latu... of...

may have previously held positions in the lower levels of government, as county or municipal agents. Thus working relations may have been established that are useful for opening avenues of communication between the state and local officials. The interaction that exists because of common interests between legislators (who are elected from districts based upon county or town lines) and county and town officials, further allows for access to the centers of state rule-making. Moreover, the state officials live, work, pay taxes, and raise families in the localities, so many of the local matters are of immediate concern to them.

On occasion, local officials, in conjunction with the legislative delegation, initiate public relations programs to influence the entire legislative membership. One effort took place in northern Virginia, where a tour was organized to bring legislators from all parts of the state to see for themselves what the area was like. The Virginia state legislators were guided by community officials through the region, and were shown commercial, educational, recreational, and historical facilities. After being wined and dined, they were faced with pleas for more state financial assistance for transportation and educational facilities and welfare programs. In general, the local officials attempted to impress on the state legislators a feeling of urgency about the problems of northern Virginia communities, and attempted to convey a general desire that the legislators develop positive attitudes toward their future requests. The importance of such a tour was to familiarize the legislators with a growing region of the state that many had not been in for several years. To most of the rural legislators, the trip came (as one reporter along with the tour wrote) "as a shocking plunge into the complexities of urban life." One legislator, from a constituency of 5,000 persons stated in astonishment, "I've never seen anything like it." [49]

Governor G. Mennon Williams, commenting on the need for state governments to be more involved with local problems, has stated that "it is important for the state to help local governments be effective." Yet, he noted that, "Presently the state government is not adequately equipped to service local governments properly or to keep abreast of their needs." [50] In a chapter (of a recent work on intergovernmental relations) entitled "The Case of the Reluctant State," Roscoe Martin has delivered an indictment of the states' failure "to reach positively and effectively to the demands of a new age." He noted that

> the atmosphere is not congenial to the embrace of new programs; and that state horizons are severely limited by prevailing mythology. . . . The vast new problems of urban America are unique in the experience of the states, which react to them in an impatient and sometimes truculent manner. Nothing would please the states more than for the cities and their problems to dematerialize into thin air. . . . [51]

In recent years, in recognition of the complexities of city problems and the need for liaison between the local officials and state rule-makers, as well as between the city and the federal agents, special state agencies have been established. Between 1966 and 1969, offices for urban affairs were created in twenty-five states.

There is a lack of uniformity of the names of the urban affairs offices, just as there is a lack of uniformity of activities performed by each and where each is placed in the state governmental framework. These may be called, for example, the Local Affairs Agency (Alaska), the Office of Local Government (Tennessee), the Division of Local and Metropolitan Government (Rhode Island), and Intergovernmental Council on Urban Growth (California). Many of these offices are in the executive departments, others are permanent legislative commissions. Their basic responsibilities have been in coordinating federal and state programs of aid, planning programs, or executing assistance programs for local governmental units. Some areas of concern for these offices are urban renewal, housing, land use, health and welfare, personnel training, and local finance regulation.

These agents assist in the state rule-making function by influencing and informing either the governor or the legislators concerned with making rules for local governments. They may develop legislative proposals, direct the legislative appropriations, or derive new program ideas for legislative and executive implementation.

A 1969 study has shown that only 14 percent of chief administrative officers, of 838 cities having a population of 10,000 or more, felt that the state office made any significant contribution to local problem solving. Basically the importance of the agencies' activities seemed to be in coordinating federal and state grant-in-aid programs. It appeared that administrators of smaller cities (*i.e.*, those under 50,000 in population) saw greater usefulness of the agencies' assistance, than did those of the larger ones (*i.e.*, those over 50,000 in population). It was concluded that the urban affairs offices were attempting to make greater efforts than ever before to serve the smaller governments. The larger cities appear to be making their own contacts with national agencies, bypassing the state offices or using these offices to assist them in establishing such contacts.[52]

In making of rules for the state, agencies take existing local rules into consideration. Existing local street patterns affect the rules made for placement and construction of major state roads, for the latter must tie in with the former so that realistic patterns of traffic movement will be obtained. Existing sewerage lines in the localities similarly affect state rules. In some issue areas, as in health and drug measures, the localities may have made ordinances before the state entered the field. In these cases, the direction taken by the state is influenced by the experiences of the local governments. If the local ordinances had proven successful, they they may be used as models for state rules; if they had proven unsuccessful, then they may demonstrate what alternative modifications are needed. In these and other fields (education, law enforcement, recreation, etc.), the local officials, through their reports, suggestions, and activities, affect the rule making activities of the legislative and executive centros, and administrative bureaus in the state capitol.

Influence of the Media on Rule-Making

The news media perform a linkage service in the political system that affects rule-making. They not only report to the people the news about governmental actions, but they convey public opinion, reactions, suggestions, and information to the rule-makers from the constituencies. The media also structure news or important events, and may set priorities for problem solving as they emphasize specific items in reporting, researching, or programming. Reporters at a press conference may question a public official in such a manner as to prod him into a re-emphasis or a rethinking of a direction of the rules to be made.

Public officials may be influenced by any one of the various media. The press, however, is by far the most influential. The newspaper, unlike radio and television, has the capacity for in depth, detailed, and interpretative news coverage. And the paper focuses more on state and local news than do the other media. Moreover, the governor, the administrator, and the legislator cannot depend on the radio and television stations in the capital city to convey information about the various localities. The various hometown newspapers can and do fill the gap for them.

The press provides various types of information helpful to rule-makers. Articles explain measures before the legislature, give general background information, analyze the effects proposals may have on problems or their impact on policy, look for hidden implications, and discuss further problems that may be raised or flaws in the proposals. In addition, rule-makers can find out what is happening among their colleagues that may have a bearing upon their own behavior patterns. All this information may be more useful to legislators than to the other state officials. Governors and administrators have better staff, internal communication systems, and access to information from other sources than do the legislative centros. One legislator has stated that:

> A lot of the time you vote on measures you really don't know much about and don't recognize what they will do. So when a newspaper points this out, it has an impact.

Another legislator has said:

> A quick glance at the paper lets me see what is happening and is quicker than hearing reports in caucus.[53]

Reactions and opinions about rules are also conveyed by the newspapers. Confronted by dozens of measures at any given moment, a public agent may rely on the paper as an instant poll that indicates reactions to specific proposals. The press acts as a source by which a rule-maker can be apprised of support or opposition by local officials, groups, or constituents. The timing of a proposal may be affected by reports that demonstrate immediate public concern or dissatisfaction. An article appearing in the paper about a bill may cause a legislator to reappraise his opinion of its importance. One Wisconsin administrator has noted that "a person would be a fool if he weren't sensitive to newspaper reactions...." [54]

Newspapers are often sources of new ideas. Columnists delineate problems and sometimes suggest solutions. Editorials, reflecting the stand of the newspapers, present statements about ways to tackle problems. If the press is interested in an issue, rule-makers may respond favorably to it, believing that in doing so they will reap favorable coverage in the future.

Citizen Participation in Rule-Making

Initiative and Referendum

Citizens can participate directly in the rule-making function where the initiative and referendum exist. In those states where there are constitutional provisions for these procedures, the public has the opportunity to "legislate" at the polls instead of through its elected or appointed public agents. Through the initiative, a group of citizens actually propose a bill; through the referendum, they are reacting to a proposal already considered by the legislature.

Twenty states, almost all in the western part of the nation, have constitutionally provided for popular initiative. Initiatives may be direct or indirect. A certain number of signatures, usually between 5 and 19 percent of the votes cast for the governor or for some other state office in the previous electron, must be obtained for a direct initiative petition. Printed upon each petition circulated among registered voters is a statement of the proposition the advocates of change wish to see on the ballot. Sometimes (as in California) that proposal will be prepared by the attorney general of the state who sees that the wording is in correct legal form. This proposed law will be placed on the ballot after the signatures on the petition have been validated by the secretary of state. If it is ratified (some states require more than a simple majority on a proposition), it will then become law without having been enacted by the legislature.

The indirect initiative differs from the direct initiative in that the petition, after having been certified by the secretary of state, is sent to the legislature. The legislature may enact the proposal, adopt a different form of the measure, or do nothing but submit it to the electorate. Should the legislature enact the proposal, it follows the usual method by which a bill becomes a law. If the legislators adopt a different form of the measure, then theirs and the citizens' proposal will be placed on the ballot for the electorate to choose the one it prefers. If both receive the required majority, then the one that receives the largest vote becomes the law. When the legislature does nothing but submit it to the electorate, the ratification stage is similar to the direct initiative.

An initiative proposal approved by the voters cannot be changed or repealed by action of the legislature. Any legislative alteration would have to be submitted to the electorate for approval. In almost all the states, the governor is prohibited from vetoing such measures. Generally, the only governmental action that can affect popularly enacted statutes is court judicial review. The people, however, may amend or repeal the measure by a later initiative.

Referenda may be optional or legislative in nature. In the states that have provisions for an optional referendum, there is a thirty to ninety day waiting period before a bill passed by the legislature takes effect as law. During this period, a group may circulate a petition to prevent the bill from taking effect. If the required numbers of signatures of registered voters is obtained, the measure is placed upon the ballot at the next regular election or at a special electron for popular approval or rejection. Constitutionally exempt from such referenda are laws pertaining to the public peace or emergency measures.

Legislative referendum permits legislators to submit proposed measures to the electorate for judgment. This usually occurs when a proposal in the chamber is considered to be controversial, such as an increase in the tax levy or a change in the tax structure. Certain matters must be referred to the public for approval before they can become the state rules. The most common matters for mandatory referenda are the issuance of bonds and state constitutional amendments. If the proposals pass (sometimes with an extraordinary majority being required), they are generally not subject to the gubernatorial veto before becoming effective.

Citizens play a major role in changing state constitutions. In thirteen states, amendments may be popularly proposed by a constitutional initiative. In those states a petition is circulated to obtain signatures of a percentage of registered voters. The basis of the necessary number of signees varies in the different states; usually it is based on a percentage of total votes cast for governor in the previous election. The petitions must also bear the signatures of a percentage of the voters residing in each county. After the petition is filed and certified as correct, the proposed amendment is placed on a ballot for citizen approval. Amendments initiated by state legislatures (in every state except Delaware) also require approval by the electorate. Ratification is based on a majority (simple or extraordinary) of those voting for the amendment, or those turning out on election day.

Direct rule-making by initiative and referendum were thought by its supporters to accomplish major reforms in the governmental process. Bertil L. Hanson has studied the impact of fifty years of popular rule-making in Oklahoma.[55] He has examined the aims of the reformers to see if they have been achieved.

First, it was expected that the initiative and referendum would increase the popular impact on rule-making, and conversely de-emphasize the impact of special groups. Yet, a review of the sponsors of the 201 questions that appeared on the ballot over the half-century period, demonstrates that this aim was not realized. Of those, eighty-four questions appeared as the result of petition drives. Table VII.1 lists the sponsors of those petitioned measures that were referred to the public for approval.

TABLE VII.1

Sponsors of Initiative and Referendum Questions in Oklahoma

Type of Sponsor	Number of Questions	Percent of Total
Business interests	21	25.0
Labor organizations	3	3.6
Farm organizations	6	7.1
Teachers associations	10	11.9
Church groups	2	2.4
Governors	17	20.2
Other public officials	15	17.8
Political parties	3	3.6
Civic reform groups	4	4.8
Other	3	3.6
Total	84	100%

Adapted from: Hanson, "Oklahoma's Experience," p. 266.

As can be seen in the table, one-half of all the questions were sponsored by business, labor, farm, professional, or religious interests. Among the questions sponsored by these groups were those that would give concessions on exise taxes, promote highway, turnpike, and hospital construction, increase teachers' salaries, and so on. Almost 40 percent of the proposals were initiated by public agents. The governors and other public officials, unable to convince the legislators of the merits of certain programs, found the initiative and referendum convenient mechanisms to bypass the legislature and appeal to the people. Only a very small number of these questions were presented by citizen groups. These were proposals for female suffrage, popular election of United States senators, and legislative redistricting.

The burdens and expense encountered in the initiative and the referendum may explain the frequency of organized sponsorship. Meeting the signature requirement is burdensome because a large number of signatures must be obtained and these come from voters scattered throughout the state. Collecting signatures necessitates a great deal of organization; having a signature-collecting arm undertake this task requires a great deal of money. Additional funds are needed for radio and television advertisements, literature, speakers, etc., to inform voters and to interest them on the issues. Hanson has shown that each recent effort has cost between $200,000 and $300,000.

The second expectation of the reformers was that the initiative and referendum would enhance the potential for change. They thought that the people would more readily instigate or accept change than would the legislators. The latter, they argued, would be prone to protect the status quo, to preserve the existing power bases. Yet, the electorate has not been the major stimulus of change. Of the total of 201 questions placed on the ballot during the fifty-year period in Oklahoma, 117 (or nearly 60 percent) have been sponsored by the state legislators. Often, these have been initiated because of the need to alter the detailed and restrictive constitution. The legislators, from time to time, have seen the need for more taxing authority, and for greater freedom to borrow money, change public salary scales, change the administrative structure, and revise election requirements. Furthermore, the electorate has not been too ready to accept changes. The voters have failed to ratify nearly 60 percent of changes initiated by the legislators. Indeed, of the 201 questions placed on the ballot, the voters have failed to ratify 67 percent of the total.

The third expectation was that the two processes of direct legislation would increase the interest and participation levels of citizens. The review of these elections, however, shows that on issue questions the levels generally have been low. When special elections have been called for initiative and referenda questions, a 40 percent turn out has been the average percentage. In December 1963, only 17 percent of the registered voters appeared at the polls to vote on a proposal to authorize a bond issue to finance a state medical center; and in September 1965, 15 percent went to vote on a proposal to increase finances for the public schools. The record turnout rate for any special Oklahoma referenda election was reached in 1959, when 65 percent turned out to express an opinion regarding the state prohibition against sale of alcoholic beverages. This turnout rate surpassed the previous high of 53.5 percent set in 1910. Even when questions were placed on the ballot at regular elections, the rate of interest on the issues (as seen by the roll-off effect) was less than it was for the candidates.

Thus, Hanson has concluded, as have observers in other states, that direct legislation appears not to have affected state politics as the reformers had hoped. It has not redistributed political power to less privileged groups, nor has it discouraged the impact of special interests. It has not appreciably enlightened the Oklahoma voters towards issues and changes.

Recall

The public may indirectly influence rule-making through the process of recall. Armed with this weapon, a concerned and aroused citizenry could remove an individual from public office prior to the expiration of his term. Approximately a dozen states permit recall for elected state officials, and a few of these permit it for appointed personnel also. Some states have imposed limitations on the use of the recall. Kansas, Nevada, and Oregon, for example, specifically exempt judges from this process. In California, an official must have been in office at least six months (and if he were a state legislator, the session must have already met for at least five days) to permit some demonstration of his conduct. Should the official not be removed at the election, another recall attempt at him could not be made within a six-month period.

As with the initiative and referendum, the process starts with the circulation of a petition. The number of signatures required is generally based on the percentage of the votes cast at the prior election for that office being recalled. After receipt and certification of the petition, a special election is called for the question of permitting the office holder to maintain his position. The ballot may (as in California) include reasons for the recall, and a statement by the office-holder justifying his conduct. The election may also be the occasion to vote on his replacement, where the candidate receiving the highest vote wins.

The recall process entails a burdensome and expensive procedure. As with direct legislation efforts, this may be a method of influencing rule-making that is more conducive to the facilities and abilities of well organized interest groups than to the public. Groups, however, which depend on goodwill for access to and influence of rule-makers, may not be willing to risk incurring the wrath that would result from any recall campaign that they had mounted. Further, it is difficult to find the large numbers of people who are knowledgeable and concerned about an incumbent, and sufficiently motivated to support what amounts to a personal attack on an official prior to the end of his term.

The recall has been invoked on a statewide basis on only two occasions. In North Dakota, a governor and two other state officials have been removed, and in Oregon, two public utilities commissioners were subject to a recall. Yet, the infrequent rate of its use does not imply that it is not an effective popular weapon to influence rule-making. A public agent, aware that his constituents are armed with the power of recall, may be more inclined to concern himself with their needs and demands. Or he may be more cautious in making rules that are too progressive or experimental, lest the citizens be prompted by the emotions of the times to recall him from office.

The Relationship of Rule-Making to the Public

State public agents, responsible for making rules affecting a broad scope of the activities of the state residents, perform within an arena limited by formal rules and inadequate facilities and resources. They must plot their course between multi-pressures and multi-demands. Final decisions made may ultimately depend on how each perceives his representational·role.

Wahlke, and his associates, have studied legislative centros (who have been assigned the prime responsibility for the rule-making function by the state constitutions) to see how public preferences are considered in the decisions to be made. It was found that the representational role patterns were of three types: "delegates," those who accept the instructions of constituents as the basis for their voting; "trustees," who use their own judgment and vote on the basis of their own principles; and "politicos," who are a blend of the other two, reacting to the articulated demands on some issues, and their own beliefs on others (*e.g.*, being a delegate on matters of local interest, and a trustee on statewide issues). Of the four state legislatures studied by Wahlke, the proportion of trustees was found to overwhelmingly dominate the composition of legislative bodies (ranging from 56 percent in the Ohio legislature to 81 percent in the Tennessee body). The delegates were the least in numbers (ranging from 6 percent of the legislators in Tennessee to 20 percent in California); with the proportion of members acting as politicos slightly higher (ranging from 13 percent in Tennessee to 29 percent in Ohio).[56]

Wahlke's explanation for the predominance of the trustee role was that the public is unable or unlikely to provide guidance because of the complex and technical nature of the problems facing modern governmental agents. However, the explanation may be that the citizens are uninterested in making attempts at providing guidance. As has been seen, levels of turnout at the polls have been low, as have levels of articulating preferences in the form of letters, telephone calls, telegrams, and personal visits. Indeed, when given the option of direct rule-making, the public, for the most part, has refused to become an active participant. Those who have articulated preferences and who have sponsored direct legislative actions have been organized special interest groups. And one may ponder what would be the outcome of the rule-making function if only articulated instructions of the groups were obeyed.

While the trustee role appears to be in conflict with the democratic beliefs (*i.e.*, representatives should act only as agents for popular preferences), one should not assume that rule-makers do not care about the public preferences. Their efforts have demonstrated concern about public interests. It has been seen that rule-makers listen to groups as these are perceived to represent public interests; that they hear party leaders and consult with local officials who are thought to convey constituent demands; and that they read the press to gauge public sentiment. And where direct legislation exists, the legislators have used the devices to obtain public responses.

Chapter VII Footnotes

1.   4 Wheat. 316 (1819).
2.   For example, the extension of the Twenty-fourth Amendment to cover state and local elections was an outcome of *Harper v. Virginia State Board of Elections*, 383 U.S. 663 (1966).
3.   The data for the state legislatures were obtained from *The Book of the States: 1970–71* (Lexington: The Council of State Governments, 1970), pp. 51–114.
4.   William J. D. Boyd, *Changing Patterns of Apportionment* (New York: National Municipal League, 1965), p. 25.
5.   328 U.S. 549 (1946).
6.   369 U.S. 186 (1962).
7.   372 U.S. 368 (1963).
8.   377 U.S. 533 (1964).
9.   Thomas R. Dye, "Malapportionment and Public Policy in the States," *Journal of Politics*, XXVII (August 1965), pp. 586–601.
10.   Herbert Jacob, "The Consequences of Malapportionment: A Note of Caution," *Social Forces*, XLIII (December 1964), pp. 256–61. See also Richard I. Hofferbert, "The Relation Between Public Policy and Some Structural and Environmental Variables in the American States," *American Political Science Review*, LX (March 1966), pp. 73–82. For an analysis of the absence of any effect of reapportionment on Key Legislative leadership positions, see Brett Hawkins and Cheryl Whelchel, "Reapportionment and Urban Representation in Legislative Influence Positions: The Case of Georgia," *Urban Affairs Quarterly*, III (March 1968), pp. 69–80.
11.   Frank M. Bryan, "Who is Legislating?" *National Civic Review*, LVI (December 1967), pp. 627–33.
12.   Allen Dines, "A Reapportioned State," *National Civic Review*, LV (February 1966), p. 74.
13.   Jack Rosenthal, "The Year of the Suburbs: More People, More Power," *The New York Times*, June 21, 1970, p. 54.
14.   Quotes and data were adopted from ibid.
15.   Malcolm E. Jewell, "How Many Members?" *National Civic Review*, LVII (February 1968), pp. 75–80.
16.   Ibid.
17.   All figures were from: U.S. Bureau of the Census, *State Government Finances in 1969* (Washington, D.C.: Government Printing Office, 1970).
18.   *National Observer*, September 15, 1969, p. 1.

19. Donald Gerwin, "Towards a Theory of Public Budgetary Decision Making," *Administrative Science Quarterly*, XIV (March 1969), pp. 33–45.

20. Ira Sharkansky, "Regional Patterns in the Expenditures of American States," *Western Political Quarterly*, XX (December 1967), pp. 955–71.

21. Richard E. Dawson and James R. Robinson, "Inter-Party Competition, Economic Variables, and Welfare Policies in the United States," *Journal of Politics*, XXV (May 1963), pp. 265–89; and Hofferbert, "Relation Between Public Policy."

22. An interest illustration is found in: Edward J. Fortier, "Oil-Rich Legislature Goes on a Spending Binge," *National Observer*, June 21, 1970, p. 1.

23. Thomas Dye, *Politics, Economics, and the Public* (Chicago: Rand McNally & Company, 1966).

24. Robert J. Huckshorn, "Decision-Making Stimuli in the State Legislative Process," *Western Political Quarterly*, XVIII (March, 1965), p. 165.

25. John C. Wahlke, *et al.*, *The Legislative System* (New York: John Wiley and Sons, Inc., 1962), pp. 245–66.

26. James David Barber, *The Lawmakers* (New Haven, Conn.: Yale University Press, 1965).

27. Charles G. Bell and Charles M. Price, "Pre-Legislative Sources of Representational Roles," *Midwest Journal of Political Science*, XIII (May 1969), pp. 254–70. See also Kenneth Prewitt, Heinz Eulau, and Betty Zisk, "Political Socialization and Political Roles," *Public Opinion Quarterly*, XXX (Winter 1966), pp. 569–82.

28. See Wayne L. Francis, *Legislative Issues in the Fifty States* (Chicago: Rand McNally and Company, 1967); Malcolm E. Jewell, *The State Legislature* (New York: Random House, 1969, 2d ed.); and Wahlke, *et al.*, *Legislative System*.

29. Victor S. Hjelm and Joseph P. Pisciotte, "Profiles and Careers of Colorado State Legislators," *Western Political Quarterly*, XXI (December 1968), pp. 719–20.

30. Hugh L. LeBlanc, "Voting in State Senates: Party and Constituency Influences," *Midwest Journal of Political Science*, XIII (February 1969), pp. 33–57.

31. Huckshorn, "Decision-Making," pp. 168–69.

32. Ibid., p. 169.

33. Stephen V. Monsma, "Integration and Goal Attainment as Functions of Informal Legislative Groups," *Western Political Quarterly*, XX (March 1969), pp. 19–28. See also his "Interpersonal Relations in the Legislative System," *Midwest Journal of Political Science* X (August 1966), pp. 350–63.

34. Wahlke, *et al.*, *Legislative System*, pp. 141–69.

35. James H. Bowhay, "Western Legislative Procedure," *State Government*, XL (Autumn 1967), p. 265.

36. G. Mennon Williams, *A Governor's Notes* (Ann Arbor: Institute of Public Administration, University of Michigan, 1961), p. 8.

37. Ira Sharkansky, "Agency Requests, Gubernatorial Support and Budget Success in State Legislatures," *American Political Science Review*, LXII (December 1968), pp. 1220–31.

38. Roy D. Morey, "The Executive Veto in Arizona: Its Use and Limitations," *Western Political Quarterly*, XIX (September 1966), pp. 504–15.

39. Coleman B. Ransone, Jr., *The Office of the Governor in the United States* (University: University of Alabama Press, 1956), pp. 181–82.

40. Roy D. Morey, "The Special Session: Asset or Liability?" *Southwestern Social Science Quarterly*, XLVI (March 1966), pp. 437–44.

41. Alan J. Wyner, "Gubernatorial Relations with Legislators and Administrators," *State Government*, XLI (Summer 1968), pp. 199–203.

42. Huckshorn, "Decision-Making," pp. 171–72.

43.   Ronald Akers, "The Professional Association and the Legal Regulation of Practice," *Law and Society Review*, II (May 1968), p. 478.

44.   From *United States v. Peters* [5 Cr. 115 (1809)] to *Sherbert v. Verner* [374 U.S. 398 (1963)]. See Norman J. Small, ed., *The Constitution of the United States of America* (Washington, D.C.: Government Printing Office, 1964), pp. 1405–1522.

45.   Paul C. Bartholomew, "Our 'Legislative' Courts," *Southwestern Social Science Quarterly*, XLVI (June 1965), pp. 11–14.

46.   Office of Economic Opportunity (Washington, D.C., 1969).

47.   R. Joseph Novogrod, Gladys O. Dimock, and Marshall E. Dimock, eds., *Casebook in Public Administration* (New York: Holt, Rinehart, and Winston, Inc., 1969), pp. 46–47.

48.   James R. Ellis, "Thrust Toward Quality," *National Civic Review*, LVIII (February 1969), pp. 56–60.

49.   *The Washington Post*, January 25, 1970, p. D1.

50.   Williams, *Governor's Notes*, p. 54.

51.   Roscoe C. Martin, *The Cities in the Federal System* (New York: Atherton Press, 1965), pp. 79–80.

52.   A. Lee Fritchler, B. Douglas Harman, and Morley Segal, *Federal, State, Local Relationships* (Washington, D.C.: International City Management Association, 1969), pp. 24–26, 40–54.

53.   Delmer D. Dunn, "Differences among Public Officials in Their Reliance on the Press," *Social Science Quarterly*, XLIX (March 1969), pp. 831–32.

54.   Ibid., pp. 832–33.

55.   Bertil L. Hanson, "Oklahoma's Experience with Direct Legislation," *Southwestern Social Science Quarterly*, XLVII (December 1966), pp. 263–73.

56.   Wahlke, *et al.*, *Legislative System*, pp. 281–82.

Chapter VIII

Rule-Making, Part 2: The Local Level

The rule-making function occurs within all local governments. Local rule-making powers originate in state constitutional provisions and state legislative enactments. The scope of local rule making activities will differ among the various governmental units.

Factors and Formal Limitations

Local rule-makers acting in general areas of responsibilities are bound by formal limitations. Within the structure of the federal system, localities are subordinate to both the federal and state governments. Local public agents, like state rule-makers, are constrained by the national constitution and laws. Rules cannot be made in those areas pre-empted by the national legislature, nor in those foreclosed by the constitution.

The primary restraining influence on local rule-making, however, is the state government. The power to create local governments is one of the powers reserved to the states within the federal system. State constitutions generally provide for the establishment of such units, and for the extent of authority that may be granted. The central principle supporting the legal basis of local governments is that they only have such rule-making powers as the state constitutions and state legislatures permit. The federal and state courts have upheld the principle that localities have no inherent or implied powers; and, in addition, should there be conflict between any state and municipal authority, the courts will resolve the question in favor of the state. The prevailing concept of restricted power is known as "Dillon's Rule" (named for its expounder, a chief justice of the Iowa Supreme Court). The dictum states:

> It is a general and undisputed proposition of law that a municipal corporation possesses and can exercise the following powers and no others: First, those granted in express words; second, those necessarily or fairly implied in or incident to the powers expressly granted; third, those essential to the accomplishments of the declared objects and purposes of the corporation—not simply convenient, but indispensible. Any fair, reasonable, substantial doubt concerning the existence of power is resolved by the courts against the corporation, and the power is denied.[1]

The establishment of local units, and the granting of rule-making authority, are accomplished by state enactments, that is, charters for local governments. There are basically four types of charters. These are, from most restrictive to least restrictive: special charters, general charters, optional charters, and home rule charters.[2]

In addition to the grant of power to make rules in specified areas, the formal procedures of rule-making are usually precisely stated in the charter. For example, some charters require that a proposal must be considered during a stated number of open meetings of a local council before it can be passed. Rule-making may be influenced by such procedural dictates. If an ordinance fails to meet in every minute detail, or to conform explicitly with the charter or state laws that set boundaries for local enactments, opponents can challenge the legality of the ordinance in the court. Many state courts have permitted suits against local governments to be brought, not only by injured parties, but by any taxpayer. Even if the suit should fail in its attempt to have the ordinance declared null and void, the delay in the implementation of the rule brought about by the litigation may successfully frustrate or hamper the actions of local government. Citizen efforts have stopped municipalities from building bridges, housing developments, and other civic projects.

Formal limitations on rule making are also placed on fiscal matters of concern to local agents. Local legislators may have certain powers over financial matters such as making budgets, imposing taxes, and incurring debts. However, state constitutions and statutes may restrain local discretion in these areas. In cities, for example, taxes may not be imposed in those areas pre-empted by state legislative action. Constitutions in nearly every state have provisions that require localities to hold popular referendum elections for approving budgets, increasing tax rates, incurring debt, or issuing bonds.

Another major formal limitation on local rule-making is the presence of overlapping boundaries of activities, responsibilities, and governmental units. First, this is present in state and local relations. In most areas of local governmental activity, there is parallel state activity; both levels, for example, are responsible for education, health, welfare, and roads. In these activities, local officials are subject to varying degrees of supervision from state administrators. For example, a permit for an electric line to be installed may be granted by a local authority, but this permission could be overruled by the state public utilities commission. Or, confusion may occur because of the overlapping boundaries. For instance, a question may arise as to who is responsible for policing a state highway running through a city.

Second, overlapping jurisdictions are present at the local levels of government. Within each municipality or county, the principal legislative board (*e.g.*, the city council or county board of commissioners) does not have exclusive rule-making authority. Several boards may co-exist within a locality, with each empowered to make rules for one activity and each free from the pressure of any other. Thus, the arrangement is a limitation on the activities and the responsiveness of the local council. For example, there are special districts within a city that have independent authority to pass ordinances, levy taxes, issue bonds, and perhaps maintain a police force. City councils are unable to influence educational policy of independent school districts. The latter, setting school curriculum, for example, are not accountable to or necessarily receptive to the suggestions of the former, which are answerable to public pressure.

Legislative Rule-Making Bodies

The prime responsibility for the rule-making function is assigned by the various charters to a legislative body. Yet, on the local level there is no uniform type of legislative body. In towns and townships, town meetings may be considered legislative assemblies. In special districts and counties, boards of supervisors or commissioners are the legislative bodies. And in many cities, there are councils that resemble state legislatures.

In addition, there is no uniform type of legislative actor. In towns or townships, he may be anyone eligible to vote who cares to attend the town meeting; or he may be the selectman, supervisor, or freeholder who is elected at the town meeting to carry on the government's business between meetings. In special districts, he may be the board member appointed to make policy decisions for a specific project. And in many cities or counties, he may be the commissioner, supervisor, judge, councilman, or alderman.

These local legislators vary with respect to their power and their ability to make rules in response to needs and demands. Their activities are affected by the conditions under which they must work. These conditions in turn are related to the composition and size of the community. For example, councilmen serving large cities that encompass heterogeneous groupings face a formidable work load. Often issues before them engender a wide range of conflict and intense feelings. Personal and group animosities often surround issues close to home matters. Thus, the numbers, salaries, and sessions of local councilmen and councils are directly related to the size of the localities.

Membership of local councils ranges from two to fifty. The size of the council appears to be related to the form of the local government, as well as to the size of the locality. Most large cities have the mayor-council form of government, most medium size cities have the council-manager form; and the commission form is most often found in small cities. The largest councils are found in the first form and the smallest numbers of councilmen in the third.

The legislative body at the county level may take any form; however, in forty-two states, the most common is the commission type. Three-member commission boards generally prevail, although five-member boards predominate in California, Minnesota, North and South Dakota, North Carolina, Mississippi, and Florida.[3]

Most councilmen and county commissioners are elected to either two- or four-year terms. Among cities, the four-year term prevails, except in those communities having populations under 5,000 persons. To assure continuity within the rule-making function, many county and city legislative bodies have staggered terms for their members. For example, in St. Louis, one half of the twenty-eight aldermen (each serving for four year terms) are elected every two years. In Seattle, where the nine councilmen also serve for four years each, four positions are filled in one election and five are filled two years later.[4]

The job of a councilman is part-time, except in very large cities. For most individuals, serving as a council member is a way to perform a community service without disruption of their usual full-time employment. County boards usually hold at least monthly meetings, with additional meetings called as pressing matters arise. In small cities, members of the council devote little time to public duty. For example, in Beloit, Wisconsin (population 33,000), the council usually meets for its regular council session on the first and third Monday evenings of each month; and on the preceding Thursday evenings, it meets as a board of public works.[5] In medium size cities, the council usually meets regularly once a week. However, it is not unusual to find additional time spent for committee meetings or public hearings. Aldermen in El Paso, Texas (population 309,000), expect to spend eight hours a week on city business. In big cities, the job of the councilmen is a full-time occupation. In Detroit (population 1,660,000), the council assembles every weekday as a committee of the whole. In Los Angles (population 2,695,000), the council members meet in session five mornings a week, and utilize most afternoon hours tending to committee business.[6]

The salaries for councilmen are nominal in most instances. Most councilmen receive an annual wage, some are paid per meeting, some receive a combination of an annual and a per meeting wage, while others receive no compensation at all. The largest proportion of councilmen are compensated by token payments that amount to a few hundred dollars annually. In about one-fifth of all cities, councilmen receive no pay. The highest paid councilmen are to be found in the large cities. For example, in Detroit, councilmen are paid $17,500 per year, and county supervisors in California receive $25,000 per year; both of these reflect the full-time council work load.[7]

The great majority of local rule-makers are not supplied with office space, staff, or clerical assistance. Those who have full-time status, or those who are presiding members or who prepare the agenda for meetings, may have the needed facilities and assistance. In Philadelphia, for example, each councilman has an office in city hall, and is provided with a secretary and an administrative assistant.[8]

The local rule-making function is performed in an environment limited by short and infrequent council sessions, by small numbers of part-time and inexperienced councilmen working without needed facilities. Thus, local legislative rule-makers, who are charged with finding solutions to complex and technical problems, may be unable to fulfill their tasks.

Apportionment and Districting

Local rule-making is affected by apportionment and districting. The size and shape of districts from which local officials are to be elected are determined by the state legislature, or in some instances, if specified by local charters, the local councils. The number of officials to be chosen from each district is also determined by either the state or local legislature. The representative nature of local governmental units, whether they be city councils or county boards, is closely related to districting and apportioning plans. However, inequalities in such schemes were to be found as late as the end of the 1960s, in localities of states in every region.

Little could be done to provide more equitable representation for the public before the Supreme Court declared that apportionment was a justiciable issue. Those communities, interests, and political parties favored by malapportionment were not willing to initiate or support changes from the status quo. In 1962, the Court's decision in *Baker v. Carr* gave promise of a legal remedy for under-representation.[9] However, the Court, during the succeeding six years, focused on malapportionment cases relating to representation at the state and national levels of government, with little attention directed to the matter of local governmental units. During that period, in several states, such as Tennessee, California, South Dakota, and Wisconsin, legislation was passed to reapportion county governing boards. But most state legislatures did little, although instructed to act by federal district courts that had anticipated that malapportionment on the local level would be considered by the Supreme Court. They chose to wait for a decision of the high court.

On April 1, 1968, the Supreme Court of the United States applied the "one man, one vote" principle to the election of councilmen in all local governments, in the case of *Avery v. Midland County, Texas.*[10] On hearing appeal from a case brought by a taxpayer and voter in Midland County, Texas, the Court overruled the Texas supreme court, which had concluded that equally populated districts need not be the basis for election of local councilmen. The situation in Midland County amply illustrated the problem of malapportionment on the local level. The county board was composed of five members; one, the county judge, was elected at-large from the entire county, and the other four were commissioners chosen from districts. The population of those districts were: 414, 828, 852, and 67,906 persons. The vast imbalance was the result of placing virtually the entire city of Midland in a single district. The city was the only urban center found in the county, and 95 percent of the county's population resided there. In effect, the Supreme Court expanded its previous rulings by enunciating that the "equal protection clause" of the Fourteenth Amendment would not permit variation from equal population in drawing districts for local governmental bodies having general powers for an entire locality. Thus, if any local legislature was composed of members from districts, then the districts were to be equal in population.

Two years later, the Court amplified the equal apportionment principle in *Della Hadley et al., v. The Junior College District of Metropolitan Kansas City, Missouri, et al.*[11] It addressed its attention to the election of members to the governing board of a special district—The Junior College District of Metropolitan Kansas City, a combination of eight separate school districts. The plaintiffs, who were residents and taxpayers of one district, alleged that their area merited more representation on the Board than they had received. In its decision, the Court affirmed that voters electing officials to any governing body that performed any governmental function be afforded protection for the equal weight of their votes. Thus, the apportionment distribution for school board members is to be treated similarly to that for the distribution of state and local legislatures.

The treatment by the Court in these cases left several problems to be resolved. One was whether there had to be uniform plans of apportionment and districting for all local governmental bodies. Another was finding an appropriate plan. Questions arose as to whether all councilmen should be elected from equally populated districts or whether there could be a weighted voting arrangement among the councilmen; whether districts should be single-membered or multi-membered; and whether the legislators should be elected at-large or from districts.

There were also differences among the states as to where the determination of reapportionment plans would be made. In many states, it was the sole responsibility of the state legislature. In some states, city councils were allowed to draw the new district lines, but county boards were not so empowered. In a few states, reapportionment plans drawn by the local councils have to be approved by the electorate.

It has been speculated that the *Avery* decision forced over 20,000 local governmental bodies, some in every state, to alter their district lines.[12] It can be assumed that the decision in the latter case will add substantially to the number of local governmental units affected. While it is too early to analyze the consequences of the Court's decisions, it is expected that the alteration in the composition of local councils would lead to changes in the emphasis of local rule-making. For example, shortly after the 1968 decision, in Shelby County, Tennessee, the city of Memphis sent six members to the previously rural dominated eleven-member board. Younger and more urban oriented members were elected to county boards in the state of Michigan. In Chicago, the number of representatives from outlying white residential areas in the county, as well as the number from central city black areas, increased.

Financial Factors in Local Rule-Making

Another factor affecting the rule-making function of local governmental units is the extent of its revenue resources and its expenditure responsibilities. The resources available to cities or counties act as important restraints on the expenditures that can be undertaken. As Henry W. Maier, long-time mayor of Milwaukee, once stated in his executive budget message:

> One area in which we lack precise knowledge is that of our own economy. All of our plans, in the long run, are at the mercy of that economy. All of our plans, in the short run, should be aimed at improving that economy. . . . Our own economy is the ultimate measure of the taxes we will have available for vital government services and programs to promote progress.[13]

The financial problems facing localities, at present, are the consequences of the general economic situation that has developed over the past several years. Though the amount of local revenue has increased one hundred percent from 1956 to 1966, it has not increased sufficiently to meet expenditures. Consequently, the amount of indebtedness during that period rose 92 percent.[14] Although all local governmental units have been experiencing difficulties in meeting expenditures, cities are particularly adversely affected. This problem has been accentuated by the flight of the middle and upper socio-economic classes to the suburbs. These people are the ones most able to pay taxes, and they are the ones who reside in single family homes, which are the basis of much of the property tax.

The cities' tax base has been further eroded by the departure of business and industry to surrounding areas. In addition, many cities have to share part of their revenue with the government of the county in which they are located. This latter outflow of funds is not generally met by any increase in services provided to the city.

The reduction of the tax base has occurred concurrently with the increase in the scope of expenditures brought about by changing living and working patterns. The emigration of the middle and upper classes to the suburbs has left the cities with a population comprised substantially of the old and the poor. These groups have increased the demands on the local government for social welfare and health services, police and fire protection, and so forth. Yet, these groups are least able to supply the revenue to support the services of which they are most in need. Moreover, the use by suburbanites of facilities found within the city also adds to the city's expenditures. The burden that extra traffic, for example, places on the streets and parking facilities maintained by the city governments, or adds to the workload of city policemen, is not offset in costs by any significant contribution made by the transients from the suburbs.

The rate of expenditures at the county and municipal levels has increased rapidly and steadily since World War II. Most of the expansion has been in the areas of established governmental activities, the greatest increase coming in the area of public education. There are more school age children attending school for longer periods of time, necessitating the extension of physical facilities. The scope of subjects being taught is wider and more complex and technical, requiring increased dependence on new equipment and skilled personnel. Welfare expenditures have also risen, as the percentage of welfare recipients in the population has increased. One reason for this last change has been the higher percentage of older people in the population due to advances in medical science. The expenditure for roads and bridges, owing to greater reliance on automobiles, has grown. The expansion of expenditures can also be accounted for by the rise of salaries and numbers of specialists employed, as well as by the rise in costs of labor and material for capital improvements.

As are other powers, local governments' financial powers are subject to state constitutional or statuatory regulations. State legislatures often set requirements for levels of expenditures that cities must make such as, for example, establishing minimum salaries for policemen and firemen. A state constitution may contain provisions specifying the proportions of funds that must be designated for specific use. One example of this is a requirement that a city's share of gasoline tax be spent for highway construction and maintenance.

State governments also retain power over the sources of revenue available for localities. Generally, tax levies must be approved by the state legislatures as must any changes in the tax rate. In addition, legislatures may specify the time period of, the conditions of, and the exemptions from a tax levy. Moreover, limits may be set on the extent of indebtedness that a locality may incur, and the conditions under which borrowing may occur.

To meet expenditures, localities have resort to a limited number of sources of revenue. The largest source of revenue is the property tax. This source may account for as much as 85 percent of the revenue raised by some cities, counties, or towns. The levy is most frequently imposed on real property, *i.e.*, so many cents per hundred dollars of the assessed value. Some localities also utilize a personal property tax on the assessed value of such tangible items as machinery, equipment, inventory, home furnishings, and jewelry. Intangible personal property taxes, on such items as stocks and bonds, also exist. The dominance of the property tax is due to the lack of alternatives caused by limitations that have been set by state provisions. A state statute in Pennsylvania, for example, has allowed local governments to utilize any tax source not preempted by the state. Though that grant of permission may appear to be broad, it is, in reality, indicative of the "state-comes-first" attitude that restricts the available alternatives which are open to local government agents seeking revenue.

The second main tax source of revenue is derived from sales taxes imposed on the value of goods and services exchanged or rendered during ordinary commercial activities. The use of local general sales tax is increasing, though it still is not prevalent throughout the country. James A. Maxwell found that in thirteen states, 2,000 governments levied such a tax.[15]

There are also selected sales taxes that are imposed on particular commodities or services, in contrast to the application of general sales taxes. Thus, additional levies would be collected from the sales of such items as motor fuel, alcoholic beverages, tobacco products, and hotel or restaurant services.

In recent years, residents of several localities have had to pay income taxes to their local government. In most places, the tax is imposed only on the income of local residents; in others, as in Philadelphia and New York City, the wages of non-resident workers are also taxed. A recent phenomenon has been the rise of the surtax, which is imposed by localities and is based on a percentage of income taxes paid to the state. In Maryland, for example, each county may levy a surtax up to 50 percent of the income tax due to state from residents of that county.

Revenue is also obtained through license taxes and fees. License taxes may have to be paid as a condition for engaging in certain businesses (such as taverns and restaurants), or occupations (such as beauticians or barbers). The granting of franchises (as, for example, to bus companies) also produce revenue. Fees are received from such items as dog, birth, or marriage registrations, or automobile inspection certificates.

Special assessments to help defray the cost of construction may be charged to residents when sewer lines are extended in their neighborhoods, or sidewalks are paved in front of their homes. Special districts raise funds from charges for their services, for example, from tolls for bridges under their authority, or from recreation facilities admission charges. A variety of fines, from traffic tickets to overdue books in the library, produce additional revenue. Municipal governments operate water supply systems, and some of them also operate other utilities (*e.g.*, electric power, gas supply, and local transit systems) that return revenue from the resident "customers." Bills for hospitals or clinic services are sent to users of these public facilities. Rents are collected from tenants of public housing projects. In addition, local governments also engage in the sale of goods. Some maintain liquor stores, others sell (on occasion) American flags, trees or shrubs, or trash containers.

The revenue received from such sources, as outlined above, are augmented by money supplied by other sources to satisfy the increasing expenditure demands. Local governments may borrow funds through the issuance of bonds. These debts are incurred mostly for capital expenditures for schools, libraries, or parkland. The extent of borrowing may be limited because of state constitutional or statutory provisions for a specified ceiling or a proportional debt ceiling related to a percentage of the property tax base. Moreover, provisions may require that the public approve the issuance of any bonds. In forty-seven states, provisions exist that require referendum elections be held for approval of bond sales.[16]

On occasion, bonds are sold for which repayment is made from the revenue received from the use of a special project instead of from the general treasury. Thus, the principal and interest on the bond for a recreation facility (*e.g.*, a swimming pool or a golf course) would be repaid by the income produced from paid admissions. Public authorities are created with the power to issue bonds. Often such an authority may have been established to bypass the regular debt limit imposed upon the local government.

Revenue is also augmented by funds or services received from the national and state governments. States contribute to local revenue, first, through grant-in-aid programs in which payments are paid by direct appropriations. The amount of the grant is usually independent of the yield from any particular source of income. Often, grants are appropriated with particular conditions. Localities may be required to match the funds, use the money for specific purposes, or they might have to meet specific regulations about the type of personnel or equipment necessary to execute the projects.

A second means by which states aid localities is shared taxes. The amount shared is usually directly related to the amount collected by state revenue processes. The states have chosen to centralize the collection system and to allocate funds according to local needs or to committed specific purposes.

Transferred funds are also received from the national government. Basically, these are in the form of grant-in-aid programs. Congress has shown a preference toward offering grants-in-aid through state programs. However, recent situations have shown that cities and counties may request funds directly to underwrite such proposed projects as urban renewal, housing, or vocational training.

The socio-economic environment of the locality has some importance for taxation and expenditure patterns as aspects of rule-making. The uneven tax base among local governments result in variations in local services. As Maxwell has noted: "In general, more will be spent by state and local governments in a rich state, that is, one with a high per capita income, than in a poor state."[17] An example of one activity, that of education, may serve to illustrate the point raised by Maxwell.

Thomas R. Dye, in his study of the education policies of sixty-seven of the nation's largest cities, found that wealth is the principal determinant of education expenditures. He studied the influence of several factors on rules made for education. These factors were governmental forms, socioeconomic characteristics of the population found within the different communities, the independence of school districts from city governments, the bases of selection of the school board members, and the partisan quality of school board elections. Dye concluded that the wealth of the community, as measured by personal income, property value, and size of the city, is the principal determining influence on how much is spent for the education of each child.[18]

However, the economic climate of a locality is insufficient in itself to determine the orientation of rule-making. Robert Eyestone and Heinz Eulau have noted that the utilization of potential resources depends on such things as how much the city councilmen can obtain from intergovernmental sources.[19] Thus, the fiscal rule-making process encompasses political pressures and public attitudes as well as the availability of potential revenue sources.

The Procedure of Legislative Rule-Making

The procedure by which bills become laws differs in the various localities, especially with the different forms of governments that exist. Though identical procedures do not exist, the enactment of a local ordinance follows a fairly common pattern.

I. The Initiation Stage

Proposals are introduced in writing by a council member. Copies of the proposed legislation are filed with the clerk or secretary of the council, or presented to each member during a session. The announcement of the filing of the proposal generally constitutes the first reading of the bill. Such drafts may have been prepared by the local executive, (*e.g.*, the mayor, manager, or county executive), by members of the bureaucracy, or by private groups or individuals, as well as by a councilman himself.

II. The Study Stage

After introduction, the bill is referred to an appropriate committee (if a council operates with some form of a committee system), and also to pertinent administrative officers for their comments or for additional data that would be useful to the legislators in weighing the merits of the proposal. During this study stage, public hearings may be held to obtain a wide range of opinions, information, or support. On occasion, modifications or changes of the original draft occur during this stage.

III. The Debate Stage

The full legislative body meets to consider the bill after a committee or a group of councilmen has studied it. The proposed ordinance is placed on the council's agenda, so that interested citizens will be aware that the measure is scheduled for open discussion, and so that they may appear before the council to express their positions. The bill is given a second reading at this stage. Informality may be the pattern of behavior within small council bodies. The process of debate can be expedited by agreement to suspend any formal rules of procedure. During this stage, additional modifications may be made on the measure.

IV. The Approval Stage

After debate and before final council action is taken, the bill is read for the third time. A bill may then be placed aside for further study (for a definite or indefinite period), or voted on. In most localities, with affirmative action by the rule-making board the bill becomes rule. However, in some governmental units the measure may have to be sent to the local executive for his approval or veto. Should he veto it, an extraordinary majority of the council members is generally required to over-ride his negating action.

V. The Final Stage

Should the measure be passed, it is published in local newspapers, and is made part of the codified ordinances. Then it becomes a public law.

Structural and Electoral Factors in Local Rule-Making

The type of governmental structure and electoral system affects the rule-making function. Whether a given governmental unit has the form of a commission, council manager, or mayor council structures; whether elections are partisan or non-partisan; or whether councilmen are elected at large or from wards may affect the extent of cohesion amongst the council members, their rule-making orientations, their influence on the rule-making function, and the types of rules made.

The Mayor-Council Form

The mayor-council form of government is generally accompanied by a ward-based, partisan electoral system. The composition of a council elected on a compact, single-member ward basis reflects the economic, religious, or ethnic cleavages that exist within the community. Such a system of compartmentalized representation allows for multiple access points to which citizens or groups can appeal; and it results in council members having to be concerned with needs and demands of a specific constituency. As each group appears before its ward's councilman, it expects him to assure that its demands will be translated into rules.

Acutely aware of constituency needs because of the small districts from which each comes, and of the benefits derived from satisfying those needs, much of the activities of councilmen are focused on performing special favors for groups or individuals. A great deal of time and energy are expended in performing "errand boy" tasks. Each councilman elected with constituency support separate from each other may have little reason to act cohesively on many issues. The process of making rules becomes a process of trading favors. For example, one legislator may say to another: "I will vote for that ordinance that will give you the low income housing development in your district, if you will vote for the municipal swimming pool to be located in mine." Usually cooperation exists when a councilman whose district would be unaffected by a proposed ordinance will acquiesce to the views of his colleagues whose districts would be substantially affected. But, where a rule will affect different councilmen differently, and conflict occurs, the result is usually a stalemate.

The large size of legislative bodies in mayor-council forms of government may also limit membership cohesion. The size of the body may prevent the presence of a stable majority coalition. Alliances may form among councilmen representing similar constituencies, yet, as issue alternatives unacceptable to the component parts are raised, the alliances may degenerate and a regrouping within a new coalition will occur. Moreover, the anonymity inherent in large bodies may lead to disruptive behavior by a few members. An ambitious councilman may be deliberately vociferous in his dissent, hoping to gain the limelight to familiarize the public with his name.

Some localities with the mayor council form of government have adopted a combination of at-large and district elections. In Philadelphia, for example, the city council is composed of ten members elected on a ward basis and seven elected at-large. However, that electoral system is no more conducive to greater cohesiveness than is the completely ward based system. As one councilman has noted: "The two kinds of members operate with different outlooks. It is imperative for a ward councilman to go along with his constituency if he wants to remain in office for more than one term. On the other hand, councilmen at-large must consider the overall view of the entire city." [20]

With limited cohesive factors, there is a need for leadership to provide direction and impetus to secure major legislative outputs. Leadership may arise from internal or external sources. But, where strong leadership has appeared the councils have been reduced, in some instances, to mere ratifying bodies.

One source of leadership may be the presiding officer of the council. He may be a council member elected by his colleagues or by the public to that post, or an individual elected in the general election to be the president but not a member of the council. The presiding officer can wield extensive influence because of his formal position. He votes in case of a tie, recognizes speakers, sets the agenda, and in most instances makes committee assignments, names the chairman, and assigns bills to them. His influence may be enhanced by his stature as spokesman for the council.

Unencumbered by the principle of seniority in the assignment of committee chairmen or members, the presiding officer of large councils may exercise his leadership through the committee system. In these larger councils most of the work is performed within the committees. In the councils of many large cities and counties there is an elaborate system of standing committees to which proposals are referred and from which guiding opinions for final action eminate. For example, in Philadelphia, there are thirteen standing committees: Rules; Finance; Appropriations; Law and Government; Public Property and Public Works; Streets and Services; Licenses and Inspections; Labor and Civil Service; Transportation and Public Utilities; Commerce, Navigation, and Airport Facilities; Recreation; Public Health and Welfare; and Public Safety; [21] with each councilman serving on about five committees. It is rare for the councilmen not to accept the report of a committee. Indeed, where committee systems exist, the entire local council often acts as a ratifying body for committee recommendations. Councilman Edward R. Cantor of Philadelphia has illustrated this point by estimating that 99 percent of the committee reports are ratified by the Council. [22]

Leadership and consensus building may be provided in a strong party system by party leaders. Local party officials, anxious to see that publicly dispensed favors are provided to groups and individuals for their support at the polls, exert influence on party affiliated councilmen. These officials communicate interests to the councilmen at caucus or committee meetings, or through such informal channels as telephone calls, ward meetings, or social gatherings. Party leaders in the council are influential in setting the legislative program. Party influence is brought to bear on the committee chairman and on the majority of the members of each committee who would be of the majority party. The same tactics would be also applicable to influence minority party councilmen.

The caucus, an organized meeting of party members in the council, is a forum for the transmission of party directives. The importance of the caucus as a tool of the political party in influencing the rule-making function has been graphically described in a publicly printed and distributed pamphlet intended to inform the citizens of Philadelphia about their city council. The section entitled "The Caucus" reads as follows:

> An institution not found in the charter or in the Rules of Council, which plays an important role in the legislative process is the majority caucus, or meeting of all the councilmen of the majority party. Since Philadelphia has a strong tradition of party government, it is actually in the caucus, rather than in meetings of the whole Council, that most legislative policy is determined. In this respect, our City Council follows the traditional practice of most legislative bodies in this country.
>
> The majority party holds a regular weekly caucus, plus a special caucus whenever important policy matters come up before Council. The caucus is particularly significant during consideration if the annual budget, at which time administrative officials may be brought in to present additional information to members of the caucus.
>
> In caucus, the members of the majority party are free to express their views on all sides of the matter under consideration. However, once a decision has been reached, it usually is binding on all the members, and they usually show a united front on the floor of Council.[23]

Thus, it can be seen that the council acts as a ratifying body to accept the decisions issuing from the caucus.

A major external source of leadership is the strong mayor. Such a mayor usually is empowered to prepare the budget, which permits him to provide a perspective for the fiscal tasks of government, and to influence those aspects of the rule-making function relying on appropriations. His position also entitles him to exercise supervision over the administration, which gives a vantage point from which to compare claims of various municipal departments, and to recommend the emphasis and direction of the rules to be made. The strong mayor commands the attention of the press, and through it, the public. These powers and advantages assist in the subordination of the council to executive leadership.

The Council-Manager Form

The council-manager structure is usually found in those communities having a non-partisan, at-large electoral system. Supporters of this system stress its efficiency in governmental operation and the expectation that government can be operated free from individual and group conflicts. It is thought that if all councilmen represent the same city wide constituency they should be able to work more in concert than those elected from single-member districts. In addition, the councilmen would hold a city wide view of politics, and could avoid the exchange of special favors.

At-large councilmen generally are adverse to a private interest serving, "errand boy" role. These councilmen tend to believe that there is a unified public interest and that it is ascertainable. They are inclined to hold the attitude that their own judgment is capable of defining the public interest and finding solutions to pressing problems. Thus, there is a tendency to postpone making decisions until the public interest can be clearly known or until there is pressure from the community about an action that must be taken.

Cohesiveness among council members, based on the sharing of similar outlooks, is enhanced by the small size of the councils found in the council-manager governmental units. In a small council, the members do not have the advantage of public anonymity, and each member's vote is crucial to the outcome of a bill's success. The desire to cooperate harmoniously is prevalent. Thus, consensus would be attempted by modifying individual stands or policy proposals to accommodate objections, or by avoiding controversial issues. If issues cannot be resolved quietly, then a basic split would occur with the result that no action would be taken.

Several studies have emphasized that when issues for which alternative solutions are controversial appear before these councils, there is a tendency not to act. Councilmen will shun any attempts at creating controversy. Moreover, councilmen do not emerge as general policy leaders or innovators. They generally have personal areas of interest and concentrate their efforts in such directions. When action must be taken but is viewed to engender controversy, the alternative selected would most likely come from the administrative officials who are removed from direct public attention.[24]

Within the council, perceived as a body of equals, little leadership is exerted. The committee system, used as an instrument of exerting direction on rule-making in mayor council systems, is not a source of leadership in this governmental form. Although a small council usually will conduct its work as a committee of the whole to take advantage of informal procedures in considering legislation or in discussing the agenda, the committee session is in essence an informal council meeting.

Nor are political parties a source of leadership. This may be explained by the political environment in which these councils are to be found. Many of the communities are nonpartisan. In these localities, councilmen may look to civic or interest groups for direction. Yet, these do not serve as substitutes for political parties, for each group is not interested in every issue before the council. In partisan situations, party officials are often constrained from exerting leadership. For in an environment that stresses efficient and business-like governmental operation (though it has a partisan election system), party organizational guidance is viewed by the public and the council members alike with disfavor.

Thus, the leadership in a council-manager plan is most likely to come from the manager, whose duties may be compared to those of a strong mayor. Although the manager, as a professional administrator, is the "servant" of the council, he is its guiding force. The councilmen, as part-time amateurs, find their abilities to supply active leadership relatively limited to those of the full-time expert administrator. It is he who sets the agenda, suggests the alternatives, supplies the supporting data, and supervises the administrative agents and the preparation of the budget.

The Commission Form

The commission form of government is usually accompanied by an at-large, non-partisan electoral system. This form is the most centralized of the various structures of local government. The small group of commissioners have vested in their office the full powers of rule-making and rule execution. Their power of the purse amply illustrates the extent of their formal abilities, in that they may draft the budget, adopt it, and administer the appropriation of funds.

The small size of this council should be conducive to cohesiveness. The typical board is comprised of from three to five members, and thus, the tendency may be for the voters to know their commissioners. Unwilling to hurt the image of one another, dissent is carefully avoided among the commissioners, and most decisions will be unanimous. In addition, cohesiveness is enhanced by the acceptance of the norm of equality of each commissioner within the group, and by the manageability of the cooperative efforts engaged into by the small number of commissioners.

Yet, such cohesiveness is not always the case in this form of government. In practice, each commissioner is assigned a separate and distinct aspect of government operations and concerns. For example, one would be the commissioner for public safety, and another for parks and recreation. Although each is elected at-large, and has a city wide view of problem solving, each is principally concerned about his own aspect of the city-wide problems. Each commissioner expends his time and energy towards the maintenance and enhancement of his own sphere of influence. Thus, the pattern of activity among the commissioners resembles the routine of trading of favors found among ward based councilmen. Cohesiveness in rule-making is generally achieved by each commissioner accepting the proposals of his colleague for the latter's area of concern in return for similar treatment of proposals in his own area.

For those city-wide matters that do not fall within the province of any separate category, such as taxation, there is the problem of coordinating the efforts of co-equal members of the board. The leadership necessary for rule-making in these matters is absent. The sources of leadership provided for in other forms of government by committees or party leaders do not exist in the non-partisan environment or in the board too small to utilize a committee system. Commissioner Tobriner of Washington, D.C. has noted the basic problems of the lack of leadership and cohesion confronting the commission form of government. In supporting the demise of the commission form in the District of Columbia he has stated:

> There is no provision for a "strong chairman" to provide leadership. . . . Under the current system, decisions must be made in a collective fashion which is often slow and cumbersome and sometimes precludes clear resolution of the issues. The effort involved in getting together the three Commissioners, all of whom have heavy schedules, for a special meeting or to meet an emergency situation, is in itself defeative of efficiency.
> Today the necessary activities of the District government, like the government of all cities, have become so diversified that three coequal Commissioners have inadequate control over many of them.[25]

Effects of Structural and Electoral Factors

Several studies have confirmed that structural differences have a bearing on the rule-making function of local governmental units. Oliver P. William and Charles R. Adrian have developed a typology that classifies four orientations of government.[26] These orientations are:

1) "Promoting Economic Growth." The public agents see the need of government to assure that the community grows in economic wealth and in population. Thus, no policy should be undertaken that might hinder growth within the community. To accomplish this, public agents should assure that the good image of the city will continue, that politics should be played down, that a friendly attitude toward business will prevail, and that there should be stability and regularity in city finances.

2) "Providing and Securing Life's Amenities," (*i.e.*, the necessities and comforts of life). The accent of policy here would be upon the "home environment," to assure attractive surroundings, and peace and tranquility.

Thus, the growth of commerce (with the accompanying problems facing governmental solution), or the economic diversities of the people (necessitating welfare expenditures) are discouraged.

3) "Maintaining (only) Traditional Services." This orientation leads to the opposition of any expansion of governmental tasks, especially if it requires additional taxes to raise revenues for the expanded expenditures. The self reliance of the individual is stressed, and the traditional nature of the community is to be preserved. Governmental agents act as "caretakers" to preserve and conserve the community's resources, and to pursue a limited role for their government.

4) "Arbitrating Among Conflicting Interests." Public agents see their tasks as attempting to satisfy (or at least, to be concerned about satisfying) all interests. Thus, governmental officials engage in political balancing of the diverse demands placed on them, and act as "arbiters."

Williams and Adrian concluded that the type of governmental structure most consistent with the arbiter and the caretaker orientations is one that includes a plural executive, district elections for councilmen, and other decentralizing devices. These characteristics permit many points of access to policy makers and, by decentralizing governmental leadership, make consolidated and unified political action more difficult. Centralization and professionalization of the bureaucracy (as in a strong mayor, or council-manager type) are characteristic of those governments supporting orientation toward the promotion of economic growth and the increasing of amenities. By strengthening the office of the mayor, by introducing an appointed city manager, and by holding at-large elections, there is a reduction in the political strength of particularistic interest groups or minorities, and an increase in the articulation of the interests of the business and suburban status groups.

Terry N. Clark, in his study of fifty-one local governmental units, found that structure was related to the number and types of rules made. In the centralized decision making structure (having few points of access) the number of outputs was high. Moreover, issues provoking controversy (*e.g.*, fluoridation and school desegregation) were readily settled. Conversely, in the decentralized type of structure (having many points of access, as with ward based representation) the number of outputs was lower. In the few localities of the latter type where the output level was high, the issues faced were primarily non-controversial in nature. Clark stressed the presence or absence of leadership in the different forms as the key factor. With leadership, direction is offered and cohesion is obtained to handle controversial issues. Without leadership, coordination between rule-makers is difficult to achieve, and the result is a smaller number of rules made.[27]

Herbert L. Lineberry and Edmund P. Fowler demonstrated that the extent of responsiveness of public agents to class, racial, and religious interests found within the community differed markedly with the type of political structure. This led to a variance in the degree that social conflicts were translated into public policy. Lineberry and Fowler noted that when a city adopted structural reforms, such as a council-manager government, with at-large and non-partisan elections, it tended to lessen the responsiveness to a variety of class, racial, and religious groupings.[28] Thus, in the "reformed" communities:

> The making of public policy takes less count of the enduring differences between White and Negro, business and labor, Pole and WASP. The logic of the bureaucratic ethic demands an impersonal, apolitical settlement of issues, rather than the settlement of conflict in the arena of political battle.[29]

Legislators' Effect on Rule-Making

The attitude patterns held by the local legislators influence their actions in the rule-making function. Eulau and Eyestone noted the existence of "normative dispositions to action" that determine individual legislative behavior. In analyzing the rule-making process for development policies of a city, for example, these authors found that such dispositions act as filters through which councilmen screen their perceptions of the problems in the city, their alternative preferences, and their conceptions of the direction of the city's future development.[30]

Perspectives

Local rule-makers may hold one of two types of perspectives toward defining and solving local problems. Robert Merton has classified these as "local" and "cosmopolitan" perspectives.[31] Those who hold one orientation conceptualize differently from those holding the other; and each relies on different types of information.

The "local's" political view does not penetrate beyond the boundaries of his community. He sees the important problems as being contained within his locality, and emphasizes that these can be solved exclusively by the local government. He looks to past governmental actions for guidance in his approach to problem solving. The information he needs to perform his rule-making tasks is basically data about immediate events and residents in the community, in the context of the locality's traditions and history. In other words, the actions of government that are best for the people are those actions in which the government has been involved in the past.

The "cosmopolitan's" political vision has a broader scope. He sees the important local problems as crossing jurisdictional boundaries, and emphasizes regional planning, coordination, and cooperation among a wider range of agents and agencies than are found within his community. He looks to different attempts made to solve similar problems in other regions of the country for guidance in his approach to problem solving. Thus, the information useful to him comes from a larger context of metropolitan experience and outside change that can supplement the immediate local information.

Cosmopolitans propose the regional approach to solving local problems for several reasons. A regional government is thought to be a more efficient arrangement to solving problems that overlap jurisdictional boundaries. The environment, cosmopolitans argue, could best be improved by matching those regional problems with regional resources by regional planning. The standard of life for most residents would be improved through a region-wide system of institutions. For example, a regional school system could provide for fully integrated educational enrollments, or a regional public housing effort could be instituted to scatter low cost housing throughout the area instead of concentrating it in the core cities. Locals, however, appear to be motivated by the factors of habit and familiarity. They support the existing governmental system and operations because these have existed for some time and people have become comfortable in their relations with them. Locals believe the local government to be well equipped to handle the problems facing the people in the individual communities.

Everett Carll Ladd referred to the different orientations as "cosmopolitan" and "parochial." He explained that parochials basically do not conceive of government as an instrument through which resources are channeled to control, shape, and direct the massive transformations the urban scene is now experiencing."[32] Cosmopolitans, he noted, believe that "government must harness resources to order and direct social change.... Conflict management, efficiency, expertise, and innovation become the golden words."[33] He saw the two perspectives as clearly differentiated in socio-economic terms. Cosmopolitans are generally professionals, well educated, and economically successful. Parochials, in contrast, are usually drawn from the lower middle class, and are small businessmen and lower white collar workers having little, if any, college education.

Ambition

Several studies have suggested that attitude patterns held by local rule-makers may be influenced by their political aspirations. Joseph A. Schlessinger has noted that "only the man with progressive ambitions is driven to explore current policies in the light of future consequences for his future career is at stake."[34]

Kenneth Prewitt and William Nowlin noted the relationship between ambition and policy perspective in their study of 372 city councilmen in the San Francisco Bay area.[35] Ambitious councilmen, they found, saw local problems as overlapping community boundaries, and saw the solutions to these problems as coming from cooperative efforts with regional, state, or national governments in accordance with aspirations for higher office; and that such rule-makers inform themselves of actions being taken in other localities, and adopted views consistent with those experiences. In contrast, the unambitious councilmen's outlook was focused narrowly toward the locality. They saw the problems of their community rooted in the rapid economic and social growth of their area, and generally opposed the expansion of the tasks of government or the introduction of outside sources of aid and influence.

Roles

Attitudes held by rule-makers that affect their perceptions may be expectation of behavior patterns known as roles. John C. Wahlke, and others, have classified a variety of such roles that exist among the rank of state legislative centros.[36] Several studies have applied these categories, in a limited manner, to particular local situations.

Williams and Adrian found that in a council-manager form, with at-large elections, the most common role was that of trustee.[37] Councilmen perceived their actions as manifestations of mandates to use their own judgment to solve problems. Among ward-elected councilmen, as in a mayor-council system, the delegate role (that one is committed to following the instructions or what is perceived to be the wishes of the constituents) was most clearly identified.

Bryan T. Downes, in his study of councilmen in thirty-seven communities surrounding St. Louis, found that 73 percent of the respondents perceived their role as trustees, 7 percent as delegates, and 24 percent as politicos (those who profess a balance between two sides on various issues). He found little relationship between socio-economic status and the roles held, and concluded that part-time legislators have little time to attempt to ascertain the public's instructions.

In addition, Downes queried the legislators about their orientation toward the purposes and processes of their positions. He found a slight relationship between these attitudes and socio-economic rank. Councilmen with high education levels tended toward the inventor role, that is, to create, formulate, and initiate programs that promote the locality as a better place to live. Those with low educational attainment appeared to orient themselves more as ritualists, involved in the routine tasks of legislative work. Those in the lower socio-economic rank favored more the role of tribune, performing the tasks of ascertaining what the people want and representing such interests in the council. High socio-economic status councilmen tended to relate with the role of broker, whose job is conceived as compromising, arbitrating, integrating, and coordinating the conflicting demands and interests with the council.[38]

Kenneth Prewitt, Heinz Eulau, and Betty H. Zisk, in their study of 129 councilmen, supported Downes' findings in that the greatest percentage of those public agents held the trustee role (54 percent), the next largest group held the politico role (31 percent), and the smallest group held the delegate role (16 percent). Their study further demonstrated how the various councilmen perceived the purposes and the processes of their positions. The largest number of councilmen held the broker orientation, and the others held (in diminishing proportions) the ritualist, the inventor, and the tribune orientations.[39]

The bases for attitudes that affect the activities of rule-makers may be influenced by the legislative setting in which the individuals find themselves. Prewitt, Eulau, and Zisk tested the assumption that early political socialization is more influential than later learning experiences in determining each legislator's behavior. They concluded that early political socialization was unrelated to an incumbent's legislative orientation. Rather, considerations and pressures found within the legislature provided direction for the councilman's relations with his constituency, his party, his colleagues, and with interest group representatives.

The Executive in Rule-Making

There is a great variance in the amount of influence that mayors wield on the rule-making function. In the council-manager and commission forms of government, a council member may be designated as mayor for the principal purpose of performing ceremonial tasks. As a general rule, however, his rule-making power is no greater than that of his colleagues. In some localities, he is the presiding officer at meetings. In a few settings, he may be restricted to vote only to break a tie; and in a few, he may have the power of veto. Sixteen percent of the mayors in the council-manager form and 15 percent in the commission form have such a veto power.[40] In the weak mayor-council structure, the mayor is the titular head of government. Although he may recommend legislation, and in a few instances exercise the formal power of veto, his rule-making power is limited by statute or charter provisions.

It is in the strong mayor-council structure that the mayor exerts a major influence on local rule-making. Indeed, he is often thought of as the "chief legislator." Typically, the strong mayor is found in the large cities. The city charter and general laws prescribe the formal powers by which the mayor can provide the leadership necessary to define major problems, suggest alternative solutions, and direct the effort for implementing those solutions.

The mayor may initiate proposals by submitting messages to the council, drafting bills for specific matters, or by preparing the budget. By these means he sets the tone of the legislative program. His proposals may reflect dissatisfaction with past programs, or recognition of needed programs.

One legal provision that permits a strong mayor to exert influence on rule-making is his power to prepare the budget. By his grant of authority over resource allocations, he is able to set the priorities for program planning. The action of the council may be legally restricted in altering his proposals. It may reduce or eliminate items but, in many instances, it may not add items or increase appropriations in the executive's budget. Thus, in budget making the council acts basically as a ratifying body.

Strong mayors in large cities universally have the power to veto all legislative proposals. The veto serves as a substantial supportive to the mayor's policy recommendations. By exercising his prerogative, he can prevent a measure from becoming a law, for it generally takes an extraordinary majority to over-ride his veto. The difficulty in over-riding a veto may enhance the influence of the mayor. By threatening to exercise the veto, he may induce councilmen to alter a proposal in accord with his wishes.

The mayor's position may be strengthened by his power to appoint and remove heads of administrative departments and other officers not elected by the people. These appointees are directly accountable to him, and thus would tend to be supporters of his programs. They are instrumental in helping him formulate policy, by presenting alternatives for him to consider. By providing the expertise on which the council must rely for information, they become advocates or lobbyists for the mayor's programs. His appointment power may be expanded into an instrument of influence over the council. His ability to dispense rewards (*i.e.*, patronage positions) may give him the necessary bargaining power to obtain needed support.

In large cities the mayor is often expected to suggest solutions to problems that reflect basic splits within the community and which appear to defy solutions. He may utilize the device of establishing "blue ribbon" commissions to study pressing and immediate problems. Members appointed to such commissions are drawn from among prominent citizens and from the dominant interest groupings of the community. Often, these panels cannot produce recommendations that satisfy the various concerned groupings. In such cases, the effort expended has at least demonstrated the concern of the mayor and his desire for reaching a settlement. Should a consensus be reached, however, the mayor is assured of popular and legislative support if he adopts the commission's recommendations. The panel members can attract publicity for their efforts, and they would act to lobby for their proposals.

The foundation of the mayor's influence is buttressed by his position as the centrally elected public agent. He is the most visible public official, and the one that the public can most readily identify. No other local personality can match his ability to command the attention of the public. Newspaper, television, and radio news agents are anxious to have him express his views about city problems. He is a welcome speaker at more functions than it is possible for him to attend.

His influence is further enhanced by his election success, which has demonstrated his ability to attract public and organizational support. His political party will muster support for his programs. The council members of the same party will be under strong pressure to adopt his proposals. Organized groups will look to him to act as arbiter between the community's dominant coalitions of interests. This popularity or support is not easily ignored by councilmen considering the mayor's policy recommendations.

There are instances in which the mayor singularly performs the rule-making function. The mayor, as chief protector of the safety and welfare of the citizenry, can in emergency situations make rules independently. Vivid demonstrations of this power occurred during the period of the riots in the mid-1960s. Mayors faced with chaotic situations issued such executive rules as setting curfews, and forbidding the sale of guns, alcoholic beverages, and gasoline. His rules had the full sanction of law, and violators were subject to prosecution.

The Administrators in Rule-Making

Bureaucrats staffing and heading administrative agencies are influential as political actors in the rule-making function. The most influential administrator is the city or county manager, found in the council-manager form of government. As the chief administrative officer of the locality, in many instances he is the dominant figure in the rule-making function. His duties are specified in the charter, and they encompass a wide range of tasks. In many respects the managers' powers are similar to those of a strong mayor. He has the power to appoint, supervise, and remove department heads and bureau chiefs, and to prepare and submit the annual budget to the council. In addition, he may make policy recommendations, and prepare and submit reports and memoranda to keep the council, and indirectly the public, advised of the financial condition of the locality, the operations of all aspects of government, and future needs and trends.

The full time, professional manager, with a virtual monopoly of detailed and technical information, is looked to by the part-time councilmen for direction in their rule-making activities. In many matters that are complex, the council would specifically request his recommendations. Most new business coming before the council is first referred to the manager for a report on its feasibility, its importance, its costs, and its consequences. His knowledge about the operations and needs of the agencies under his supervision, enables him to be a prime initiator of policy proposals. He presents alternative choices to priorities and by setting the agenda, presents their arrangement for council consideration.

A counterpart to the manager has been created (by recent charter amendments or ordinances) in many large cities having the mayor council form of government. He is called a chief administrative officer; and, because he is appointed by and directly accountable to the mayor, he is known as the "deputy mayor." His powers and duties are similar to that of the manager in that he is responsible for such things as appointing and supervising administrative agents and agencies, preparing the annual budget proposals, and making policy recommendations. Thus, he is able to exert influence on the rule-making function; this is accomplished by influencing directly the strong mayor, and through him the council.

The city attorney (also called city solicitor or corporation counsel), is another particularly influential bureau. He drafts bills in correct legal form and presents them to the council. He steers the rule-making activities of the council by advising them regarding the areas and methods in which they are permitted (by state constitution, statutes, or charter provisions) to make rules. Without proper counselling, the council members would be seriously handicapped in performing their tasks. For example, as a staff member of the City Council of the District of Columbia related, the council members had always relied on the corporation counsel situated in the office of the mayor for advice about the areas and methods permitted to them for action. However, they had discovered that they had been misled in regard to their formal powers. Believing this was due to a "power play" by the mayor, the council members hired their own attorney. The councilmen then discovered "quite a few more avenues for action." [41]

Career bureaus are actively involved in the rule-making function. These agents are full-time, experienced, specialized professionals. Their integral positions within the organization of government and their contacts with pressure groups and officials in other levels of government enable them to be important actors. Because of their experience and knowledge about operations and programs, they are looked to by executive and legislative centros for initiating, analyzing, criticizing, and supporting policy proposals.

Harry W. Reynolds Jr.'s study of the Los Angeles council, illustrated the dominant influence that administrators exert on the rule-making function. [42] Both the top level politically appointed and the middle level civil service personnel played a significant part in initiating proposals and maneuvering them to successful passage. Table VIII.1 shows the number and type of legislative proposals initiated by bureaucrats in comparison with those by the mayor, councilmen, citizens, interest groups, and special "blue ribbon" committees.

The table indicates that the greatest proportion of measures considered by the city council were initiated by the bureaucrats (80 of the 206 total).

TABLE VIII.1

Legislative Proposals Introduced in Los Angeles City Council by Subject Matter and Source of Authorship*

February 27–March 30, 1959

Subject Matter Breakdown of Legislative Proposals†	Total No. of Bills by Topic	Authorship of Proposed Legislation by Source						
		Private Citizen	Private Group	Mayor	Council	C.A.O.‡	Dept. of City	Committee of City
Public safety . . .	16	3		1	1		8	3
Police	14	2		1			8	3
Fire								
Traffic. . . .	2	1			1			
Public works . . .	89	19	8	5	6	15	19	17
Streets.	67	16	7	3	6	8	13	14
Sidewalks. . . .	1						1	
Water-power . . .	3	1						2
Sewers	12	1		2		6	2	1
Rubbish	1		1					
Right of way . . .	4	1				1	2	
Public buildings . .	1						1	
Building and safety . .	9	2	2	1			2	2
Health and welfare . .	14	3	1			3	5	2
Health	10	2				3	3	2
Recreation . . .	4	1	1				2	
Planning.	23	2	1			1	5	14
Personnel	10		4		1	4	1	
County, State and Federal affairs	20	1	2		1	5	9	2
Industry and Transportation	11		1					10
Finance (authorization).	14	1	1	4	1	2	1	4
Totals	206	31	20	11	10	30	50	54
Percentages of total		15.1	9.2	5.3	4.8	14.5	24.7	26.4

* The Los Angeles City Council is comprised of 15 members chosen for 4-year terms in non-partisan elections. Half the members are elected every two years. The Council's business is transacted through 15 standing committees. The mayor is elected for four years, appoints 5-man boards to administer the city's 19 departments. With few exceptions, all departmental personnel beneath the commissions is under the merit system.

† The legislation under consideration here relates substantively to questions of enlarging or modifying municipal services, and to matters of administrative authority, organization, and procedure. Revenue, appropriation, and private bills are omitted. In preparing this study the writer has had access both to the complete legislative histories filed with the city clerk and to the impressions and memorabilia of legislators and interest groups participating in the lawmaking process of the city.

‡ The C.A.O., or chief administrative officer, handles budgetary and organization and management matters. He is appointed by the Mayor, confirmed by the Council, answerable to both.

Source: Reynolds, "Career Public Service," p. 626.

However, further analysis by Reynolds showed what the table did not. Career bureaucrats were highly involved in the formulation of measures initiated by the other groupings. The administrators reviewed the justification of the desired objectives and the feasibility of desired programs initiated by the others. They reviewed, wrote, or rewrote drafts of twenty-seven of the thirty-one bills initiated by the private citizens, eleven of the twenty by the interest groups, eight of the ten by the city councilmen, and all eleven by the mayor. Few of the fifty-four measures proposed by the special "blue ribbon" committees were drafted or cosponsored by one or more of the department agents.

In many instances thereafter, the bureaus became advocates for the proposals. Among the techniques they used to exert influence during the deliberative council stage were making personal contacts with and submitting memoranda and position papers to council members; presenting testimony at formal hearings; and exploiting outside medias (such as newspapers, civic organizations, and influential citizens).

The high percentage level of passage of the proposals initiated by bureaucrats and of the proposals that they helped others to initiate demonstrated the potency of influence exerted by administrators on city council decisions. Of the eighty bills initiated by the chief administrative office and other bureaus, sixty-one were approved; as were twenty of the thirty-one bills by private citizens, fourteen of the twenty bills by pressure groups, eight of the eleven bills by the mayor, and nine of the ten bills by the council. In contrast, of the measures initiated by the select committees (the only groups that had not engaged the services of the administrators), only six bills were successfully passed.

During the period of the study, 109 of the 118 bills passed by the council were signed into law by the mayor. Practically every one of the bills the administrators had reviewed, written, or rewritten was approved. Thus, the administrative influence was seen to be present also in the executive performance in the rule making function.

Illustrative of the recognition by others of the bureaucratic importance in the rule-making function are two statements made to Reynolds by private individuals:

> "We find the Council checks with the departments on our requests and lets itself be governed by what they say."
> "If the administrators oppose us, we're sunk."[43]

Administrators, though greatly influential, do not all work towards the same goals and purposes. They are not to be considered as a monolithic entity, but a collection of groupings of bureaus each of which has its own interests, its own personal "bread and butter" concerns (such as pensions, salary, and promotion scales), and its own desires to protect, maintain, or expand its activities, offices, and responsibilities. Melvin W. Webber has noted that:

> Among the most powerful of the interest groups affecting governmental policies are the professional staff within the municipal government who hold vested interests in their own brands of programs and projects. Each tends to see the road to social betterment through the biasing lenses of its own profession's filters and each therefore competes with others for the limited financial resources they must divide.[44]

The administrators' struggle for their agencies' autonomy and self direction is supported by citizens who strive for efficiency in government, or for keeping "politics out of government." They may also receive the support of the councilmen who view them as voters at the polls, especially in non-partisan cities where public employees may form the largest collectivity of voters.

The bureaus also participate in the rule-making function by interpreting rules. The execution of each rule made is subject to the discretion of the administrator charged with its execution. For example, federal public assistance grants-in-aid programs specify that there be no inter-city differences within a state in its application under the state's rules. Yet, a study in Massachusetts showed that uniformity in application did not exist among twenty-nine cities and towns.[45] Martha Dierthick found that the dissimilarities were due to the variance of the discretion used by the professional administrators, particularly the respective heads of the local agencies. As she explained, "It is his values and preferences that are expressed in the local government's application of state laws and rules."[46]

In addition, administrative agents make rules. The head of each agency is usually given the authority to promulgate rules and regulations for the administration of matters within the concern of his department. For example, officials in local health departments can make rules for quarantine, compulsory vaccination, inspection of products and premises, elimination of unsanitary conditions, and closure or condemnation of an establishment for non-compliance.

The Judges in Rule-Making

The subordinate legal status of local governments and the prevailing concept of restricted local rule-making power, enunciated in "Dillon's Rule," leads to the pervasiveness of the judiciary in local rule-making. Though local legislation is subject to state and federal court review, the enforcement of Dillon's principle has been accomplished mainly by state judges.

State judges, in reviewing local legislation, have not placed narrow restraints on their activities. Local charters are carefully scrutinized to determine not only if a particular locality has the power to make specific rules,
but also if the local councils have performed the rule-making function in the
prescribed manner. Any individual who feels that his local rule-makers
have stepped beyond their prescribed province of activities can appeal to the
courts. A local resident need not have suffered personal injury to have legal
standing in the court; his status as a taxpayer permits him to challenge any
local rule in an action referred to as a "taxpayer's suit."

Decisions of state judges are based not only on a narrow reading of local
charters, but on standards deemed judicially appropriate. Two such standards
have been: (1) that municipal ordinances must be "reasonable," and (2) that
local councils, in making rules, give adequate consideration to all affected
interests in the community. Yet, although there are no clear guidelines as to
"reasonableness" or to procedures by which judges can evaluate whether
adequate attention was paid to all interests, justices have invalidated local
ordinances on those grounds.

Another principle that has been used in court decisions is that tax money
can be spent only for "public purposes." In this respect, "public purposes"
has been defined as those tasks that have traditionally been considered
activities of the government (as opposed to those traditionally engaged in by
private entrepreneurs), regardless of any public benefit which may be derived.
For example, this principle has been the basis of the arguments used by
private parking garage owners who have challenged the decisions of local
councils to construct public parking garages.

Because judges have not placed limiting restraints on their activities in
reviewing local legislation, and because of their receptivity to challenges, the
threat of judicial action exists in the minds of local rule-makers during their
deliberations. Although not all judicial challenges to local rules are successful,
the councils are cognizant of the burden entailed in proving to the courts that
the local government has the power to do what it sought to do. Litigation
involves the expenditure of time, energy, and money. Attorneys for the local
government may have to spend weeks, months, or years (costing taxpayers
thousands of dollars) to prevent a rule from being invalidated by the courts.
In many instances, such delays have the effect of obstructing a necessary rule
from being executed, or a needed program from being started or completed.
Thus, council members will try to act within the areas permitted, and to
carefully pass legislation in the wording and manner consistent with their
powers.

Judges perform the rule-making function through their actions in interpreting rules of local legislative and administrative agents. Legislative enactments
rarely are so worded as to include all contigencies that may arise. Therefore,

the judges may act to interpret the intent of the council. In applying the rule to a particular case, or in claiming to interpret the council's intent, the judges are making rules.

In some instances, court decisions affect the initiation of rules, in that they stimulate local officials to act in implementing the new decisions. Thus, legislative agendas or prescribed areas are set. In this regard, the decisions of the Supreme Court of the United States are illustrative. For example, when the Supreme Court, in the *Avery v. Midland County, Texas* decision, ruled that the election of county councilmen must be based on the "one man one vote" principle, the county boards were being told to make rules to reapportion. Should councils fail or refuse to act, the courts will make the prescriptions for conduct in such areas. Thus, by declaring whether a rule is constitutional, by interpreting what a rule means, and by implementing a disputed rule, the judges are rule-makers.

Intergovernmental Influence on Rule-Making

As problems become less local in nature, so does the rule-making function. Rule-making on the local level is affected by the state government, the federal government, and by the governments of surrounding jurisdictions.

The State and the Locality

The formal relationship between the city and the state is a primary factor in intergovernmental influence on local rule-making. The powers of local governments are derived from state constitutions and statutes. Such powers may be taken away through constitutional amendments or revisions of statutes.

The amount of autonomy that localities may enjoy is clearly spelled out in their charters. Some enjoy a relatively high degree of independence in making rules to meet the needs of local citizens. Others enjoy relatively little autonomy, and in the absence of home rule powers rely on the state legislature to perform the rule-making function for them. The state legislature acts by passing special and general legislation. Special legislation refers to laws dealing with a specified locality; and general legislation refers to laws affecting all localities.

State and local intergovernmental relations are complex arrangements, due to the intertwining of state and local responsibilities. In some areas of activity, both the state and local governments have concurrent responsibilities for making rules. Thus, local and state rule-makers may coordinate their activities to avoid unnecessary duplication, or to plan for orderly servicing of the people's needs.

In some specific areas states influence local rule-making by providing some form of assistance for programs. They do this through financial or technical assistance. Principally, financial assistance takes the form of grants-in-aid.

Nearly two-thirds of all state financial assistance goes for elementary and secondary education. Other sizeable state financial assistance programs are public welfare, health, and highways. In these areas, the local government is empowered to make rules for the administration of the various projects. However, local agents are subject to state rules and oversight. Thus, a local school board may make rules for the hiring of teachers and the curriculum to be taught; yet, the teachers must meet the state certification requirement and the curriculum must conform to the guidelines set by the state. States assist in non-financial ways by providing a variety of technical aids and equipment. In addition, advice and information may be furnished for planning and administering programs.

Local officials are forced to make rules for activities made mandatory by state statutes. These are areas of state responsibility that have been delegated to the local governments. They include rules for local elections, fire and police protection, courts and jails, health programs, and sewage disposal.

Local agents are prohibited from making rules in some areas by state legislative pre-emption. In Maryland, for example, the list included censorship. An example of such pre-emption restricting local rule-making was seen in 1969, in Montgomery County, Maryland. Many residents were aroused by the distribution of a weekly "smut sheet" published by an underground press. There were vociferous demands that the county council take action to prohibit further circulation of the paper in the county. While the council members acknowledged the complaints, they made clear to the residents that the council was unable to act because legislation concerning censorship could only come from the state government.[47]

In recent years, many states have established special agencies for local governmental matters. For example, New Jersey's Division of Local Government (in the State Department of Finance and Taxation) is charged with the continuous investigation of programs of local governments. The Division has the power to regulate local methods of budgeting and financial procedures. It can force a locality to provide enough funds to meet debts or reduce deficits. The Local Government Board, which establishes policies for the Division, has the power to take actual control of a municipality in the event of bankruptcy or financial crises.

Most states have agencies specifically for overseeing local fiscal matters. Most of these audit municipal accounts. Nearly one-half of the states require localities to submit periodic financial reports and they supervise municipal debts.

Despite the states' relationship with local rule-making, most state legislatures have been reluctant to become involved with the complex and vast problems of the cities. The reluctance and demonstrated incapacity of state agents to play an effective role in solving these problems has led to the involvement of federal agents, for contemporary urban problems have become national concerns. The relationship between the national and local governments is not a new phenomenon, but the extent and directness of this involvement is relatively new.

The Federal Government and the Localities

Local rule-making has always been affected to some extent by the federal government. Along with the parent states, the localities are subject to the enumerated powers and supremacy clauses of the Constitution of the United States. In some areas, permission from the national government must be obtained before local action can be taken. For example, if a city wanted to operate a radio station, it must obtain a license from the Federal Communication Commission. If it wants to build a bridge, plans must be approved by the Army Corps of Engineers.

Morton Grodzins has established five categories of federal activity on the local level. Most of these have been established by the federal government since the depression period of the 1930's.[48] Table VIII.2 lists the modes of national activities.

It is in the categories of federal grants-in-aid that the national governmental influence over local rule-making has been markedly exerted. Urban problems, previously ignored and minimized, have recently received national recognition through the creation of agencies and a series of federal programs. In the 1960s, for example, three agencies were established whose programs focused on urban problems. The department of Housing and Urban Development supervised programs aimed at improving the urban physical environment. The Department of Transportation had major interest in urban mass transportation. The Office of Economic Opportunity had such programs as employment, education, and legal assistance for the disadvantaged members of various ethnic, age, economic, and racial groupings clustering mostly in the main urban centers.

The predominant intergovernmental relationship has been a federal-state-local arrangement in which most assistance payments have been channelled through the states for local projects. On occasion, however, the national government has given assistance directly to the localities. Yet, this last arrangement has not been an exclusively federal-local one, for state governmental agents remain involved. The approval of state agents for local proposals may be required by the federal government. For example, the Economic Opportunity Act of 1964, which provided federal aid for job corps projects, work study programs, and community action programs, required that local proposals be submitted to the governor for approval prior to the granting of any funds. Federally assisted local projects may have to meet state plans and rules of standards for construction and operation. Localities desiring

TABLE VIII.2

Channels of Federal Activity on the Local Scene

Modes of Activity	Examples
1. Federal direct-to-people activities.	Old age and survivors insurance. Veterans benefits. Mail delivery. Licensing.
2. Federally engineered local governments, relatively independent on state or local governments.	Soil conservation. Agricultural stabilization and conservation. Grazing service advisory board.
3. Federally engineered local governments, relatively dependent on state or local governments.	Selective service. Civil defense. Public housing and urban development (in some states).
4. Federal grants channeled through states.	Welfare. Highways. Employment. Forestry. Vocational education. Public health.
5. Federal grants and other aid directly to local governments.	Airports (in some states). Public housing and redevelopment (some states). Flood control. School construction (some states). Disaster relief (some cases).

Adapted from: Grodzins, "Federal and State Impacts," p. 60.

direct federal aid for airport construction have to consult with state officials about planning designs and location. In addition, state legislation may be necessary (as in the case of building an airport) before localities are permitted to construct facilities and operate a program. Localities, in all instances, need enabling acts from the state legislature to permit them to participate in programs directly funded by the federal government. And, the state may enter as a participant (to the extent it so desires) in every federal program designed to assist localities.

Federal grant-in-aid programs have had an impact on local rule-making. Such aid has encouraged localities to launch needed programs they were not previously able financially to undertake. Most of the localities have found it easier to obtain funds from the federal government than by appealing to the state legislatures. One example is the urban renewal programs first provided for by the Housing Acts of 1949 and 1954. These acts called for federal assistance to be given to localities for slum clearance and community development projects. Cities were in special need of such projects, yet, state legislators generally had never displayed any interest in assisting in the finances of urban renewal. The need can be seen by the large numbers of localities that have chosen to participate in federally assisted renewal programs. As of June 1969, a total of 2,583 urban renewal projects in 1,042 localities had been initiated.[49]

Grants-in-aid have eased many localities' financial rule-making plight. Much of the difficulty localities faced in providing programs to meet the needs of their residents had been due to the lack of funds. State and federal taxes had pre-empted most of the revenue fields that might have been sources for local revenue income. Thus, receipt of federal funds has provided an additional source of income, and it has affected rules that would be made for increasing tax rates or for dispersing the previously limited revenue. Moreover, officials in financially depressed localities have been able to make rules in areas on a more equal basis with their counterparts in richer communities.

Federal assistance programs have influenced localities to pass rules in accord with national standards. For example, grant programs from the Department of Health, Education, and Welfare require that projects it funds are to be administered by merit service personnel. In addition, the priorities to be set by localities for allocation of funds are affected by the national programs offered. Local officials may be induced to reorder their programs so as to obtain the outside revenue. They may further be enticed into providing additional aspects to programs for which the federal government offers additional funds.

For some programs the federal government has created functional special districts. These have had the impact of fragmenting local rule-making. For other programs, cumbersome and inflexible regulations have narrowed the discretion of local agents. However, federal grants have had the countereffect of strengthening local governments by opening areas of activities to local agents previously not engaged in because of limited funds. Where federal funds have been provided, local governments were able to improve services by hiring more expert and professional staff members.

A recent development that has underscored the importance of federal programs to localities has been the creation by local governments of federal liaison departments or officers. By 1969, 16 percent of all cities (principally the large and central cities) had established a special office to keep aware of, plan for, make proposals for, and coordinate the receipt of available federal grants. In the past few years, several localities have established lobby offices in Washington, for the purpose of having a city employee watch congressional legislation and try to influence congressmen to pass additional assistance programs. Some localities with such urban lobbies have been Atlanta, Birmingham, Boston, Chicago, Dade County, Long Beach, and San Diego. The explanation for these recent developments is the belief held by local agents that such federal liason officers and lobby attempts have proven helpful in obtaining federal funds for the localities.[50]

Interlocal Cooperation

As local governments have found it more difficult to provide the professionally trained personnel and the costly plants and equipment necessary to provide modern governmental services, an ever increasing number of interlocal contracts and agreements have come into existence. These have occurred among localities within the same state or among localities of different states. Permission for such cooperation has been granted through state legislative enactments (as in Minnesota, Nebraska, New York, Pennsylvania, Virginia, and Wisconsin), or through state constitutional provisions (as in Alaska, California, Hawaii, and Missouri). Cooperative interlocal ventures have taken many forms.

Cooperative Agreements

The cooperative agreement is the oldest form of interlocal cooperative ventures. Such agreements have usually been undertaken by adjacent communities. Fire fighting was the first specific area in which interlocal cooperation was attempted. Fire protection agreements may be made by one locality with another for temporary emergency service, or for a more permanent mutual aid arrangement. As local agents recognized financial savings, increased efficiency of service, and community identity retained in these agreements, more were undertaken for other areas. Agreements were most often entered into for law enforcement, public health, waste disposal, vocational education, recreation, and ambulance service. In recent years, local agents have also recognized that better service to the public can be made at lower costs by the joint sponsoring of costly facilities. For example, in 1968, eleven cities in Los Angeles County jointly organized a data processing system.

Interlocal agreements may be temporary or permanent in nature. Temporary agreements are usually formed to develop a solution to an immediate pressing problem. One of these occurred during the riots that erupted in Washington, D.C., in April 1968. The Washington chief executive entered into agreements with surrounding counties for their police to patrol the District's boundaries, and to enter into the District should they be needed to maintain peace. Temporary agreements may, however, develop into permanent arrangements.

Contractual Arrangements

Another form of interlocal cooperation is a contractual arrangement for the provision of services. Some of these contracts provide for service charges while others do not. Central cities may supply water to outlying communities for a fee. County governments, in addition to the traditional provisions of services to unincorporated areas, have been called on to provide a wide variety of services by contract to incorporated cities or towns. For example, in Los Angeles County, several incorporated cities have voluntarily entered into contractual arrangement with the county government to receive (for a fee) such services as building inspection, fire and police protection, library, animal regulation, street maintenance and construction, and traffic signal maintenance.[51]

Conferences and Leagues

Interjurisdictional cooperation has also taken the form of conferences and associations of local officials. These officials meet to study common problems and to propose possible alternative solutions. The oldest of these associations is the various state leagues of municipalities. First conceived as a means to coordinate pressure at the state capitals (in the late nineteenth century), for the purpose of protecting and advancing the interests of local governments, they have developed into instruments for interlocal cooperation. State municipal leagues are found in all but two states (Hawaii and Rhode Island). The leagues are called by different names, among which are Alabama League of Municipalities, League of Arizona Cities and Towns, Pennsylvania State Association of Boroughs, and New York State Conference of Mayors.

Each league, supported by dues paid by member municipalities, maintains a permanent office headed by a full-time director and a small staff. League members meet annually at a conference or convention for the purpose of discussing current problems. The leagues' staffs perform such services for their members as data collection and analysis, training programs for municipal employees, central purchasing for small municipalities, and advising and sponsoring legislative programs.

The National League of Cities is a federation of state leagues. It conducts research on municipal problems and serves as a national clearing house for information on such problems. In addition, it keeps localities informed about new federal programs and lobbies for federal legislation that benefits member localities. The National Association of Counties provides the same services for county officials.

Specialized associations have been organized for cooperative efforts among various types of local officials. These include Municipal Finance Officers

Association, International City Management Association, National Association of Housing and Redevelopment Officials, and the International Institute of Municipal Clerks. The United States Conference of Mayors is, perhaps, the most notable of these. Mayors of cities with populations of over 30,000 join together to improve municipal administration, interchange ideas, and foster relations with the national government. The exchange of proposals, data, and ideas may influence local officials as they consider ways to deal with their own local problems.

Metropolitan Governments

A special concern within local rule-making is the realization that problems do not respect jurisdictional boundaries. The population residing within a metropolitan geographic area shares common interests and problems, such as transportation, water and sewerage systems, air pollution, and public health. Yet, local governmental units are severely limited in their abilities to solve problems that are metropolitan area-wide in nature. One reason is that each government is not able to solve a problem that will not be contained within the geographic boundaries of its jurisdiction. Various attempts have been made to cope with this reality.

Special Districts

Until the mid-twentieth century, state rule-makers sought to solve metropolitan problems by creating special districts. Yet, the establishment of these districts served further to fragment local rule-making. While special district governments are independent units for specific problem areas, in that they each have rule-making authority and some power to finance their programs, their rules affect the rule-making function performed by other governmental agents who serve similar constituencies. To illustrate the complexity, imagine that the members of a special district sanitary commission pass a rule to build a sewer line extension into an undeveloped land tract. This decision would ultimately affect the economic, political, and social conditions of the community. Specifically, the extension would affect the direction of home building, business locations, transportation routes, schools, parks and recreation, police and fire protection, library services, and street construction. The rules made for each would be the responsibility of a variety of governments. Thus, the rule made by the special district would affect rule-making by county and municipal agents, as well as those of other special districts.

Cooperative Planning

Another attempt to handle interjurisdictional problems has been cooperative planning. Multijurisdictional planning agencies were created, beginning in the mid-1950s, by local governments with the approval of state legislatures.

The primary purpose of these agencies is comprehensive planning. The members conduct general planning studies, population and economic analysis, and land use studies. They are generally required by state statutes to draw a comprehensive ("master") development plan. In addition, they provide planning advice, information, or special studies for local governments or special districts. They may review zoning or subdivision cases, or review and comment on local, state, or federal programs sponsored within a jurisdiction.

The metropolitan planning agency is comprised of members selected by the local governments they are to represent. Generally, the majority of the members are sent from the associated cities and counties, while the remaining ones are sent from towns or special districts, and the states. Membership in and withdrawal of membership from an agency are at the discretion of each associated local council.

The actions of planning agencies may or may not affect local rule-making. Local councils may defer to the expertise found within the agencies, but there is no requirement that they do so. Local councils need not adopt the comprehensive plan, nor accept the agencies' services or recommendations.

Councils of Government

A significant recent attempt to solve metropolitan problems is the establishment of councils of governments (COGs). The first metropolitan council of government was established in the Detroit metropolitan area in 1954. Officials in other metropolitan areas recognized the need for interlocal cooperation, but were slow to form such councils for lack of funds. By 1965, only twenty-five COGs had been organized. After 1965, the federal government gave impetus to the movement. The Housing and Urban Development Act of 1965 provided for federal financial support for general planning programs undertaken by such councils. Further impetus was provided by the Demonstration Cities and Metropolitan Development Act of 1966, which required that comprehensive metropolitan plans for such areas as housing and mass transportation be devised. In addition, as a condition for federal grants-in-aid, these plans are to be reviewed and approved by area-wide councils prior to the submission to appropriate national departments. With federal impetus, the number of councils of governments had grown to 142 by 1969.[52]

The councils are generally comprised of equal numbers of representatives from each county and municipal governing body within a metropolitan area. The members selected from each locality are usually drawn from the ranks of its elected officials. A locality's membership in and withdrawal from a council is accomplished through the passage of a resolution by the local governing body.

The councils provide mechanisms for studying problems, obtaining and reconciling the views of the various local governments, and provide guidance for metropolitan development and planning. In addition, they serve to represent the needs of the metropolitan area to state and federal agencies and legislatures. Yet, their influence on local rule-making may be no more than suggestive in nature. A COG cannot take effective action on an area-wide problem if a majority of the members oppose the proposal, and it has no coercive power to enforce or implement any decision made. It relies on the fact that its membership is comprised of members of associated local councils, and that these councilmen would return home to persuade their colleagues of the merits of the COG's recommendations and proposals. Each member locality is under no legal requirement to be bound by its membership, and may join into or refrain from any COG actions at its own local council's discretion. Yet, councils of governments have made officials from local governmental bodies aware of what problems their neighbors have, what solutions they are proposing, and what actions they are taking.

Jurisdictional Changes

Several attempts have been made to alter jurisdictional boundaries as a means to solve regional problems. These have included annexation, whereby a municipality expands its jurisdiction over surrounding unincorporated territories; and complete or partial city-county consolidation, whereby a new governmental structure is formed that amalgamates the county and all or some of the municipalities found within the county. The creation of metropolitan county governments and metropolitan federations represents a two-level approach, whereby the rule-making function is shared between municipal governments and strengthened or newly created area-wide governments. For example, Metropolitan Dade County Government (a metropolitan county plan in Florida) makes rules for county wide traffic regulation, building codes, mass transportation, and urban renewal, among other things, while incorporated localities within the county retain responsibility for such matters as water supply, police departments, and waste collection.

Changes that alter jurisdictional boundaries may, on occasion, occur by state legislative action, as when the Indiana General Assembly (in 1969) acted to consolidate Indianapolis with Marion County. However, almost all changes require the approval of voters in a referendum election. While the various plans offer such advantages as increased cooperation, consolidated responsibility, flexibility, simplified governmental structures, and avoids duplication of services, the voters have been generally reluctant to give their approval. Several reasons have been offered for the public's resistance to change.[53] There may be fears of higher tax rates, lower levels of service, and conflict between races. Groupings benefitting from the governmental arrangements that are in existance are reluctant to support a change from the status quo. People may hold feelings of local pride and prefer small population centers. Generally there is little understanding of centralization, and there is distrust of a governmental system in which community control over rule-making is diminished.

Influence of Community Power on Rule-Making

For many years, sociologists and political scientists have conducted investigations to determine who actually makes the decisions that influence the rule-making function in local areas. These studies have been called "community power studies." Muncie, Illinois, a homogeneous and small, compact midwestern city was one of the first communities studied to see if elected public officials actually make the important decisions. Sociologists Helen and Robert Lynd found that in Muncie, during the mid 1920s,[54] and again later during the mid 1930s,[55] that the dominant influentials were the heads or owners of the principal industry or businesses, and bankers. The power of this coalition was based on control of the economic sector of the city. These persons not only provided the major means of employee income, but also controlled the means of credit. The policies that they were interested in promoting were supportive to their self interest. Political and elected leaders were subordinate to those business leaders. Thus, the Lynds found that the rule-making function in Muncie was controlled by a tightly knit closed business elite.

Over a decade later, another sociologist, Floyd Hunter, conducted a study of the power structure in Atlanta, Georgia.[56] He confirmed the existence of an elite, but found a complex arrangement of influentials in that large, heterogeneous, southern city. Hunter saw the presence of a pyramidical structure of power that consisted of several layers of influentials. Power to influence the rule-making function flowed downward. At the top layer of the influence arrangement were the owners and heads of major business concerns. These individuals formulated public policy. The decisions reached in these meetings were channelled down to the next layer, comprised of institutional and associational organizations (as, for example, religious, educational, civic associations, and a few public officials). The spokesmen from these groups acted as "front men" to communicate and initiate specific rules to the public and political arena. The elected public officials, who in name performed the rule-making function, were within the lower level structure that was charged with the implementation of rules formulated elsewhere. Most rules formulated by the top layer influentials were city-wide in nature. Yet, there were public issues with which they did not concern themselves, although they carefully screened such issues to assure that implementation would in no way threaten their interests or dominant values.

A study by E. Digby Baltzell in the mid-1950s found an arrangement of influence in Philadelphia that was based on social standing.[57] The "old wealth" aristocracy made the public decisions and its interests were business oriented. Those representing old wealth believed that holding public office was not necessary for them to exercise power over the rule-making function. Here too, the public agents were subordinate to that influence, possessing the formal titles but not the power.

Thus sociologists have provided, for consideration, an elitist theory of community power. This theory depicts society as being stratified primarily according to economic levels. In the uppermost level is a clearly defined, small, continuing, elite comprised of business and financial leaders. Public officials are to be found in lower levels, and their recruitment and formal rule-making performance are under the aegis of the elite.

In contrast, recent studies of community power by political scientists have stressed a pluralist model of influence. Their studies do not indicate the existence of elite dominated decision making, but rather an arrangement of multigroups struggling for positions of influence. The pluralist model emphasizes that the base for influence is interest and activity in the political arena, rather than the ability to control economic resources.

One of the earliest and most influential of the pluralist studies was Robert Dahl's research report of New Haven, Connecticut.[58] Dahl found that every individual or group had access to some resources for influence. Yet, not every group or individual utilized these resources to the same extent or with equal skill. For each issue Dahl studied, he found that there were leaders and subleaders who had exerted predominant influence on the outcome. However, these individuals were not drawn from the same interests, or social or income strata, nor were they members of a permanent clique. Indeed, there was a different set of influentials active for each issue, that is, leaders in one issue area did not exert influence on other issue areas. Although some individuals were actively involved for more than one issue, these were usually elected public officials, most frequently the mayor. Dahl found that business and economic leaders, rather than being the ruling group, were only one of the many groups exerting influence. It was on specific business oriented decisions that their interests did generally prevail.

Aaron Wildavsky conducted his investigation of Oberlin, Ohio, and supported the pluralist theory.[59] As had Dahl, he found that neither wealth nor family standing was important as a base for exerting influence. Rather, the resources that were important were information, energy, time, and skill. These resources were widely dispersed, and were open for exploitation and employment by any person or group who wished to exert influence on the rule-making function. Wildavsky noted four reasons that might explain pluralistic community power. First, different issues are salient to different individuals or groups, and in varying degrees. Second, no one group or individual controls all the resources necessary for influence. Third, the level of activity exerted towards influencing issue outcomes differs with the nature of the group and the nature of the issue. Fourth, there are few issues that fail to engender some degree of controversy. Thus, there are groups or individuals in constant conflict with one another, as each strives to see their opposition or support of an issue predominate.

The pluralist theory was further confirmed and defended by the investigations of Nelson Polsby in New Haven, Edward C. Banfield in Chicago, Wallace S. Sayre and Herbert Kaufman in New York, and Frank J. Munger in Syracuse.[60] They all noted that there exists multiple power centers within each community, with each center exerting influence on different issue areas. People participate to the extent that they are interested in a particular issue.

Several students of community power structure have reached other conclusions about who actually makes the decisions that influence the rule-making function. In their studies they have found the existence of individual or group influentials, but that these do not comprise a compact ruling elite. M. Kent Jennings investigated Atlanta a decade after Hunter did, to see if Hunter's premise was correct.[61] He confirmed the political influence of individuals in key economic positions. However, he concluded that Hunter's ruling elite model had to be revised, for he found that the owners and heads of major business concerns comprised only one of several groups influential in formulating public policy. Moreover, business leaders were not a monolithic grouping. All did not share similar outlooks and policy orientations, nor did they all exercise uniform levels of political activity. Although there was some relationship between influence and social status, the influentials were not drawn only from the higher socio-economic status levels. Actors other than those business leaders were involved in decision making. Jennings found that at least one-half of the influentials were central or minor governmental officials. Thus, there was no clear elite, although there was a coalition of interests that exerted influence on more than one issue area.

William A. Gamson found that individuals having a reputation for influence were influential in the eighteen New England communities he studied.[62] The basis for the reputation of the individuals was their high level of political involvement and activity. The effect of this reputation was that when these individuals took the same public position on an issue, more than 75 percent of the time their stand was translated into the rule made. However, those enjoying reputations of influence were not found to have been a cohesive force, for on different issues different individuals aligned on different positions. Thus, Gamson concluded that a group of individuals was recognized as being influential, but they could hardly be considered a ruling elite.

Peter Bachrach and Morton S. Baratz suggested an approach to study community power that is referred to as a "neo-elitist" theory.[63] They contended that power is not only manifested by influencing the direction of rules made by public agents, but that power can also be exerted to suppress issues or alternative suggestions from being raised. Thus, a study of community power must include the concept of "non-decision making."

In addition, Bachrach and Morton held that power to influence the rule-making function does not exist only in situations of conflict, wherein one group's interests prevails over others (as the elitists maintain), or whereas multi-interest groups struggle to affect the outcome of an issue (as the pluralists maintain). Instead, Bachrach and Baratz postulated that power may be present in consensus situations. They recognized that there may be an elite within a community whose interests prevail within the rule-making arena. However, interests of the elite are not necessarily divergent from those held by the rest of the community. They contended that the members of the elite, as opinion leaders, are able to transmit their values and aims between themselves and the leaders, and consensus is reached without conflict.

Robert E. Agger and his associates further supported the importance of viewing "non-decision making" as consequences of power exerted over the local rule-making function.[64] They found, in their study of four cities, that political ideology (*i.e.*, a set of beliefs and attitudes toward the political system held by most of the people) was important in understanding community power. They postulated that a community is comprised of many groups that are differentiated by ideology rather than by interests. The ideologies are articulated by active, small, influential inner cliques. By influencing the passive public to accept a set of beliefs and attitudes, these elite groups are able to create a consensus to obtain rules consistent with their own ideological ends.

Citizen Participation in Rule-Making

There exists today several localities where people are directly involved in the rule-making function. These are principally small New England towns. Annually, or more frequently, as necessary, the qualified voters meet together to initiate, discuss, debate, and make rules for pressing matters. At these meetings, citizens participate in the making of the budget, or decide upon such other items as street lighting or improvements, a new library, or the raising of teachers' salaries. Yet, these are isolated instances of direct rule-making. For localities with a large and heterogeneous population, the only mechanisms for direct involvement have been the referendum and initiative elections, and for direct influence, the recall election.

Recall

Recall is a means by which the electorate can remove public agents from office before the expiration of their terms. This process provides a means to influence rule-making because it may be used as a threat to induce officials to alter or modify their attitudes more in line with those of the constituents. While provisions for recall exists in many localities in each section of the United States, its most frequent use has been in the West, especially in California where it was first used (in 1903).

In California, the recall has been used frequently against county, municipal, and special district officials (*e.g.*, sanitary districts, school districts, and water agencies). For example, during the 1960s, school board members of nine school districts were recalled, as were a mayor, and several city and county councilmen. Recall elections have taken place in Marin County, and in such cities as Sacramento, Kern, Fresno, Pasadena, Long Beach, San Fernando, Durante, Irwindale, and Lawndale.[65]

Recall attempts in large cities rarely get beyond the initiation stage because of the large number of signatures needed on the petitions. In January 1969, residents of the northeast section of Philadelphia initiated petitions to recall their councilman. Though he was elected on a ward basis, the petitioners needed to obtain the signatures of 28,109 registered voters in that ward (based on a state requirement that a minimum of 25 percent of those voting in the prior councilmanic election sign a recall petition). This large number of signatures was not obtained. Again, in January 1970, an attempt was made to recall another councilman by the same residents. This attempt, too, was unsuccessful because the large number of signatures could not be obtained.[66] In contrast, an attempt to recall three councilmen in Tempe, Arizona (where 25 percent of those voting in the prior election was the basis for the number of signatures needed) required only 617 signatures for each petition. This number was relatively easy to obtain.[67]

Incumbents subjected to recall attempts have been charged with corruption, or they have been attacked for holding an unpopular stand on an issue. In the attempts in Philadelphia, residents signed recall petitions in reaction to a councilman's vote for tax increases (in 1969), and a councilman's vote to change the zoning restrictions to favor large scale developers (in 1970). In the attempt in Tempe, Arizona, the petition drive to recall three councilmen was completed by an ultra-reactionary group after whispered general rumors were spread throughout the community that the three men were Communist sympathizers.

Planning a petition drive, seeking signatures, and conducting a campaign against officials demands organized effort, time, energy, and financial resources. For this reason it is rare that individual citizens can and will initiate this mechanism as a device to more directly exert influence on the rule-making function. However, the threat of its use, buttressed by the occasions where it has been successful, may serve to influence the elected rule-makers. For officials may have to expend their own resources of time, energy, and finances to defend their positions; and their work is disrupted until the conflict is settled.

Initiative

The initiative represents one mechanism whereby the electorate participates directly in making local rules. Through the initiative, residents may by way of a petition propose a measure to be placed upon the ballot. If approved by the voters, the measure becomes an ordinance. State constitutions and local charters prescribe the various requirements for completing and submitting a petition, and for ratification of the proposal.

This mechanism has been used infrequently. Examples of its use in recent years include the establishment of merit service, police and fire pension plans, and wage policies by city employees in various California localities. Petitions may be raised to repeal a local ordinance. The voters in Santa Barbara adopted a proposal (sponsored by local realtors), which repealed a council-adopted real estate transfer tax. In those localities where provisions for the initiative exists, there may be limitations as to the subjects that can be affected by initiative petitions. Some examples of items left exclusively to elected officials are street improvements, location of public buildings, purchases of supplies, tax rates, and appropriations.

Referendum

A widely utilized mechanism whereby people can directly affect rule-making is the referendum. The referendum is an election at which the voters may accept, reject, or modify charter provisions or council approved ordinances. A measure to be placed upon the ballot can be initiated by the council or by the public.

The council may refer a bill to the public at its own discretion, or when required by law to do so. Usually, councilmen will only refer those measures they consider controversial in nature. Fluoridation of drinking water has been such a controversial issue. Although fluoridation has been unanimously supported by medical groups (such as the American Dental Association, and the American Medical Association), much opposition has arisen from groups that consider it to be either an infringement of individual liberty, an affront to religious freedom, an ineffective means to prevent tooth decay, or a Communist plot to physically and spiritually weaken the youth of America. From 1950 through 1966, 925 referenda were held on this issue. This high figure is illustrative of the propensity of local councilmen to avoid taking decisive action on such a controversial issue. The outcome of these elections illustrates the typically negative reaction toward issues referred to them. Of the 925 referenda, 566 were rejected at the polls.[68]

Measures may also be referred to the public by the council because of state constitutional requirements. Popular approval of budgets (*e.g.*, school budgets), and increases in property tax rates, are examples. The largest number of referenda is for proposed bond sales. In all but three states (Alabama, Hawaii, and Indiana), localities are required to hold a referendum before they may issue bonds for public sale. In 1971, a total of 2,299 bond election referenda were held. The public was asked to approve the sale of bonds to raise funds for such purposes as education, transportation, utilities, conservation, social welfare, and public services. These referenda also met a considerable rate of negative reaction from the electorate. Of all the bond issues referred in 1971, 43 percent were rejected.[69]

In addition, many states require that a referendum be held for charter amendments, and most states require that one be held for territorial changes. The Advisory Commission on Intergovernmental Relations studied proposed changes in local government structure, and found that in ten of the eighteen localities where referenda were held from 1950–1961, the proposed changes were rejected.[70]

Citizens may call legislative ordinances to a referendum by circulating a petition. The procedure is similar to that of the initiative and the recall. As are the others, referenda petitions are likely to be sponsored by organized groups. Civil rights issues may provide illustrations of referenda sponsored by groups. In Berkley, the California Real Estate Association, and in Detroit, the Detroit Home Owner's Council, sponsored propositions that asked voters to reject fair housing ordinances passed by the respective councils. Both propositions were so worded that voters were not blatantly asked to reject any rights of blacks. Instead, they were asked to uphold the over-riding right "to privacy and to the free use, enjoyment, and disposition of residential property." Both of these referenda were adopted, although they were later declared unconstitutional by the courts.[71]

The Use of Initiative and Referendum

The initiative and referendum are mechanisms by which the individual can directly participate in the rule-making function. However, a review of the utilization of these mechanisms indicates that individual citizens have not or could not participate in or exert influence on the making of rules. For the initiative and referendum to be potent instruments of making rules, the individual citizens have to be knowledgeable about the mechanisms and about the proposals. It is difficult for a voter to be knowledgeable about a proposal, because the propositions may be so worded as to camouflage the real issue (as was seen in the fair housing referenda). Propositions stated in legal terms or in abbreviated terms may lead to confusion in the minds of a voter. In addition, despite a need for change, conflicting opinions about the merits of a proposal, or the absence of cues (as usually provided by party labels or leadership identification), in this issue election lead to a voter predisposition of maintaining the status quo (as was seen the fluoridation issue). Voter reaction to a proposal, moreover, may be based on a misunderstanding of or failure to recognize its long range implications as compared to its short range benefits. For example, in 1969, voters in Fremont and in Youngstown, Ohio, rejected proposed property tax increases that were necessary for funding the operations of the public school system. The voters gained the immediate benefit of forestalling higher tax payments, but they failed to see the implications to the school system. Formal education ground to a halt as the schools closed for lack of funds.

To be effective, the people must also be able and anxious to use the mechanisms. It appears that these mechanisms are conducive to a minority or a special interest group interest. The amount of time, energy, and money needed to circulate petitions and campaign has limited the use of these mechanisms to organized groups having the necessary resources at their disposal. Also, twelve states have required extraordinary majorities to approve the referred questions. Thus, a minority of voters may have been sufficient to thwart the desires of a majority. For example, in California, which has required for passage a majority of two-thirds of those voting, slightly more than one-third of the voters could have prevented a measure from passage. Moreover, a majority of the electorate seldom vote in these issue elections. Unless an issue is "really hot" (as was the fair housing referenda in Berkley), the turnout rate is usually 20 to 30 percent of the registered voters. Thus, it would appear that in practice the use of the initiative and referendum has not significantly permitted individual participation in the making of rules.

Community Control

In recent years there has been heard in many localities a call from the public for "community control." Generally, the call has been for the decentralization of governmental institutions, with agencies established throughout the city, and with residents participating in the rule-making activities engaged in by public agents. The orientation of the proponents has been for a return to neighborhood "town meetings," or at least, for the creation of boards of elected neighborhood residents to be able to directly influence the agencies that have immediate effect on some daily activities of the people. While in almost all instances the results have been citizen participation in rule administration, some scattered attempts have been made to include citizens in the rule-making function.

One example has been the community control program of the Thomas P. Morgan Elementary School in Washington, D.C.[72] Although the budget for the Morgan School was determined by the District of Columbia Board of Education, neighborhood residents have been able to determine budgetary priorities, the educational policy, and the rules for hiring personnel. The school is located in the Adams Morgan neighborhood, which is comprised mainly of lower and middle income black families. The community elected fifteen members of a newly established eighteen-member neighborhood school board, which included seven parents, five adult community representatives, and three young people from the community (who, by prescription, had to be selected from youths between the ages of sixteen to twenty-three). The remaining three members of the board were representatives of the school's staff. The board was charged with making rules concerning the personnel and the curriculum for the school. This project has been hailed as being a success. The principal of the school has stated that

> It is important to the attainment of educational objectives for community standards to prevail in school. We won't define what the norms should be and push the children into them. Instead we change the norms. We arrange the environment to fit the kid.

The Morgan school board members felt that community control was one way to raise the level of public school education in the inner city. However, they have expressed the belief that community control might not be the way for every community. As one board member stated, "A lot depends on the community."

The Relationship of Rule-Making to the Public

Despite means that allow for the public to perform actively in the rule-making function, the principal rule-makers are essentially the elected and appointed public officials. Their task is generally accepted to be the satisfaction of the needs and interests of the public. Yet, should they follow the desires of the public, or should they attempt to satisfy what they see to be the needs of the public? A fundamental question is, however, do these men and women know what the public wants?

Roberta S. Sigel and H. Paul Friesema attempted to provide a partial answer to the fundamental question.[73] They compared the preferences stated by a sample public with the perceptions that community leaders held of the public's view on any given issue. The study was undertaken in Detroit, where the non-partisan board of education had established a special advisory committee to design a new high school and community center. The neighborhood for which this was planned was a multi-problem area, with high levels of delinquency, illegitimacy, and unemployment. The population was 55 percent black, and predominantly comprised of low socio-economic groupings. The new facilities were to meet the social, economic, and educational needs of the community.

In contrast to the general characteristics of the residents, the members of the special committee were all highly educated, middle and upper class individuals. These individuals were small businessmen, PTA officials, ministers, social workers, and housewives. They were not drawn from the "big names" of the city, though each had roots and deep interests in the community.

Sigel and Friesema interviewed most of the committee members, and 101 parents of children who would be enrolled in the new high school. The parents were asked to state their attitudes toward or levels of satisfaction with such items as racial conditions, living conditions, governmental performance, tax levels, urban renewal programs, compulsory training of unemployed adults, and school curriculum. The committee members were asked to estimate what they believed were the responses of the parents.

The findings of the study showed that the leadership's perception of the public's preference was most inaccurate. Only 29.8 percent of the estimates made by the leaders were accurate reflections of the parents' responses. The general dissimilarity was found to be for every issue question asked. Black leaders were no more cognizant of the popular attitudes than were their white colleagues. The leaders were much more concerned with bringing about social change and respecting individual rights than were the residents. The parents were not nearly as dissatisfied with the living conditions in their district, as resentful or cognizant of their deprivations, nor as adverse to compulsory action by the government as the better educated, middle class leaders thought they were.

The authors felt that their findings would be discouraging to those who held the view that responsive rule-making must be based on accurate leadership perception of the preferences of the public. Yet, they noted that the task of community representatives may be:

> 1) to recognize and gratify community needs—not just desires; and 2) to be vastly more dissatisfied with social inequities than are those they lead and to work for reform but 3), at the same time, not to lose sight of basic constitutional rights in this search for reform.[74]

Chapter VIII Footnotes

1.   John F. Dillon, *Commentaries on the Law of Municipal Corporations* (Boston: Little, Brown, and Company, 1911, 5th ed.), Vol. I, Sec. 237. For the Supreme Court's decision supporting Dillon's rule see, for example, *City of Trenton v. the State of New Jersey*, 262 U.S. 182 (1923).

2. See Chapter II for a discussion on charter types.

3. Herbert Sydney Duncombe, *County Government in America* (Washington, D.C.: National Association of Counties Research Foundation, 1966), p. 42.

4. Edward C. Banfield, *Big City Politics* (New York: Random House, Inc., 1965), pp.122, 135.

5. Warner E. Mills, Jr., and Harry R. Davis, *Small City Government* (New York: Random House, Inc., 1962), p. 7.

6. Banfield, *Big City Politics*, pp. 69, 53, 82.

7. *Municipal Year Book, 1968* (Washington, D.C.: International City Managers' Association, 1968), p. 62; Duncombe, *County Government*, pp. 46–47.

8. Interview, Mr. Edward R. Cantor, councilman-at-large, city of Philadelphia, March 10, 1970.

9. 369 U.S. 186 (1962).

10. 390 U.S. 474 (1968).

11. 397 U.S. 50 (1970).

12. William J. D. Boyd, "Local Governments Progress on Remap," *National Civic Review*, LVIII (February 1969), pp. 67–68.

13. Henry W. Maier, *Challenge to the Cities* (New York: Random House, Inc., 1966), p. 120.

14. Lynder Manner, "Trends in Municipal Finances," *Municipal Yearbook, 1968*, p. 247.

15. James A. Maxwell, *Financing State and Local Governments* (Washington, D.C.: Brookings Institution, 1965), p. 159.

16. U.S. Office of Education, *Bond Sales for Public School Purposes: 1967–69* (Washington, D.C.: Government Printing Office, 1969), p. 3.

17. Maxwell, *Financing Governments*, p. 36.

18. Thomas R. Dye, "Governmental Structure, Urban Environment, and Educational Policy," *Midwest Journal of Political Science*, XI (August 1967), pp. 353–80.

19. Robert Eyestone and Heinz Eulau, "City Councils and Policy Outcomes: Developmental Profiles," in James Q. Wilson, ed., *City Politics and Public Policy* (New York: John Wiley and Sons, Inc., 1968), pp. 37–65.

20. Interview, Mr. Edward R. Cantor, March 10, 1970.

21. *The Council of the City of Philadelphia, 1968–1972*, pp. 8–9.

22. Interview, Mr. Edward R. Cantor, March 10, 1970.

23. *The Council of the City of Philadelphia, 1968–1972*, pp. 9–10.

24. See for example: Charles R. Adrian, "Leadership and Decision-Making in Manager Cities," *Public Administration Review*, XVIII (Summer 1958), pp. 208–13; and Oliver P. Williams and Charles R. Adrian, *Four Cities* (Philadelphia: University of Pennyslvania Press, 1963).

25. U.S. Congress, House Committee on Government Operations, *Reorganization Plan No. 3, of 1967*, (90th Congress, 1st Session, House of Representatives Report No. 537, August 3, 1967), p. 126.

26. Williams and Adrian, "Leadership and Decision-Making."

27. Terry N. Clark, "Community Structure, Decision-making, Budget Expenditures and Urban Renewal in 51 American Communities," *American Sociological Review*, XXXIII (August 1968), pp. 576–91.

28. Robert L. Lineberry and Edmund P. Fowler, "Reformism and Public Policies in American Cities," in Wilson, *City Politics*, pp. 97–123.

29. Ibid., p. 112.

30. Heinz Eulau and Robert Eyestone, "Policy Maps of City Councils and Policy Outcomes: A Developmental Analysis," *American Political Science Review*, LXII (March 1968), pp. 124–143.

31.   Robert Merton, "Patterns of Influence: Local and Cosmopolitan Influentials," in his *Social Theory and Social Structure* (New York: The Free Press, 1968), pp. 441–74.

32.   Everett Carll Ladd, Jr., *Ideology in America* (Ithaca: Cornell University Press, 1969), p. 318.

33.   Ibid., p. 315.

34.   Joseph A. Schlessinger, *Ambition and Politics* (Chicago: Rand McNally and Company, 1966), p. 209.

35.   Kenneth Prewitt and William Nowlin, "Political Ambitions and the Behavior of Incumbent Politicians," *Western Political Quarterly*, XXII (June 1969), pp. 298–308.

36.   John C. Wahlke, *et al.*, *The Legislative System* (John Wiley and Sons, Inc., 1962), pp. 237–376.

37.   Williams and Adrian, *Four Cities*.

38.   Bryan T. Downes, "Municipal Social Rank and the Characteristics of Local Political Leaders," *Midwest Journal of Political Science*, XII (November 1968), pp. 514–37.

39.   Kenneth Prewitt, Heinz Eulau, and Betty H. Zisk, "Political Socialization and Political Roles," *Public Opinion Quarterly*, XXX (Winter 1966), pp. 569–82.

40.   *Municipal Year Book, 1968*, p. 56.

41.   Interview, January 6, 1970.

42.   Harry W. Reynolds, Jr., "The Career Public Service and Statute Lawmaking in Los Angeles," *Western Political Quarterly*, XVIII (September 1965), pp. 621–39.

43.   Ibid., p. 631.

44.   Melvin M. Webber, "Comprehensive Planning and Social Change," in Bernard J. Frieden and Robert Morris, eds., *Urban Planning and Social Policy* (New York: Basic Books, Inc., 1968), p. 16.

45.   Martha Dierthick, "Inter-city Differences in Administration of the Public Assistance Program: The Case of Massachussetts," in Wilson, *City Politics*, pp. 243–66.

46.   Ibid., p. 257.

47.   Interview, Mr. David B. Collier, Clerk to the Montgomery County (Maryland) Council, February 25, 1970.

48.   Morton Grodzins, "Federal and State Impacts," in Edward Wilson, ed., *Urban Government* (New York: The Free Press, 1969), pp. 59–66.

49.   *Report of Urban Renewal Operations* (Washington, D.C.: U.S. Department of Urban Development, Renewal Assistance Administration, June 30, 1969), pp. 2–3.

50.   A. Lee Fritchler, B. Douglas Harman, and Morley Segal, *Federal, State, Local Relationships* (Washington, D.C.: International City Management Association, December 1969), pp. 7–12.

51.   Robert O. Warren, *Government in Metropolitan Regions: A Reappraisal of Fractionated Political Organization* (Davis, Calif.: University of California, Institute of Governmental Affairs, 1966).

52.   B. Douglas Harman, "Councils of Governments and Metropolitan Decision-Making," *The Municipal Year Book, 1969* (Washington, D.C.: The International City Management Association, 1969), pp. 10–16.

53.   See for example, Advisory Commission on Intergovernmental Relations, *Factors Affecting Voter Reactions to Governmental Reorganization in Metropolitan Areas* (Washington, D.C.: Advisory Commission on Intergovernmental Relations, May 1962); Brett W. Hawkins, "Public Opinion and Metropolitan Reorganization in Nashville," *Journal of Politics*, XXVIII (May 1966), pp. 408–18; Thomas R. Dye, "Urban Political Integration: Conditions Associated with Annexation in American Cities," *Midwest Journal of Political Science*, VIII (November 1964), pp. 430–46.

54.   Robert S. Lynd and Helen M. Lynd, *Middletown* (New York: Harcourt Brace and Jovanovich, Inc., 1929).

55. Robert S. Lynd and Helen M. Lynd, *Middletown in Transition* (New York: Harcourt Brace and Jovanovich, Inc., 1937).

56. Floyd Hunter, *Community Power Structure: A Study of Decision-Makers* (Chapel Hill: University of North Carolina Press, 1953).

57. E. Digby Baltzell, ed., *The Search for Community in Modern America* (New York: Harper and Row Publishers, Inc., 1968).

58. Robert A. Dahl, *Who Governs?* (New Haven: Yale University Press, 1961).

59. Aaron Wildovsky, *Leadership in A Small Town* (Totawa, N.J.: Bedminster Press, 1964).

60. Nelson Polsby, *Community Power and Political Theory* (New Haven: Yale University Press, 1963); Edward C. Banfield, *Political Influence* (New York: The Free Press, 1961); Wallace S. Sayre and Herbert Kaufman, *Governing New York City* (New York: W. W. Norton, Inc., 1965); Frank J. Munger, *Decisions in Syracuse* (Bloomington: Indiana University Press, 1961).

61. M. Kent Jennings, *Community Influentials: The Elites of Atlanta* (New York: The Free Press, 1964).

62. William A. Gamson, "Reputation and Resources in Community Politics," *American Journal of Sociology*, LXXII (September 1966), pp. 121–31.

63. Peter Bachrach and Morton S. Baratz, "Two Faces of Power," *American Political Science Review*, LVI (December 1962), pp. 947–52.

64. Robert E. Agger, Daniel Goldrich, and Bert E. Swanson, *The Rulers and the Ruled: Political Power and Impotence in American Communities* (New York: John Wiley and Sons, Inc., 1964).

65. Winston W. Crouch, *et al.*, *California Government and Politics*, (Englewood Cliffs, N.J.: Prentice-Hall, Inc., 1967, 4th ed.), pp. 119–20.

66. *The Evening Bulletin* (Philadelphia), January 15, 1970, p. 26.

67. Ross R. Rice, *Extremist Politics: An Arizona Recall Election* (New York: McGraw-Hill Book Company, Inc., 1964).

68. Harvey M. Sapolsky, "The Fluoridation Controversy: An Alternative Explanation," *Public Opinion Quarterly*, XXXIII (Summer 1969), pp. 240–48.

69. Securities Industry Association, *Municipal Statistics Bulletin*, LVIII (February 1972), p. 4.

70. *Factors Affecting Voter Reactions to Governmental Reorganization in Metropolitan Areas* (Washington, D.C.: Advisory Commission on Intergovernmental Relations, 1962), p. 1.

71. Thomas W. Casstevens, *Politics, Housing and Race Relations: California's Rumford Act and Proposition 14* (Berkeley: University of California, Institute of Governmental Studies, June 1967); and Harlan Hahn, "Northern Referenda on Fair Housing: The Response of White Voters," *Western Political Quarterly*, XXI (September 1968), pp. 483–95.

72. Susan Eddy, "Community Control Guides Morgan School," *Public Management*, LI (July 1969), pp. 11–13.

73. Roberta S. Sigel, and H. Paul Friesmer, "Urban Community Leaders' Knowledge of Public Opinion," *Western Political Quarterly*, XVIII (December 1965), pp. 881–95.

74. Ibid., p. 894.

Chapter IX

Rule Execution

Within the states and localities, rule-makers have established elaborate organizational structures to provide for the implementation, application, and enforcement of the rules. The performance of such tasks comprise the rule execution function. The responsibility for the day-to-day performance of rule execution rests with those public agents known as bureaucrats.

The scope of the rule execution function is so broad that it touches the lives of all members of the community. Many people, however, are not aware of the extent to which they depend on the routine operation of rule execution until the function abruptly ceases to be performed. Thus, the realization of dependency becomes clear when, for example, the children are home for an extended period because the schools are closed in mid-semester, or the garbage piles up on the street because the sanitation workers have not collected the trash. Yet, other people—especially the poor—are very aware of the scope and breadth of bureaucratic activity. For them the government is often a network of executive agencies that directly and continually affect many important aspects of their lives. Welfare agents supply checks for food, clothing and rent; housing agents arrange for shelter; public nurses and doctors tend to health needs; employment agents aid in finding jobs; and so on.

By the beginning of 1970, nearly 10 million people were publicly employed to carry out the tasks of rule execution in state and local governments.[1] It costs the taxpayers over $63 billion to pay for their services. The governments are expending over $140 billion (including the payroll for bureaucrats) for the activities engaged in by the agents of rule execution.[2] A detailed presentation of employment, payroll, and expenditure data appears in Table 1.

TABLE IX.1

Employment, Payrolls, and Expenditures of State and Local Governments

Functions	All Employees (full-time and part-time) (thousands)			Payroll (millions of dollars) (October 1979)			Expenditure Amount (millions of dollars)		
	Total	State Government	Local Government	Total	State Government	Local Government	Total	State Government	Local Government
Total	10,147	2,755	7,392	5,906.3	1,612.1	4,294.2	131,332	48,749	82,582
Education	5,297	1,182	4,115	3,169.7	630.2	2,539.4	52,718	13,780	38,938
Local school	3,928	18	3,910	2,442.4	12.1	2,430.2	37,461	437	37,024
Institutions of higher education	1,298	1,094	204	680.1	570.9	109.2	12,924	11,011	1,914
Other education	71	71	—	47.1	47.1	—	2,332	2,332	—
Highways	607	302	305	341.4	192.8	148.6	16,427	11,044	5,383
Public welfare	259	99	159	149.5	59.8	86.6	14,679	8,203	6,477
Hospitals	879	450	429	446.5	247.1	199.3	7,863	4,002	3,861
Health	130	51	79	82.8	36.3	46.5	1,806	786	1,019
Police protection	508	57	451	338.6	43.1	295.5	4,494	688	3,806
Local fire protection	266	—	266	152.5	—	152.5	2,024	—	2,024
Sewerage	65	—	65	38.2	—	38.2	2,167	—	2,167
Sanitation other than sewerage	133	—	133	71.3	—	71.3	1,246	—	1,246
Local parks and recreation	160	—	160	66.3	—	66.3	1,888	—	1,888
Natural resources	183	151	33	103.6	89.9	13.7	2,732	2,158	574
Housing and urban renewal	59	—	59	37.5	—	37.5	2,138	23	2,115
Airports	14	—	14	9.1	—	9.1	969	178	791
Water transport and terminals	21	4	17	13.2	2.9	10.3	444	173	271
Correction	146	92	55	99.5	62.7	36.8	1,626	1,051	575
Local libraries	79	—	79	29.3	—	29.3	700	54	646
Employment security administration	80	80	—	52.8	52.8	—	769	767	2
Financial administration	240	95	145	131.2	61.3	69.9	2,030	1,022	1,007
General control	369	51	319	167.9	37.8	130.0	2,652	698	1,954
Local utilities	277	—	277	195.5	—	195.5	7,820	—	7,820
Liquor stores	16	16	—	8.7	8.7	—	1,627	1,404	223
Other and unallocable	357	125	232	200.1	85.9	114.1	6,140	2,282	3,858

Note: Statistics for local governments are subject to sampling variation. Because of rounding, detail may not add to totals.
— Represents zero or rounds to zero.

Sources: Census Bureau, *Public Employment in 1970*, p. 9; Census Bureau, *Governmental Finances in 1969–70*, pp. 21, 23.

There has been tremendous growth in the numbers of administrative public agents over the course of time. The 200 percent increase of bureaucrats within the last generation may serve to illustrate the upward trend. After the Second World War, the total employment of state and local government was approximately 3.2 million persons; by 1970, it was over 9.7 million individuals. While there are many reasons for this growth, one explanation is that expanded governmental activities necessitate an expanded public work force.

Much of the expansion of state and local governmental activity has been directed into the social and economic aspects of community life. As the expansion touched the immediate interests of larger numbers of people, increased demands were heard for citizen participation in the function of rule execution. The demands reflected the belief that people affected by public programs ought to have access to and influence on the process by which decisions about their lives are made. In doing so, the public has called into question the century-old American administrative doctrine that public needs are best met by professionally competent bureaucrats in an orderly arranged executive structure.[3]

Doctrines of Administration

I. Professionalism and Neutral Competence

Professionalism and neutral competence have long been the standards and criteria for the recruitment of bureaucrats, the organization of administrative structure, and the performance of the rule execution function. The implementation of this doctrine has been largely guided by the concepts of the ideal bureaucracy as espoused by Max Weber.[4] The central objectives of that model were to produce administrative efficiency, and impersonal and rational decision making. The efficient bureaucracy would be marked by a hierarchy of agents who, by the process of division of labor, perform specialized tasks. The administrative agents are to make decisions and conduct themselves in a detached, rational manner, guided by clearly formulated and uniform rules. Such agents, furthermore, are to be hired and promoted on the basis of their skill, experience and ability.

Political disillusionment and administrative necessities were historical bases for the acceptance of Weber's concepts. As it became clear to many citizens that the public agents responsible for rule execution were using the offices obtained through political favoritism for personal gain, political dissillusionment set in. Charges of bribery, corruption and fiscal mismanagement were levied against those "political hacks" who were recruited by party bosses to fill administrative posts. Yet, more importantly, it was becoming clearer that those types of administrators were unequipped to handle the demands of the specialized and technical areas of activities and services into which the state and local governments were moving.

The need for expertise increased as both legislators and judges delegated and permitted additional responsibilities to bureaucrats. The legislators, who saw that their part-time positions and constituent demands left them with little time to formulate anything but general rules, assigned the administrative agents greater discretion in implementing specific programs. As governmental activities expanded into such areas as licensing, regulating utilities, and directing social services, conflicts arose from the implementation of programs. The judges, admitting their own institutional shortcomings, permitted bureaucratic settlement of controversies. Thus, the increased rule-making and rule adjudication functions performed in the executive structure also strengthened the demand for competent professionals.

To enhance the recruitment and promotion of individuals who had the requisite skills, experience, and training, the merit service system was introduced. By creating merit system boards to administer the recruitment and testing of applicants to vacancies and to review the recommendations for promotion, it was intended that bureaucrats were to be removed from the immediate influence of those central executives and legislative agents who were directly involved with partisan activities.

The acceptance by the public of a system of merit service was based on the belief that such a system might assure that staffing would be based on ability, or that, at the least, it would withdraw the selection and promotion processes from political favoritism. The excesses of corruption in the state capitols and city halls during the late nineteenth century stimulated many citizens to demand reform. Leonard D. White has noted that the public was concerned about "the moral purification of public life, the deterioration of which they declared threatened the existence of a self-governing republic."[5]

The federal government has been instrumental in promoting adoption of the merit system by the state and local governments. The enactment of the Pendleton Act in 1883, which created the federal civil service, and its success on the national level (as seen by the extension of its coverage in the succeeding years), had set the example for the other governments to follow. In addition, many states and localities were prodded into establishing some merit system to meet the requirements of federal grant-in-aid provisions that insisted on professional competence in the administration of federally funded programs.

The merit system first appeared in the states in 1883 when New York followed the national lead in enacting its own merit law. Today all states have some form of merit system. All but eighteen states have general coverage; in the remaining, either select categories of public servants (*e.g.*, state police) are covered, or coverage is limited to those working in programs requiring it as a condition for obtaining federal grants-in-aid (*e.g.*, health and welfare).[6]

At the local level the system has been more widely adopted in the cities than in the counties. The percentage of those cities having merit service ranges from over 95 percent of those with populations of 250,000 or more persons to approximately 50 percent of those with populations of under 25,000 persons.[7] Across the nation, only about 10 percent of the counties utilize merit examinations.[8] As counties have become more urbanized, however, there has been an increase in adoptions. One survey of 200 urban counties has reported approximately half of them having such systems operative.[9] Not all employees are recruited by examination in each of these localities. As on the state level, coverage may be restricted to those engaged in specific activities (*e.g.*, firemen or policemen), or in administering federally financed programs.

Concomitant with the increased size of bureaucratic personnel was the growth of professionalism within the public service. As labor was divided and tasks became differentiated, specialists and generalists were called upon to perform the rule execution function. Specialists were needed to perform "line" services, that is, those activities that are substantive or direct in their contribution to administrative objectives. For example, doctors and nurses were recruited to carry out the aims of the public health programs, and social workers for the welfare programs. Generalists were needed for "staff" services, that is, those activities that are important for the orderly operation of the administrative machinery. Thus with a large bureaucracy, trained persons are needed for such administrative tasks as personnel recruitment, procurement of materials, record keeping, and financial estimating and fiscal accounting.

The differentiation of positions led to an emphasis on professionalism. Standards were adopted as an integral part of the bureaucratic operation. Formal educational preparation became a requisite for entrance into many line and staff positions. Associations or unions were established that promoted solidarity and opened channels for the transmission of information and reference cues. Codes of ethics were written by the various associations to prescribe formal and informal patterns of professional behavior. The professionals began to look to each other for guidance in their public responsibilities, as they met together in conferences sponsored by such associations as National Association of State Mental Health Program Directors, Association of State and Interstate Water Pollution Control Administrators, Public Personnel Association, and the Municipal Finance Officers Association.

The movement to make politics and administration distinct and separate spheres and processes went beyond the professionalization of the bureaucracy to that of structural change. One widely adopted new form was the council-manager plan. The supporters of this plan believed that it would compartmentalize two basic processes. The political sphere would be the realm of the council, and the manager would supervise the "nonpolitical" rule-execution sphere. As White had noted, it was the task of the managers to "administer the affairs of the city with integrity and efficiency . . . without participating in or allowing their work to be affected by contending programs or partisans."[10]

The manager, a graduate of a university program in management training and public administration, is charged with the supervision of the city or county bureaucrats in their daily tasks. As a full time "chief-of-staff" he is aware of administrative difficulties, problems, and performance and is in a position to coordinate efforts for the effective execution of rules. In doing so, the manager is guided by the principle of neutral competence as set forth in the "code of ethics" drawn up by his professional organization, the International City Management Association. Amongst the provisions of the code are:

> The city manager considers it his duty continually to improve his ability and his usefulness and to develop the competence of his associates in the use of management techniques.
> He recognizes that the chief function of the local government at all times is to serve the best interests of all the people on a nonpartisan basis.
> The city manager handles all matters of personnel on the basis of merit.
> The city manager curries no favors. He handles each problem without discrimination on the basis of principle and justice.[11]

Independent agencies, boards, commissions and special districts were other structural changes adopted at the state and local levels to further divorce administration from politics. If a special governmental activity or service had to be undertaken or an industry or utility had to be regulated, then a governmental body whose sole energy was expended in that direction would be created. For example, park and planning boards, library boards, boards of health and dozens of others came into being. Independence was assured by isolating each agency from central political supervision. Board members were appointed or elected on a non-partisan basis, with secure tenure of substantial terms staggered to overlap those of the governors and mayors. Thus, the energies of the various agencies could not be diverted to other activities, reduced in effectiveness or totally abandoned by changes in the offices of the chief executive or the legislative councils. The aim was to protect the administrators from the daily pressures of politics, as manifested in the executive office or legislative branch. In recent years, the creation of independent agencies has had its impetus from federal grants-in-aid program provisions.

Members of the boards were recruited on the basis of their experience and knowledge in the areas of activities they were to oversee. In many states and localities, statutes or customs prescribe that professional associations have representatives on the board or be consulted in the nomination of panel personnel. For example, the state medical associations might choose the state's chief health officer. For the professional groups were thought to be best able to know what standards should be enforced, what programs should be emphasized, and what persons are best suited to implement programs and service public means.

Special districts were independent not only from other agencies, but also from other governments. These were political units having their own charters created with responsibility to perform a particular public service. They were given their own fiscal autonomy with powers to tax and borrow, as well as the power to hire personnel, and execute their own rules. The geographical jurisdiction of the special districts augmented their own independence, for many cut across the boundaries of other local governments.

II. Executive Leadership and Centralization

Professionalism, neutral competence, and administrative structures free from political pressures did not insure effective, efficient, and economical rule execution. Rather, what was most often produced was chaotic, costly, and conflicting administration, a system of fragmented government and policy making.

State and local administrative structures were marked by a proliferation of independent agencies. These tended to become separate centers of rule execution. Administrators carried out policies and implemented programs with no reference to the practices of other governmental bodies. This lack of coordination between agencies engaged in related fields of endeavors resulted in duplication of services and increased governmental costs. An array of independent agencies and agency heads pursuing policies not always in accord with one another bred chaos. Few individuals (least of all members of the public) knew what the operation of programs was or how to exert effective influence.

Administrative officials rarely welcomed or looked for direction from a chief executive. It was not uncommon for members of boards or commissions to struggle to protect their respective realms from central executive hegemony, in order to enhance their own personal chances for obtaining higher office. Those who were elected looked to their own constituencies for support and tried to develop their own vote-getting prowess. Administrators elected on a non-partisan basis were freed from the constraints of having to coordinate their individual views with those elected with the backing of a political party. Administrators who were appointed to terms that overlapped those of the governor or mayor were similarly unconstrained by central executive leadership and direction.

The problem of fragmented government was enhanced by professionals and specialists in the bureaucracy who were appointed, promoted, and retained through the merit system. They felt themselves capable of formulating policy for their own agencies and tended to resent interference from the "layman" or "amateur" chief executive. Civil servants, who could rely on their own resources or ally with client groups having similar interests and goals, could thwart an overall administrative program that they felt should be modified or delayed.

Legislative Controls

The fragmentation of rule execution could not be effectively countered by state legislatures and local councils. The legislative bodies have the capacity to exert influence over the bureaucracy, in that they have diverse rule-making, agency creating, financial, and investigative powers. Yet, inherent legislative limitations hamper them from exercising much control over the activities of administrative agents.

One principal means by which the legislature exerts influence on the rule execution function is through its powers to create agencies and to make rules that shape the broad objectives, purposes, and goals of administrative tasks and responsibilities. To enhance program implementation, it can (within the boundaries set by the basic rules) establish, consolidate, or abolish administrative agencies. In addition, it may expand or limit the number of bureaucratic positions to be filled within a particular agency.

Through legislative prescriptions, the rule-makers may set the limits of authority to be exercised by the public servants. Administrators may be permitted a wide latitude of discretion in planning how rules should be executed, or they may be directed by provisions in the laws passed to take clearly specified actions. Should the legislators be displeased with the manner in which administrators are executing programs (as a result of discretion or directed action), then new rules or modifications of old rules can be passed.

Control over administrative actions can also be exerted through the power of regulating appropriations. Much of what an agency does and how it does it depends on the public funds it receives and the freedom the agency has in allocating the monies. For example, the legislature may be highly restrictive. It may set ceilings on expenditures, specify to which item or program a set amount of money is to be applied, and it may prohibit transfer of funds from one program to another or from one agency or another. The power of the purse can be a potent instrument of persuasion, for administrators are aware that the displeasure of legislators over program implementation could lead to agency funds being slashed.

Hearings provide a fourth basic means by which legislative controls may be exerted. Legislators may review the performance of an agency or that of agency personnel. This is accomplished in the state legislatures by permanent or special committees. Local councils may conduct their investigation through ad hoc committees or by the entire membership. Bureuacrats may be called on to answer penetrating questions about acts of commission or ommission. Records and documents could be reviewed to see what and how actions have been taken, and audits of financial accounts may be made. Such hearings provide the opportunities to legislators, in face-to-face meeting, to directly tell administrators what to do or what not to do. The threat of an investigation is often, in itself, a potent means of exercising control. Administrators may gear their activities in accord with the wishes of the legislators, rather than submit their agency to critical scrutiny and themselves to what can be a time-consuming, extra-energy-expending, and personally unpleasant experience.

Occasionally, constituents request their legislator to intercede on their behalf with an administrative agency. As such requests or complaints are heard, the legislators become acquainted with the operations of an agency. In the performance of the case work tasks for their constituents, the legislators may transmit their own ideas as to how to better discharge the responsibilities of rule execution.

The power to appoint or confirm persons to administrative office may be another means of exercising legislative control. To assure that policy implementation will proceed in agreement with legislative intent, this power would not be taken lightly. Nominees will have their previous record of performance and publicized statements reviewed so that their views may be assessed. To aid them in this assessment, the legislators may call on the candidates to clearly specify the standards that will guide them in pursuit of fulfilling their administrative responsibilities. Should doubts still remain, the potential appointees might be asked to pledge that they will conduct their affairs along prescribed guidelines before confirmation will be given. Knowledge that inattention to pledges made could bring subsequent retribution may encourage administrators to follow those guidelines. For example, a breach may come back to haunt him when he seeks legislative approval for appointment to another executive position.

Despite the capacity to exert influence over the bureaucracy, the legislators are hampered by perceptual, institutional, and political factors in controlling the fragmentation of rule execution. Legislators may perceive their role to be different from that of the administrators. They may conceive themselves as being generalists and the bureaucrats as being specialists. As generalists, they feel that they are to set broad policy objectives, flexible rules, and minimum standards; while the bureaucrats, as specialists, are looked upon as being capable of attending to the details necessary for effective rule execution. The legislators may choose to minimize their role as overseers of administration, preferring to maximize their rule-making and constituent serving roles.

In addition, the legislators may feel inhibited in correcting administrative fragmentation, should they perceive the bureaucracy as being a complex and incomprehensible maze.

Brief legislative sessions is one institutional factor that hampers oversight efforts. State legislative bodies meeting a few months each year or biennium, and local councils meeting in weekly or bi-weekly sessions, leave long intervals during which bureaucrats can carry on their own respective operations without control. Limited staff and the lack of an independent information gathering service further hampers legislative efforts and ability to cope with the vast array of administrative actions. The legislators themselves are too busy to interview witnesses, obtain and peruse documentary evidence, and define issues of contention for investigative or normal committee hearings.

The third institutional factor is the lack of any effective mechanisms through which legislators can exert oversight. Committees designed to some extent to enhance the legislators' familiarity with administrative operations (through division of labor) have proven to be ineffective mechanisms for control. Moreover, the opportunity to familiarize themselves has been lessened by the necessity for legislators (whether in large or small legislative bodies) to serve on more than one committee or on a committee handling more than one subject. Unassisted by any professional staff and rushed for time, the legislators develop little administrative expertise and have little chance for in-depth administrative surveillance. Indeed, the committee members have to rely on the bureaucrats for information—a situation not conducive to oversight. The proliferation of administrative agencies has also hampered legislative committee control. Should there not be sufficient numbers of committees to carefully scrutinize the large number of activities undertaken by agencies, then a gap in the scope of legislative oversight of rule execution results.

The fervor with which legislators pursue oversight activities is often influenced by political considerations. As such, the legislative body, comprised of members elected by constituencies with divergent demands, rarely will agree on the level of control to be exercised. Legislators may have to work and maintain good relations with agencies so as to serve better the constituent's needs. Should a large segment of the residents in a district have frequent and amiable contact with an administrative agency, a legislator would be reluctant to interfere with that relationship. For example, an assemblyman representing a farming constituency would be more inclined to investigate the department of welfare's operations than those of the department of agriculture. Another political consideration is that of party of affiliation. A desire to embarrass the administration of an executive whose party affiliation is other than that of a majority of the legislators may provide the impetus for that majority to initiate oversight activities. Conversely, the avoidance of embarrassment to one's own party members may stifle such attempts.

When legislative oversight is exercised, it is most often in response to some specific stimulus. Investigations start, for example, when charges of poor administrative practices are raised by citizens who have been aggrieved by bureaucratic action or inaction, from an employee inside an agency who believes that there has been some ethical or legal wrong doing, from newspaper accounts of malfeasance, or from an ethnic, racial, or other interest group which feels that a prejudicial act has occurred. Other times oversight is undertaken when a legislator's particular and immediate interest in a subject is aroused. Legislative control appears at best to be spotty, transitory and remedial, rather than systematic, continuous, and preventive.

Judicial Control

The governmental system of the states and localities vests some power to oversee administrative actions in the judicial structures. However, the scope of judicial control is narrow. Judges are limited in that they act in the settlement of disputes and that they focus on only one controversy arising from executive action at a time. Moreover, the courts are not in a position to provide direction and leadership to check fragmented administrative action and policy. Judges act after the fact, that is, when cases are brought to them by parties affected by bureaucratic action or inaction.[12]

Individuals may contest administrative actions by bringing cases before a court for review. Actions of an official that have been performed outside the scope of his powers or the geographical boundaries of his government may be one cause for the initiation of a suit. Secondly, a claim may be made that an official has abused his powers of discretion. A third type of action that may be challenged is an official's error in procedure; that is, the administrator can be seen not to have followed the prescribed routine of administering a program. Other cases may be based on errors of law or errors of fact found to have been made by bureaucrats. In the first instance, an official may have misconstrued the law he is empowered to execute, as when a building inspector orders a fire escape to be placed on a two story building, although the law requires it to be placed on those buildings that are three or more stories in height. As an instance of errors of fact, a county animal health inspector might misjudge the symptoms of a sick cow and conclude that the animal had contracted a contagious disease, ordering the entire herd slaughtered.

Should a court decide in support of an individual's complaint, there are various types of orders that can be issued to administrative agents. One type of order is the injunction, which is issued to stop a specific action, either permanently or temporarily, until a formal court hearing can be held. The writ of mandamus may be issued to an administrative agency or official to do a specific action he is required to perform, but which he had failed to do. A third type of order is the writ of habeus corpus. This is designed to bring a person placed in custody by an administrative officer before a judge to determine the legality of the detention.

Generally, the complaint is lodged by a citizen aggrieved by an administrative action. Yet, state and local courts have facilitated efforts to obtain judicial review of administration by permitting "taxpayer suits." The initiation of these suits may be made by any taxpaying resident, even if he were not directly and immediately affected by the execution of a program. Taxpayers suits are most often initiated to stop or delay a bureaucratic action thought to be illegal, fraudulent, or detrimental to the interests of the community.

Certainly the courts can not exert leadership or provide direction to resolve administrative fragmentation, for they are not designed to perform such tasks. As they must wait for cases to come to them, the judges can only act to correct what they have deemed to be an improper administrative action. Moreover, the courts are severely constrained in the degree to which they can control or influence those performing the rule execution function. Many cases in which judicial oversight could be exerted go unnoticed. Citizens, for financial, personal, social, or psychological reasons, fail to initiate a suit. A second constraint is the burden of heavy caseloads confronting contemporary courts, which acts to discourage judges from frequently getting involved with administrative matters. Lastly, the recruitment process for the bench does not usually produce judges who are trained in the variety of technical matters in which bureaucrats are engaged; nor do they have available to them staff skilled in such matters. Deference is often paid to the decisions and discretion of those over whom the judges are to oversee.

Strengthening Executive Control

The inability of existing structures to bring order to the disorder created by the proliferation and fragmentation of administrative agencies led to efforts to reorganize the executive structure. It was felt that coordinated, efficient, and effective rule execution could be accomplished if agencies were to be arranged under the direction of a single executive, who is accountable to the public at election time. To exert leadership over the centralized administration, the chief executive would be given tools to enhance his capacities of control, and thus advance his abilities to carry out his constitutional mandate to "faithfully execute" the rules.

Several basic changes were deemed necessary to strengthen the control of a chief executive over the administrative process. The principal ones are these:

1. *Centralized organization.* To overcome the problems of fragmented administration, it would be necessary to simplify and integrate the complex array of offices and independent agencies into one centralized organization. Agencies responsible for performing similar tasks would be consolidated. Consolidation would be undertaken for the dual purposes of eliminating the duplication of services and reducing the number of agencies to a manageable proportion. The consolidated agencies would be grouped together into departments charged with overseeing broad areas of public services. In turn, the new departments would be under the direct control and supervision of a single central elected chief executive.

2. *Executive appointment and removal.* To enhance executive leadership, it would be necessary to grant the chief executive powers of appointment and removal. By having top level bureaucrats answerable to the chief executive, the independent determination by agencies of how rules should be executed would be diminished. The governor or mayor, thus empowered, could pursue his policies without dissension from those responsible for executing the programs. And the knowledge that the executive has the power to remove those administrators who deviate from the stated goals makes them reluctant to do so.

3. *Executive office.* To aid him in formulating the direction of rule execution, the chief executive must have assistance. One source of such assistance is that set of administrators he has appointed to head the various administrative departments. Such men may meet regularly as a cabinet to assist in setting priorities, coordinating programs, planning policy implementation, and solving major and pressing administrative problems. A second source would be that of a personal staff attached to the office of the executive. The men and women of his immediate staff would relieve him of much of the minor routine tasks of office and act to coordinate the flow of communications to his office, thereby permitting the governor or mayor to act more expeditiously in fulfilling his administrative responsibilities.

4. *The executive budget.* The executive's power of supervision and leadership could be intensified by centralizing the budgetary process within his office. This important tool enables the chief executive to propose a comprehensive plan for program application and goals. By budgeting items, he could introduce, expand, modify, or eliminate offices, officers, and programs. The executive's power of supervision could be enhanced by requiring the agency heads to direct requests for funds through the executive office, rather than independently negotiating with the legislature. Placing the initiation of the budget under the executive enables him to provide rewards to agencies as incentives to follow a given course of direction or punishments for recalcitrant officials. To assist the chief executive, a budget officer or finance department would be established and responsible to him for sifting through

the various demands for funds and fitting them into the comprehensive scheme designed by the governor or mayor.

5. *Executive tenure in office.* The prescriptions of many states and localities that limited executives to short and single terms in office proved to be a detriment to effective executive leadership and control. An executive was unable to utilize the experience gained in office, establish a basis for administrative strength, or provide continuity in program implementation. Thus, all proposals for executive reform included the removal of restrictions of the number of terms that a chief executive could serve consecutively and the lengthening of each term to four years.

In recent years, nearly every state has made at least overtures toward simplifying the administrative institutions and strengthening the central executive office.[13] Although Illinois had taken steps to streamline its executive branch as early as 1917, the principal stimulus for changes in the other states came from the national government. In the aftermath of the proliferation of New Deal agencies, the Congress, reviewing the 1937 report of the President's Committee on Administrative Management, passed the Reorganization Act of 1939. A decade later, Congress accepted and enacted several recommendations of the Commission for the Organization of the Executive Branch of Government (the Hoover Commission).

In several states, the consolidation of agencies responsible for similar type services or interrelated programs has occurred. The new agencies have most often been placed under the direction of the governors. Cabinet forms of executive structure were instituted in three states (California, Maryland, and Massachusetts) in the late 1960s and early 1970s. The governor's appointment power has been enlarged in several states, as has been his removal power. To further strengthen the control of the governor over the administrative structure, the number of elected department heads has been reduced.

Provisions for longer and consecutive terms have been other steps taken to enhance gubernatorial leadership. In forty-one states, the term of office for governor is four years. A governor may seek reelection to office an unlimited number of times in eighteen of those states granting four year terms. While reelection is possible in the other states, in twelve he may serve only two consecutive terms; in nine he may not immediately succeed himself; and in two he may not seek election after having served two terms. In nine states, the governors are still limited to two year terms; yet, in all but two (New Mexico and South Dakota stipulate a maximum of two consecutive terms) he may retain office so long as he enjoys electoral success.

The governors' ability to exert influence has been strengthened by provisions that grant them fiscal responsibilities. Forty-six governors have budget making authority in that they (assisted by their own budget staffs) are required to draft and transmit a comprehensive budget proposal to the legislature. The legislatures in forty-two of those states have unlimited power to change the budget. In the four others, some limitations exist. The legislatures in Maryland and West Virginia, for example, may decrease but not increase itemized figures. Although the legislatures generally have the power to alter the budget, it must be emphasized that the exigencies of the legislative process rarely allow more than a discussion of and reaction to parts of that budget presented to them. Should legislative changes prove unacceptable, the governors of all states but North Carolina can veto the appropriation bill. In forty-three states, the governor need not veto the entire bill to express his dissatisfaction; he may exert an "item" veto over just those parts of the bill he refuses to accept. The veto power gives the governor important leverage in shaping the fiscal affairs of the state, as well as administrative policies, for it takes an extraordinary majority of legislators to override his action.

Structural changes to centralize the direction over administrative activities had been made at the local level prior to those made at the state level. Many municipalities, in seeking efficiency, professional, and neutral competency in administration, had adopted commission or council-manager forms of government. An essential characteristic of both those forms was the consolidation of agencies under the group of elected officials who comprised the council or the board of commissioners. Those men were usually the only elected officials, and they were ultimately responsible for the rule execution function. The two forms were especially popular in localities having small to medium size populations.

As the demands for governmental services increased and the number of agencies that were established to provide the services grew, the trend to adopt the commission form came to a halt. Indeed, localities abandoned the plan as it became recognized that the boards could not exert leadership over the proliferation of agencies responsible for the new and diverse services.

Many of the localities that abandoned the commission plan joined the ranks of those that had already seen the merits of adopting the council-manager form of government. The major advantage was believed to be the presence of a full time, professionally trained administrator charged with managing the daily operations involved in the execution of programs. Yet, in those cities and counties that experienced rapid urban growth and problems, as well as escalating numbers of administrative responsibilities, the advantage became a disadvantage. For a part-time council was unable to adequately supervise the manager. Though the manager was able to assume expanded responsibilities, diminished supervision led to autonomy from the electorate or their representatives. As a consequence, several counties and municipalities replaced the council-manager form with the executive-council plan.

The executive-council form has been traditionally the pattern of government in large cities. Large localities having heterogeneous population characteristics and diverse demands to satisfy resembled states in geographic miniature. Their efforts in accomplishing efficient and competent administration had resulted in as great a problem in fragmentation as confronted many of the states. Thus, the search for solutions to overcome the problems took the similar route for central leadership. A single executive with added formal powers, who would be directly accountable to the electorate, was sought. Attention was directed toward establishing appointment, removal, budget and veto powers, and lengthening the tenure of office.

Among the mechanisms to strengthen the executive office, the veto is the most prevalent. Mayors in over two-thirds of the cities can veto council measures. The expansion of terms has been the least prevalent. Mayors are elected to four year terms in 42.4 percent of the cities, to three year terms in 1.1 percent, to two year terms in 53.6 percent, and one year terms in 2.7 percent. In almost half the cities the mayor's appointive power is enhanced by the fact that only the executive and the council are elected. In many localities, the executive is not hampered in fiscal matters by having elected officials follow independent courses of action. For in only 4.8 percent of the cities is the controller elected, in 10.6 percent is the assessor elected, in 11.4 percent is the auditor elected, and in 35.1 percent is the treasurer elected.[14]

Additional assistance was given to the mayor of many large cities and the executives of urban counties to enable them to exert leadership over the administrative structure. Such assistance was provided in the structural reform of the chief administrative officer. What the cabinet and budget officers were to the governor, and the manager to the council, the chief administrator officer was to the local executive.

It is interesting to note that those powers associated with central leadership were felt by executives who lacked them to be most necessary for exerting direction over the administrative process. When governors were asked, "What powers, both formal and informal, do you lack which could aid you significantly in effecting your programs?" 66.6 percent of the respondents replied "appointive," 30.8 percent replied "veto," and 28.2 percent replied "tenure." Only 7.7 percent of the responding governors mentioned "budgetary" constraints. That such a low percentage mentioned fiscal restraints might indicate that the governors have already been granted sufficient power over their state budgets. In addition, 46.2 percent believed that the absence of administrative reorganization powers in the hands of the governor severely restricted them in directing the administration.[15]

Limitations on Executive Control

Although efforts to reorganize the bureaucracy and to enhance central leadership have been somewhat successful, the changes in themselves have not led to executive control. Situational, political, psychological, and practical factors act to limit such control. The size of the bureaucracy and the scope of its activities are so great as to inhibit the capacity of one individual to be an omnipresent and continual overseer of the administrative structure.

The executive centro, faced with many constituencies and a variety of responsibilities, and having only a twenty-four hour day at his disposal, must choose which aspects of the rule execution function he will emphasize. Personal preference is one criterion that the governor or mayor may use in selecting those issues upon which he will focus his attention and energies. An individual who has an elderly parent who needs constant medical attention is likely to be concerned about the enforcement of health standards of nursing homes; one who is an outdoorsman may stress conservation programs; and one who has a rural background may hesitate to cut the programs of the farm bureau. He may choose, as another criterion, to closely supervise the implementation of those programs that command the largest proportion of the state or local budget. Thus, for example, education and welfare programs usually qualify as areas for close executive scrutiny.

Political considerations enter into the choice of agencies and programs to be given special attention. Campaign promises made may have to be fulfilled during his administration. For example, Richardson Dilworth, who successfully won the office of mayor of Philadelphia on a "reform" platform, spent a great deal of his time during his tenure attempting to retain his image as champion against the corrupt administrators of City Hall.[16] A politically ambitious executive may cautiously select issues on the basis of the risk involved or the visibility to voters. He may avoid pressing the implementation of programs he anticipates would arouse negative reactions from prominent and important supporters; or he may aggressively activate the execution of those programs he perceives to be those most salient to his constituency. Should he aspire to national office, he may devote his attention to those programs that would attract notice beyond the bounds of his jurisdiction. Hence, attention to regional issues may necessitate his absence from the center of administrative activities, thereby limiting the number of issues on which he could focus at home. In addition, administrative success, a means to demonstrate one's competency in office, can be attained through the careful selection of issues (*e.g.*, those problems that can be readily rectified, such as better and more numerous street lights, or playground and recreation facilities).

Alan J. Wyner has shown how governors may attempt to gain political advantages by following the path of least administrative resistance. The governor, pursuing that course of action, may endeavor to bring industry into his state. Should his attempts be successful, he reaps many political benefits. Increasing the industrial base of the state is an objective that would win the support of most groups within the constituency, for few people will react negatively to improving the economy. Moreover, industrial immigration is a visible accomplishment of an administration. Thus a governor is inclined to undertake a task that would not necessitate public, time consuming, and energy absorbing clashes with the bureaucracy.[17]

The number of choices available to the executive in planning his oversight activities is limited by inherited commitments and long established practices. Previous administrations may have begun programs that cannot be too readily interrupted or reversed. No matter how zealous a governor or mayor may be in relation to a program of interest, he is constrained from acting in other than an incremental fashion. For example, the boards of education of many large cities are hearing criticisms that the children are not being educated by current practices and curricula. Yet, neither they nor the mayors can radically alter an ongoing process. Most often that which can be accomplished is limited to piecemeal innovations through test pilot programs.[18]

Federal grant-in-aid programs may act to diminish the latitude of executive choice. Any major shifts of rule execution practices may be prohibited because financial commitments have resulted in some budget rigidities. For example, gasoline taxes may have already been earmarked as matching funds for a federal highway project and therefore cannot be diverted to finance any redirection of executive priorities. Moreover, it is most difficult, if not politically unfeasible, to halt a federal-grant-in-aid program already in progress. Downtown urban renewal projects serve as a good illustration. Though citizen groups may vocalize dissent over the continuation of a project, they will most likely be unable to influence the mayor to order development agencies to cease action. For the workable programs, often representing years of time and manpower in drafting and planning, have already been approved by the federal agency.[19] Blueprints for rebuilding the center city have been drawn, private loans have been secured, businesses have settled plans to relocate, and so on. Moreover, one may ask, what is to fill the vacant area left after the homes and commercial sites have been razed?

The priorities of the issues to receive attention can be influenced by expressions of interest transmitted to the executive.[20] A number of grievance letters from citizens regarding a particular administrative procedure or agency may alert him that his immediate scrutiny is necessary. Newspaper articles, task force reports and recommendations, party personnel and friends are other sources of stimuli for oversight. The activities of neighboring states and localities can provide impetus for the restructuring of priorities. When a governor attends meetings of the National Governors' Conference or the mayor attends the Conference of Mayors sessions, he hears what his colleagues are striving to do and may return home with the intentions of matching or surpassing such administrative efforts.[21]

For many executives, the principal administrative task is the management of crises. Instead of choosing areas on which to focus his attention, he may find a series of exigencies commanding all his time and energy. Governors may find that they are diverted because of scandals arising from administrative mismanagement, or riots in prisons or colleges. Mayors may find that much of their time is spent bringing order out of the disorder caused by welfare and housing demonstrations, race riots, or work stoppages of teachers, garbage collectors, and policemen. The problems of private enterprises may have public ramifications which absorb the energies of the mayor. For example, Mayor John Lindsay was confronted by two such experiences during his first term of office. Citizens of New York looked to his office to remedy the crises caused by a fuel strike in the midst of a flu epidemic during the coldest period of winter, and that of an electrical failure in the midst of the evening rush hour on the hottest day of summer.[22]

The central executive can be stymied in his administrative efforts by the very agents over whom he is to exert leadership and control. It is difficult for him to direct the actions of those who possess greater expertise and technical knowledge in specific areas of public activity. Moreover, the executive centro must rely on those experts for the information necessary to pursue the oversight of a particular public activity. Even if there is a skilled and loyal staff within the executive office, the assistants rarely can match the expertise of the bureaucrats in the respective departments.

Governors or mayors responsible for overall execution of rules must contend with bureaucrats who have their own goals, their own causes and interests, their own needs for resources and power, their own constituencies and allies, and their own established ways of operation. Administrators are aware of their own power to circumvent the chief executive. Should there be a subject of contention, the bureaucrat can remain recalcitrant, knowing full well that the executive will eventually be diverted by other pressing matters. Moreover, protected by the merit service, they know that they may very well remain in office longer than the elected leader. Should the governor threaten an appropriations cut, the bureaucrats can appeal to friends in the legislature or act to mobilize client groups to agitate on their behalf. Should the mayor threaten to fire an appointed administrator, the latter may know that the mayor would be hesitant to provoke a public struggle that could reflect negatively on his judgment in selecting personnel or that could embarrass his administration.

The administrative hierarchy established by centralized reorganization schemes often isolated the executive from many agencies and agents. This arrangement may act to diminish executive oversight. He may not be fully knowledgeable about the operations of the agencies as such information is usually filtered through top level administrative officials and his staff. Any action taken to remedy that situation, such as direct communication with lower echelon personnel, may be interpreted as an act of interference and lower the morale or foster the resentment of hierarchically minded public servants.

The extent to which the executive exerts leadership and control may be influenced by his personal orientations toward his office. He may like the glamour of the office, rather than the hard work necessary for administrative control. He may perceive his role as being a caretaker or innovator, rather than a manager, and act accordingly. He may lack the ingredients of leadership, such as the ability to inspire confidence and loyalty, or the inclinations for bargaining, compromising, pleading, or deferring action when necessary. Most importantly, he may lack the "know-how" of the intricacies associated with the formal powers of office granted to him. For no amount of formal powers is worthwhile unless the individual possessing them knows how to use them to move others to action.

Administrators' Perceptions of Executive Control

Several researchers have surveyed state administrators in order to determine the effectiveness of gubernatorial control. Deil S. Wright interviewed 933 top level bureaucrats in all the fifty states.[23] The administrators were asked to assess the extent of gubernatorial control over the affairs of their respective agencies. In making comparisons between the influence exerted by the governors and the legislators, 32 percent of the agents responded that the governor exercised greater control, 44 percent responded that the legislature did, and 22 percent said that they perceived that both exercised equal control. It did not appear that the extent of formal powers granted to the executive had a significant bearing on administrators' perceptions of his control. As Wright has noted:

> Our findings show that even in states where governors are the strongest they are far from having dictatorial, monopoly, or predominant control in the eyes of top state administrators.[24]

When those administrators were asked whether they thought that the governor or the legislature was more "sympathetic to the aims and purposes" of their agency, 55 percent responded that they perceived the governor as being more sympathetic, 20 percent perceived the legislature as being so, and 14 percent thought each was equally sympathetic. Administrators from states with strong governors felt that their chief executive was more sympathetic to their agency's goals than did those from states with weak governors. Moreover, in those states where the governors were involved with the appointment of agency heads, the administrators ascribed greater gubernatorial support than did those where such appointment power was limited.

It is not surprising, therefore, that when Wright asked the administrators whether they would rather be controlled by the governor, the legislature, or an independent commission, the most preferred control was that of the central executive. Such preference was expressed by 42 percent of the respondents, while 28 percent preferred an independent commission and 24 percent favored legislative control.

These findings led Wright to the conclusion that "there appear to be deep cleavages within state administration along the relational dimensions of perceived political control, fiscal control, goal congruence, and preferred types of control."[25] Thus, though the chief executives in the states have been granted increased formal powers, "the governor apparently is not viewed as the primary powerwielder over state administrators."[26]

That formal power does not automatically confer control was seen by Thomas J. Anton in his study of state budget making.[27] Although the governors have been given principal responsibility for preparation of the budget, it was seen that the bureaucrats do not readily acknowledge gubernatorial pre-eminence in fiscal affairs. The experienced top level administrators would not immediately give him their cooperation and assistance in preparing a comprehensive and coordinated budget plan. To gain control over the administrative structure through the budget, he must first overcome the attitudes of the bureaucrats that he is "an outsider—a 'new boy,' come to meddle in their affairs." As Anton stated:

Neither the governor's lack of financial sophistication nor the ambiguity about his staying power is likely to encourage a warm reception from the old hands. The new boy must prove himself first, and he must do so in the face of a formidable array of obstacles.[28]

The expansion of the gubernatorial office staff may act to further dilute the extent of personal influence he may exert over the administrative structure. After interviewing the staff members in the governors' offices of forty states, Donald P. Sprengel found that in performing their tasks the staff insulated the governor from administrative demands. Approximately 90 percent of the sample responded that they handled "problems from beginning to end without consulting the governor." Over 95 percent of the respondents attested that they handled "correspondence from beginning to end without consulting the governor." About three-fourths of the staff personnel answered affirmatively to the question: "Are people desiring to see or speak with the governor referred to you first for discussion or consideration of the business they have on their minds?" Sprengel found that the staff developed their own criteria in handling the demands, rather than having strict gubernatorial guidelines as the bases for their decision making. Personal criteria used in solving problems and replying to correspondence included: "common sense, personal experience, or good judgment;" "an interpretation of the situation itself;" and "the desire to avoid consulting the governor if possible." Among the personal criteria utilized for granting conferences were: "the nature, urgency, seriousness, or importance of the matter;" "the insistence or demeanor of the caller;" and "a desire to handle the matter, if possible, without referral to the governor."[29]

A case study of the executive office of Rhode Island illustrated how independence of the administrators from the governor is created. When former Governor Chafee was asked how a chief executive keeps control on rule execution, he responded:

> Everybody, I suppose, has different ways of operating. My system is to find the very, very best directors I can—that is, my immediate subordinate chiefs who run the departments—and then I let them run it. I have confidence in them and I don't look over their shoulders.[30]

Wyner's conclusion drawn from his study appears to succinctly summarize the findings of other studies focusing on executive-administrator relationships. He stated that "a substantial segment of the state bureaucracy operates without much contact with or influence by the Governor."[31] Thus, though the advocates of executive leadership and direction had seen many of their reform proposals adopted, the governor or mayor has not become the complete conductor and coordinator of the rule execution function.

Administrative Unionization

The twentieth-century phenomenon that runs counter to the trend toward centralization has been the unionization of public employees. Whereas a premise of central leadership is that the bureaucrats are working for a common administrative purpose, the organization of public employees has been based on the assumption that they are motivated for personal gains as well as by performance goals. Although unionization has become an established reality in administration, conflict over these assumptions surrounds the appropriateness of employee organization. There are those who believe that the administration of public services for the citizens is the paramount objective, and that the implementation of those services should not be impaired by private demands; and there are those who hold that it is no less necessary to collectively discuss and negotiate wages and working conditions for public workers than it is for employees in the private sector. Public employees assert that they have the right to form unions for collective bargaining, and to be deprived of that right relegates them to the status of "second-class citizens." Many government officials, on the other hand, have thought that it is one thing to have a right to petition the government, and another to demand a share in decision making in the allocation of public resources or in the making of administrative policies. Some public officials feel that granting the right to unionize and bargain collectively would diminish the sovereignty of the government that grants it, or would set up an adversary relationship between agency management and the employees; others feel that it is a modern way of administering governmental affairs.

The insistence of public employees to unionize has led states to provide for collective bargaining at the state and local levels.[32] By the end of 1970, forty states had passed legislation that authorizes some form of employee organization and recognizes such organizations as agents for the negotiation of economic and other worker demands. With such impetus, the number of public employees who have joined unions has risen dramatically in recent years. In New York, for example, 96 percent of all city employees are represented by unions or associations; and in nine other states the proportion of municipal workers who are unionized exceed 65 percent. Large cities are more likely to have unions than are small ones; urbanized counties have seen more organization of workers than have the rural ones; and industrialized and urbanized states are the most frequent settings for employee unionization. Thus, as would be expected, the number of unionized public employees is largest in the Northeast region, followed closely by the Western region; and the smallest numbers of organized workers are to be found in the North Central and Southern regions respectively.

In every state, employee organizations are to be found. The largest organization is the American Federation of State, County, and Municipal Employees Union. Its membership includes employees engaged in the full range of governmental activities. The Teamsters, Chauffeurs, Warehousemen, and Helpers of America Union has had the second greatest success in organizing employees in a variety of governmental activities (though they have been most energetic in recruiting among the public works department employees). Other organizations have specialized in unionizing those engaged in particular activities. The largest of these has been the International Association of Fire Fighters (which has a virtual monopoly in representing firemen); the Fraternal Order of Police (which accounts for most of the policemen); and the American Federation of Teachers (which has actively tried to become the leading association for school teachers). In many instances, unions that had initially organized in the private sector have expanded to include public employees.

A consequence of unionization has been an increase in the number of public employee strikes.[33] Union leaders, familiar with the tactics of labor unions in the private sector, believe they should have the strike as a weapon in dealing with public employers. To be forbidden the right of strike, they believe, would detract from their bargaining power. Their willingness to engage in strikes quite often is in contradiction to the rules of the state. Only four states given legal sanction to strikes by government workers. Hawaii has permitted strikes by all employees in the state; and Pennsylvania has authorized strikes by all employees except prison guards, policemen, firemen, and personnel in the courts and mental hospitals. Both have, however, forbidden strikes when one would create "a clear and present danger or threat to the health, safety, or welfare of the public." Vermont has granted municipal employees and teachers the right to strike, and Montana has permitted nurses a limited right to strike. The other states have remained silent on the matter or have expressly prohibited the right to strike either to all employees or to those whose strikes would endanger the public health or safety. The prohibitions often carry with them penalties to be imposed should a strike be undertaken. These penalties have included fines (to be levied against the union's treasury or against the strikers), imprisonment of union leaders, and suspension or dismissal of striking employees.

The penalties have generally proven ineffective as deterrents to work stoppages. Employees usually know that the penalties are lightly applied, if at all, to preclude making labor martyrs, to alleviate bitterness and tension, and to prevent further work stoppages in retaliation. They also know that the public employer cannot suspend or dismiss all of them if they went out on strike.

State and local governments when faced with strikes have sought relief through the adjudication process. The state courts have decided against striking public employees by holding that strikes are not to be engaged in unless the state statutes expressly permit such action. The Kentucky Court of Appeals, for example, has declared that strikes by public employees can be regulated by state statute, and their prohibition is not in violation of due process, equal protection, prohibitions against involuntary servitude or the abridgement of free speech and public assembly (as protected by the Kentucky and federal constitutions).[34]

Herbert Haber, New York City's Labor Relations Director, has called for a pragmatic prospective on the right to strike. Thus, he has noted:

> From a realistic standpoint . . . irrespective of whether they have a right or don't have a right, whether they should have it or not—we have strikes. Public employees are striking. And I must conduct my business as though for all practical purposes they've got a de facto if not a de jure right to strike—because they *are* striking.[35]

The period of extensive work stoppages began in 1966. The total for that year alone exceeded the total number of strikes of the five previous years. To illustrate the extent of strikes and the upward trend in recent years, data are presented in Table IX.2. As can be noted in the table, most of the work stoppages have occurred on the local level. The general pattern of strikes by regions, in recent years, has remained unchanged. The most active section of the country, measured by the number of strikers, has been the Northeast (most notably in New York). The greatest number of strikes have occurred in the Midwest (especially in Michigan, Illinois, and Ohio); but these have involved fewer numbers of workers than have the strikes in the Northeast. The lowest number of instances of work stoppages has been found in the West (California accounting for most of the walkouts), although that region ranks higher than the South in the number of people on strike.

TABLE IX.2

Strikes, by Level of Government, 1966–1970

| | State Government | | Local Government | |
Year	Number of Strikes	Total Workers Involved	Number of Strikes	Total Workers Involved
1966	9	3,090	133	102,000
1967	12	4,670	169	127,000
1968	16	9,300	235	190,900
1969	37	20,500	372	139,000
1970	23	8,800	386	168,900

Sources: Bureau of Labor Statistics, *Work Stoppages in Government, 1958–68*, p. 9; *Government Work Stoppages, 1960, 1969, and 1970*, p. 3.

Rule Execution and the Citizenry

After nearly a quarter of a century of low public attention to the problems of poverty, a reawakening of interest occurred in the decade of the 1960s. As the cost, inadequacies, and failure of programs that were started during the New Deal period became publicized, attention began to be focused on the administrative structure. Bureaucrats were depicted as being unable to attain the goals of ameliorating the various conditions of poverty, as being in search of inappropriate or incompatible means toward the objective, or of failing to consider the consequences of actions taken in pursuit of those goals.

Programmatic failures were believed to be the failures of administrators, not those of elected officials. The previous decades of reforms had resulted in an enlarged bureaucracy with responsibilities beyond that of routine program implementation. Those elected to office had abdicated much of their rule-making responsibilities to the professional, competent, and permanent bureaucracy. Legislators enacted programs that were essentially broad policy objectives; they delegated to the bureaucrats the tasks of interpreting what the policy goals were and deciding how those were to be pursued and implemented. Similarly, the bureaucrats were integral to the initiation and planning of executive programs, as well as to their execution.

Moreover, the lack of concrete ends and clear priorities of the social and economic programs made the goals of past reforms unobtainable. Neutral competence, professionalization, and structural changes to enhance rational decision making were the reformers' means to promote efficiency and economy. Yet, for bureaucrats to execute rules in the most efficient and economical manner, they must have a clear idea of what is to be accomplished, and such specific guidelines were lacking. As Gilbert V. Steiner noted: "Even with a willingness to add to the public investment in relief of the poor, it is clear that how to do it is no less difficult a question than is how much to do." [36]

Citizen Participation

Since elected officials did not have the answer to those questions, and the administrators' answers were not producing effective results, the new demand was for the direct involvement of the poor in programs that were affecting their lives. The demand for citizen participation had begun as early as the mid-1950s. It denotes a disillusionment with the professionals, those who took charge and failed to "deliver the goods." The demand for citizen involvement can be viewed as an expression of unwillingness to trust or a rejection of expert planning and rule execution.

Several reasons have been posited for the inclusion of citizens in the rule execution function. Each reason has been based on unfavorable perspectives about the bureaucracy. Some advocates of citizen inclusion believed that bureaucrats were unable to recognize that their actions affected individuals differentially. That became clear in the development of urban renewal projects, when bureaucrats, who had failed to realistically assess the reaction of all the publics to be affected, met resistance.

The urban renewal program (inaugurated as Title I of the Housing Act of 1949) began among high hopes. Mayors of many of the larger cities gave top priority to renewal in their own community when they perceived that they had the backing of liberals, planners, newspapers, and businessmen. There was initially widespread enthusiasm generated over the possibilities of restoring the decaying central city. Yet, the enthusiasm began to wane as it became apparent that urban renewal was not a program to be implemented simply. From 1949 to 1954, the urban renewal agencies had little to show in results. While approximately 211 localities were interested in some form of inner-city development, only 60 had reached the land acquisition stage.[37] What had gone wrong? The planners had planned for the various projects themselves. Yet, they failed to consider one crucial factor—resident resistance.

The failure of urban renewal projects has been traced to citizen resistance. William L. Slayton and Richard Dewey, for example, wrote that such projects had been killed primarily because of opposition within the redevelopment area. They found that residents who were not aware of a proposed project until they heard of it via the media, were likely to take a dim view of its value. Thus, they concluded:

> From a purely practical point of view, as a means of easing redevelopment through the perils of resident opposition, the community organization . . . can become a valuable tool.[38]

When formulating the Housing Act of 1954, Congress provided for community involvement. The new act contained a requirement that each applying locality would have to submit a "workable program." Such a program would have to be produced with the consultation of those in the community affected by the renewal projects. Although the usual reaction was to create citizen committees, with representatives drawn primarily from city-wide interests rather than from the project areas, most of the successful projects were completed where the residents were actively included in the planning. As William L. Loring, Jr., Frank L. Sweetser, and Charles F. Ernst have noted:

> Having had a hand in the planning, residents are already predisposed to accept the plans which they feel they have helped create, even though the plans finally involve changes in the neighborhood they would not have agreed to without prior discussion and change of their attitudes.[39]

Thus, the call for citizen participation in the urban renewal program was stimulated by practical necessity. It was believed that by coopting the residents of the area into the planning and implementation stages of renewal, one could practically ensure the success of the program.

Other advocating citizen participation believed that programmatic failure was due to the misdirected energies of bureaucrats. Richard A. Cloward and Lloyd E. Ohlin, in their studies of juvenile delinquency, showed how the wrong programs are executed because of a lack of awareness of the real causes of problems.[40] They saw delinquency as a product of a juvenile's rejection of the values of the greater society, and of a sharing, instead, of the norms of a "delinquent subculture." The members of that subculture attribute their everyday failures to prevailing societalinstitutional arrangements. Thus, Cloward and Ohlin emphasized that the present modes of handling delinquents helped form and maintain the subculture, rather than eliminate it. For the treatment of deviant behavior was based on an assumption that it is an individual adaptive problem, instead of recognizing that the development and maintenance of a delinquent attitude is a collective enterprise.

Cloward and Ohlin have explained that a youth commits his first act of delinquency with fear and uncertainty; his defiance of the dominant social norms is tentatively undertaken. He needs encouragement and reassurance to defend his own position, and he finds these in others who have faced similar experiences. Without such support he will have difficulty in creating a firm basis for his defiant attitudes. The traditional means of dealing with the delinquent was to reject and to isolate him from society; and in doing so, it placed him in closer approximation with others sharing similar views with whom he could communicate and be reassured. Moreover, most attempts to reform juvenile delinquents were made through clinical therapy that assumed the "patient" would have a "guilt feeling" that could be used to get him on the road to rehabilitation. Yet, the authors posited that the delinquent, having already rejected society's norms, does not have a society imposed sense of guilt. It is necessary then for the public workers to execute programs which would get at the heart of the subculture's belief system.

Following Cloward and Ohlin's line of reasoning, it was felt that the way to break the delinquent subculture was to make those individuals who were alienated from the institutions of society feel that they were accepted and involved. Thus, by participating in the programs which were aimed at helping low income communities in dealing with their problems, the alienated individuals would become motivated to reexamine and change their opinions of the institutions.

Cloward and Ohlin's work laid the foundation for the Juvenile Delinquency and Youth Offenses Control Act of 1961. Under the act, the Office of Juvenile Delinquency was charged with developing citizen participation programs. This office funded several experimental demonstration projects. Among the several projects were Mobilization for Youth and HARYOU-ACT, both in New York City; Crusade for Opportunity, in Syracuse; and Action for Boston Community Development, in Boston. Each project established neighborhood service centers. Youths and other residents were hired to work in the centers. These indigenous non-professionals were to establish contact with other ghetto residents, and organize self-help projects in their respective neighborhoods. Community residents were to meet and set priorities and types of services to be undertaken by the neighborhood centers.

Citizen participation was also seen as a means to counteract the tendency of professional bureaucrats to see problems in the narrow perspective of their own specialization. Frederick C. Mosher has seen that professionalism breeds differentiation of one field of public activity from another and embues those within each field with a sense of exclusivity of knowledge and prerogative to operate in that activity. He has noted that:

> Except for those professionals who grow beyond their field, the real world is seen as by a submariner through a periscope whose direction is fixed and immutable.[41]

Daniel P. Moynihan has noted that administrative agents were trying to attack the problems of poverty from single purpose perspectives. Those individuals believed that by attempting to solve the most serious aspect of the problem (that is from their agency's vantage point) other problems would dissipate. Thus, trying to gain a commitment from governmental agents to engage in long range and generalized policy planning, he wrote:

> The problem is so interrelated, one thing with another, that any list of program proposals would necessarily be incomplete, and would distract attention from the main point of interrelatedness. . . . Whatever the specific elements of a national effort designed to resolve this problem, those elements must be coordinated in terms of one general strategy.[42]

Moynihan was not alone in proposing an interrelated attack. Planners had stressed that the time had come for comprehensive examination of solutions to the problems of the decaying city. Weber has written:

> We are coming to comprehend the city as an extremely complex social system, only some aspects of which are expressed as physical buildings or as locational arrangements. . . . We can no longer speak of the physical city versus the social city or the economic city or the political city or the intellectual city.[43]

The Demonstration Cities Act of 1966 was the governmental response to this view of interrelatedness. The framers of the Act believed that for comprehensive planning to be successful there was a need for citizens to participate. The Department of Housing and Urban Development's workable program guide clearly stated that the implementation of the Act required the active involvement of citizens residing in the model neighborhood areas in planning and carrying out the program. The guide noted that the requirement

> Grows out of the conviction that improving the quality of life of the residents of the model neighborhood can be accomplished only by the affirmative action of the people themselves. This requires a means of building self-esteem, competence and a desire to participate effectively in solving the social and physical problems of their community.[44]

The requirement for citizen participation was also a means to overcome the doubts that professionals could plan without such help. As a 1968 Model Cities Technical Assistance Bulletin noted:

> Many best intentioned officials and technicians by their training, experiences and life-styles, are unfamiliar with or even insensitive to problems and aspirations of neighborhood residents.[45]

Let the residents meet with the bureaucrats, these advocates thought, and the merging of indigenous needs with technical skills would produce effective and useful programs.

The creation of the Office of Economic Opportunity and the ensueing OEO programs were other outgrowths of the belief that problems were interrelated and could not be solved by focusing on any specific one alone. Nathan Glazer has indicated that a new agency was established to oversee the anti-poverty programs as a revolt against professionalism. That is, a revolt against the professionalism of welfare agencies, schools, employment agencies, and so on, all of which had coexisted too comfortably with poverty, and thus were unable to break through the cycle with innovative execution. As Glazer explained:

> For some years, progressive social workers had been attacking the public agencies for a number of faults—their inability to cooperate in handling a "multi-problem" family or individual, their emphasis on their specific function as against all the client's needs, their insistence on professional qualifications for workers (making it difficult for them to absorb new views from outsiders), their limited, middle-class orientation in dealing with the problems of lower-class people.[46]

The Community Action Program provision of the Economic Opportunity Act required that the poor were to participate in programs for their aid. Indeed, it marked the first time in social welfare history that such a requirement was made based on the belief that the involvement of the poor would precipitate the development of dynamic new ideas and programs. In addition, it was believed that community action projects would serve as vehicles through which traditionally, politically, powerless groups could exert influence. This sentiment was articulated in the Community Action Workbook:

> One of the major problems of the poor is that they are not in a position to influence the policies, procedures, and objectives of the organizations responsible for their welfare.[47]

The program provisions for the participation of the poor was, thus, aimed at rectifying the status of the powerless.

Kenneth Clark and Jeannette Hopkins, in their nationwide study, evaluated the extent to which the Community Action Programs had actually altered the status of the poor clientele in their relationship with the bureaucracy.[48] The research led the two authors to conclude that the poor have not been able to participate effectively in or instigate planning of programs which would produce significant changes in their life conditions. Several reasons were seen to account for this ineffectiveness. First, organizations that are financed by public funds inevitably become controlled by public officials, rather than by those the funds were appropriated to assist. Such political officials have not been amenable to nurturing programs which could directly or indirectly threaten the maintenance of their own political power and position.

Secondly, the poor were seen to remain powerless because they had not been given any authority or machinery to plan, regulate, or determine their own Community Action Programs. The poor comprised only a fraction of the members on the Community Action Boards (the directing bodies). They often found that they did not have the skills necessary to compete with the others on the board, namely the middle class and professionals. Usually the leadership fell to the middle class members, whose views would many times conflict with those to whom the poverty programs were directed.

Citizens' Advocates

Lisa R. Peattie has argued that those who lack education and technical sophistication are ill-equipped to confront the "experts."[49] As a consequence, citizen participation in urban renewal programs has been reduced on many occasions to approving or reacting to plans that have been prepared by the agencies instead of proposing their own concepts to be integrated. The disadvantaged are handicapped by their lack of technical knowledge. They are not able to cope with the professionals who "speak the language of maps, diagrams, and statistical tables."

The recognition that the poor are in a disadvantageous position when dealing with the bureaucracy has led to reform proposals based on the premise that professionals are needed to counteract the actions of other professionals. One reform proposal calls for the establishment of the office of ombudsman. Such an office would be fully and legally empowered to investigate citizen complaints against administrative agencies and to correct inequities and abuses. Proponents of the ombudsman contend that:

Only a specialized, full-time official, wise in the ways of bureaucracy, having a vested interest in correcting its errors, and supported by adequate staff and authority, can perform this function effectively.[50]

The interest in the office of ombudsman has been stimulated by the adoption of this plan (already over a century old in the Scandinavian countries) in eight countries during the past two decades.[51] In the United States, measures to create an office of the ombudsman have been introduced at both the state and local levels. The legislatures of twenty-six states have wrestled with the reform proposal, but only in Hawaii (in 1967) and Oregon (in 1971) was the office created. On the local level, the statutes or charters of nearly a dozen cities, townships, and counties were changed to permit the appointment of agents having ombudsman type tasks.

The basic task of the ombudsman is to bring complaints to the attention of offending agents, with the expectation that corrective action will be taken. Although procedures for performing such a task vary, a general pattern can be described. After an individual writes or calls to register a complaint, the ombudsman transmits it to the appropriate agency head and asks for an answer to the complaint raised. Once he receives the necessary information, he proceeds to determine whether the department has acted correctly or whether the bureaucrat's original action is to be modified. If change be desired, then there is a time period stipulated for implementation. Should the department head refuse to implement the ombudsman's recommendation, he must decide whether to publicize the bureaucrat's reticence by informing the governor, the legislature, or the public through the press.

In nearly all the localities that have provided for some form of ombudsmanship, the activities are engaged in by information or public relation type offices. Nowhere is the office called "ombudsman;" instead one finds such words in the titles of the agencies as information, inquiry, citizens' assistance, and so on. The major weakness of these offices is the lack of formal power. They generally cannot subpoena records to conduct investigations. Nor do they have any power to coerce malfunctioning bureaucrats to redress any wrongdoing. Moreover, none has any status independent from a central executive, having been appointed to the post. Their capacity to assist citizens is based primarily on their abilities to persuade bureaucrats and to focus publicity against the offending agency. In effect, as Jack H. Stephens has said, "the final decision is left to the top administrator, the representatives of the people or the people themselves."[52] Thus, the agencies created are, as Paul Dolan has called them, "pseudo-ombudsman."[53]

Reform proposals have also been made to have professionals hired to represent groups in the constituency, especially the poor, in dealing with professional bureaucrats engaged in urban planning. In the belief that the poor and uneducated need the assistance of professionals to express the indigeneous interests within a technical framework, support has been expressed for advocacy planning. The advocate planners would present their clients' interests to the independent planning commission or department responsible for drafting plans for the entire locality. That would permit a range of alternative proposals to be presented, which would reflect the interests of groups of residents in the constituency who might otherwise have been unable to conceptualize their interests for incorporation into the public agency's plan.

Paul Davidoff, in discussing the advocate planners, believed that they have a variety of responsibilities. The advocate planner should be more than "a provider of information, an analyst of current trends, a simulator of future conditions and a detailer of means." Beyond drafting plans for the client, he would aggressively plead their case before the planning agency. He would also have the responsibility of being an educator. As such, he would inform other groups and public agencies of the problems and outlook of his clients. He would inform his clients of the operations of city government, of particular programs likely to affect them, and of their rights under planning and renewal codes. In addition, he is to help them clarify and articulate their views, as well as aid in the expansion of the size and scope of the client organization so they may continue to act to influence future plans.[54]

Clark and Hopkins have contended that for the poor to plan and see implemented effective programs for social change, they need the assistance of concerned, committed, and independent professionals. Such professionals would develop realistic programs and train the poor in the utilization of the necessary skills to effectively confront public officials. Their principal goal would strive for the self sufficiency of the poor in representing their own interests in anti-poverty programs. The success in reaching that goal would be achieved when the poor no longer require such aid.[55]

Citizen Criticism

The most critical evaluations of the performance of the rule execution function has occurred since the riots of the mid-1960s. One stimulus was the *Report of the National Advisory Commission on Civil Disorders*.[56] That report clearly established that residents of the riot areas, in the twenty cities studied, were greatly dissatisfied with administrative practices and with the level of public services they received. The Commission members noted that in almost all cities the topics of grievances among black communities were the same. In the report, the topics were categorized according to the level of intensity at which the grievances were held. Within the category of the highest range of intensity were included complaints against police practices, employment and underemployment, and inadequate housing. Inadequate education, poor recreation facilities and programs, and ineffectiveness of the political structure and grievance mechanisms comprised the second category. These were followed by grievances about discriminatory administration of justice, inadequacies of federal programs, inadequacy of services provided by municipal governments, and inadequate welfare programs.

The second stimulus has been the increasing number of black spokesmen who have been vociferous in their denunciation of the professional bureaucrats—who are most often white. Stokely Carmichael and Charles V. Hamilton have voiced the antagonisms against such bureaucrats:

> The man in the ghetto sees the white policeman on the corner brutally manhandle a black drunkard in a doorway, and at the same time accept a pay-off from one of the agents of the white-controlled rackets. He sees the streets in the ghetto lined with uncollected garbage, and he knows that the powers which could send trucks in to collect that garbage are white. . . . He looks at the absence of a meaningful curriculum in the ghetto schools . . . and he knows that the school board is controlled by white. . . . Black people have seen the city planning commissions, the urban renewal commissions, the boards of education and the police departments fail to speak to their needs in a meaningful way.[57]

That type of sentiment has not been exclusively espoused by militant blacks; it has been heard from those considered more moderate. For example, Sterling Tucker, a black spokesman with close governmental ties, has written defiantly:

> Whitey has become the symbol of oppression because the systems and institutions in America that oppress blacks are all controlled—and controlled unjustly—by white people. It is bad enough when individuals behave in a discriminatory manner. It is something else again when the discriminatory behavior of individuals is institutionalized. . . .[58]

Work stoppages of government employees have been the third stimulus for critical evaluations of the bureaucrats. These actions have been primarily strikes, although other forms of work stoppages (*e.g.*, slow downs, sick call-ins, lateness) have also occurred. Although such phenomena have occurred sporadically throughout the century, 1966 ushered in a period of extensive work stoppages.

The strikes have run the gamut of public agencies, the largest proportion involving public school teachers and librarians. The next largest proportions have been found in the areas of sanitation, and protective (*i.e.*, police, prison and probation, and fire) services. Workers in publically owned transportation and utilities have engaged in work stoppages, as have welfare, hospital and health service employees, among other types of bureaucrats.

The millions of citizens who have been immediately affected by the stoppage of essential public services have clearly seen that many bureaucrats are motivated for personal gain. The principal reason for strikes has been economic; two-thirds of all work stoppages have been for higher wages, and supplementary benefits. Other issues provoking strikes have been working conditions (*e.g.*, work assignments, work rules, overtime, and safety measures), administrative matters (*e.g.*, number of pupils per class, or case loads for welfare workers), and union recognition (that has been marked not only with struggles to get collective action accepted by government agencies, but also between unions competing to be the sole recognized bargaining agent with the government). Citizens have also seen strikes as the bureaucratic response to structural reform proposals for citizen inclusion. For example, policemen have reacted with sick call-ins to proposed civilian control boards, and teachers have struck to demonstrate dissatisfaction with decentralized schools having neighborhood school boards.[59]

The cessation of public services always causes inconvenience to the populace, although the range extends from nuisance to extreme hardship. The half day strike of bridge tenders (in 1971), who lifted the drawbridges around Manhattan Island before they left their jobs, brought considerable inconvenience during the evening rush hour traffic that day. The twenty-eight day strike of New York City welfare workers immediately influenced the daily lives of thousands of families. Cincinnati residents faced a major health threat (in 1970) by the accumulation of garbage resulting from its not having been collected for over a month by striking city sanitation workers. The fifty-four day strike of New York City school teachers (in 1968) wrought inestimable hardship to schoolchildren and their families.

Community Control

The evaluation prompted by the stimuli of the late 1960s have focused on the bureaucracy as the source of problems in rule execution. Researchers have sought to explain how bureaucrats respond to the multi-pressures directed toward them from their work situation, and from the community environment. One administrative response has been to treat entrenched interest groups more deferentially than newly emerging articulate client groups. In doing so, administrators are reacting by considering as reference groups those that have established a long relationship with them and will continue to do so in the future. If, for example, urban renewal agencies are more prone to listen to business groups than to the poor resident groups, it is, as Clarence N. Stone has suggested in his study of Atlanta, a response to the businessmen having established a continuing and undiverted interest and involvement in many issues, rather than a sporadic involvement in singular ones. As Stone explained, the absence of follow-through at subsequent stages of a decision permits the bureaucrats in the long run to succumb to those who are consistent in their vigilance. Thus, while neighborhood citizen groups may develop organizational and leadership skills that enable them to succeed in a particular policy implementation decision, it is the business groups that prevail over the direction the program eventually takes.[60]

Bureaucrats may, secondly, respond by becoming more sensitive to the set of interests and values of the general public than to that of their clients, when each set conflicts with the other. For example, welfare and public housing agencies are generally faced with negative reactions from the overall public, whose tax dollars must pay for the services rendered. Bureaucrats recognize that middle class Americans hold negative attitudes toward the relief system and the poor. Thus, when relief rolls expand or public housing is scheduled to be built in urban or suburban residential neighborhoods, the middle class public vents its disapproval with the appropriate agency. To ward off such attacks, the bureaucrats resort to a variety of abrasive practices, such as making service rendering seem punitive and degrading, in order to discourage requests for aid and to lighten the agencies' responsibility. Richard A. Cloward and Frances F. Piven have explained that this is made easier by the poor's lack of ability to exert influence as long as they are dependent on the bureaucracy for material resources. Knowing that the clients will not try to exert pressure for fear of having benefits cut off, the bureaucrats can more readily respond to the pressures of those who pay the bill than they can to those who are recipients of the aid.[61]

Bureaucrats may also respond by developing psychological and organizational mechanisms, such as simplification and routinization of tasks and perceptions of their clientele. Simplification may be defined as the manner by which individuals "order their perceptions to make the perceived environment easier to manage;" and routinizations as the "establishment of habitual or regularized patterns in terms of which tasks are performed." Such mechanisms are utilized, as Michael Lipsky explained, when administrators try to cope with the problems they face in their work environment, such as inadequate resources, psychological, or physical threat, and ambiguous or contradictory job performance expectations.[62]

The employment of such mechanisms may be manifested in one or more alternative forms. Decisions may be made expediently, and short cuts may be adopted that decrease the adequacy of task performance. Clients may be viewed with suspicion, and be stereotyped or discredited. The recognition of the individuality of each client's needs and bureaucratic involvement with each client may be minimized. Means may be created by which client demands or grievances are discouraged or contained within the agency. Reports of the difficulty of tasks and of professional competence and successes may be exaggerated. Bureaucrats may disclaim responsibility over the results of their work. Programmatic goals and job expectations may be altered. Or administrative agents may satisfy public expectations by focusing their attention on serving the clientele most conducive to being aided.

Steven A. Waldhorn has discovered another type of response being made. Bureaucrats have been said to displace the goals assigned to their agency. In place of the goals, new purposes have been adopted, which can be achieved more easily. Such a psychological phenomenon has led Waldhorn to label the public agents as "pathological bureaucrats." [63]

David Rogers has also called the bureaucracy "sick." He has defined the term to encompass those agencies "whose traditions, structures, and operations subvert their stated missions and prevent any flexible accommodation to changing client demands." [64] The bureaucrats then respond to pressures in several ways: by compulsive rule following and rule enforcing; insulating themselves from clients; placing personal career interests over the interests in serving various publics; focusing on agency needs to protect and expand their power; making decisions in committees, so as to make it difficult to pinpoint responsibility; and yielding to strong informal pressure from peers toward conformity to codes.

Those scholars and black spokesmen who are most disillusioned with the professional bureaucracy and most unwilling to trust them in the performance of the rule execution function have advocated the most drastic reform. For them, the remedy is not merely citizen participation in the planning of programs, but for citizen direction over those governmental activities that affect their daily lives. The black spokesmen have called the demand "Black Power;" the scholars have called it community control.

One component of black power as called for by Carmichael and Hamilton has been:

> The black community as a base of organization to control institutions in that community. Control of the ghetto schools must be taken out of the hands of "professionals". . . . Black parents should seek as their goal the actual control of the public schools in their community: hiring and firing of teachers, selection of teaching materials, determination of standards, etc. . . . We have come to a stage in our history where the old approaches of doing *for* a people will no longer suffice.[65]

Sterling Tucker has written of this type of power to be wielded by the poor and black residents over rule execution:

> We need power bases, and our neighborhoods can be those bases if we can but take them over. . . . By taking control of our own ghetto schools, we can help build black pride in our youth and insure black success in the near future; by creating our own housing development corporations, we can come to have some control over the course of urban renewal, contracting practices, public housing developments, freeways and the like.[66]

The concept of power as community control has been defined by Alan A. Altschuler as a demand for the legal right to have neighborhood councils comprised of neighborhood residents to oversee the implementation of public programs. The demand denotes, according to him, a number of reforms—principally institutional decentralization. Citizens in neighborhoods would design policies for their neighbors. They would hire bureaucrats to carry out those policies, and would directly supervise those charged with administering tasks.[67]

Herbert Kaufman has noted that the demand by the blacks and the poor for community control denotes, in part, a quest to obtain a significant impact on the administration of programs. It is also an effort to overcome the impersonality of the huge bureaucracy that is "indifferent to their uniqueness and their humanity." But principally, it is a recognition by the newly organized minority groups that they have to compete with groups already long entrenched in relationships with agencies, and that success in the competition takes patience and time. Thus, no longer able to wait to for equal footing with highly mobilized and experienced groups, they "have adopted a strategy of deriding those institutions and seeking to build new ones in which they can have greater, perhaps dominant, influence."[68]

Yet not all agree that citizen control is the panacea. Some, reacting to the racial premises of citizen control plans fear that it:

> would be a step toward racial separatism; that it would intensify rather than alleviate social friction; that it would prove a dead end for blacks themselves, leading them to expend a great deal of effort in return for negligible or even negative returns.[69]

Others see the negative aspects of fragmentizing the administration of programs by neighborhoods, which would lead to a reduction in the "capacity of local government for vigorous action, and for action based on citywide rather than more parochial considerations."[70] Excessive fragmentation, they believe, is already at the root of the urban problem, for problems span small territorial boundary lines, and need regional solutions. Neighborhood councils would have to look to state and national authorities for added assistance, and would, thereby, be defeating the concept of local control. Moreover, decision making is slower when negotiations have to be made with a variety of special decentralized authorities.

Aside from such criticisms, focus has been directed at what are considered formidable obstacles to indigenous citizen participation.[71] One obstacle is the lack of administrative experience and technical competence on the part of the poor and poorly educated, who would be members of the various councils. They would then be in an untenable position overseeing "expert" professionals and experienced bureaucrats. Such citizens, it is said, would be unable to conceive of long-range and unfamiliar implications of their actions, and be reduced to short-range, specialized pursuits.

A second, and more important, obstacle is the lack of unified needs or a consensus of purpose in a neighborhood. "There are," as Robert C. Seaver has noted, "in most communities many interests, usually advancing demands which are at cross purposes or mutually exclusive." [72] Thus, even an organized community will pose problems in the implementation of programs, as even the most assiduously made plans will leave some areas untouched and ripe for resistance. This is compounded by the probability that community representatives on the neighborhood councils would not be of equal mind in developing the policies or in overseeing the implementation of programs. "Virtually everyone who is a party to a renewal or planning process operates from a different set of imperatives," Seaver observed. [73] And the mixture of professional administrators and demanding citizens might not lead to the implementations of commitments.

Kaufman envisioned the inevitability of a variety of problems arising in community control projects. Differences in the human and financial resources will be found among the neighborhood units. Competition will ensue, and some units will become more advantaged in terms of talent and money than others. A new system of patronage will spring up (as factions in the neighborhood struggle to maintain control), which could lower the quality of services rendered. Costs will mount in the absence of the economies of larger scale expenditures, and will divert some resources from the substance of programs to the operations of governing. These and other consequences will initially be tolerated, Kaufman explained, but eventually demands will come for "central intervention to restore equality and balance and concerted action," and "inspire a clamor for unification and consolidation." It is at this time that the century old doctrines of administration (professionalism and neutral competence, and executive leadership and centralization) will be reasserted. [74]

Anthony Downs has taken note of the consternation that Americans feel about the growth of bureaucracy, and over the "fear that society will become dominated by empire building, wasteful spending, egregious blunders, miles of red tape, frustrating delays, 'buck-passing,' and other horrors they attribute to bureaucracy." [75] He finds it ironic that the bureaucracy has become an object of derision. One is asked to remember that if government is created to perform a variety of activities that individuals cannot perform themselves, then it is necessary to have a segment of the population charged with that responsibility. Bureaucrats and bureaucracy, thus, become indispensable. If they have grown large, it is because the magnitude of the tasks that have been placed on state and local government requires large numbers of administrators to perform them. And if the bureaucracy has become a professionalized body of men and women, it is because the substance of governmental services requires "continuous attention from trained specialists." This is necessary, because some services cannot be performed intermittently (such as the performance of the public safety activity), nor can they be performed without skilled agents (as in education and health services).

Downs has stated that "neither praise of the technical superiority of bureaus nor condemnation of their inefficiency makes sense unless the exact context of their operations is specified." [76] Their performance should be evaluated in terms of the possible; bureaucrats are human, and work in a human situation where perfect knowledge about problems, priorities, programs, alternatives and consequences is not attainable. It also may be necessary to judge the performance in relation to what it is society wants its administrators to do. Bureaucrats may be able to do very little when a society blinds itself to problems, like poverty, which are blemishes on this technically advanced and affluent nation. Thus, though attacks have been made on the administrators, prompted in this generation by their inability to eliminate poverty conditions, one must remember that the bureaucrats did not make the problems, nor can they solve them without public support—in the form of willingness to change cultural values and willingness to supply resources.

Chapter IX Footnotes

1. Bureau of the Census, *Public Employment in 1969* (Washington, D.C.: Government Printing Office, 1970), p. 7.
2. Bureau of the Census, *Governmental Finances in 1969–70* (Washington, D.C.: Government Printing Office, 1971), pp. 20–26.
3. Several studies have analyzed the development of such administrative doctrines. See, for example: Herbert Kaufman, "Administrative Decentralization and Political Power," *Public Administration Review*, XXIX (January/February 1969), pp. 3–15; Wallace S. Sayre, "Premises of Public Administration: Past and Emerging," *Public Administration Review*, XVIII (Spring 1958), pp. 102–105; Herbert Kaufman, "Emerging Conflicts in the Doctrines of Public Administration," *American Political Science Review*, (December 1956), pp. 1057–73; and York Willbern, "Professionalization in the Public Service," *Public Administration Review*, XIV (Winter 1954), pp. 13–21.
4. See, for example; H. H. Gerth and C. Wright Mills, *From Max Weber: Essays in Sociology* (New York: Oxford University Press, 1946).
5. Leonard D. White, *Introduction to the Study of Public Administration* (New York: The MacMillan Company, 1955, 4th ed.), p. 19.
6. *Modernizing State Government* (New York: Committee for Economic Development, 1967), p. 58.
7. *The Municipal Year Book, 1967* (Chicago: The International City Managers' Association, 1967), pp. 161–62.
8. Herbert S. Duncombe, *County Government in America* (Washington, D.C.: National Association of Counties Research Foundation, 1966), pp. 59–60.
9. *The Municipal Year Book, 1970* (Washington, D.C.: The International City Management Association, 1970), pp. 178–80.

10.   Leonard White, *The City Manager* (Chicago: University of Chicago Press, 1927), p. 301.

11.   "The City Manager's Code of Ethics," *Public Management*, XXXIV (October 1952), p. 218.

12.   See the following chapter for a more complete analysis of rule adjudication.

13.   See Chapter I for a more detailed presentation of the reorganization of the executive structure. For up-to-date figures, consult the most recent issue of *The Book of the States.* Figures in this section were derived from data in *The Book of the States, 1970–71* (Lexington: The Council of State Governments, 1970), pp. 145–64, 78–79.

14.   Figures were derived from data in *The Municipal Yearbook, 1967*, pp. 103–10, and *The Municipal Yearbook, 1968*, pp. 52–63.

15.   Thad L. Beyle, "The Governor's Formal Powers: A View from the Governor's Chair," *Public Administration Review*, XXVIII (November/December 1968), pp. 540–45.

16.   See James Reichley, *The Art of Government: Reform and Organization Politics in Philadelphia* (New York: Fund for the Republic, 1959).

17.   Alan J. Wyner, "Governor–Salesman," *National Civic Review*, LVI (February 1967), pp. 81–86.

18.   See, for example, David Rogers, *110 Livingston Street* (New York: Random House, 1968).

19.   Charles Abrams has noted: "It takes at least two years to get a project into the preparatory stage for execution, another three before it is put up for bid. Clearance may take another two years." Charles Abrams, *The City is the Frontier* (New York: Harper and Row, Publishers, 1965), p. 102.

20.   David J. Olson, "Citizen Grievance Letters as a Gubernatorial Control Device in Wisconsin," *Journal of Politics*, XXXI (August 1969), pp. 741–55.

21.   These points were explained by Governor John Chafee (Rhode Island) in R. Joseph Novogrod, Gladys O. Dimock and Marshall E. Dimock, *Casebook in Public Administration* (New York: Holt, Rinehart, and Winston, Inc., 1969), pp. 48–49.

22.   John Lindsay has graphically demonstrated the crises confronting his office in *The City* (New York: W. W. Norton and Company, Inc., 1969).

23.   Deil S. Wright, "Executive Leadership in State Administration," *Midwest Journal of Political Science*, XI (February 1967), pp. 1–26.

24.   Ibid., p. 13.

25.   Ibid., p. 11.

26.   Ibid., p. 6.

27.   Thomas J. Anton, "Roles and Symbols in the Determination of State Expenditures," *Midwest Journal of Political Science*, XI (February 1967), pp. 27–43.

28.   Ibid., p. 32.

29.   Donald P. Sprengel, *Gubernatorial Staffs: Functional and Political Profiles* (Iowa City: The Institute of Public Affairs, The University of Iowa, 1969), pp. 31–52.

30.   As quoted in Novogrod, Dimock and Dimock, *Casebook*, pp. 47–48.

31.   Alan J. Wyner, "Gubernatorial Relations with Legislators and Administrators," *State Government*, XLI (Summer 1968), pp. 202–203.

32.   Data for this section on unionization were derived from: *The Municipal Year Book, 1969*, pp. 31–57; *The Municipal Year Book, 1970*, pp. 173–81; *Report of Task Force on State and Local Government Labor Relations* (Chicago: Public Personnel Association, 1967); *1970 Supplement to Report of Task Force on State and Local Government Labor Relations* (Chicago: Public Personnel Association, 1971; Advisory Commission on Intergovernmental Relations, *Labor-Management Policies for State and Local Government* (Washington, D.C.: Government Printing Office, 1969); Frederick C. Mosher, *Democracy and the*

Public Service (New York: Oxford University Press, 1968); and Chester A. Newland, "Trends in Public Employee Unionization," *Journal of Politics*, XXVI (August 1964), pp. 586–611.

33. Data for this section on strikes were derived from: Bureau of Labor Statistics, Department of Labor, *Work Stoppages in Government, 1958–68*; Bureau of Labor Statistics, Department of Labor, *Government Work Stoppages, 1960, 1969, and 1970*; in addition to the works cited in note 32, above.

34. *Jefferson County Teachers Association v. Board of Education*, 75 LRRM 2486 (Ky. Ct. App. 1970).

35. As quoted in: Novogrod, Dimock and Dimock, *Casebook*, p. 89.

36. Gilbert Y. Steiner, *The State of Welfare* (Washington, D.C.: The Brookings Institution, 1971), p. 12.

37. Abrams, *The City*, p. 86.

38. William L. Slayton and Richard Dewey, "Community Organizations and Redevelopment," in Coleman Woodbury, ed., *The Future of Cities and Urban Redevelopment* (Athens: Ohio University Press, 1963), p. 427.

39. William C. Loring, Jr., Frank L. Sweetser, and Charles F. Ernst, *Community Organization for Citizen Participation in Urban Renewal* (Boston: Cambridge Press, Inc., 1957), p. 220.

40. Richard A. Cloward and Lloyd E. Ohlin, *Delinquency and Opportunity: A Theory of Delinquent Gangs* (New York: The Free Press, 1960), pp. 124–43.

41. Mosher, *Democracy and Public Service*, p. 108.

42. Lee Rainwater and William L. Yancey, *The Moynihan Report and the Politics of Controversy* (Cambridge: The MIT Press, 1967), p. 93.

43. Melvin M. Webber, "Comprehensive Planning and Social Responsibility," *Journal of the American Institute of Planners*, XXIX (November 1963), p. 235.

44. *Workable Program for Community Improvement—Answers on Citizen Participation, Program Guide No. 7* (Washington, D.C.: Department of Housing and Urban Development, February 1966).

45. *HUD Guide to Citizen Participation, Model Cities Technical Assistance Bulletin* (Washington, D.C.: Department of Housing and Urban Development, December 1968).

46. Nathan Glazer, "The Grand Design of the Poverty Program," in Chaim I. Waxman, ed., *Poverty: Power and Politics* (New York: Grosset and Dunlap, 1968), p. 285.

47. As quoted in Charles E. Silberman, "The Mixed-Up War on Poverty," *Fortune*, LXXII (August 1965), p. 158.

48. Kenneth Clark and Jeannette Hopkins, *A Relevant War Against Poverty* (New York: Harper and Row, Publishers, 1968).

49. Lisa R. Peattie, "Reflections on Advocacy Planning," *Journal of the American Institute of Planners*, XXXIV (March 1968), pp. 80–88.

50. Kaufman, "Administrative Decentralization and Political Power," p. 6.

51. For general discussions of the ombudsman, see (among others): Stanley V. Anderson, ed., *Ombudsmen for American Government* (Englewood Cliffs, N.J.: Prentice-Hall, Inc., 1968); Walter Gellhorn, *When Americans Complain* (Cambridge: Harvard University Press, 1966); Walter Gellhorn, *Ombudsmen and Others* (Cambridge: Harvard University Press, 1966); and "The Ombudsman or Citizen's Defender: A Modern Institution," *The Annals*, CCCLXXVII (May 1968).

52. Jack H. Stephens, "Hawaii's Ombudsmen," *National Civic Review*, LIX (February 1970), p. 83.

53. Paul Dolan, "Pseudo-Ombudsmen," *National Civic Review*, LVIII (July 1969), pp. 297 ff.

54. Paul Davidoff, "Advocacy and Pluralism in Planning," *Journal of the American Institute of Planners*, XXXI (November 1965), p. 333.

55. Clark and Hopkins, *A Relevant War*.

56. *Report of the National Advisory Commission on Civil Disorders* (Washington, D.C.: Government Printing Office, 1968).

57. Stokely Carmichael and Charles V. Hamilton, *Black Power* (New York: Vintage Books, 1967), pp. 9–10, 42.

58. Sterling Tucker, *Black Reflections on White Power* (Grand Rapids, Mich.: William B. Eerdmans Publishing Company, 1969), p. 68.

59. See footnote 33, above.

60. Clarence N. Stone, "Demand Processing, System Bias, and Policy Formation in Atlanta's Urban Renewal Program," (forthcoming).

61. Frances F. Piven and Richard A. Cloward, *Regulating the Poor* (New York: Pantheon Books, 1971).

62. Michael Lipsky, "Street-Level Bureaucracy and the Analysis of Urban Reform," *Urban Affairs Quarterly*, VI (June 1971), pp. 391–409.

63. Steven A. Waldhorn, "Legal Intervention and Citizen Participation as Strategies for Change in Public-Serving Bureaucracies," (mimeographed).

64. Rogers, *110 Livingstone Street*, p. 267.

65. Carmichael and Hamilton, *op. cit.*, pp. 166–67, 182.

66. Tucker, *Black Reflections*, p. 71.

67. Alan A. Altshuler, *Community Control* (New York: Pegasus, 1970).

68. Kaufman, "Administrative Decentralization and Political Power," p. 5.

69. As listed in Altshuler, *Community Control*, p. 18.

70. Ibid.

71. Robert C. Seaver, "The Dilemma of Citizen Participation," in Hans B. C. Spiegel, ed., *Citizen Participation in Urban Development* (Washington, D.C.: NTL Institute for Applied Behavioral Science, 1968), pp. 61–71.

72. Ibid., p. 68.

73. Ibid., p. 64.

74. Kaufman, "Administrative Decentralization and Political Power," pp. 11–12.

75. Anthony Downs, *Inside Bureaucracy* (Boston: Little, Brown and Company, 1967), p. 253.

76. Ibid., p. 40.

Chapter **X**

Rule Adjudication

In every political system, the function of rule adjudication is performed to insure that there is compliance with public rules. Rule adjudication includes ascertaining whether a violation of a rule has occurred in a given instance, evaluating the degree of severity of that violation, and applying appropriate penalties against the violator.

A degree of certainty in community life is an outcome of rule adjudication being performed. Each person becomes aware of what is expected of him and what he may expect of others when he knows that sanctions will be applied to enforce accepted patterns of behavior. Therefore an individual might confidently enter into contracts to make a purchase, sell property, or work because he knows that there is adjudicatory recourse should there be a violation of the terms of agreement.

Every member of the community is affected by the adjudication function either directly or indirectly. He may be a participant in the adjudication process, either as a defendant or a plaintiff in a civil suit (*e.g.*, a case arising from an automobile accident), or a criminal suit (*e.g.*, having been involved in a street corner brawl). He may find his pocketbook affected as a result of an adjudicatory action, as when the telephone or electric company is successful in obtaining a rate increase. Decisions reached by agents of adjudication may determine whether his child is bussed to an integrated elementary school, his landlord rents to blacks; his boss provides equal opportunities to job seekers, or his union or country club opens membership to all racial and religious groups. Thus, many aspects—major or minor—of a person's life may be altered by the outcome of conflict resolution in the arenas of adjudication, irrespective of whether he runs afoul of the law or is "law abiding."

Agencies of Adjudication

There are three major categories of controversies: civil, criminal, and administrative. Civil conflicts are disputes between persons arising from economic, property, social, and personal injuries or damages. Those involve controversies over such matters as wills, contracts, property, insurance, marriage, divorce, adoption, and so on. Individuals claiming injuries or damages usually seek monetary compensation or a writ of specific performance. Criminal conflicts arise when acts forbidden by the rules of the political system are committed. If a person commits any criminal act, he is considered to have acted against society and is liable for the punishment society (through its rules) prescribes. The spectrum of criminal activities is very broad; it ranges from murder and rape to jay walking or parking in a no parking zone. When persons feel that they have been adversely affected by actions taken by administrative agencies or by actions of others in violation of administrative rules, controversies of an administrative nature ensue. The substantive content of such conflicts may encompass zoning, sanitation, franchises, licenses, rates, and safety.

The institution in which the adjudication process is initiated may be determined by the nature of the controversy. Persons contesting administrative decrees and violations thereof may (where prescribed by statute) initiate action in a designated office of the appropriate bureaucratic agency. Where an agency is not empowered to perform adjudicatory proceedings, the action may be initiated in a court specified by law. The arena for settling criminal and civil controversies is the court.

There are a variety of courts in which cases may originate. These may be classified as courts of limited jurisdiction or courts of general jurisdiction. Some courts are limited in that they are established to handle specialized types of cases. Usually their names reflect the types of responsibilities delegated to them, so that one finds juvenile courts, traffic courts, domestic relations courts, probate courts, and so on. Other courts (*e.g.*, magistrate courts, justice of the peace courts, municipal courts, and county courts) are limited in that the cases that appear before them involve small amounts of monetary damages and minor criminal offenses. Cases representing severe criminal violations and civil controversies involving substantial monetary amounts are initiated in courts of general jurisdiction. Several states label these circuit courts; others label them superior courts; and still others call them district courts.

When a party in a controversy is not satisfied with the decision reached by the institution of original jurisdiction, and can demonstrate cause, he may choose to appeal. Every state has established appellate institutions. These may be comprised of one or two tiers. At the highest level of the state court system is a supreme court (referred to as courts of appeals, supreme judicial courts, supreme courts of error, or supreme courts of appeals in several states). Because of large numbers of petitions for appeal or state requirements for mandatory appellate hearings, supreme courts have been burdened with heavy case loads. In order to ease the work of those courts, nearly one-third of the states have created an intermediate appellate court level. This level may be comprised of several courts, with divisions for geographic jurisdiction and civil or criminal controversies.

Some institutions of adjudication have jurisdiction over both original and appellate controversies. For example, administrative agencies empowered to settle conflicts usually have appellate divisions. Persons not satisfied with administrative decisions must try all administrative remedies before bringing their controversy into the court system. Once all administrative channels have been exhausted, appeals are taken to the courts of general jurisdiction, although laws may prescribe that some type of controversies may be taken directly to the appellate level. In addition, courts of general jurisdiction, focused basically on original controversies, are empowered to hear appeals made from minor courts. In most states, the appellate level courts have been granted limited original jurisdiction. Such controversies as those relating to the state constitution, public revenue, and habeas corpus may be initiated in the supreme and intermediate appellate courts.

Procedures of Adjudication

The Fourteenth Amendment to the national constitution guarantees that no state shall "deprive any person of life, liberty, or property, without due process of law." Every state has established formal procedures for "due process' in the adjudication of criminal, civil, and administrative controversies. Differences of procedures exist among (1) the types of controversies; (2) the institutions of adjudication (*e.g.*, trial court procedures differ from those of administrative agencies); (3) the nature of the subject matter within each category of controversy (*e.g.*, the procedures for misdemeanors and felonies differ within the category of criminal conflicts); (4) stages of adjudication; and (5) states and localities. There are, however, important procedural aspects common to the performance of the adjudication function. Six steps can be identified.

1. Notice

The first step in the process of adjudication is to give notice to an individual that he is being accused of having committed a specified violation. In a civil suit, this is accomplished by a plaintiff filing a detailed statement of complaint with a clerk of an appropriate court, and thereafter, the court issuing a summons to the defendant which explains the nature of the grievance and requests a response. In a criminal controversy, the arresting officer and/or a minor court judge notifies an accused individual about the charges made against him and his legal rights. Formal charges may be brought against those accused of a felony by indictment of a grand jury or by a prosecuting officer. Administrative agents, either orally or in writing, communicate the facts, arguments, nature of the proceedings and the time period for response to the parties involved in an administrative controversy.

2. Response

The defendant, usually with an attorney (who may be appointed by the court for indigents accused of a major felony), responds to the notification of charges made against him. His response determines the direction of the subsequent adjudication process. Should he plead guilty to a criminal charge, agree to satisfy the demands of a civil complainant, or choose to comply with an administrative ruling, then there would be no trial or formal hearing. In the first instance, he would be sentenced or fined; and in the others, performance and compliant action would be expected.

However, if none of the above occur, then the adjudication process would continue. A trial date is set when the defendant denies criminal guilt or the allegations of the civil charge. A hearing is scheduled when a respondent claims that an administrative action is injurious to his property interests, or it might be scheduled upon his denial of the charges brought against him.

3. Pre-trial Meeting

Prior to a formal trial or hearing, an exchange of information takes place among all parties to a controversy. The major issues of the case would be raised, and evidence to be introduced and witnesses to be called at the trial would be made known. This enables the parties to go into the trial stage fully prepared and expecting no major surprises. The information may be obtained at a scheduled meeting, a preliminary hearing, or through individual written or oral communication.

4. Trial and Hearing

A trial is an adjudicatory examination of the issues between the parties engaged in a civil or criminal controversy. Witnesses are called to give testimony and evidence is introduced, and both are subject to close scrutiny. The proceedings may take place before a jury, unless the defendant chooses to waive a jury trial (where permitted). Cases that involve minor criminal offenses and minor civil claims would be heard only by a judge.

Administrative conflicts are brought before an examining board at a formal hearing in the appropriate agency. To expedite matters, testimony is prepared in advance and presented to the members of the panel, limiting the oral aspect of the hearing to cross-examination. Witnesses may be called to offer additional, and often expert, information. Juries are not a part of this form of proceedings; the panel sits as both judge and jury.

5. Decision

After conclusion, possibly with summation of arguments, a decision is to be reached as to whether a violation has occurred, the degree of severity of that violation, and the appropriate penalties or damages to be applied. If a jury is present, the judge will instruct the jurors on the applicable law and outline the framework within which they must determine the conflicting facts of the case, and request a verdict from them. In civil suits, he will offer additional instructions as to assessing the damages to be awarded to the winning party.

Having deliberated, the jury announces its decision as to guilt or fault. Should it be unable to reach a decision, a new trial may have to be ordered. Damages are assessed by the jury in civil cases, and penalties are pronounced by the judge in criminal controversies. When the jury trial has been waived, the responsibility for the entire decision rests with the presiding judge.

Prior to the decision of an administrative panel, the parties to the controversy are afforded the opportunity to submit their views. At such time they can propose conclusions, and exceptions to the initial rules made by the administrative agency, as well as offer supporting arguments for such statements. The panel in issuing its decision must take into account and answer each statement made by the parties. Its decision must clearly state the basis for its findings and conclusion, which includes the rules and precedents it believed appropriate in forming the decision.

6. Appeals

After the decision has been made, the losing party may choose to seek satisfaction through continuing the adjudication process into the appellate stage. Usually his petition for appeal must be submitted within a specified period of time and to a prescribed institution. Although individuals may have a legal right to appeal any adverse decision, they usually base their petition on a point of fact, law, or procedure. For example, an appellant may allege that there was an erroneous ruling of the judge on motions or objections during the trial, that improper instructions were given to the jury, or that an imprecise statement of findings and conclusions was made by an administrative hearing board.

The route of appeal may be simple or complex, depending on the judicial structure of the state or the nature of the case. In those states having intermediate courts of appeals, cases arising from courts of general jurisdiction go first to that level, unless a major constitutional question has been raised that permits direct access to the supreme court. Without the intermediate level, the highest court of appeal would be the direct target for most civil and criminal appeals. In contrast, appeals from decisions of courts of minor jurisdiction and administrative agencies may be made to a series of institutions. For example, the decision reached in a controversy involving a major criminal offense might only be appealed to the state supreme court; whereas, an appeal of an administrative decision may be brought in sequence to an administrative appeal board, a court of general jurisdiction, an intermediate appellate court, and as a last resort to the supreme court. If a national constitutional question can be raised as a point in a controversy, an ultimate appeal may be directed to the Supreme Court of the United States.

Appeal procedures differ from those of trials. At this level, attention is paid to briefs and records of the original trial proceeding. Neither testimony nor new evidence and issues may be introduced. A panel of judges sits to review the record presented to it, rather than a single judge sitting with or without a jury. The only time that a trial is held for appeals is when a court of general jurisdiction accepts a petition of an appellant from a minor court of no record.

Alternative actions are available to appellate panels. They may affirm or reverse (in whole or part) the previous decision or finding. On occasion they may choose to remand the case to a lower court for a retrial or a rehearing. When a case has been remanded, the adjudication process may begin anew. The process of adjudication ceases when a losing party chooses to accept a decision, or when all avenues of redress have been exhausted.

Factors Influencing the Performance of the Adjudicating Function

The function of rule adjudication is intertwined with the functions of rule-making and execution. Those performing the rule adjudication function look to the rules made to evaluate violations and look to the prescriptions in the rules for the penalties to apply. The agents of adjudication operate within the institutions and jurisdictions that may be set by the basic and statutory rules. However, the rules are often ambiguous in nature and substance, and the penalties they prescribe are inexact. Because those prescriptions are loosely drawn, a wide range of discretion is available to the agents. At each step of the procedures of adjudication, influence is exerted on that discretion by a variety of formal and informal factors and actors.

Notice

Not every controversy enters into the arenas of adjudication. For a variety of reasons individuals, policemen, prosecuting attorneys, judges, administrative agencies, and grand juries may choose not to give formal notification of intent to bring an individual or corporation before an adjudicatory body to ascertain whether a violation has occurred. The decision to charge or initiate adjudicatory action is not readily made. One must determine whether the advantages ensuing from starting an action is sufficient to overcome the pressures against so doing.

Individuals may fail to utilize the adjudication process because they are unaware that legal remedies exist. Others may be reluctant to take action against those with whom they come in daily contact (*e.g.*, neighbors, relatives, and business associates). Individuals may fear going before a court or an administrative agency, suspicious that their grievance will not receive a fair and impartial hearing.

The recognition of excessive delays caused by backlogs of cases before courts of general jurisdictions and administrative agencies may cause persons to hesitate before bringing charges. A recent study of the time it took personal injury cases to appear before a jury trial clearly demonstrated the problem confronting potential complainants.[1] The average delay is nearly two years, ranging higher in heavily populated cities and countries. For example, it was found that it might take three and one-half years in New York City to have a case heard, four years in Philadelphia, and five and one-half years in Cook County, Illinois. Such a time span may dampen the enthusiasm to undertake adjudicatory action, for with the passage of time witnesses might die or move away, or forget necessary details, and facts may become blurred, evidence may be lost, and legal costs may increase.

Financial costs may be a major deterrent to instituting litigation.[2] Although the amount of monetary damages sought may total several thousands of dollars, the expenditures needed to utilize the adjudication process may be beyond the means of an individual. Filing fees, witness expenses, experts' fees, investigation costs, and jury and transcript fees must be paid. By far the greatest expense is that of acquiring the services of competent attorneys.

The complexities and intricacies of the adjudicatory machinery virtually requires individuals to be assisted by lawyers. Indeed, little chance of success exists without the aid of competent attorneys. The Supreme Court has recognized the importance of legal assistance in adjudicatory proceedings through its "right to counsel" decisions,[3] and the states have made provisions to hire lawyers for indigents accused of criminal violations.

It has been recognized that the inability to pay lawyers has prevented individuals from utilizing the channels for legal redress in civil controversies. While states have not provided for free legal services, in recent years there has been an increase of such services for the poor through the establishment of legal clinics under the anti-poverty programs and expansion of private legal aid agencies. However, the staffs of those offices have not been large enough to meet the demand for legal representation, nor have the staffs been noted for their competency, for the most experienced and skilled attorneys have been attracted to more lucrative practice than the defence of the poor.

Even those with the financial means to hire a lawyer may find it difficult to obtain one. Attorneys may refuse to represent clients or to become involved with cases or causes that are considered to be unpopular by the community. Their rejection may be based on their fear of jeopardizing their reputation and thereby their future practice.

Yet, individuals do initiate litigation. The decision to overcome the obstacles may be affected by the particular goals of the participants. These may include a desire to right a civil wrong or to get adequate compensation for damages sustained to one's property, person, or reputation. Certainly many persons go to the arenas of adjudication because they are unable to gain satisfaction elsewhere. An individual who has a particular claim to press may find that he has more leverage in the courts than in the legislative and executive institutions. Or individuals collectively may satisfy their intent to prevent or delay governmental action (*e.g.*, construction or zoning changes) by initiating appropriate charges.[4]

Administrative agents review a variety of considerations before initiating an action.[5] Consideration must be given to the availability of staff, funds, and time needed to conduct an investigation, prepare exhibits, obtain expert testimony, and fully prosecute the case. Relationships with client groups is another consideration. It is difficult to bring charges against groups that have assisted the agency in the past by offering useful information and services, lobbying legislators in the agencies' behalf, obtaining reappointments for administrative officials, and holding promise for further employment.

An agency may initiate action to satisfy the demands of client groups. For example, such groups may see agressive agency action as a means to protect their business, profession, or occupation from loss of prestige or substandard practices. A decision may be predicated on legislative, executive, and popular pressures, for gaining the support of public officials or constituents may be crucial to the well-being and enhancement of the agency and ambitious agency staff members. An agency's success in obtaining funds and useful legislation from the legislative and executive centros often depends on its ability to demonstrate support from the electorate or support from groups that can influence the electorate. Thus, an active crusade of charging violators in an area of intense public interest, or conversely, overlooking the violations of powerful political supporters may be strategies adopted as means to achieve the goals set by top level bureaus.

In criminal cases, the principal actors involved in the notice stage are the policemen and the prosecuting attorneys. The role of those persons in the performance of the adjudication function is extremely important, for they enjoy a wide latitude of discretion in initiating the process against alleged violators. Unless a warrant is issued, the policemen's discretion in the initiation of an action encompasses the decision to arrest, hold for a charge, or issue a summons for a misdemeanor (*e.g.*, parking or traffic violations).

The laws of the states and localities do not expressly grant discretion to policemen, but neither do the laws specify police action for every situation. Although the patrolman is expected to know the law and at a minute's notice be able to ascertain which legal prescription has been violated and by whom, the decision of whether an arrest is to be made may depend on other considerations. The law may be complex or judicial interpretation of rules may be so unclear as to confuse action to be taken. The policeman may be inhibited by his knowledge that a mistake might make him liable for civil damages and administrative penalties. The nature of the offenses might affect the decision. An armed bandit, for example, might be more subject to arrest than would a jaywalker. Similarly, the policeman may be more strict with certain types of people than with others; thus, a recognized criminal might attract his attention more than a well dressed, innocuous looking individual. The decision to arrest may be influenced by factors of the neighborhood to which he is assigned. His action may be tempered by the need to maintain a good relationship with the people and the amount of prestige police may enjoy in the community. He may be affected by the attitudes of the neighborhood toward the offense and toward the offenders, or the characteristics (*i.e.*, ethnic, racial, religious) of the residents. A rough neighborhood or dangerous situation may heighten his awareness of possible personal harm and serve to dampen his enthusiasm for attempting to make an arrest. Lastly, should he be a member of a special unit (*e.g.*, a vice squad), he may be under pressure to make arrests to demonstrate that the unit's existence is necessary.

After an arrest, the police have some discretion over whether an individual will be held for a charge. Several studies of juvenile offenders indicated the factors that enter into the determination to hold or release alleged violators.[6] Among such factors were the severity of the offense; the age and background of the child; the policeman's attitude, experiences, and perception of his role (*e.g.*, social worker *vs.* law enforcer); his concern for his status, prestige and goodwill in the community and with his colleagues on the force; and his perception of the court's reaction to the case, as well as his expectation of the severity of the penalty to be imposed by judges. In addition, the decision to hold for charge may be based on the existence and effectiveness of other agencies doing related work. For example, where present, policemen may believe that social welfare agencies rather than adjudicatory institutions might be best suited to satisfactorily arrive at a solution.

The policy of a particular police department may have an important bearing on the extent to which policemen issue summonses. Police chiefs may emphasize campaigns against traffic violations through the issuance of tickets, or they may stress other aspects of police work. They may try to minimize citizen hostility by deemphasizing minor traffic offenses, hoping that the goodwill generated by merely giving warnings to drivers will establish future citizen cooperation. Often policemen may see the possibility of deriving personal advantages through issuing such charges of violation. Through the number of tickets he hands in, the police officer can demonstrate to his superiors that he has earned his salary (especially if he is assigned to a traffic squad). Moreover active ticket writers may find that they are rewarded for their endeavors by such incentives as more preferable tours of duty, promotions, extra income assignments, and so on. Certain disadvantages may dissuade an officer from over-zealously enforcing traffic codes; having to appear in court on one's day off is an example of a negative incentive.[7]

The prosecuting attorney (or, as he is known in different jurisdictions, the prosecutor, county solicitor, state attorney, or criminal district attorney), becomes involved early in the adjudication process of most major criminal violations. A citizen may come to his office to request that he institute a criminal proceeding, or he may be called on by a policeman to authorize the holding of an apprehended criminal. Most often he must obtain auxiliary authority from grand juries or minor court judges to issue a warrant or notice. Yet, whether the prosecutor undertakes the task alone or with others, he is principally responsible for deciding if an individual should be charged and with what violations. His choice is made in light of proximate and remote pressures placed on his office.

The pressures may be based upon practical, personal, political, or social considerations, and they may affect the roles the prosecutor plays. As a judicial administrator, he is concerned about the costs of prosecution as related to the time and energy to be expended by his usually understaffed office and low budget. He must decide whether it is worth spending part of his limited resources on preparing for relatively minor offenses, violations that may be best settled elsewhere, or cases he perceives as difficult to prove guilt beyond a reasonable doubt. In addition, he must be concerned about the practical problem of securing witnesses to appear at a trial; that is, will they be available, believable, cooperative, and so on. Moreover, his enthusiasm to press charges may be constrained by his awareness that the jails are overcrowded with persons awaiting trials (those unable to obtain bail), and that the courts are strained by a backlog of cases awaiting the trial stage of adjudication.

As protector of society and defender of justice, the prosecutor is the target of constituent pressures. Victims of offenses seeking restitution, the return of stolen property, or just revenge or retaliation demand action. General public opinion may direct his action in the extent to which he enforces the laws. For example, community mores may condone certain types of illegal activities as violations of Sunday closing laws or social gambling. Often public opinion is led by the media, which may undertake campaigns denouncing certain crimes against society. Thus, the prosecutor may decide to focus his energies toward selecting specific problems. He may strive to appease policemen by issuing formal notices to those arrested, so as not to depreciate their crime fighting efforts.

Whether elected or appointed to his office, and especially if he is ambitious for a higher position, the prosecuting attorney plays a political role. In that capacity another set of factors may influence his decision to issue a notice. The prosecutor's office is one that can attract public attention. He who holds it may court publicity by concentrating on those violations that have been the focus of constituent interest. He may seek to build a reputation as a successful prosecutor and project an image of toughness. That may be accomplished through the selection of cases in which he can readily demonstrate guilt. Moreover, the decision to bring charges or not may be influenced by political leaders who are concerned with repaying previous campaign commitments or building credits for future support.

In several states, the office of the prosecuting attorney is permitted by law to issue a notice through writs of information. Yet in most jurisdictions, the formal notice by law must eminate from the office of minor court judges or magistrates, or from grand juries. The major responsibilities of those actors are to determine whether a crime has been committed and whether it is probable that the one accused has committed the offense. The prosecutor exerts pervasive influence on such decisions. Although those actors may hold hearings and investigate the facts before deciding their course of action, they almost always react to the case as presented to them by the prosecutor and follow his suggestions. They have the power to summon witnesses and secure evidence, but rarely utilize that power. They normally hear only the evidence presented to them by the prosecuting authorities; and though they may question the witnesses directly, they usually rely on the prosecutor to do so. Moreover, they are inclined to follow his instructions and suggestions as to the nature and degree of the violation to be charged, for they respect his competence, expertise, and familiarity with legal technicalities.

The pressures involved in initiating the adjudicatory process affect various constituencies differently. Those who have the necessary resources of knowledge, skill, time, energy, money, and interest, as well as organization, have been able to utilize the process more often and more advantageously than those who have not. Studies have shown that high socio-economic status individuals have brought notice in civil and administrative proceedings more frequently and have been charged less frequently in criminal proceedings than have poor and black individuals.[8] Poor and black persons have not actively and traditionally sought to further their interests through the adjudication process. For, in addition to lacking the necessary resources and organization, they have not perceived that state and local administrative agencies and courts have been sympathetic to their grievances. Southern state courts, for example, have not been considered the best arenas for blacks to contest the validity of state segregation laws. When civil rights cases have arisen, most actions have been taken into the federal court system.[9] Awareness that individual action has not been a viable means of utilizing the adjudicatory machinery has led to court decisions permitting class action. As a result, efforts have been made by community action groups and legal service agencies (among others) to organize and represent the poor in initiating formal notices.

Response

Having received a notice, an individual is required to respond within a prescribed period of time. Usually the initial response is made by the defendant or (more likely) his attorney, through written communication. The type of controversy defines the alternative responses that can be made.

The defense in civil controversies may file a response in the nature of a preliminary motion to dismiss the charge. He may question the legality of the notice process, the correctness of the court's jurisdiction, or the precision of the notice. In lieu of filing a preliminary motion (or in response to a denial by the court of that motion), the defendant may either deny the allegations or offer no dispute to the claim made against him. In administrative cases, the defendant may respond by filling a consent decree in which he agrees to cease and desist from the disputed practice, or deny the charges and press for a formal hearing to contest them.

Although in major criminal cases the accused may have to enter a simple plea of guilty or not guilty at the time of indictment or arraignment, the initial response generally is to move to have the formal notice dismissed by the court. Such a motion takes the form of a demurrer or a motion to set aside the notice, claiming that reasonable or probable cause for the indictment or commitment of the defendant has not been shown. In addition, a motion may be made to remove the adjudication of the conflict from a particular court (one that may have proper jurisdiction but in which it is feared by the defendant a fair and impartial trial cannot be obtained) to another. If no preliminary motions have been made or if those made have been denied by the court, then the accused individual must respond with a formal plea.

Among the several kinds of pleas that can be made by defendants are (1) not guilty; (2) guilty; (3) nolo contendere (translated as "I will not contest it," that is, a plea that is in effect an admission of guilt, but which if selected cannot be used as an admission of guilt in any subsequent civil action arising from the violation); (4) prior conviction or acquittal of offense charged; (5) prior jeopardy; or (6) not guilty by reason of insanity.

The type of response that one selects is influenced by the magnitude of the offense, psychological and personal predispositions, resources available to the defendant, and perceptions of the outcome of the adjudication process. For minor offenses, such as motor vehicle violations, littering, or permitting pets to roam unleashed, the alleged violator may abridge the process by selecting not to contest the particulars of the notice. Many states and localities have established procedures to facilitate that effort. For example, persons may be permitted to pay a fine by mail instead of having to appear in court. An individual may not desire to appear in court, if he would lose a day's work and pay, if he believed that his word would not be given credence or as much weight as that of the arresting officer, or if he felt that he would be intimidated by appearing before a judge.

Those accused of civil or administrative violations may choose to contest the notice believing it is to their advantage to do so. If found guilty the defendant would be required to cease some action or pay some monetary damages, neither of which he may be immediately anxious to do. Thus, if one had the money, organization, and legal talent available, then achieving delay in the process may be the most effective course of action. Delay may lead to success should the resources of the plaintiff be exhausted before those of the defendant. Even if success is not achieved or there is seen to be little prospect of eventually winning, an extended interim period allows the continuance of business as usual. Such a strategy is aided, if not by the legal manipulations of experienced attorneys, by the extreme backlog of cases characteristically found in administrative and civil arenas of adjudication.

In major criminal cases, where there is a likelihood of conviction, there are many pressures on the accused to enter a plea of guilty. The decision to make such a plea may be based on the desire to avoid the trial stage. An individual may wish to evade the psychological trauma of a trial and shun the accompanying publicity, which might have adverse affects upon his reputation and his family. Moreover, he may see no benefit deriving from a trial by jury. For as Abraham S. Blumberg has noted, the defendant may know intuitively or learn from his jail companions or his lawyer that

> Juries are notoriously known to convict. In simple terms, the outcome of any jury trial often turns upon the question of whom the jury will believe—the assertions of the police, law enforcement officials and their witnesses, or the accused. The answer forthcoming with frequent regularity is: the police and those offering testimony in their behalf.[10]

Inducements by the prosecuting attorney may also serve as pressures for a plea of guilty. The prosecutor might promise to present the case to the judge in such a manner so as to cast the defendant in a favorable light. That could be accomplished by withholding information about some facts of the case, the defendant's past criminal record, and by emphasizing his cooperation, willingness to make restitution, or by presenting other factors that would elicit sympathy. He could offer to influence the judge's decision in sentencing by requesting leniency, recommending concurrent sentences, suggesting probation, or at least agreeing not to oppose probation. And he could propose to dismiss or consolidate several of the multiple charges (if more than one were initially made in the notice) or pledge to reduce a charge to a less serious one. Charge reduction (such as changing a charge of burglary to petty theft, molesting a minor to loitering around a schoolyard, and selling marijuana to possession of drugs) would have the effect of lessening the penalty or bringing the violation within probationary categories.[11]

The benefits derived from these promised activities do not only accrue to the defendant, for the prosecuting attorney obtains several advantages from engaging in "plea bargaining." Obtaining guilty pleas expedites his tasks and reduces the administrative pressures on his office. It reduces the expense, workload, and time of his underfinanced and understaffed office in preparing cases to go to trial (*e.g.*, obtaining evidence, conducting investigations, and securing witnesses). Not going to trial avoids any legal questions of the admissability of evidence or the propriety of police investigations and arrest practices. In addition, by obtaining a plea of guilty, he can avoid upsetting his schedule with the unpredictable length of time to be consumed by a trial. The prosecutor might suggest reduction of charges to enhance his image, and to demonstrate the effectiveness of his office. Far more convictions can be obtained within a given time period and there is greater certainty of conviction for lesser offenses than for major ones. In addition, a prosecutor may feel that stiffer penalties accompanying major offenses might be unjustly applied to juveniles, first offenders, or violators who had acted under the pressures of mitigating circumstances.

Policemen also may engage in plea bargaining with accused violators. As arresting officers, they have the information about the accused and the facts of the case which the magistrate and prosecutor rely on almost exclusively in the formulation of a charge. They may be able to negotiate by offering to withhold or modify some information and consequently a lesser charge could be made. They may seek a reduced charge to induce a violator to give evidence against others suspected of committing more serious offenses. Or they may negotiate to get a guilty plea so that they themselves can avoid long, frequent, or inconvenient court appearances; can escape potential challenges to their arrest or interrogation practices; can demonstrate productivity; and can expeditiously complete their records on that particular case.

The major premise underlying plea negotiation is a willingness to compensate the accused for his willingness to save the state the expense and time of a trial. While the prosecuting attorney cannot technically grant lenient sentences or probation, he greatly influences the deliberations of the judges. Quite certainly, no system could operate for long if promises were not frequently kept. It can be inferred that the system operates relatively successfully and effectively, for it is a commonly noted fact that approximately 90 percent of the defendants brought into the state and local court systems plead guilty to some charge.[12]

Pre-trial Meetings

Release

Once a response has been entered in criminal cases, the first pre-trial consideration is whether to commit or release the suspected violator until the trial begins. Since a period of weeks, months or, in some instances, years may elapse before the accused is actually tried, all states have provisions for release (except for those accused of the most heinous crimes). The state's concern with the defendant's appearance at the proper time and place for the trial has affected the conditions for obtaining release that have been established. In some situations, a promise to appear is sufficient, and thus release is based on personal recognizance. In others, a monetary amount must be deposited with the court to guarantee trial attendance. A person may post collateral (*e.g.*, cash, negotiable securities, personal property) as a condition for his release. This condition is based on the premise that since the collateral would be forfeited upon failure to appear (in addition to possible arrest and extra penalties imposed because of his flight), the individual would be present in court. The most common type of deposit is the bail bond. The bond is posted by a bondsman, who pledges the necessary security for the defendant. The fee for such a service is equal to from 2 to 20 percent of the value of the bail set by the court. If the individual fails to appear for trial, then the bondsman must pay the full amount of the bond to the court and seek to be reimbursed by his client.

The decision to grant release and the conditions by which it can be obtained rests with an adjudicatory agent (usually a magistrate or a minor court judge). At this stage of the process, the judge has little time to conduct an inquiry into the reliability of the accused. Thus, he usually relies on the information presented by the prosecuting attorney and the police. The police report would contain such information as the nature of the offense, circumstances surrounding the violation and apprehension, and the demeanor of the defendant at the time of arrest and while being held in custody. The prosecuting attorney offers the criminal and biographical record of the accused and an opinion of the likelihood that, if released, another offense might be committed by the defendant. In addition, the judge's decision might be affected by the physical appearance of the accused individual. As one judge remarked:

> I take into consideration his appearance, whether he is well dressed and looks like he is established in the community—if he is dressed like a bum it is likely he is a bum.[13]

The amount required to be deposited with the court for release, as noted above, was to be set to assure appearance. However, the current general practice is that the amount is related to the nature of the crime. Thus, higher bail figures are set for more serious crimes, regardless of the perceived reliability of the defendant.

Though state constitutions usually contain prohibitions against "excessive bail," the definition of excessive is left to the judge's interpretation. On many occasions a judge has set high amounts as conditions for release. He may do this in the belief that the defendant will not be able to raise the set amount. He might also levy an amount for each alleged crime listed in a multiple charge or he might even refuse to set bail. Any of these would be done when the judge believes he has to protect society from a criminal, teach the defendant a lesson, or punish the alleged violator by retaining him in custody.

For those whose family and friends do not have sufficient assets to post collateral, the bondsman may hold the ticket to freedom. Occasionally, the accused awaits his trial in jail because the bondsman refused to do business with him. The refusal may be based on a dislike for the defendant or disapproval of the crime committed; but, most often the bondsman's refusal is based on a fear of economic loss. Thus, he may reject a client if the fee involved is too small to defray the expense of processing the bond; if he fears the loss of future local business stemming from his assisting an unpopular individual; or if he perceives that there is a high probability that the defendant will not appear or be found on the date of the trial. In some instances, the bondsman may be willing to post bail but the accused may be unable to pay the fee asked.

The bail system has had its critics. A major criticism has been that regardless of how objectively it is administered, there is an inherent bias against the poor. Inability to post collateral or pay a bond fee results in punishment prior to conviction. For if one has to remain in jail to await trial, then he loses his freedom, loses his salary from work, receives the societal stigma of imprisonment, finds his family subjected to pressures arising from his absence, and so on. In addition, incarceration may act to his detriment during the subsequent steps of adjudication. He cannot actively assist in the investigation and gathering of evidence in preparation for his defense. By being detained he does not have the opportunity to demonstrate that he can operate in society without any trouble, and that he would meet his commitment to appear in court on the prescribed day. Moreover, the judge and jury might look with suspicion upon someone who was confined after his arrest. Other critics have focused on the inordinate power of the bondsman who, by acting in an arbitrary and self-serving manner, can foist the above disadvantages on defendants. The criticisms of the bail system have been succinctly summarized by a supreme court justice who noted: "At best, it is a system of checkbook justice; at worse, a highly commercialized racket." [14]

Several states have responded to the criticisms by initiating bail reform experiments. Illinois, for example, has focused attention on the abuses of the bondsman. It has instituted a plan whereby the defendant may post with the court a percentage of the bail amount. When he appears in court, his deposit would be returned, less a minimal charge for administrative expenses. While the fee is generally equal to that charged by a bondsman, the individual has the advantage of not being dependent on the discretion of the bondsman. A more sweeping reform has been the experiment in New York City, known as the "Manhattan Bail Project." Believing that criminal justice procedures should not be predicated upon the ability to pay, the Vera Foundation sponsored a plan by which alternative measures are applied to evaluate an accused individual's reliability. A trained staff investigates the defendant's residential and family stability, employment history, and prior criminal record. Utilizing a prescribed formula, a total score of points per factor is derived. The staff evaluates the score and makes a recommendation to the court. The judge may then permit release upon personal recognizance to those who received favorable recommendations.

The bail project has been so successful that it has stimulated similar changes in approximately 100 communities, in more than half the states. A report to the National Conference on Bail and Criminal Justice has noted:

> The Manhattan Bail Project and its progeny have demonstrated that a defendant with roots in the community is not likely to flee, irrespective of his lack of prominence or ability to pay a bondsman. To date, these projects have produced remarkable results, with vast numbers of releases, few defaulters and scarcely any commissions of crime by parolees in the interim between release and trial. [15]

Exchange of Information

Pre-trial meetings may be arranged to exchange information between the parties to a controversy. The principal actors in such activities are the attorneys, with their clients playing a passive role. This is so because the training and experience of attorneys provides them with the legal expertise needed to recognize technical flaws or loopholes in the notice; be aware of the implications of conceding or contesting an issue; know which information is important to obtain or withhold in order to prepare for a successful defense or prosecution; and to accurately assess the potential value of informal agreements or settlements.

Information is exchanged to assist the attorneys in the preparation of each party's case. The legal representatives of the clients in the controversy may meet to discuss the case. For example, in administrative controversies, the defending lawyer and administrative agents confer about which issues each is in agreement on, the desirability of amending pleadings, the possibility of obtaining admission of facts and of evidence that would avoid unnecessary proof, and which issues are being contested. Such conferences are prescribed by law for civil cases in nearly all the states. A judge may be present to hear and guide the lawyers' discussions of the issues, the admission and examination of facts and evidence, the disclosure of witnesses, pending motions, considerations of consolidation of charges, specification of damages, and to make an estimate of trial duration.[16]

The attorneys may arrange meetings with the defendants, plaintiffs, or their witnesses. Those individuals may be questioned so that the attorneys may become familiar with the nature and manner in which they conduct themselves and present their testimony and evidence. At such meetings, the attorneys may note weaknesses in the other's case and begin to plan trial strategy.

Settlement

A major advantage of these meetings is that they provide opportunities for expediting matters at the trial or formal hearing. Agreements made not to contest some of the original issues or facts and evidence save time, expense, and energy in the preparation of the case. For example, if parties agree to fault in civil controversies, all that would remain to be done is to determine the punitive or compensatory damage.

Settlement is an informal bargaining process in which the parties to a dispute evaluate the advantages and disadvantages that may accrue from reaching a legally binding decision without proceeding through the trial stage. Administrative agencies, short of staff and resources, and pressured by a backlog of cases, may be anxious to bargain in the hope of closing their records without further costly delays and efforts. Individuals or small corporations may be readily persuaded to settle, fearing a continued drain on their resources (to prepare exhibits, pay for records, hire experts, retain lawyers) if the case goes to trial. They may also wish to avoid damaging publicity that might arise from a formal hearing, or they may want to seek a swift decision so that they may return to their normal course of business.

Larger corporations, in contrast, may find it advantageous not to agree to a swift settlement. They can afford the expense of a hearing, and they have in their employ a staff of lawyers and technical experts equipped to handle the complexities of administrative adjudication. Those corporations may seek to delay settlement, choosing to evade admissions of defects in their products or services, or hoping that time will bring a new administration or agency official favorable to their stance.

The continuation of plea bargainings may lead to a settlement in criminal controversies. Weaknesses noted during the exchange of information might influence a defendant to change his plea, or a prosecutor to offer inducements. Should the state's attorney find that he lacks the necessary supporting evidence to his charge, he may offer the ultimate settlement—nullification of that charge.

Opposing parties to a civil controversy may find it beneficial to compromise and reach a prompt settlement. Each may prefer to forego the psychological strains and the costs of a trial. The plaintiff may believe it advantageous to receive some compensation promptly in light of pressing bills; while the defendant may find this an opportunity to pare down the size of the claim made against him. Both may perceive that the amount agreed upon is a better one than would have been acquired from a judge or jury.

Most often it is the lawyer's recommendation that influences the decision of the parties to settle. Such advice may be given when he thinks that the cost of further litigation would exceed the return from the bargain he could make outside the courtroom; or that the certainties of a settlement are preferable to the uncertainties of the trial outcome. He may be personally motivated to encourage compromise. A profit motive may prompt him to initiate a settlement, for instead of devoting his time in a long trial procedure, he could be investing his time handling the legal affairs of other clients. Moreover, his future professional enhancement and advancement might be based on his being cooperative and a skillful negotiator.

Pre-trial settlements may not earnestly be negotiated until immediately before the trial convenes. Often this timing is a calculated strategy. Each party may attempt to out wait the other expecting that the approaching trial date will heighten the pressure sufficiently to induce a favorable compromise. Furthermore, defendants, especially automobile insurance companies, may be in no rush to proffer large amounts of money that they could invest profitably during the period of delay.

Trial

A trial or hearing is that step in the adjudication process at which evidence is submitted and subjected to cross examination and rebuttal. The presentations for civil and criminal controversies are offered to the judge, or to the judge and the jury; and those for administrative controversies are offered to a tribunal of hearing examiners for evaluation.

The task of submitting evidence and arguing the case generally rests with the defense attorneys, prosecutors, or administrative agents handling the suit. The attorney's objective of success may lead him to attempt to influence the scheduling of cases before judges he considers friendly. Should the lawyer perceive that success may be best achieved with only the trial judge, he may recommend that a jury trial be waived.

The Jury

Trial by jury is not a right of the defendant in every controversy. Administrative procedures do not provide for the presence of juries at hearings. The magnitude of the civil or criminal charge determines, in most states, whether the option exists for a jury to be called. Where the option is available, a jury will be impanelled unless the individual accused of a criminal charge waives his right or both parties to a civil controversy decide against the presence of a jury.

Should the case be presented before a jury, then members to that panel are selected immediately prior to the commencement of the trial proceedings. Statutory prescriptions outline the population from which potential jurors are to be selected. Among the basic requirements set for eligibility are residence, citizenship, and literacy. Persons who are physically handicapped, mentally incompetent, convicted felons, or members of certain professions (as, for example, lawyers, doctors, veterinarians, accountants, undertakers) are generally ineligible to serve. Others may request exemptions on the basis of health, or personal hardship.

The clerks of the local courts compile a list of potentially eligible jurors, relying on such sources as tax or voting rolls, volunteers, and suggestions from community leaders (*e.g.*, party or civic group officers). The persons on that list are contacted to ascertain whether they meet statutory prescriptions. Thereafter, names are drawn at random, and twelve individuals (or fewer for non-capital offenses in several jurisdictions) are sought for a jury.

The attorneys and the trial judge are the principal participants in the selection of the jurors. The attorneys seek to find friendly or non-hostile members for the panel, and the judge looks to see that objective and impartial jurymen are selected. Individuals called are questioned by the attorneys, and their answers determine whether they will be selected. Each attorney may challenge the selection of a prospective juror whom he feels would not listen fairly and evaluate the evidence impartially. A challenge may be raised if it appears that the individual has already formed an opinion, has already discussed the case, has been in similar circumstances, has predispositions that might influence his perception of the parties and the issues raised in the controversy, and so on. Challenges may be denied by the judge if he feels that sufficient cause for rejection has not been shown. In addition, each attorney has a limited number of peremptory challenges, that is, he may request dismissal of an individual without offering a reason. The selection process may be a lengthy one, especially where the case has attracted a great deal of media attention. Extensive coverage by press, television, and radio may make it difficult to find persons in the community who are unfamiliar with the case and free from prejudgments.

The American tradition of trial by jury is based on the premise that an impartial panel is drawn from a cross section of the community. Yet, it is not possible that every jury contains representatives of all economic, social, religious, racial, ethnic, and political groups. The sources from which prospective jurors are drawn do not list all members of the community. Thus, if property tax and voter registration rolls are the source of names, then those who do not own property or register to vote will not be called for jury duty. Moreover, the demands of jury duty act to deter certain segments of the community from serving. For example, young mothers might be unable to leave their children unattended or afford substitute care; and laborers might not be able to afford long absences from their jobs.

Studies have shown that the composition of the average jury over-represents the middle class, small businessmen, managers, older housewives, and retired persons.[17] John H. Vanderzell has studied several methods used to select juries, and has shown that there is a relationship between the method of selection and the composition of a jury. However, he found that no method produced a cross section in miniature of the community.[18]

Several questions regarding the composition of juries have been brought before the Supreme Court of the United States.[19] At each instance, the Court has reiterated that purposeful discrimination against certain groups is not to be permitted. As the Court has stated:

> Perspective jurors shall be selected by court officials without systematic and intentional exclusion of any groups. . . . That fact lies at the very heart of the jury system. To disregard it is to open the door to class distinctions and discriminations which are abhorrent to the democratic ideals of trial by jury.[20]

However, neither the national nor the state courts have yet held that a jury panel must perfectly reflect a cross section of the community to meet the constitutional requirements for "due process of law."[21]

The Trial Procedures

After the jury has been impanelled, the clerk of the court calls the case and the trial begins. Throughout the proceedings, each of the competing attorneys directs his energies toward influencing the jury to accept the correctness of his arguments. The attorneys get the first opportunity to convey their respective perspectives of the controversy at the outset of the trial, with the opening statements. The accusing party's representative speaks first to outline how he will prove the charge, and this is followed by the defending attorney who outlines how he will demonstrate that his client is not guilty of the allegations made.

Thereafter, the activities revolve around the presentation of the evidence. The burden of proof rests with the accuser; and, as such, he presents his case first to demonstrate the validity of the charge. Witnesses are sworn in and questioned about the facts or asked to recall information relevant to the issues at point. Physical evidence (such as exhibits, photographs, charts, and sketches), is presented to support witness testimony. The witnesses may be cross-examined to test their perceptions, memory, and ability to state accurately their observations. Efforts would be made to cast doubt on the credibility of those who have testified. Should the cross-examination weaken the testimony of the witness or elicit new evidence, then a redirect examination might occur (a recross is possible afterwards, if the judge permits). In criminal cases, the defendant need not testify if his attorney believes it detrimental for him to be questioned and cross-examined. Certain individuals may be permitted the privilege of withholding some evidence to protect prized social and professional relationships. For example, doctors need not reveal what their patients have told them, clergymen need not relate what was revealed to them, wives need not testify against their husbands, and so on.

During this round of the procedures, objections may be raised to a question asked or to evidence that has been introduced. The objecting party must state the grounds upon which the objection is based (*e.g.*, hearsay testimony, evidence produced by wire tapping, or by illegal search and seizures). The judge must decide whether to uphold or to overrule the objection. He must ascertain whether the evidence or question has some relationship to the fact it is meant to establish; the significance of that fact to the case; and the danger of prejudiciously influencing the jury. In addition, he must see that the rules of evidence and constitutional prescriptions are followed. By objecting, the attorneys are trying to affect the immediate course of the trial, the decision process of the jury (for the objection and the judge's ruling may be an end in itself), or the record for future appeal.

At any time prior to the final round of the trial, the parties may choose to negotiate. For example, the accused in a criminal controversy may feel that the case is not proceeding in his favor and choose to change his plea to guilty, hoping for leniency; or in civil proceedings, the defendant may agree to a monetary settlement. Should the judge affirm the settlement of all parties to a controversy, then the jury is dismissed and the case proceeds, if necessary, to the next step of adjudication.

If no settlement has been reached, the attorneys present their closing arguments. These summary statements offer the last chance to affect the jury. Each attorney rises (the accusing going first) to persuade the jury to adopt his own version of the facts, emphasize the strengths of his case, and highlight the weaknesses of his opponent's.

Following the closing statements, the judge addresses the jury. He instructs the members of the panel as to the law applicable to the case and the alternative offenses to which they could find the defendant guilty. In many state and local jurisdictions, the judge may make remarks on the evidence to "guide" the jury. Sometimes he may be permitted to express his opinion regarding the guilt or innocence of the alleged offender (provided he informs the jurors that they may disregard his opinion and make the final decision themselves).

The jurors have sat quietly through the entire proceeding, and have listened and watched. They may have sat for hours, days, weeks, or months. Now they listen to the instructions, and retire in the charge of the bailiff (or another court officer) to arrive at a decision. The court reporter ceases his efforts to await the reconvening of the court for the issuance of the decision.

There are modifications from the trial procedure described above. Where a jury has been waived, the attorneys have directed their presentations of the case toward persuading the judge. Such presentations differ from those addressed to a jury, for it is from a trained and experienced perspective that the judge will access the evidence.

In minor cases, the procedure may be more informal and less complex. Often the only testimony given is that of the parties involved in the civil or criminal controversy. The judge asks most of the questions, and private attorneys are usually not present.

Procedures also differ in administrative hearings, which are held before a tribunal of hearing examiners. Opening statements are usually dispensed with, and arguments are directed to those issues that have been delineated at the pre-hearing meetings. The testimony is usually submitted in writing, prior to the hearing; and during the formal hearing, the cross-examination is directed to such testimony. The rules of evidence are looser than that for a trial court; for example, amicus curiae briefs may be submitted, as well as any evidence resonably related to the issues.

Decision

To describe the decision stage is to reiterate the definition of the function of rule adjudication. Once the trial or hearing has ended, the decision must be made as to three questions: has a violation of a rule occurred? what is the degree of severity of that violation? and what appropriate penalty is to be applied? However, the procedures prior to this stage may have alleviated the necessity for those responsible for making decisions to answer each of the three questions. For example, where a plea of guilty was submitted, the violation has been demonstrated; where a plea bargain was negotiated, the severity of the violation has been set; and where settlements were reached, the penalty has been agreed upon. Yet, in the absence of any shortcutting of the procedures, the questions are to be answered at this stage, and all that has gone before has a direct or indirect affect on the deliberations.

Those empowered to decide (*i.e.*, a judge, and/or jury, or administrative panel), are permitted a degree of discretion in their actions. However, this latitude is exercised within some limitations. A judge, for example, may be bound to a promise made during plea bargaining. Although a charge against a defendant may be altered to a less severe one or multi-offenses reduced to a lesser number, the charge cannot at this stage be enlarged to a more serious violation. Moreover, each criminal and administrative charge carries with it a range of prescribed statutory penalties.

The psychological predispositions toward the individuals and the issues affect the perceptions of the decision makers about what they have each seen and heard. The atmosphere of the trial or hearing affects the reflection of what has occurred. Extensive press coverage and mass public attendance enhances the image of the importance of the controversy. Outbursts, unruly behavior, and other extreme reactions by the audience to the defendants, witnesses, or evidence create lasting impressions that influence the decision making process. Conversely, an atmosphere of audience sympathy may be sensed and remembered. The judge may permit television cameras, photographers, and reporters to be present, which creates an aura of sensationalism that is not conducive to calm and objective reasoning.

During deliberations, it is the manner by which the evidence and testimony has been presented that is recalled. Those who have sat and watched have to evaluate whether the evidence indicated definite proof that a violation was committed by the accused, or whether the evidence has been sufficiently refuted to cast doubt upon its validity. They have seen how witnesses have given testimony and have conducted themselves during cross-examination. The introduction of expert witnesses, to whom the court may have shown deference, may effectively impress the decision makers.

Moreover, the demeanor of the plaintiff, the defendant, and the defendant's family may be crucial in affecting the outcome of the controversy. Different individuals evoke different reactions from members of a jury. Jurors may be more favorably disposed to mildmannered, neat, articulate, attractive persons than to unkempt, uncouth, unattractive, loud mouthed individuals. Studies have shown that jurymen have sympathy for the young and the elderly, females, cripples, clergymen, and war veterans. For example, they may not wish to spoil a youth's record or they may feel that society owes something to wounded soldiers. Sympathy may be generated for the defendant who shows remorse, has been seen to be punished enough (as when he was injured in the course of the crime, or has been jailed for an extensive period of time awaiting his trial), has been accused of violating an unpopular law (*e.g.*, social gambling, drunkenness, etc.), or has an elderly mother or pregnant wife present and weeping in the courtroom. Sympathy could also be evoked by the sight of a victim or plaintiff who has suffered serious pain, injury, or damages, and the jurors feel that such should be compensated or avenged.[22]

Of the many variables that affect the decisions, the performance of the attorney is most critical. His presentation of the case, his handling of the witnesses (*i.e.*, his ability to direct, twist, reconstruct, badger, humiliate, or support individuals giving testimony), his objections, his organization of the evidence, his demeanor and his reputation may be most effective in a courtroom. The jury may be impressed by a defense attorney who has an outstanding reputation and is a recognized personality, or who has had a long established practice in town. Similarly, the jurors may look favorably upon the prosecuting attorney who enjoys a good reputation, has built a record of "crime busting," or is a prominent political figure in the community.

Stuart S. Nagel has shown that certain factors or personal attributes relate with an attorney's success.[23] Older attorneys, those with many years of trial experience, those from prestigious law firms, those who hold or have held public office, and those with Anglo-Saxon names tend to win more cases than do others. But by and large, the greater proportion of attorneys do not have spectacular reputations and dramatic personalities. For most, their success is based on hard work, diligence, conscientiousness, and energy.

Some lawyers may be at a disadvantage in the competition for success. Public defenders or court appointed lawyers for indigents may be unable to prepare their cases extensively, due to the low amount of renumeration available for investigation and research. Should such a lawyer be willing to spend his time for a client (even though he receives minimal salary) he operates under a handicap, for he may be appointed only at the start of the trial and meet his client for the first time in court. His performance during the trial may be limited, for without pre-trial efforts to secure the facts to enhance or destroy a witness's testimony or the credibility of evidence, he must rely on spotting surface inconsistencies (when he is not busy trying to catch up with the background of the case). He is further handicapped if his client is not out on bail. For then the attorney must visit the client in the jail, the client cannot assist in getting witnesses, and there cannot be any lunch or recess conferences and last minute "warm-ups."

States attorneys may be similarly disadvantaged. Often they do not receive a file on the case they are to prosecute until the day they are to appear in court. Though cases may be received by the prosecutor's office in advance of a trial date, pre-trial investigation and the search for facts or witnesses could be inadequate. These offices are often staffed by an insufficient number of full-time and well-financed individuals who would be able to present a well prepared argument. Moreover, many of the prosecuting attorneys are young, recent law school graduates who lack the experience to compete well against lawyers who have acquired courtroom techniques over a long period of legal practice.

Jurors are also influenced by the demeanor of the judge during the trial. The judge, who commands respect in the courtroom and is considered knowledgeable about the law and procedure, is looked to by the jurors for cues. Inexperienced in and unfamiliar with the intricacies of the rule adjudication function, the members of the panel watch and listen to the judge rule on objections; address the attorneys, the witnesses and the parties to the controversies; and offer comments and instructions. Overt deference and respect shown to an attorney, an expert witness, or a party, for example, can make a lasting impression.

The judge, acting as a decision maker in the absence of jurors, is also subject to a variety of influences. His background, legal training, and experience affect his perception and behavior. His knowledge of the law and legal interpretations permit him to decide whether a violation has occurred by evaluating the issues of the controversy more than the drama of the courtroom. Thus, he may be less sensitive to the personal attributes of the defendant, less swayed by sympathy for the victim, less prejudiced by infractions of societal norms, and less affected by the presentation of attorneys than would be a jury. But he is not a neutral observer.

The neutrality of the judge may be affected by the additional information he is able to obtain. As the central official of the court, he is privy to data that show the prior criminal record of an accused violator, pre-trial negotiations, and pre-trial behavior (including the attitudes of the police and the presecutor towards the defendant charged with a criminal offense). Moreover, he is able to question parties and witnesses in the courtroom to extract relevant testimony that has not been developed by the contending attorneys.

Judicial, political, and societal pressures may bear on his decision. He may be aware of the consequences that a criminal record may hold for an individual, especially for young, or well-established, respectable citizens. He is influenced by the opinions and the advice of the prosecutors, especially those whose diligence he has come to respect over a period of close contact. A lawyer who appears to plead a case before him may be looked upon with greater favor than others. The attorney may be a friend, a fellow member of the bar, a graduate of the same law school, instrumental in recruiting judges, or a part-time judge himself. The possibility of appeals may serve to restrain the scope and manner of his decision, for the judge is cognizant of political and professional consequences of reversals in appeal. It has been said:

A judge is allowed a couple of reversals by the appellate courts before he loses his stature, but if he passes that invisible line, he becomes the butt of jokes among members of the bar. In a state where judges are appointive, this sort of derision is deadly, and even in elective states, such judges may find themselves speedily dropped from the ticket or not recommended by the bar for re-election.[24]

As a politician, the judge may be influenced by pressures eminating from his relationships with individuals important to his recruitment and election. It is difficult for the judge to totally ignore the interests or plight of those party leaders, prominent community residents or civic group officials who may have helped in his election campaign. Furthermore, it is difficult to consciously thwart the wishes of those governors, mayors, legislators, or select panels that were directly or indirectly responsible for his judicial appointment.

A sample of Hawaiian judges were asked to rate factors they believed to be influential in deciding a case. While one-third of the judges gave a high rating to "precedent, when clear and directly relevant," the remaining respondents rated subjective factors as most influential. "Common sense" and "my view of justice in the case" were the highest ranked subjective factors. "Highly respected advocates" were rated somewhat influential. Interestingly, "what the public needs" was rated as a significant factor, but "what the public demands" was not.[25]

The administrative hearing panel members deliberate through their perspective as experts. Most have risen to their present position through the ranks of the agency for which they are adjudicating controversies. Their past work experience has involved them with similar types of conflicts. They are cognizant of how bureaucrats prepare for the case before them. They may have had contacts with the company that is now a party to the controversy or has entered an amicus curiae brief. They may have worked closely with the defending attorneys in previous agency-client interactions. They may aspire someday to become employed by the company pleading the case before them. All those factors may be present as informal influences on the decision to be made.

Verdict and Sentencing

Having completed their deliberations, those responsible for decision making announce the verdict that has been reached. The decision written by the administrative panel first notes whether the accused has been found at fault or innocent. The opinion includes reasons for the finding. The administrators indicate that the agency has jurisdiction over the controversy, why each issue in the case has been so decided, and why the type of penalty imposed is justified. For those found guilty, cease and desist orders may be issued, and/or fines may be levied. No criminal penalties, such as imprisonment, can be applied. For that the administrators must go to a court, which alone is empowered in states and localities to levy such serious sanctions.

In the courtroom, where a jury has been present, the foreman of the panel is asked by the judge for the verdict. The foreman may have to announce that a decision could not be reached. The jury, he explains, has been unable to attain the consensus required by the state. In criminal cases, all states require a unanimous consensus for capital offenses; and some states lower the proportion of agreement for less severe offenses. Half the states impose the unanimity rule for civil cases, the others permitting an extraordinary majority. If the judge is satisfied that further deliberations by the jurors would fail to produce the required consensus, or to obtain anything other than the "hung jury," he will declare a mistrial. If the prosecutor or plaintiff wishes (believing that the chance for success is sufficient to expend additional resources), he may request a new trial. Otherwise, the controversy ceases and the defendant is free of the charge.

In most instances, the foreman announces that a decision has been reached. Should it find against the defendant in civil cases, the jury has to arrive at the amount of compensation to award the plaintiff. The amount may be nominal, if no tangible damage has been charged. In such cases (as for example, in libel or slander suits), the decision may reflect the intent of the plaintiff for obtaining vindication rather than an actual sum of money. Although the jury is able to assess any amount it wishes, the judge can set aside the award (when he considers the amount excessive or inadequate) and order a new trial.

For criminal cases, if the jury does not find the accused innocent of the charges made, then it may find him guilty of the charge, of a less severe violation, or of only some of the multiple charges brought against him. In about one-fifth of the states it may then pronounce a sentence; in the other jurisdictions sentencing is solely the province of the judge. Should the judge feel that the jury has pronounced too harsh a sentence or has arrived at a penalty beyond those limits a statute permits, he is not bound by its decision. He can modify a penalty by giving probation, lower fines, or shorter imprisonment sentences.

Where a jury is not present, the judge decides guilt or innocence alone. He also is responsible for deciding the amount of compensation to be given a civil plaintiff and the appropriate penalty for a criminal violator. Penalties in criminal cases take the form of (1) fines, (2) imprisonment with or without fines, (3) imprisonment to be followed by a period of probation, or (4) suspended sentence (*i.e.*, probation for a period of time during which certain conditions are imposed, as: good behavior, abstaining from liquor, etc.).

Much has been written about the discrepancies of sentencing practices.

The diversity can not be explained entirely by the personal predispositions of trial judges. Partly the diversity in sentencing practices among the states is explained by the variety of forms of sentencing permitted by statutes, differences in statutory penalties for the same categories of violations, and by varying parole policies. The penal codes of most jurisdictions are the products of piecemeal construction. Over the years, legislatures have prescribed punishments for newly defined crimes and have adjusted penalties for existing offenses as societal thoughts and beliefs changed. In about half the states, indeterminate sentences are the legal practice. That means that the judge must specify a minimum and maximum period of time (parole may be possible after the minimum number of years has passed), or that the judge is limited to the imposition of a fixed statuatory maximum number of years (parole may be possible after a proportion of the time has been served in prison). In the remaining states, definite sentences are prescribed by law; that is, a single specified term of years is to be levied by the judge (parole may be possible after some portion of that time has been served in the penitentiary).

The laws of several states provide mandatory minimum sentences for particularly dangerous crimes (*e.g.*, armed robbery). Most states make a heavier punishment for repeated offenders mandatory (*e.g.*, life imprisonment for the third or fourth conviction on a felony charge). Some require consecutive sentences for a defendant found guilty of more than one charge. Statutes in a number of states prohibit probation for those who have committed serious offenses or those who have prior criminal records.

The limits to the amounts of fine that can be imposed may be fixed by statute. The alternative, that is imprisonment for those not paying the fine, is also set. Often a rate is established by law, which prescribes the ratio between the fine payment and imprisonment (as, for example, one day in jail for each dollar of the fine not paid).

Disparity in sentencing practices exists within states as well as between states. In making rules about penalties, legislators have seen fit to prescribe a range of punishments and to delegate to judges the power to set a penalty within a fixed minimum and maximum limit. The justification for judicial discretion has been that allowance must be made for extenuating circumstances that may underlie a violation, variations in community mores, and types of offenders. Support of such discretion has come from police and prosecutors, who use offers of leniency to negotiate with defendants for information or testimony to aid in the investigation of crime. Moreover leeway permits negotiation for guilty pleas, which save the state the time and expense of preparing a case and going to trial.

Several considerations enter into the judge's deliberation in applying sentences. The judge recognizes that society has delegated to him the responsibility for applying sanctions to criminal offenders so as to (1) isolate offenders for the protection and safety of the community; (2) discourage other potential offenders; (3) rehabilitate deviants from the rules of society; (4) express the community's condemnation of certain acts; and (5) reinforce the values of acceptable conduct. He recognizes the need to maintain and defend the judicial roles, offices, actors, and process. He may try to fulfill the promises made in plea bargaining negotiations, for he knows it is a major tool for the prosecutor in expediting the adjudication procedure. Although the judge cannot override a jury's verdict, he can use his sentence power to modify the panel's penalty decision when he considers it too harsh or too lenient. However, he is prone to accept the jury's decision or its recommendation for mercy, for he does not wish to discredit the stature of the jury system. His knowledge of prison conditions (as well as the pressures from prison administrators who are beset by poor facilities, overcrowded conditions, and inadequate resources), could affect his decision whether to imprison convicted offenders. Furthermore, it has been seen that a judge's decisions are influenced by his interest in maintaining the integrity and dignity of the judicial position. Thus, harsher sentences are decreed for those defendants who articulate expressions of disparagement for the courts, law, or police; for those who fail to use honorific titles; and for those who disagree with the judge, who use sarcasm, or who raise their voices in anger.[26]

To meet the demands of adjudicating the heavy daily docket of misdemeanors, the judges presiding over minor courts are often forced to develop practices that appear to resemble assembly line justice. A long line of defendants move before the bench does not allow the judge time to ponder the complexities of each individual case. To cope with the situation, many judges have decided upon a penalty for each type of offense. And that penalty is automatically levied after an accused individual is found guilty.

In sentencing, a judge may rely upon his own personal beliefs and values toward punishments. Although imprisonment is a most severe penalty, he may feel that it is the most appropriate one for some offenses and offenders. It is unlikely that a court would consider a fine an adequate punishment for a violent offense. Judges may believe that to protect society, imprisonment is the proper sentence for those who have the potential to repeat or who have repeatedly committed crimes. He may consider that confinement in a penal institution is the best method to discipline, train, or rehabilitate some of those who have breached the legal codes of the community.

Personal motivations can also direct the judge in the making of his sentencing decision. In some localities, financial renumeration is a factor in convicting and levying penalties. Some justices of the peace, for example, receive their income directly from the fines they collect. Where judges are elected, they may strive to court citizen support by reflecting their community's biases or prejudices, or swaying with popular sympathies or antagonisms towards individuals brought before the bench. Most judges attempt to be objective in meting out sentences in order to protect their reputation. They are cognizant that too harsh a sentence may result in a reversal at the appellate level, and too lenient a sentence may free a criminal to commit other offenses. In either event, a reputation may be damaged by a projected image of one who exercises faulty judgment.

Judges also rely on the recommendations and information of others to arrive at sentences. These may be received or sought from juries, policemen, prosecutors, attorneys, and probation officers. Such individuals may be called upon for information (such as the accused's prior criminal record, family status, educational and employment history, and financial, mental, and physical conditions), which could be useful to predict the possibility of rehabilitation.

Judges may hold pre-sentencing hearings, investigations or reports before sentencing felons. Statutes in one-fourth of the states make such reports mandatory for that class of offenses. In the other states, the initiation of those efforts is left to the discretion of the trial judge. Probation officers (usually rushed and overworked) are the principal agents preparing the documents for the investigation. The prosecutors may also submit reports, as they endeavor to fulfill plea bargaining promises. Psychiatric examinations of those who have committed certain offenses (*e.g.*, sex crimes) may be mandatory. Or the judge may request psychiatrists or psychologists to examine the mental state of the convicted felon.

Whether pre-sentencing procedures are conducted (where not mandatory), often depends on the interest that defense attorneys display for their client's fate. The attorneys could submit reports, meet with the judges, probation officers, or prosecutors, and enter pleas or motions that would impress upon the court the necessity for special consideration. However, those endeavors are infrequently performed, for the attorney may be disinterested, busy, or unwilling to expend such energies for those who are unable to pay him adequately for his time (as, for example, indigents who are assigned to him by the court).

The judge does not have to accept the recommendations given him. However, he usually is influenced by the pre-sentencing reports. Studies have shown a high relationship between the recommendations and the judicial dispositions. For example, in California superior courts about 97 percent of the recommendations for (and about 80 percent of recommendations against) probation have been followed. Several reasons have been offered for the high rates of agreement. It may be that probation officers and prosecutors try to "second guess" a judge's personal predisposition, or that the decision was so obviously appropriate that concurrence was the natural outcome. Moreover, judges who request such reports usually have high regard for the professional qualities and competence of those charged with making them.[27]

The deliberation over the appropriate penalty may have taken moments or months. If it were to extend over an appreciable amount of time, the convicted individuals may have been granted bail, or imprisoned (if not permitted release or if unable to raise the necessary funds). Once the penalty has been decided, the defendant stands before the bench to hear the judge pronounce the sentence. That statement of punishment is the final entry in the trial record.

Appeals

Should a losing party feel that an error has been committed during the adjudication procedure, the decision may be appealed. In civil suits, either party of a controversy may initiate an appeal; however, only the defendant in administrative and criminal cases is permitted this opportunity. For capital crimes several states have provisions that make appeals of the verdict automatic, and in such instances the judge may initiate the process on behalf of the convicted individual. All states have rules that permit review of some aspect of sentencing. Most, however, restrict such review to penalties that do not conform with statutory limits. Almost one-quarter of the states permit a convicted individual to appeal his sentence on its merit. Most states require review of death penalties.

Those who appeal must demonstrate that an injurious action had occurred that had affected the outcome of the trial or hearing. One may appeal on a matter of proper pre-trial procedure, such as errors of charge, failure to be told of legal rights, forced confessions, inadequate time to prepare a defense before the case was scheduled to be heard, and that the court or administrative agency lacked the jurisdiction to hear the case. One may contend that the outcome of the trial was adversely affected by the composition of the jury. It may be claimed that the panel was not representative of the characteristics of the population or of the defendant's race, or that the attorney's challenges to the selection of some jurymen were inaccurately denied by the judge.

An appeal may be made contesting an action of the judge. He may not have dutifully maintained an atmosphere conducive to sober and objective consideration, especially in those cases that have aroused community emotions and hostilities. Perhaps, it might be argued, the judge improperly denied motions to postpone the trial to a calmer day or grant a change of venue; or he did not sequester the jury to isolate it from receiving information other than that which had been introduced in the courtroom; or that he added to the sensationalism of the atmosphere by permitting television cameras, lights, photographers, and reporters to be present throughout the proceedings. In addition, the judge's instructions to the jury as to what it may find, what verdicts it may reach, and what evidence is relevant could be challenged.

Judges' and hearing officers' rulings on attorneys' motions and objections, on the admissability of evidence and witness testimony, or on some technical procedure may be pointed to as sufficient cause for appeal. Excessively harsh penalties may be contested. Attacks may be made on the validity of the law under which the controversy arose. For any point raised in challenge, the appellant must show that it had served to prejudicially affect his cause.

Many believe that anyone who has lost a case and has cause to feel that prejudicial treatment was present should appeal. Yet, not all who qualify can or do appeal. Those who do not know that they are entitled to an appeal, or how to handle the technical complexities of the procedure (and can not obtain the services of those who do), rarely go beyond the trial stage. Those who cannot afford to await the delays or the costs accompanying appeals will not do so. Appeals are expensive. Transcripts must be obtained, briefs must be filed in correct form, court fees must be met, and lawyers who know the proper procedures must be paid for their services and expenses. Should the aggrieved party perceive that there is minimal chance for success, he will not proceed (as, for example, when a court has a reputation of deferring to the opinions of specialized and technically trained agency personnel).

If the resources are available and the possibility for success seems reasonable, then persons will most probably initiate appeals. Often the decision to file is made by the attorney, who does it pro forma, or is convinced that a better decision can be obtained. Individuals may be assisted and prompted by permanent or ad hoc interest groups that have the resources and the desire to test the validity of a law and the propriety of its enforcement. Corporations that do not wish to readily acquire the stigma of guilt, or that wish to delay the execution of a judgment against them, may be motivated to go the route of appeals.

Appeals are generally initiated with a petition directed to the proper court. One files a notice of appeal, transcripts of the trial record, and a brief that outlines the reason for appeal. This must be done within a prescribed time period after the trial or hearing. The respondent (*i.e.*, the party against whom the appeal is taken) files an answering brief, setting forth the reasons why the decision of the lower court or administrative agency should not be reversed. For example, an agency whose jurisdiction is questioned sets forth the facts upon which it relied in assuming jurisdiction.

There is little further preparation required at this stage, for appellate judges usually confine their attention to the prior written records. They do not frequently hear additional testimony or review further evidence (although they may permit short oral arguments in support of the reasons for appeal). That the judges focus on the documents partly explains why attorneys are anxious to get certain data included in the trial record, and why administrative decisions are written in fine detail.

Where review is not mandatory, or the statutes are silent, the decision to accept an appeals case is left to the discretion of an appellate court. Appellate judges may establish their own criteria or rules for accepting cases. They may require that all previous remedies have been exhausted (for example, that an appellant has first petitioned for review to all appeal boards in an administrative agency). Technical criteria may have to be met. Courts, for example, may refuse to hear a case if the appeal was not filed within the prescribed time, or if the briefs were incorrectly written. The proper form of relief may not have been asked for by the appellant. The judges may not feel that the party is sufficiently adversely affected. For example, they may refuse to entertain a case they perceive only to be designed to test the validity of a rule or administrative procedure.

While awaiting the acceptance, hearing, and decision of the appellate court, the convicted criminal may apply for bail. The decision to permit bail rests with the judge of the trial court in which he was found guilty. Should a death or monetary penalty have been imposed, the execution of that penalty will be suspended during the appeal process. Should he have been sentenced to imprisonment and granted bail, the sentence does not begin until the final appellate decision has been reached. If he had not been granted bail and was imprisoned during the interim, then usually (but not always) the time spent behind bars is credited towards the completion of his sentence.

Should an appeal court agree to review a decision, the controversy is heard by a panel of justices. The aura of the appellate courtroom is quite different from that of the trial courtroom. The drama that arises from the appearance of defendants, plaintiffs, witnesses, etc., is absent as a pressure on judicial decision making. In its place is substituted another set of influences.

The fact that they are not making the original determination on the controversy before them serves to reinforce the sense of responsibility that the appellate justices bring into their deliberations. Perhaps the first pressure felt by the justices is that of upholding the decisions of the lower courts, for a major responsibility of the higher courts is to maintain the integrity of the system of adjudication. To overturn decisions may be considered a rebuke to the objectivity and wisdom of judges and juries. Indeed, such pressure may be intensified when lower court judges are friends or are held in high esteem by the legal community. The responsibility of maintaining system integrity may, conversely, lead to a reversal of a lower court decision. Although appellate justices are rarely favorably inclined to overturning the prior decision, they may feel compelled to do so where an error of procedure or the lack of impartiality has been demonstrated.

Another pressure recognized by the justices is the responsibility of the appellate court to maintain the continuity and uniformity of rules so that there is predictability within the adjudicatory process. The stable operation of any political system depends on the members of the community knowing what the rules are and that sanctions will be imposed when those are broken. More particularly, the stable operation of the adjudicatory subsystem depends on its members (*i.e.*, policemen, prosecutors, lawyers, and judges) knowing the rules in order that they can bring charges against violators, and prosecute or defend those individuals charged.

Because of these awesome responsibilities, the judges often look beyond the written record of the immediate controversy. They search for relevant precedents, by examining earlier decisions of the courts of their state, their sister states, or those of the national hierarchy. Law review articles, which suggest appropriate precedents and analyze alternative decisions of similar controversies, may also be read. Amicus curie briefs may be invited to provide analysis of the possible consequences the prevailing decision or alternative decisions may engender.[28] To aid him in the gathering of such additional information, each justice enlists the assistance of the law clerk assigned to him.

Though the justices seek the additional information, the sources of that data are taken into consideration and weighed subjectively in their deliberations. They may weigh more heavily the precedents set by state courts that hold eminent reputations, nearby courts that have close cultural contacts and common sectional problems, or those courts that are empowered to overrule their decisions (*e.g.*, Supreme Court of the United States). Extra consideration may be given to those law journals that are sponsored by prestigious law schools, and/or the judges' alma mater, as well as those that have published articles written by one (or more) of the justices. They may look favorably upon the arguments included in well written briefs or those posited by attorneys who have earned the respect of the legal community for outstanding competence. The reception accorded to ideas presented in amicus curiae briefs may be related to the judges' image of the group, their perception of the group's importance to the controversy, and the group's stature within the constituency. In addition, the perceptions, energies, knowledge, interest, and thoroughness of the law clerks (who screen the various inputs) combine to form an important influence on the judges.

Personal characteristics are important factors in the decision making process of all judges. The principal research on the relationship between the background factors of state appellate court judges and their decisions has been undertaken by Stuart S. Nagel.[29] One set of factors he has examined included the justices' socioeconomic, religious, and ethnic origins. Those judges who were members of racial, ethnic, or religious minority groups and whose families were of low socio-economic status were shown to have a more "liberal" perspective (in that they were more prone to favor the defense in criminal cases, the injured party in motor vehicle cases, the debtor in creditor-debtor cases, the claimant in industrial related cases, the administrative agency in business regulation controversies, and labor in labor-management disputes) than were those from white, Protestant, higher socio-economic status families. Nagel has suggested that those who had not grown up within a favored societal position may have developed predispositions of empathy towards the plight and problems of the "underdog."

Nagel also examined the political party affiliation of the judges and concluded that there was a relationship between their affiliation and their voting decision. This, he felt, was due to the common backgrounds and values shared by persons affiliating with the same political party. Yet, such a relationship cannot be entirely explained in terms of the judges' personal background traits. For it was seen that under different methods of judicial selection the rate that judges voted with their party colleagues on the bench varied. Nagle found that when judges were elected to their positions there appeared to be a high rate of party consensus; and where judges were appointed party agreement was less frequent.[30]

A judge's occupational background was also seen to be related to judicial decision making. Most justices had been practicing attorneys and had brought to their positions on the bench predispositions gained from their experience in arguing cases for certain types of clients. For example, those who had been insurance and corporate lawyers appear to be more positively prone toward insurance companies or business parties; and former prosecutors appear to be less predisposed toward the defense. Few judges have had public administrative experience. Thus, they may not feel competent to overturn those decisions made by specialized and technically trained administrative hearing examiners.

After the records and briefs have been read and the arguments heard, the justices retire to deliberate. In many of the states, the decision is reached by a vote (after discussion) and the chief justice assigns one judge to write the court's opinion. In other states, an opinion is written first by one assigned judge; and a vote is then taken to affirm, reject, or modify the written opinion. During the deliberations, deference may be paid to the opinion of the judge who is considered by his colleagues to be more experienced, or more knowledgeable about the subject, and who is most persuasive.[31]

A person may have more than one opportunity to appeal a decision. He may petition the appellate court to rehear his case; but more frequently he seeks redress from a higher level appellate court. For example, an appeal of an intermediate appellate court's decision would be directed to the state court of last resort. Once the highest state appellate court has made a decision, the appellant may endeavor to bring his case into the federal court system.

Petitions (*i.e.*, technically requests for writs of certiorari) can be made to the Supreme Court. The appellant must show that his case involved an infringement of an important principle of the federal constitution. The Court is free to decide if a "federal question" of substance is indeed involved; and, indeed, it may grant removal of cases from a state court to a federal court when appeals demonstrate that a continuence of the trial in the state court may produce a clear threat to a constitutional right. Conversely, Supreme Court justices may decide not to accept the petition if they have reason to believe that the review system provided by the state courts is adequate. Most federal judges are predisposed to respect the independence of state judicial actions, and rarely will interfere with the adjudicatory process of the states.

Refusal by a higher court to hear an appeal has the effect of affirming the lower court decision. Agreement to hear an appeal may result in acceptance, modification, or rejection of the lower court's decision. Should the appellate court decide to remand the controversy to a lower court, it would set guidelines as to what should be done.

Appeals to the Executive

When appeals to the judicial system fail, clemency may be sought from the governor. Petitioners may request a pardon, commutation, reprieve, or parole. A pardon erases the legal consequences of the crime for the party found guilty, giving the appearance that a conviction had never occurred. Granting a pardon, in about half of the states, is left to the sole discretion of the chief executive; in the others, the concurrence of some type of pardon board is required. Several states permit the governor to commute, or reduce a sentence; as for example, reducing a death sentence to life imprisonment. A reprieve postpones the execution of a penalty for a brief period, allowing the appellant additional time to petition the courts for review. A parole is a conditional release of a convicted individual who has served part of the term for which he was sentenced to prison. The responsibility for this last action is usually shared by the governor with an established state probation board.

The governor also participates in the adjudicatory process in matters of extradition. Extradition is the returning of an accused person to a state from which he had fled (where a charge was brought against him). The process begins with the governor of the state in which a crime has been committed requesting the governor of the state to which the accused has taken refuge to "deliver up" the fugitive. The fugitive may petition the latter governor not to grant the extradition request. The chief executive may summarily send him back, grant him sanctuary, or hold hearings to ascertain the merits of the arguments.[32]

Public Attitudes Toward the Function of Rule Adjudication

"Law and order"—a simplistic slogan—helped carry a candidate into the White House, in 1968. That millions of voters could rally around such a slogan was an indication that the function of adjudication was not being performed to the satisfaction of many Americans. Dissatisfaction may always have been present, but the turbulent events of the sixties served as catalysts to bring negative attitudes into sharp and clear focus. Riots in the cities, increasing crime rates, campus disorders, and other events that shattered domestic tranquillity broadened the scope and depth of public discontent.

While some groups or individuals were actively hostile to law enforcement agents, others were looking to them for relief. But the adjudicatory system was perceived by neither as responding satisfactorily. A nationwide poll conducted in the spring of 1971 showed that 77 percent of the adult population thought that the system of justice in America was not working well.[33] Probes into public attitudes discovered the broad scope of underlying dissatisfaction. No sphere of adjudication escaped criticism. While the most vociferous discontent was directed toward the handling of criminal controversies, expressions of frustration also were heard concerning the spheres of civil and administrative processes.

Clarence N. Stone has identified four major dimensions of contention found within the public. One dimension of this conflict surrounded the issue of how to balance the rights of individuals with the security, safety, and order of the society. The second was whether all economic and racial groupings within the community receive equitable treatment by the agencies of adjudication. The clash over the causes and prevention of violative behavior was the third dimension. The last was the question over the proper role of adjudicative agencies.[34]

While an increasing number of persons have become indignant over the institutional invasion of individual rights, an increasing number of others have become concerned that governmental action has been neither far-reaching nor fast-moving in the protection of public security, safety, and order. Organizations of welfare mothers have decried administrative adjudication that has upheld the premise that:

> in exchange for assistance given to them the recipients must give up control over their lives and subject themselves to a series of controls and regulations of any work they do, any movement or travel arrangements they make, their living arrangements, family relations, and how they spend the money they receive.[35]

Civil rights leaders have denounced southern state courts for having refused to rectify governmental activities that have limited the political and individual rights of blacks. Rioters and protesters have witnessed criminal court procedures become oriented to mass justice at the expense of individual rights. It has been reported, for example, that in a single day in Detroit, 1,000 defendants were arraigned; while an all-day grand jury session in Newark handed down indictments naming 100 or more defendants, after an average deliberation of less than two minutes per case.[36] The report on Detroit further highlighted that

> there was little chance to screen out those cases that could best be handled out of court or which could not survive trial. Defense counsel were not allowed to represent defendants during arraignment. Some judges failed to advise the defendants of their legal rights. After one group-arraignment, a Detroit judge told the next group of defendants, "You heard what I said to them. The same things apply to you."[37]

However, public dissatisfaction with the adjudication function has not been activated by the concern that there has been an institutional invasion of individual rights. On the contrary, nearly two-thirds of a nationwide sample appear to have been more disturbed over the loss of public safety, security, and order than over the loss of constitutional rights. Three-fourths of those respondents agreed that every American should be required to be finger-printed for governmental files; half of them approved of police stopping and searching any individual who appeared "suspicious"; and two-fifths supported police wire-tapping and holding those under suspicion up to twenty-four hours before initiating procedures for bail.

Throughout this chapter it has been indicated that there is a basis for concern that lower economic groupings are disadvantaged when utilizing the cumbersome, complex, and technical procedures of adjudication. Affecting favorable decisions in administrative controversies is more difficult for the poor, who do not have the access, familiarity, skill and rapport with administrative agents and proceedings, than for those who have established through experience and long standing interactions the capabilities to deal effectively with the system. Lacking the resources to hire lawyers and pay court fees, or unable to afford the time spent in court and the delay in awaiting renumeration for damages, the poor all too infrequently utilize the court process for the redress of civil grievances.

Moreover, a large proportion of the population recognize that all economic and racial groupings do not receive equitable treatment by the agencies of adjudication in criminal proceedings. Charges have been made that discrimination exists in practices from the arrest stage through the decision stage of adjudication. Surveys have shown that between 50 and 86 percent of blacks perceive that police engage in discriminatory and excessively brutal practices during arrests. Seventy percent of blacks have expressed a belief that a black man is far more likely than a white man to be convicted and sentenced for a crime. More significantly, overwhelming majorities of blacks (84 percent) and whites (77 percent) hold beliefs that the poor are more likely to be convicted and sentenced for a crime than are the wealthy.[38]

The focus of concern over the causes and prevention of violative behavior has generally been directed to the leniency and laxity of adjudicative agencies. While those concerned acknowledge that individuals violate rules because of a breakdown of societal and cultural norms or for personal, selfish motivations, there is a prevailing belief that adjudicatory agents are failing to deter violative behavior. For example, the deplorable conditions found in substandard rental properties have been attributed to the failure of administrative agents to enforce housing codes or initiate adjudicatory procedures against landlords who fail to comply with code regulations. Moreover, there is little stimulus for the landlord to comply when he finds that those sanctions applied against him for violations are minimal in comparison to the cost of upgrading his property. Civil court proceedings have not acted to discourage civil controversies from arising. There is little compulsion for civil wrongdoers to quickly correct their actions. For there is a recognition that a high probability exists that aggrieved parties will not see the advantage of initiating civil proceedings that are expensive to utilize, delayed in action, and devoid of enforcement capabilities.

The nationwide sample uncovered widespread agreement that the adjudicative process did not deter crime. Seventy-five percent of the sample thought that convicted criminals were let off too easily; 68 percent felt that the quality of justice was seriously impaired by the lengthy delay in bringing accused individuals to trial; and 40 percent thought that lenient judges were contributing to the increase in crime. Respondents volunteered such comments as "Judges should take a harder line," and "Judges should stand for the majority of people, not for the minority." Although there was a consensus that the prison system is in need of reform (for example, over two-thirds believed that prison rioters' complaints are probably well founded), it is unlikely that an effort to abolish the system would be supported. Most respondents saw value to preventive detention. Nearly three-fourths of white respondents supported that concept, and approximately one-half of the blacks did.

The last dimension of contention within the public is over the proper role of adjudicative agencies. Questions have been raised about the effectiveness of an administrative agency in regulating groups or businesses with which they have developed close working relationships; and about the propriety of agents adjudicating controversies arising from the execution of rules they themselves have made. The passive role of the civil courts has been questioned. Should such courts be active and accessible arenas for the protection of those who do not have resources or social standing, yet nevertheless who have legitimate civil grievances? Or should they be inert arenas to which disputants come who cannot settle their controversies elsewhere? And questions are raised about the role of the agents of criminal adjudication. Are they to be the protectors of society's order and well being or the defenders of individual, constitutional rights? Are they to undertake a punitive or a rehabilitative role? And are they to assume a role of neutrality from public demands, or one of accountability to public sentiment in arbitrating the controversies before them?

Such widespread dissatisfaction may reflect a widespread sense of frustration—people feel that they lack the ability to affect change and that the adjudication system is not readily amenable to change. The traditional methods of articulating dissatisfaction (*i.e.*, voting, impeachment, or recall) seem fruitless. None is geared to settle any of the four major dimensions of contention within the public. Each merely permits the removal of a judge, who by his behavior has provoked a high degree of negative reaction. New structures have been instituted in several states and localities to provide channels for the expression of grievances. These have included police review boards and commissions on judicial qualifications, which are empowered to handle complaints lodged against the respective agents of adjudication. The structures have the potential to recommend changes to alleviate tensions; in receiving complaints, they are apprised of those public demands that are not being met. However, the brief history of such boards and commissions has demonstrated that they have not realized such potential. Instead, they have shown a propensity to limit their attentions to a narrow range of activities. Each has reviewed individual complaints against specific agents, evaluated the evidence and recommended whether disciplinary action should be taken. Commentators have maintained that these bodies have been overly concerned with the efficient administration of their respective agencies, with upholding the morale of professional personnel, and with sustaining public respect for the existing adjudicatory process.[39] Thus, it has been contended that the panels have offered palliatives rather than remedies for the underlying dimensions of dissatisfaction. However, as long as the public cannot agree upon an effective remedy, it can only be expected that palliatives will be proposed.

Chapter X Footnotes

1. Charles J. Desmond, "Current Problems of State Court Administration," *Columbia Law Review*, LXV (April 1965), pp. 561–68. See also Institute of Judicial Administration, *State Trial Courts of General Jurisdiction Calendar Status Study—1965: Personal Injury Cases* (New York: Institute of Judical Administration, 1965).

2. See, for example, David J. Saari, "Open Doors to Justice: An Overview of Financing Justice in America," *Judicature*, L (May 1967), pp. 296–308.

3. *Gideon v. Wainwright*, 372 U.S. 335 (1963); *Escobedo v. Illinois*, 378 U.S. 478 (1964); and *Miranda v. Arizona*, 384 U.S. 436 (1966).

4. See, for example, Kenneth M. Dolbeare, *Trial Courts in Urban Politics: State Court Policy Impact and Functions in a Local Political System* (New York: John Wiley and Sons, Inc., 1967).

5. See, for example, Robert S. Lorch, *Democratic Process and Administrative Law* (Detroit: Wayne State University Press, 1969).

6. See Nathan Goldman, *The Differential Selection of Juvenile Offenders for Court Appearance* (New York: National Research and Information Center of the National Council on Crime and Delinquency, 1963); and Stanton Wheeler, ed., *Controlling Delinquency* (New York: John Wiley and Sons, Inc., 1967).

7. John A. Gardiner, "Police Enforcement of Traffic Laws: A Comparative Analysis," paper delivered at Annual Meeting of the American Political Science Association, 1966.

8. Dolbeare, *Trial Courts*; Goldman, *Differential Selection*; Stuart S. Nagel, "The Tipped Scales of American Justice," *Transaction* (May/June 1966), pp. 4–9; Stuart S. Nagel, "Disparities in Criminal Procedure," *U.C.L.A. Law Review*, XIV (1967), pp. 1272–1305; Herbert Jacob, "Politics and Criminal Prosecution in New Orleans," in Kenneth N. Vines and Herbert Jacob, *Studies in Judicial Politics, Tulane Studies in Political Science*, Vol. VIII (1963), pp. 77–98; and Jerome E. Carlen, *et al.*, "Civil Justice and the Poor," *Law and Society Review*, I (November 1966), pp. 85–89.

9. See, for example, Kenneth N. Vines, "Federal District Judges and Race Relations Cases in the South," *Journal of Politics*, XXVI (May 1964), pp. 337–57; and Kenneth N. Vines, "Southern State Supreme Courts and Race Relations," *Western Political Quarterly*, XVIII (March 1965), pp. 5–18.

10. Abraham S. Blumberg, "The Criminal Court as Organization and Communication System," in Richard Quinney, ed., *Crime and Justice in Society* (Boston: Little, Brown and Company, 1969), p. 280.

11. See Donald J. Newman, *Conviction: The Determination of Guilt or Innocence without Trial* (Boston: Little, Brown and Company, 1966).

12. See, for example, The President's Commission on Law Enforcement and Administration of Justice, *Task Force Report: The Courts* (Washington, D.C.: Government Printing Office, 1967), p. 4.

13. As quoted in Brian A. Grosman, *The Prosecutor: An Inquiry into the Exercise of Discretion* (Toronto: University of Toronto Press, 1969), p. 53.

14. As quoted in Ronald Goldfarb, *Ransom* (New York: Harper and Row Publishers, 1965), p. IX.

15. *Task Force Report: The Courts*, p. 39.

16. Maurice Rosenberg, *The Pretrial Conference and Effective Justice* (New York: Columbia University Press, 1964).

17. See, for example, *Task Force Report: The Courts*, p. 147.

18. John H. Vanderzell, "The Jury as a Community Cross-Section," *Western Political Quarterly*, XIX (March 1966), pp. 136–49.

19. For example, the Court has stated that women cannot be excluded from juries because of their sex, *Ballard v. United States*, 329 U.S. 187 (1946); that Mexican–Americans cannot be excluded, *Hernandez v. Texas*, 347 U.S. 475 (1954); and that blacks cannot be excluded, *Patton v. Mississippi*, 332 U.S. 463 (1947), and *Carter v. Jury Commissioners of Greene County*, 396 U.S. 320 (1970).

20. *Thiel v. Southern Pacific Company*, 328 U.S. 217 (1946).

21. See *Atkins v. Texas*, 325 U.S. 398 (1945); and *Cassell v. Texas*, 339 U.S. 282 (1950).

22. The most comprehensive study of juries is Harry Kalven, Jr., and Hans Zeisel, *The American Jury* (Boston: Little, Brown and Company, 1966).

23. Stuart S. Nagel, *The Legal Process from a Behavioral Perspective* (Homewood, Ill.: The Dorsey Press, 1969). See also: Arthur Lewis Wood, *Criminal Lawyer* (New Haven: College and University Press, 1967).

24. James L. Blawie and Marilyn J. Blawie, "The Judicial Decision," *Western Political Quarterly*, XVIII (September 1965), p. 590.

25. Theodore L. Becker, "A Survey Study of Hawaiian Judges: The Effect on Decisions of Judicial Role Variations," *American Political Science Review*, LX (September 1966), pp. 677–80; and his "Judicial Structure and its Political Functioning in Society," *Journal of Politics*, XXIX (May 1967), pp. 302–33.

26. Dean Jaros and Robert I. Mendelsohn, "The Judicial Role and Sentencing Behavior," *Midwest Journal of Political Science*, XI (November 1967), pp. 471–88.

27. Robert M. Carter and Leslie T. Wilkens, "Some Factors in Sentencing Policy," *The Journal of Criminal Law, Criminology and Police Science*, LVIII (December 1967), pp. 503–14.

28. See, for example, Lucius J. Barker, "Third Parties in Litigation," *Journal of Politics*, XXIX (February 1967), pp. 41–69.

29. Nagel, *The Legal Process, passim.*

30. There is agreement with Nagel's findings in several studies. See, for example, S. Sidney Ulmer, "The Political Party Variable on the Michigan Supreme Court," *Journal of Public Law*, XI (1962), pp. 352–62. Some disagreement with the findings may be found in David W. Adamany, "The Party Variable in Judges' Voting," *American Political Science Review*, LXIII (March 1969), pp. 57–73.

31. For an example of the process see Robert J. Frye, *The Alabama Supreme Court: An Institutional View* (University: Bureau of Public Administration, University of Alabama, 1969).

32. The principle that a governor may utilize his discretion in granting a request for extradition was established by the decision reached by the Supreme Court in *Kentucky v. Dennison*, 24 How. 66 (1861).

33. *Newsweek*, March 8, 1971, pp. 39–43. All statistics noted in this section (unless otherwise cited) are derived from the nationwide public opinion survey, conducted by The Gallup Organization, as reported in *Newsweek*.

34. Clarence N. Stone, "Patterns of Voting on Mallory, Durham, and other Criminal Procedure Issues in Congress," in Carl Beck, ed., *Law and Justice* (Durham, N.C.: Duke University Press, 1970), pp. 95–120.

35. Paul Jacobs, *Prelude to Riot: A View of Urban America from the Bottom* (New York: Vintage Books, 1967), p. 70.

36. National Advisory Commission On Civil Disorders, *Report* (Washington, D.C.: Government Printing Office, 1968), p. 341.

37. Ibid.

38. In addition to *Newsweek*, previously cited, see *Task Force Report: The Police*, pp. 146–49.

39. See, for example, Jacobs, *Prelude to Riot*, and Sidney H. Asch, *Police Authority and the Rights of the Individual* (New York: Arco Publishing Company, Inc., 1971).

Name Index

Abrams, Charles, 350n, 351n
Adamany, David W., 395n
Adrian, Charles R., 95n, 274–75, 278, 307n, 308n
Agger, Robert E., 300, 309n
Agnew, Spiro T., 196
Akers, Ronald, 237, 256n
Alford, Robert R., 35n
Allen, Tip H., Jr., 57n
Almond, Gabriel A., 2, 3, 5n, 59, 63, 93n, 94n, 95n, 96, 124, 130n, 132n, 133, 160n
Althoft, Phillip, 200n
Altschuler, Alan A., 346, 352n
Anderson, Stanley V., 351n
Anton, Thomas J., 330, 350n
Asch, Sidney H., 395n

Bachrach, Peter, 300, 309n
Baer, Michael A., 130n, 172n, 200n
Bailey, John, 166
Bain, Henry M., 95n
Baker, Charles W., 208
Baltzell, E. Digby, 298, 309n
Banfield, Edward C., 35n, 160n, 161n, 168, 187, 199n, 200n, 201n, 299, 307n, 309n
Baratz, Morton S., 300, 309n
Barber, James David, 163, 164, 165, 168, 199n, 200n, 201n, 223, 255n
Barker, Lucius J., 131n, 395n
Bartholomew, Paul C., 239, 256n
Beck, Carl, 395n
Becker, Theodore L., 395n
Bell, Charles G., 255n
Berelson, Bernard R., 94n
Berkley, George E., 83, 95n
Beyle, Thad L., 350n
Blank, Blanche D., 200n
Blawie, James L., 395n
Blawie, Marilyn J., 395n
Blondes, Leonard, 67, 98

Blumberg, Abraham S., 365, 394n
Boesel, David, 146, 161n
Bone, Hugh A., 95n, 131n
Bowhay, James H., 255n
Bowman, Lewis, 135n, 160n, 200n
Boyd, William D. J., 208, 254n, 307n
Boynton, G. R., 135n, 160n, 200n
Bryan, Frank M., 210, 254n
Bullitt, Stimson, 161n
Burke, Edmund, 132n
Burns, James MacGregor, 200n

Campbell, Angus, 94n, 160n, 161n
Cantor, Edward R., 270, 307n
Carlen, Jerome E., 394n
Carmichael, Stokely, 126, 127, 132n, 343, 346, 352n
Carr, Joe C., 208
Carter, Richard F., 95n
Carter, Robert M., 395n
Casstevens, Thomas W., 309n
Chafee, John, 243, 331, 350n
Childs, Richard S., 35n
Claque, Christopher, 95n
Clark, Kenneth, 340, 342, 351n, 352n
Clark, Terry N., 275, 307n
Cloward, Richard A., 336–37, 345, 351n, 352n
Coleman, James S., 5n, 133, 160n
Collier, David B., 308n
Collins, John, 86
Colombotos, John, 94n
Conway, Margaret M., 161n
Cornwell, Elmer E., 57n
Crain, Robert L., 95n
Crotty, William J., 175, 200n
Crouch, Winston W., 309n
Cutright, Phillips, 75, 76, 94n, 146, 161n

Dahl, Robert A., 60, 93n, 298, 309n
Daley, Richard, 137, 165, 187
Davidoff, Paul, 342, 352n

Davis, Harry R., 307n
Dawson, Richard E., 255n
Delaney, William, 201n
Desmond, Charles J., 393n
Dewey, Richard, 336, 351n
Dierthick, Martha, 308n
Dillon, John F., 11, 306n
Dilworth, Richard, 326
Dimock, Gladys O., 256n, 350n, 351n
Dimock, Marshall E., 256n, 350n, 351n
Dines, Allen, 254n
Dohrenwend, Barbara Snell, 94n
Dohrenwend, Bruce P., 94n
Dolan, Paul, 341, 351n
Dolbeare, Kenneth M., 394n
Donaldson, William, 200n
Downes, Bryan T., 278, 279, 308n
Downs, Anthony, 348–49, 352n
Duncombe, Herbert Sydney, 35n, 201n, 307n, 349n
Dunn, Delmer D., 256n
Dye, Thomas R., 210, 254n, 255n, 267, 307n, 308n

Eddy, Susan, 309n
Eldersveld, Samuel J., 136, 160n, 165, 199n
Ellis, James R., 256n
Epstein, Leon D., 85n, 95n
Ernst, Charles F., 336, 351n
Eulau, Heinz, 108n, 131n, 255n, 267, 276, 279n, 307n, 308n
Eyestone, Robert, 267, 276, 307n

Field, John O., 35n
Fiellin, Alan, 201n
Fishburne, Charles C., Jr., 34n
Flinn, Thomas A., 136, 160n, 200n
Fortier, Edward, 255n
Fowler, Edmund P., 35n, 275–76, 307n
Francis, Wayne L., 255n
Frederickson, H. George, 201n
Freedman, Robert S., 57n
Frieden, Bernard J., 308n
Friesema, H. Paul, 305–06, 309n
Fritchler, A. Lee, 256n, 308n
Froman, Lewis A., Jr., 53, 57n, 124, 131n
Frye, Robert J., 395n

Gallup, George, 80, 94n
Gamson, William A., 299–300, 309n
Gardiner, John A., 394n
Gellhorn, Walter, 95n, 351n
Gerth, H. H., 349n
Gerwin, Donald, 161n, 215, 255n

Gibson, Frank K., 201n
Gilbert, Charles E., 95n
Glazer, Nathan, 339, 351n
Glick, Henry Robert, 94n
Goldfarb, Ronald, 394n
Goldman, Nathan, 394n
Goldman, Sheldon, 198n
Goldrich, Daniel, 309n
Goodman, Jay S., 57n
Green, William J., Jr., 165
Greenstein, Fred I., 57n
Greenstone, J. David, 161n
Grodzins, Morton, 289, 290n, 308n
Grosman, Brian A., 394n

Haber, Herbert, 333
Hadden, Jeffrey K., 95n
Hagensick, A. Clarke, 141, 161n
Hahn, Harlan, 95n, 131n, 309n
Hamilton, Charles V., 126, 127, 132n, 343, 346, 352n
Hamilton, Howard D., 95n
Hanson, Bertil L., 131n, 250, 251, 256n
Hanson, Royce, 58n
Harman, B. Douglas, 256n, 308n
Harris, Joseph P., 95n
Hatcher, Richard, 85
Hawkins, Brett W., 35n, 58n, 254n, 308n
Heard, Alexander, 200n, 201n
Hecock, Donald S., 95n
Herring, Pendleton, 122, 131n, 132n
Hirschfield, Robert S., 173, 200n
Hjelm, Victor S., 255n
Hodges, Robert W., 164n, 199n
Hofferbert, Richard I., 254n, 255n
Hopkins, Jeannette, 340, 342, 351n, 352n
Huckshorn, Robert J., 225, 255n
Humphrey, Hubert, 196
Hunter, Floyd, 297, 299, 309n

Ippolito, Dennis, 200n
Irwin, Theodore, 132n

Jacob, Herbert, 130n, 201n, 210, 254n, 394n
Jacobs, Clyde E., 131n
Jacobs, Paul, 395n
James, George A., 201n
Janovitz, Morris, 201n
Jaros, Dean, 395n
Jennings, M. Kent, 60, 93n, 136, 160n, 161n, 299, 309n
Jewell, Malcolm E., 110n, 191, 201n, 211–12, 254n, 255n
Jones, David, 95n, 132n

Kalven, Harry, Jr., 394n
Katz, David, 136, 160n
Kaufman, Herbert, 299, 309n, 347, 348, 349n, 351n, 352n
Keefe, William J., 200n
Kessel, John H., 35n
Key, V. O., Jr., 94n, 124, 132n, 194, 201n
Kingdon, John W., 95n

Ladd, Everett Carll, Jr., 277, 308n
Lane, Robert E., 94n
Latham, Earl, 161n
Lazarsfeld, Paul F., 94n
Le Blanc, Hugh L., 225, 255n
Levin, Murray B., 86, 95n
Levy, Leonard W., 35n
Liebman, Charles, 35n
Lindsay, John, 71, 72, 91, 123, 187, 328, 350n
Lineberry, Herbert L., 275–76, 307n
Lineberry, Robert L., 35n
Lipsitz, Lewis, 95n
Lipsky, Michael, 345, 352n
Lockard, Duane, 201n
Longley, Lawrence D., 117, 131n
Lorch, Robert S., 394n
Loring, William L., 336, 351n
Luttberg, Norman R., 130n
Lyford, Joseph P., 166, 200n
Lynd, Helen, 297, 308n, 309n
Lynd, Robert, 297, 308n, 309n

Maier, Henry W., 263, 307n
Manner, Lynder, 307n
Marshall, Chief Justice, 48
Martin, Roscoe, 245, 256n
Massotti, Louis H., 95n
Maxwell, James A., 267, 307n
McAnaw, Richard L., 201n
McPhee, William N., 94n
Mendelsohn, Robert I., 395n
Merton, Robert K., 161n, 276, 308n
Milbrath, Lester W., 94n
Mills, C. Wright, 349n
Mills, Warner E., Jr., 307n
Monsma, Stephen V., 255n
Morey, Roy D., 231, 255n
Morris, Robert, 308n
Mosher, Frederick C., 337–38, 350n, 351n
Moynihan, Daniel P., 142, 161n, 338
Munger, Frank J., 299, 309n

Nagel, Stuart S., 377, 387–88, 394n, 395n
Newland, Chester A., 351n

Newman, Donald J., 394n
Novograd, R. Joseph, 256n, 350n, 351n
Nowlin, William, 277, 308n

O'Alemberte, Talbot, 34n
Ogul, Morris S., 200n
Ohlin, Lloyd E., 336–37, 351n
Olson, David J., 350n

Patterson, Samuel C., 110n, 160n, 166, 172, 192, 199n, 200n, 201n
Peattie, Lisa R., 340, 351n
Perlman, Robert, 95n, 132n
Pisciotte, Joseph P., 255n
Piven, Frances F., 345, 352n
Polsby, Nelson, 299, 309n
Pomper, Gerald, 174, 200n
Powell, G. Bingham, Jr., 5n
Press, Charles, 95n
Prewitt, Kenneth, 108n, 131n, 255n, 277, 279, 308n
Price, Charles M., 255n

Quinney, Donald J., 394n

Rainwater, Lee, 351n
Ranney, Austin, 85n, 95n
Ransone, Coleman B., Jr., 57n, 230
Reichley, James, 350n
Reynolds, Harry W., Jr., 77, 94n, 118, 131n, 282, 283n, 284, 308n
Rice, Ross R., 309n
Riordon, William L., 137, 138, 161n
Robinson, James R., 254n
Roche, John P., 35n
Rogers, David, 346, 350n, 352n
Rose, Alex, 123
Rosenberg, Bernard, 131n
Rosenberg, Maurice, 394n
Rosenthal, Donald B., 95n
Rosenthal, Jack, 254n
Rossi, Peter H., 199n
Rustin, Bayard, 126, 132n

Saari, David J., 393n
Sapolsky, Harvey M., 131n, 309n
Savard, William, 95n
Sayre, Wallace S., 299, 309n, 349n
Schattschneider, E. E., 124, 131n
Schlessinger, Joseph A., 277, 308n
Schnore, Leo F., 35n
Scoble, Harry M., 35n
Scott, Thomas M., 35n
Seaver, Robert C., 348, 352n
Segal, Morley, 256n, 308n

Sharkansky, Ira, 254n, 255n
Sherbenov, Edgar L., 35n
Siegel, Paul M., 199n
Sigel, Roberta S., 305–06, 309n
Silberman, Charles, 351n
Slayton, William L., 336, 351n
Small, Norman J., 256n
Smith, Paul A., 62n, 93n
Snowden, James H., 58n
Sokolow, Alvin D., 131n
Sorauf, Frank J., 199, 201n
Sprengel, Donald P., 330, 350n
Steiner, Gilbert V., 335, 351n
Stephens, Jack H., 341, 351n
Stokes, Carl, 85
Stokes, Sybil L., 57n
Stone, Clarence N., 344, 352n, 390, 395n
Swanson, Bert E., 200n, 309n
Swanson, Wayne R., 57n
Sweetser, Frank L., 336, 351n

Templeton, Fredric, 64, 94n
Thiessen, Victor, 95n
Thomas, Norman C., 58n, 136, 160n
Tobriner, Commissioner, 274
Truman, David B., 113, 131n
Tucker, Sterling, 343, 346, 352n
Tydings, Joseph, 98

Ulmer, S. Sidney, 395n

Van Dalen, Hendrick, 103, 104n, 130n
Vanderzell, John H., 373, 394n
Veeder, William J., 61, 93n, 94n
Verba, Sidney, 59, 63, 93n, 94n, 95n, 96, 124, 130n, 132n
Vine, Kenneth N., 94n, 130n, 394n
Vose, Clement E., 131n

Wahlke, John C., 60, 93n, 94n, 108, 130n, 131n, 161n, 167, 168n, 192, 200n, 201n, 223, 227, 253, 255n, 256n, 277, 308n
Waldhorn, Steven A., 345–46, 352n
Wallace, George, 124
Warren, Robert O., 308n
Waxman, Charm I., 351n
Webber, Melvin M., 285, 308n, 351n
Weber, Max, 312, 338
Wheeler, Stanton, 394n
Whelchel, Cheryl, 254n
White, Leonard D., 180, 201n, 313, 315, 349n, 350n
Wildavsky, Aaron, 298–99, 309n
Wilkens, Leslie T., 395n
Willbern, York, 349n
Williams, G. Mennon, 228, 245, 255n, 256n
Williams, Oliver P., 95n, 274–75, 278, 307n, 308n
Wilson, Edward, 308n
Wilson, James Q., 35n, 86, 95n, 125, 126, 130n, 132n, 142, 160n, 161n, 307n, 308n
Wirt, Frederick M., 136, 160n, 200n
Wolfinger, Raymond E., 35n, 57n
Wood, Arthur Lewis, 395n
Wood, Robert C., 148, 161n
Woodbury, Coleman, 351n
Wright, Deil, 201n, 329–30, 331, 350n
Wright, Neil S., 201n
Wyner, Alan J., 234, 255n, 326, 350n

Yancey, William L., 351n

Zeigler, Harmon L., 60, 93n, 103n, 107, 130n, 161n, 171, 172, 172n, 200n
Zeisel, Hans, 394n
Zisk, Betty H., 108n, 131n, 255n, 279, 308n

Subject Index

Access: 105–07
Ad hoc groups: 96–8, 151
Adjudication notice: 358–64; delays, 359, financial costs, 359–60; warrants, 361
Administration: 9–35; doctrines, 312–34; executive leadership, 316; professionalism, 312–16
Administrator: characteristics, 197; citizen articulation, 77; executive control, 329–31; political recruitment, 178; lobbying, 117–18; media, 247; professionalism, 28–9, 312–16; rule making, 235–37, 281–85; unionization, 331–34
Advisory Commission on Inter-governmental Relations: 43, 303, 308
Advocate: 340–42
Aldermen: 24, 259
Allied Civic Groups: 152, 153
Amateur politicians: 147–48
Amendment: initiation, 39, 40, 41; ratification, 30, 40, 41; rule making, 249
American Federation of State, County and Municipal Employees: 332
American Independent party: 124
American Institute of Public Opinion: 74, 94n
American Legion: 124
Appalachian Regional Development Act: 243
Appeal: 357–58, 384–90
Apportionment: 207–11, 261–63
Arrest: 361
Articulation: group, 96–132; individual, 59–95, 124–30; interest, 59–132; trends, 124–30
Assessor: city, 25; town, 24
Associations: civic, 98–9, 151; organized, 96–100; membership, 101–102; permanent, 98–100; private oriented, 98–9, 151; public oriented, 98–9, 151–54; strengths, 102–09

Atkins v. Texas: 394n
Auditor: 15; city, 25; state, 16; town, 24
Auditors, Board of: 24
Avery v. Midland County, Texas: 262, 287

Bail bond: 367, 368, 369, 386
Baker v. Carr: 208, 209, 261
Ballard v. United States: 394n
Ballot: group articulation, 120; long, 18; short, 140, 141, 143
Bill: 216–17, 284; committees, 221; local rule making procedures, 268; state rule making procedures, 216–22, 268
Board: 25–8, 92, 315–16; also see specific type
Bondsman: 368
Bribery: 114
Budget: 215, 229–30, 322, 323
Bureaucracy: centralization, 275; citizen articulation, 77, 78; citizen participation, 334–40; lobbying, 117–18; local bureaus, 178–79; professionalism, 275; public attitude, 179–81; rule execution, 331–34, 344–49; sick, 345–46; state bureaus, 177–78; strikes, 332–34, 343–44; unionization, 332–34
Bureaucrats: 140; career, 282–84; interest aggregation, 134, 154–55, 156, 159, 160; lobbying, 117–18; political recruitment, 177–81; professionalism, 312–16; public attitude, 179–81; rule making, 235–37, 281–85
Bureaus: definition, 177; local bureaus, 178–79, 281–85; public attitude, 179–81; state bureaus, 177–78

Cabinets: 323
Calendar: 218
Campaign: 148, 190–91

400

Candidate: characteristics, 197–99; direct primaries, 143, 145, 182; financial resources, 190–91; group endorsement, 120, 142; incumbency, 189–90; motivation for office, 195–97; nominating conventions, 182; nominating panels, 184; non-partisan, 194–95, 196; party competitiveness, 191–94; party reforms, 142–43, 144; political recruitment, 166, 169–70, 181–99; qualifications, 184, 187, 188, 189

Caucus: 218, 220, 225–26, 271

CBS Television Network: 75, 94n

Centralization: 19, 20, 22–3, 30–1, 141, 143, 275, 316, 322

Centros: 181–99, 326; characteristics, 197–99; definition, 181; environment, 186–89; financial resources, 190–91; incumbency, 189–90; motivation for office, 195–97; nominating conventions, 182; nomination panels, 183–84; non-partisan, 194–95; party competitiveness, 191–94; polls, 191;. primaries, 182–83; qualifications, 184; recruitment, 181–95

Charter: 36; apportionment, 261; changes, 46–7; intergovernmental influences, 50–2, 287; judicial review, 286; political recruitment, 181; rule making, 258, 281; types, 44–6, 258

Citizen: advocates, 340–42; articulation, 59–93, 124–30; attitude toward public office, 163–65, 305–06; blacks, 125–27, 346; civic obligation, 59; criticism, 342–44; efficacy, 63, 84; elderly, 129–30; interest 60–1, 84; interest aggregation, 138, 143, 145, 146; knowledge, 61–2, 84, 162; participation, 334–42; political recruitment, 162; poor, 127–29, 347; rule adjudication, 363–64, 390–93; rule making, 248–54, 300–05; voting, 80–9

Citizen Complaint Centers: 90–1

Citizen Complaint Officer: 71, 90–1

City attorney: 282

City of Clinton v. Cedar Rapids & Missouri River Railroad Company: 34n

City of Phoenix, Arizona v. Emily Kolodziejski: 80

City of Trenton v. State of New Jersey: 34n, 306n

Civic associations: 98–9, 151–54, 157, 160

Civic Federation: 152

Clerk: city, 25; town, 23

Coalitions: 116–17

Coat-tail phenomenon: 191

Cohesion: 104–05

Colegrove v. Green: 208

Commission form: 25–8, 240, 244, 268, 273–74, 279, 324

Commissioner: non-partisan, 194–95; political recruitment, 181; qualifications, 187; rule making, 259, 273

Commissioners, Board of: 26, 27, 140

Commissioners of Hamilton County v. Meghels: 34n

Committee: appropriations, 218; bills referred, 217; chairman, 222; committee action, 217, 220; conference, 219; influence, 221 joint, 222; membership, 221–22; rule making procedure, 216–22, 270

Committee for Economic Development: 43

Communication: direct channels, 110–14; financial resources, 190; interest articulation, 65–71, 109–17; indirect channels, 73–83, 114–17; institutional channels, 68–71; legislative channels, 222–28; new channels, 89–93; personal channels, 65–8, 110–14

Community action: 334–40

Community Action Program: 128

Community power: 297–300

Community Services Act: 92

Compacts: 240

Competitiveness: 191–94

Comptroller: 25

Conference: 240–41, 293–94

Conference of Chief Justices: 241

Conference of Mayors: 327, 244, 294

Congress: 209

Conservative Party: 124

Constituent: 138, 188, 269

Constitution: change, 39–41, 48, 53; courts, 49, 50; electorate input, 54–7; intergovernmental influences, 48–52, 289; interest groups, 53; national, 202, 289; political recruitment, 181; ratification, 42; reform, 43–4; revisions, 41–2; rule making limitations, 203–06, 258; state, 36–7, 38, 39, 2–3–06

Constitutional Conventions: 40, 41–2; delegates, 54–5, 56; electorate input, 54

Contractual arrangements: 293

Cooperative agreements: 292

Cooperative planning: 294–95

Corporation counsel: see City attorney

Council of State Governments: 43, 241

Council-Manager form: 272–73, 279
Councilmen: 24, 149, 159; ambition, 277–78; at-large elections, 188, 269; characteristics, 177, 260, 272–73; citizen articulation, 78, 115–16; communication channels, 66, 67; grass root pressure, 115–16; non-partisan, 194–95, 269; perspective, 276–77; political recruitment, 178, 181, 186; roles, 278–79; rule making 259, 269, 272–73; salaries, 261
Councils of Government: 30, 71, 108, 295–96
Counties: 9, 11, 26, 27
County executive: 24, 25; communication channels, 115; group articulation, 115; interest aggregation, 155; intermediaries, 115; lobbying, 117; non-partisan, 194–95; political recruitment, 181
Courts: appellate, 22; circuit, 21; district, 21; federal, 239; lobbying, 118–20; magistrate, 21; malapportionment, 208–09; political recruitment, 183–84; of appeals, 22, 384–90; rule execution, 320–21; rule making, 237–40; state supreme, 22, 239; superior, 21

Defendant: 368, 376
Defense attorney: see Lawyer
Democratic Party: 123, 126, 137, 141, 142, 144, 146, 147, 148, 167, 182, 183
Demonstrations: 115, 124
Dillon's Rule: 11, 50, 257, 287
District primary: 143, 145, 182
Districting: 211–12, 261–63
Districts: 188; multi-member, 211; school, 9, 13; single member, 211–12; special, 9, 12–13, 28, 71, 266, 290, 294, 315–16; type of government, 28
Dunn v. Blumstein: 80

Economic Opportunity Act: 92, 127, 289
Efficacy: 63, 84
Elections: at-large, 188, 197; direct primary, 143, 144; form of articulation, 85–9; initiative, 87–9, 121, 302, 303–04; interest aggregation, 136, 137; interest groups, 105, 106, 120; nominating process, 145; non-partisan, 194–95, 268; participation, 83, 84; referendum, 87–9, 121, 302, 303–04; reform, 139–40; rule making, 268–76
Electorate: 54–57; apathy, 56; civic obligation, 87; demographic characteristics, 83–5; direct primaries, 143, 145,

182; efficacy, 84; interest, 84, 144, 164; interest articulation, 85–9; knowledge, 84, 89, 143, 144; party reforms, 143–44; rule making, 249; voting, 80–9
Elites: 298–300
Escobedo v. Illinois: 393n
Ewing v. Hoblitzelle: 34n
Executive: administrative opinions, 329–31; appeals, 389; central direction, 20; citizen articulation, 78; consolidation, 20; control, 321–31; election, 144; historical development, 16–8; interest aggregation, 134, 155–57; limitations, 325–29; lobbying, 117–18; political recruitment, 177–81, 181–89; power, 15–6; qualifications, 184; reorganization, 19–20; rule execution, 316; rule making, 228–35, 279–81; structure, 15–6; tenure, 323; veto, 230–31, 280
Executive-Council pattern: 24–5, 324
Extradition: 390

Farmer Labor Party: 122
Federal Communication Commission: 289
Federal government: 289–92
Federal Highway Act: 242
Financial resources: 190–91; intergovernmental influences, 287–88; rule making, 212–16, 263–67
Floor leaders: 220
Foreman: 380
Freedom Organization: 124
Function: 3, 4, 5
Gideon v. Wainwright: 393n
Government: factors relating to, 31–4; responsibilities, 37–44; also see under specific type

Governor: 15–20; appeals, 389; appointees, 184; budget, 229–30, 323; characteristics, 197–99; communication channels, 66, 115; direct rule making, 325; intermediaries, 115; legislators, 232–34; lobbying, 117; media, 247; political recruitment, 178, 181; qualifications, 184; rule making procedures, 216–22, 228–35; veto, 230–31
Grants-in-aid: 241–43, 289–91, 327
Grass root pressure: 115–16, 146
Grey v. Saunders: 209
Group: 96–132; channels of communication, 109–17; coalitions, 116–17; electoral process, 120; factors, 102–09; grass roots, 115–16; influence, 102–09;

informal legislation, 226–27; interest aggregation, 151–54; political parties, 121–24; resources, 102–03; strength, 102–09; techniques, 109–17; also see under specific group

Group articulation: 96–132; blacks, 125–27; channels, 109–17; coalitions, 116–17; elderly, 129–30; electoral process, 120; fluidity, 100–01; lobbying, 109–17, 117–18, 118–20; membership, 101–02; political parties, 121–24; poor, 127–29; strengths, 102–09; techniques, 109–17

Harper v. Virginia State Board of Electors: 80, 254n

Hearings: caucus, 218; legislative control, 317; rule execution, 317; trial, 371–72

Hernandez v. Texas: 394n

Hoover Commission: 19, 323

Human Rights Commission: 210

Hunter v. Pittsburgh: 34n

Incumbent: 166, 170, 189–90, 301

Inflos: 170–75; definition, 170; lobbyists, 170–72; party officials, 173–75

Initiative: appointment, 208; citizen participation, 248–52; expense, 251; form of articulation, 87–8, 121; rule making, 248–52, 302; turnout, 88; use of, 303–04; voting, 88–9

Interest aggregation: 3, 4, 133–61; bureaucrats, 154–55; chief executive, 155–57; interest groups, 151–54; legislators, 157–60; political parties, 133–50; reforms, 139–42

Interest articulation: 3, 4, 59–93; blacks, 125–27; bureaucracy, 77; citizens, 59, 61, 63; citizen complaint center, 90–1; channels, 64–71, 89–93, 109–17; coalitions, 116–17; collective actions, 96–132; demographic factors, 63–5; elderly, 129–30; elected officials, 77–8, 115; grass root pressures, 115–16; intermediaries, 114–15; lobbying, 109–17, 117–18, 118–20; media, 73–5; political parties, 75–7, 121–24; polls, 78–80; poor, 127–29; prerequisites, 59–63; public officials, 71–2, 113–14, 115; riots, 89–90, 115, 124; techniques, 109–17; trends, 124–30; voting, 80–9, 120

Interest groups: 96–132; access, 105–07; channels, 109–17; coalitions, 116–17; cohesion, 104–05; constitutional commissions, 55; electoral process, 120; grass root pressure, 115–16; influence, 53, 102, 103; interest aggregation, 134,

151–54; interest articulation, 72–3, 96–132; lobbying, 109–17, 117–18, 118–20, 170–75; party reforms, 142–43; political parties, 121–24; political recruitment, 168; receptivity, 107–09; resources, 102–03; strength, 102–09, 142; techniques, 109–17

Intergovernmental Council on Urban Growth: 246

Intermediaries: 114–15

International City Management Association: 178, 315

Judge: appeals, 384–90; characteristics, 197, 387, decision, 375–79; lobbying, 118–20; neutrality, 378; political recruitment, 178, 181, 183–84; qualifications, 187; recall, 252; rule adjudication, 353–95; rule execution, 320–21; rule making, 237–40, 259, 285–87; trial, 371–72; trial procedures, 372–84

Judicial: appeals, 384–90; lobbying, 118–20; pre-trial period, 367–70; public attitude, 390–93; response, 364–67; reorganization, 22–3; rule adjudication, 353–95; rule execution, 320–21; rule making, 237–40, 285–87; sentencing, 379–84; settlement, 370–71; structure, 21–2 trial, 371–84, verdict, 379–84

Judicial review: 238

Jury: 359, 365, 372–73, 374, 375, 380, 382

Jurors: 378

Juvenile delinquency: 336–37

Justice of the Peace: 21, 382

Kentucky v. Dennison: 395n

Kramer v. Union Free School District: 80

Laws: see Rule making, execution, and adjudication

Lawyer: 359, 360, 370, 371, 372, 377, 385

League: 293–94

League of Women Voters: 43, 54, 99, 120, 124, 152, 153

Legislator: ambition, 277–78; bribery, 114; caucus, 225–26; citizen articulation, 77, 78; characteristics, 197; communication channels, 66; drawbacks, 185, 186; facilitators, 108; function, 228, 317–20; governors, 232–34; informal groups, 226–27; informal rules, 227–28; interest aggregation, 134, 155,

156, 157–60; judicial, 239; leadership, 219–20; local influence, 243–47; lobbying, 106–09, 113–14, 115; perspective, 276–77; referendum, 249, 302–04; receptivity, 107–09; resistors, 108; rule making, 158, 217–22, 222–28, 259–61, 276–79; role, 222–24, 269, 278–79, 317–32; salary, 206; revenue, 216

Legislature: apportionment, 207–11, 261–63; bicameral, 14, 15, 205; caucus, 225–26; districting, 211–12, 261–63; fiscal consideration, 212–16; informal groups, 226–27; leadership, 219–20; rule execution, 317–20, rule making procedure, 216–22, 259–61, 267–68; size, 205, state, 14–5, 202–56; structure, 204–05; unicameral, 14, 15

Liberal Party: 122, 123, 124

Lieutenant governor: 16, 220

Limited government: 37

Lobby: 108, 233, 235; bribery, 114; executive branch, 117–18; judicial branch, 118–20; public opinion, 172; techniques, 109–17

Lobbyist: 106, 107, 108, 109, 109–17; bribery, 114; executive branch, 117–18; grass roots, 115–16; indirect channels, 114–17; informal legislative groups, 226–27; judicial branch, 118–20; personal contact, 113–14; political recruitment, 168, 170–75; public opinion, 172; testifying, 110–13

Local government: interlocal cooperation, 292–94; jurisdictional boundaries, 296; perspective, 276–79; rules, 44–7; rule making, 257–309; structure, 23–31

Localities: council of government, 295–96; interlocal cooperation, 292–94; jurisdictional boundaries, 286; relationship with federal government, 289–92; relationship with states, 10, 11, 287–89; rules, 44–7

Magistrate: 367

Malapportionment: 207–10

Manager: 28, 29, 30, 140, 155, 158; duties, 281, 314–15, 324; non-partisan, 194–95; political recruitment, 178, 181; rule making, 281–85

Mayor: 25, 26, 140, 155; characteristics, 197, 324–25; chief administrative officer, 282; communication channels, 66, 115; influence, 271; intermediaries, 115; lobbying, 117; media, 280–81; non-partisan, 194–95; political recruitment,

178, 181; public hearings, 70; rule making function, 271, 279–81; tenure, 324; veto, 280, 325

Mayor-Council form: leadership, 270; legislative bodies, 269; party influence, 270–71; rule making, 269–73, 279, 282

McCulloch v. Maryland: 48, 57n, 203

Media: editorials, 248; grass root pressure, 115–16; interest articulation, 73–5, 115–16; press, 247; publicity, 143; trials, 376; rule making, 247–48

Merit system: 145, 156, 176, 313–14

Metropolitan government: 29–31, 294–97

Miranda v. Arizona: 393n

Mississippi Freedom Democratic Party: 124

Municipalities: 9, 11–2

National Advisory Commission on Civil Disorders: 89–90, 95n, 342, 395n

National Association for the Advancement of Colored People (NAACP): 119, 125

National Association of Counties: 293

National Governor's Conference: 240, 327

National League of Cities: 293

National Legislative Conference: 241

National Municipal League, 43, 44, 47, 57n, 244

National Opinion Research Center, 164n, 199n

Neighborhood Service Centers: 92

Nominating conventions: 182

Nominating panels: 183–84

Non-partisan systems: 194–95, 196

Ombudsman: 340–42

Open meetings: 70–1

Organization of the Executive Branch of Government, Commission on: 35n

Organized associations: strength, 102–09; types, 96–100

Pardon: 389

Party identification: 86, 136–37, 144, 224

Party leaders: activities, 135, 137–39; amateurs, 147–48; functions, 137, 144; interest aggregation, 136, 146, 148, 149–50, 159, 160; minority party, 193; nominating process, 145; party competitiveness, 191–94; party organization, 136, 142; patronage, 141–42, 145, 176; political recruitment, 165–67, 173–75; reforms, 139–42

Patronage: 141–42, 145

Patton v. Mississippi: 394n
Penal code: 381
Pendleton Act: 51, 313
Permanent associations: 98–9, 151–54
Petition: 249, 301, 385, 389
Plaintiffs: 370, 371, 376
Pluralism: 298–99
Police: 361, 362, 366
Police powers, 38–9
Political communication: 3
Political parties: amateur, 147–48; constitutional commissions, 55; definition, 134; direct primaries, 143, 145, 182; executive, 156, 231–32; factional alignments, 194; financial resources, 190–94; image, 144; incumbency, 189–90; interest aggregation, 133–50, 160; interest articulation, 72–3, 75–7, 86, 121–24; leadership, 165, 173–75; minor party, 121–24, 169, 193; nominating conventions, 182; organization, 136, 142, 148, 167; partly competitiveness, 191–94; party identification, 136–37, 144; patronage, 141–42, 176; political recruitment, 165–67, 173–75; primaries, 182–84; reforms, 139–42; rule making, 224–25, 231–32, 270
Political power: political parties, 135; rule making, 297–300
Political recruitment: bureaus, 177–81; centros, 181–99; characteristics of nominees, 197–99; environment, 186–89; financial resources, 190–91; incumbency, 189–90; inflos, 170–75; interest groups, 168; merit system, 176; motivation for office, 195–97; nominating conventions, 182; nomination panels, 183–84; non-partisan, 194–95; party competitiveness, 194; party leaders, 165–67; patronage, 176 polls, 191; primaries, 182–84; qualifications, 184; self-recruitment, 169–70; service personnel, 175–77
Political socialization: 3
Political structures: 3, 9
Political system: 9, 133, 163, 176, 247
Politician: see under specific type
Polls: indirect channel, 78–80; interest articulation, 78–80; political parties, 136; political recruitment, 191; problems, 78–80; surveys, 79
Precinct committeeman: 138, 146
Precinct leaders: 165
Precinct worker: 146
President of the Senate: 220

Pressure groups: 114, 115–16; also see under interest groups
Primary: blanket, 183; closed, 182; direct primary, 143, 145, 182; non-partisan, 183, 194–95; open, 182–83; partisan, 182
Probation officer: 383
Progressive Party: 122
Proposals: 268, 284
Prosecuting attorney: 362–63, 367, 370, 373, 374, 377, 383
Public: see Citizen
Public hearing: group articulation, 110–13; 155; individual articulation, 69; media, 70
Public office: competitiveness, 193; non-partisan, 194–95, 196; motivation for office, 195–97
Public officials: characteristics, 197–99, 297; citizen articulation, 71–2, 77–8; citizen attitude, 163–65, 179–81, 305, 306; elections, 140; group articulation, 109–17; incumbency, 189–90; interest aggregation, 154–55, 160; lobbying, 109–17, 117–18, 118–20; media, 73–5, 247, 280–81; motivation for office, 195–97; non-partisan, 194–95, 196; political recruitment, 174, 181; recall, 252, 301–02
Public relations men: 170
Public servants: See Service personnel
Public trust: 195

Recall: definition, 301; expensive, 252; rule making, 252–53, 301–02
Receptivity: 107–09
Referendum: citizen participation, 248–52; expense, 251; form of articulation, 87–8, 121; rule making, 248–52, 302–03; turnout, 88; use of, 303–04, voting, 88–9
Regulatory agencies: 236, 237, 264
Republican National Committee: 94n
Republican Party: 122, 144, 146, 147, 148, 167, 182, 183
Resources: 102–03, 190–91
Revenue: 213–15, 216, 265–67
Reynolds v. Sims: 14, 209
Riots: 89–90, 390
Rule adjudication: 3, 9, 353–94; agencies, 354; appeals, 384–90; decision, 375–79; definition, 353; influencing factors, 358–90 notice, 358–64; pre-trial period, 367–78; procedures, 355–58; public attitude, 390–93; response, 364–67; sen-

tencing, 379–84; settlement, 370–71; trial, 371–72, 372–84; verdict, 379–84
Rule application: 3
Rule execution: 310–52; administrative, 312–16, 331–34; citizen participation, 334–40, 340–44; community control, 344–49; executive control, 316, 321–31; judicial control, 317–20
Rule making: apportionment, 207–11, 261–63; administrator, 235–37, 281–85; budget, 229–30; caucus, 225–26; citizen participation, 248–53, 300–05; community power, 297–300; districting, 211–12, 261–63; electoral, 268–76; executive, 228–35, 279–81; factors, 202–16, 257–59; informal factors, 22–28; informal groups, 226–67; informal rules, 227–28; interest groups, 153; intergovernmental effects, 240–43, 287–97; judges, 237–40, 285–87; fiscal consideration, 212–16, 263–67; leadership, 219–20, 270; legislative bodies, 259–61; legislators, 158, 206, 217–28, 276–79; legislator's role, 222–24, 278–79; limitations, 202–16, 258–59; local influences, 243–47, 297–300; local level, 257–309; media, 247–48; political parties, 148, 224–25 procedure, 216–22, 267–68; recall, 252–53, 301–02; relation to public, 353–54, 306–06; special session, 231; state level, 202–56; structure, 268–76; veto, 230–31, 280

Sanctions: 228
Secretary of State: 15
Senior Citizen Clubs: 129
Sentencing: 379–84
Service personnel: merit system, 176; patronage, 176; political recruitment, 175–77
Settlement: 370–71, 375
Sherbert v. Verner: 256n
Slaughterhouse cases: 49, 57n
Speaker: influence, 220; state house, 219–20
Special districts: 9, 12–3, 28, 71, 266, 290, 294, 315–16
Special interests: see Interest groups
Socialist Party: 122
State: 9–10, 202
State Attorney General: 15, 371, 377

State government: 202; rule making, 257, 287–89; structure, 13–23
Strikes: 332–34, 343–44
Structural-functional approach: 2, 3, 4
Superintendent of Public Education: 16
Supervisors, Board of: 24
Supreme Court, U.S.: 48, 49, 80, 203; appeals, 389; districting, 211–12; juries, 373; malapportionment, 209, 261–63; rule making, 239, 287

Tammany Hall: 137, 138
Tax: 264–66, 286
Testifying: 110–13, 237
Thiel v. Southern Pacific Company: 394n
Thomas P. Morgan Elementary School: 305
Ticket: see Adjudication notice
Town meeting: 23–4, 68
Township: 9, 12, 259
Treasurer: city, 25; state position, 15–6; town, 23–4
Trial: 371–72; pre-trial, 367–70; release, 367–69
Trustees, Board of: 24, 237

U.S. Bureau of the Census: 5n, 34n, 172n, 254n
U.S. Commission on Civil Rights: 94n
United States Attorney General: 51
United States v. Peters: 256n
Unionization: 331–34
Urban League: 100, 125
Urban planning: 336, 338, 339

Verdict: 379–84
Voters: direct primary, 143, 145, 182; group pressure, 120; incumbent, 190; precinct workers, 146; support, 137
Voting: civic obligation, 87; direct primary, 143, 145; eligibility, 80–1; forms of articulation, 80–9; initiative, 88–9, 248–52, 302–03; party identification, 86, 224; protest, 144; referendum, 88–9, 248–52, 302; state legislature, 218, 224; turnout, 81–5, 253; demographic characteristics, 83–5
Voting Rights Act: 51, 81, 123
Warrant: 359
Witness: 363, 370, 374
Work stoppages: see Strikes